Peter G. Aitken

SAMS
Teach Yourself
Internet
Programming
with Visual Basic® 6
in 21 Days

SAMS

A Division of Macmillan Computer Publishing

201 West 103rd Street, Indianapolis, Indiana 46290

Sams Teach Yourself Internet Programming with Visual Basic 6® in 21 Days

Copyright © 1999 by Sams Publishing

International Standard Book Number: 0-672-31459-2

Library of Congress Catalog Card Number: 98-87212

Printed in the United States of America

First Printing: December 1998

00   99   4

Trademarks

All terms mentioned in this book that are known to be trademarks or service marks have been appropriately capitalized. Sams cannot attest to the accuracy of this information. Use of a term in this book should not be regarded as affecting the validity of any trademark or service mark.

Warning and Disclaimer

Every effort has been made to make this book as complete and as accurate as possible, but no warranty or fitness is implied. The information provided is on an "as is" basis. The authors and the publisher shall have neither liability or responsibility to any person or entity with respect to any loss or damages arising from the information contained in this book or from the use of the Web page or programs accompanying it.

EXECUTIVE EDITOR
Chris Denny

ACQUISITIONS EDITOR
Sharon Cox

DEVELOPMENT EDITOR
Anthony Amico

MANAGING EDITOR
Jodi Jensen

SENIOR EDITOR
Susan Ross Moore

COPY EDITORS
Kate Talbot
Rhonda Tinch-Mize

INDEXER
Heather Goens

PROOFREADER
Cynthia Fields

TECHNICAL EDITOR
Per Blomqvist

SOFTWARE DEVELOPMENT SPECIALIST
Andrea Duvall

TEAM COORDINATOR
Carol Ackerman

INTERIOR DESIGN
Gary Adair

COVER DESIGN
Aren Howell

LAYOUT TECHNICIANS
Brandon Allen
Timothy Osborn
Staci Somers

Contents at a Glance

Contents

About the Author

Peter G. Aitken started programming on one of the first PCs to roll off the assembly line and has been at it ever since. His first efforts were laboratory data acquisition and analysis programs for use in his position as a research scientist. He started writing about computers and programming not long afterwards. Peter has well over 100 magazine articles to his credit, having written for publications such as *PC Tech Journal*, *PC Magazine*, and *PC Techniques*. Peter's first book was, like this one, about Basic programming, even though it was long before the introduction of Visual Basic. Since then, he has written more than 25 books and has more than a million and a half copies in print. Some of his more recent titles include *Visual Basic 6 Programming Blue Book*, *Teach Yourself C in 21 Days* (with co-author Brad Jones), *Digital Camera Design Guide*, and *Ten Minute Guide to Word 97*.

During daylight hours, Peter is an associate research professor at Duke University Medical Center, where he conducts research on the function of the nervous system. His education includes a bachelor of science degree from the University of Rochester, a master of science degree from the State University of New York, and a doctorate from the University of Connecticut. Peter has two children, Benjamin and Claire, and lives with his wife, Maxine, in Chapel Hill, North Carolina. His favorite recreational activities include fishing, stamp collecting, cooking, and travelling.

Dedication

To my wife, Maxine, with appreciation for all you had to put up with while I wrote this book.

Acknowledgments

Like most books, this one was a team effort. My name alone is on the cover, but I certainly had a lot of help. My acquisitions editor, Sharon Cox, first approached me about the book and then guided me through the process, from the first outline to the final review. Development Editor Tony Amico helped at every stage of the writing, making sure that my explanations made sense and my text was readable. Per Blomqvist, technical editor, made sure that my code worked properly and, when it did not, helped to fix it.

Tell Us What You Think!

As the reader of this book, *you* are our most important critic and commentator. We value your opinion and want to know what we're doing right, what we could do better, what areas you'd like to see us publish in, and any other words of wisdom you're willing to pass our way.

As the Executive Editor for the Visual Basic Programming team at Macmillan Computer Publishing, I welcome your comments. You can fax, email, or write me directly to let me know what you did or didn't like about this book—as well as what we can do to make our books stronger.

Please note that I cannot help you with technical problems related to the topic of this book, and that due to the high volume of mail I receive, I might not be able to reply to every message.

When you write, please be sure to include this book's title and author as well as your name and phone or fax number. I will carefully review your comments and share them with the author and the editors who worked on the book.

Fax: 317-817-7070
Email: vb@mcp.com
Mail: Chris Denny, Executive Editor
        Visual Basic Programming Team
        Macmillan Computer Publishing
        201 West 103rd Street
        Indianapolis, IN 46290 USA

Introduction

For the past several years, what have been the hottest buzzwords in the world of computers? You've got it—*Web* and *Internet*! Wherever you turn, it's the *Web this* and the *Internet that*. If you don't have your own Web page, you might feel that you have been left back in the Stone Age. Companies have Web pages, movies have Web pages, universities have Web pages, charities have Web pages, and millions upon millions of individuals have their own personal Web pages. If you went to some remote valley in the Himalayas, you might get away from all the Internet fuss, but probably not for long.

The Internet is for more than just fun, of course. More and more, businesses are turning to the Internet as a valuable tool for exchanging information, keeping employees informed, and selling and buying products. The amount of commerce conducted over the Internet is already large and is expected to grow very quickly in the near future. Even today, things that we used to do via mail, by telephone, or in person are often done over the Internet. In the past week, for example, I used the Internet to order some clothing, rent a video, check my credit card balance, and look up the air fares for a trip I am planning. As the Internet grows and more people become familiar with it, this sort of activity will only increase.

One unavoidable result of the Internet's growth is that there will be greater need for programmers to create the applications that run on the Internet and make all these wonderful capabilities possible. Web sites don't just grow on trees, you know! A well-designed Web site takes a lot of planning and work by a skilled developer. The demand for Web programmers will continue to increase. Because you are reading this book, I assume that you're interested in developing your own Web programming skills.

Like most other tasks, Web programming demands the proper tools. You have plenty of choices, and the most of them do a good job. Even so, if you use an inappropriate tool, your ability to create sophisticated and attractive Web applications will suffer. Web development tools have been changing at a rapid rate, with greater ease of use and more sophisticated features being added with each new product.

In my opinion, the new release of Visual Basic, version 6, is one of the very best Web development tools available. One of its most important advantages is the millions of Visual Basic programmers out there. If you have experience using Visual Basic to create standard applications, almost everything you already know can be leveraged to use Visual Basic for Web development. Rather than learn a new language and a new development environment, you can stay with your tried and true tool.

What capabilities does Visual Basic bring to the world of Web development? Let's take a brief tour:

- Easy creation of ActiveX controls for deployment and installation from the Web
- Packaging of entire Visual Basic applications as ActiveX documents, permitting execution and distribution by means of the Internet
- Internet-aware controls that enable you to create Web-aware desktop applications
- VBScript for writing both client-side and server-side scripts
- Dynamic HTML for creating sophisticated Web-based business applications
- Active Server Pages for creating custom dynamic Web content
- Sophisticated database tools for creating data-aware Web applications

Some of these technologies you'll find enabled within the Visual Basic development environment. Others work outside the development environment, using Visual Basic syntax and tools to add functionality to Web pages, browsers, and servers. All in all, Visual Basic provides you with an extremely powerful and flexible set of Web development tools, which I have not seen bettered by any other product. I don't think you can go wrong choosing Visual Basic as your Web development tool.

Who Should Read This Book

If you fall into one or more of the following categories, this book was written specifically with you in mind:

- You have just recently started using Visual Basic, and you want to start learning about its Web development capabilities.
- You are an experienced Visual Basic programmer and want to leverage your existing knowledge to Web development projects.
- You have tried another Web development tool and have become frustrated by how difficult it is to accomplish anything.
- You have already used Visual Basic to do some Web programming and now want to learn about its full range of features.
- You have used Visual Basic for regular database programming and now need to extend your database applications to the Internet.

To use this book, you need at least a little experience with Visual Basic. This is not meant to be an introductory Visual Basic book, and I do not cover the basics of using the Visual Basic development environment, writing Basic code, using controls, and so on. If you do not have previous experience with Visual Basic, you might want to obtain an introductory book on the topic.

What This Book Contains

This book is divided into 21 lessons, with each lesson designed so that it can be easily completed in one day. It's up to you to determine the pace that suits you best. Some readers might be able to complete two lessons per day, whereas those of you with busy schedules might take more than one day for each lesson. Don't worry if you think you are progressing too slowly; you are the only one who can judge whether your progress is satisfactory.

The new lessons are designed to be read from start to finish, in order. The early lessons cover more basic material, and some of the later lessons build on this material. As much as possible, I have tried to combine *telling* you how to do something with *showing* you how to do it. There are lots of demonstrations and examples throughout the book, many of which you can continue to modify and develop on your own if you want. At the end of each lesson, you'll find a question-and-answer session, a quiz, and, when appropriate, an exercise for you to complete. These elements are intended to help you test your knowledge. If you have obtained a good grasp of the material in a lesson, you should be able to complete these with little trouble. If you find that the quizzes and exercises are difficult for you, it might be a sign that you need to review the material in the lesson.

What You Need to Begin

To use this book, you must have either the Professional or the Enterprise edition of Visual Basic version 6 installed on your computer. Many of the advanced features required for Internet programming are not included in the Learning edition of Visual Basic. You also need an Internet connection, via a modem or a local area network. As I mentioned before, you should have at least a fundamental knowledge of how to use Visual Basic.

Okay, it's time to begin. You have a lot of material to learn, but it will be worth it. When you are finished, you will be ready to tackle just about any Internet programming task that comes your way.

Peter G. Aitken
Chapel Hill, North Carolina
October 1998

WEEK 1

At a Glance

The goal of this book is to teach you how to use Visual Basic version 6 to create Web applications. In week 1, you will start off learning some Web and Internet basics, as well as the importance of providing dynamic Web pages. Then you will spend the remainder of the week learning about ActiveX technology, a central part of Microsoft's Web strategy. At the end of this week, you will have a good understanding of Web and Internet basics and will be able to use ActiveX technology to solve some of your Web programming problems.

Where You Are Going

On the first day, you will learn the basics of how the Web and Internet work, and you'll also learn some essential Web-related terminology. Day 2 introduces you to ActiveX technology, which is an underlying part of many of Visual Basic's Web-related capabilities. On Days 3 and 4, you will learn about ActiveX controls and actually create your own ActiveX control that can be used on your Web pages. Day 5 covers some more advanced control techniques and walks you through creating a more sophisticated control. Days 6 and 7 cover ActiveX documents, complete Visual Basic applications packaged for deployment on the Web.

1

2

3

4

5

6

7

DAY 1

Saying Hello to the World

If you want to say hello to the entire world, the Internet is the best way to do it. If you need to develop pages and applications for the World Wide Web, Visual Basic is a terrific choice of tools. Because you're reading this book, I assume you want to learn how to use Visual Basic, Microsoft's powerful visual development tool, to create programs for the Web and the Internet. I also assume that you already have at least a fundamental familiarity with Visual Basic, but are new to using it for Internet and Web programming.

That's the goal of this book—to teach you in 21 easy lessons how to leverage the power of Visual Basic to create just the applications you need. First, however, you need some background information about the Internet, what it is and how it's changing, and about the tools that Visual Basic provides for Internet development. Today you will learn about

- The origins and history of the Internet and World Wide Web
- "Web-speak"—URL, HTTP, FTP, and more
- Domain names and IP addresses

- Static versus dynamic Web content
- Active Server Pages and dynamic HTML
- Database connectivity on the Web

A Brief History of the Internet and World Wide Web

Many people do not realize it, but the Internet and the World Wide Web (or *Web* for short) are not the same thing. They are closely related, to be sure, but you need to understand the differences in order to effectively work with them. Briefly, the Internet consists of all the computers connected to it, the connections between them, and the methods used to transfer information from one computer to another. The Web comprises the sum of all interlinked information available on the Internet. Now let's look at some details.

The Internet

The beginning of the Internet can be traced back to the days of the Cold War, when there was a very real possibility that the United States and the Soviet Union would start tossing nuclear-tipped missiles at each other. The Department of Defense realized the potential value of a communications system that could not be easily disrupted in the event of an attack. The initial project, called ARPANET, was started in 1968. It achieved the astounding feat of connecting four computers located in four different cities. Well, it seemed astounding back then!

It soon became clear that this sort of network had many potential uses beyond the goals of the Defense Department, including permitting research scientists and engineers to rapidly and efficiently exchange information. It also became obvious that a single network would never be able to provide the desired functionality. Rather, connecting existing networks was seen as the way to go, in other words, *internetwork* communication, or the Internet. The early Internet primarily connected universities and research labs. Because it was funded by the government specifically for defense-related and research-related tasks, it was not available for use by individuals or businesses.

Major changes for the Internet were in the wind in 1991. The National Science Foundation, which had provided most of the financial support for the Internet, withdrew most of its funding and opened the Internet to commercial organizations. Change was gradual at first because corporations and individuals were slow to realize the enormous

1

potential of this newly available technology. This situation was not to last, however, and what started as a trickle of change soon became a torrent, leading to the Internet as we know it today. Much of this change had to do with the emergence of the World Wide Web.

The World Wide Web

The Internet itself existed for quite a while before the Web was born. This early Internet was used primarily for the transfer of data files and for exchanging electronic mail. The birth of the Web dates to the period of 1989–1991 when its initial specifications were developed by a fellow named Tim Berners-Lee working at the European Laboratory for Particle Physics (CERN) in Switzerland. His reasoning went something like this.

The information that people need is located in documents, or files, that are stored in computers. Almost all documents make reference to other documents that contain related or supporting information. Those documents in turn reference other documents. What if a document could not only reference other documents, but could also provide an easy way to view (link to) those other documents? Equally important, what if it didn't matter where the documents were located? A document located on a computer in New York could link to a document on a computer in Bombay as easily as it could link to one down the hall. The concept of a *hyperlink* was indeed powerful, permitting the creation of a web of related information, therefore the term *World Wide Web*. Figure 1.1 illustrates the idea of hyperlinks between documents.

FIGURE 1.1

Links between documents on the Web.

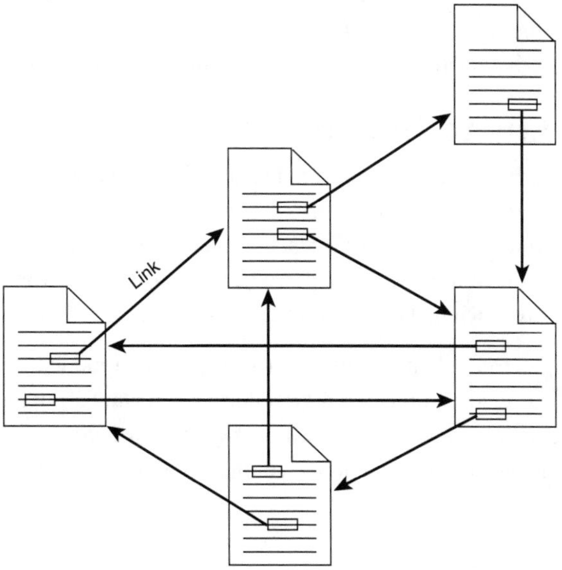

The concept of a World Wide Web was indeed intriguing, but actually implementing the idea was more involved. Two essential developments were required: an agreed format for the documents on the Web, and an agreed technique for transmitting these documents over the Internet. These technologies, Hypertext Markup Language (HTML) and Hypertext Transfer Protocol (HTTP), will be covered later in this chapter.

The Physical Internet

You might be wondering exactly *where* the Internet is. Will you find it in the basement of a building in Washington, D.C.? Perhaps it's in a closely guarded warehouse in St. Louis. Nope, in fact, it's impossible to answer this question in a meaningful way. When you understand the structure of the Internet, you will realize why the question makes no sense.

As I mentioned earlier in this chapter, the Internet consists of all the computers connected to it and the connections between them. The Internet is not some separate "thing" to which people connect their computers. Rather, the Internet is what results when all these people connect their computers together. When you log on to your Internet service provider (ISP), your computer becomes part of the Internet.

The only thing that might be considered to be the "center" of the Internet is the specialized hardware used to transmit information from one location to another. All sorts of communications links are used by the Internet, ranging from simple telephone lines to high-speed fiber-optic cables and satellite links. If the communication links are the highways of the Internet, its traffic cops are the *routers*, specialized computers that direct traffic, seeing that each and every packet of information is sent to the proper destination.

Connecting to the Internet

The vast majority of people connected to the Internet have either a *direct connection* or a *modem connection*. You are most likely to have a direct connection if you are using a computer at your job, school, or library. With a direct connection, your computer is connected to a local area network (LAN) by means of a network adapter card, such as Ethernet or Token Ring. The LAN, in turn, is connected to the Internet.

If your computer is at home, you are probably using a modem connection. A *modem* is a device that can send and receive digital data over a standard telephone line. You dial your ISP and establish a modem connection between your computer and the ISP computer. The ISP computer, in turn, is connected directly to the Internet.

To be honest, a direct connection has all the advantages over a modem connection. It permits much faster transfer of data, as much as 20–30 times as fast as a modem. It is also always "on," requiring no dialing or waiting before you can begin working. It is also free of potential problems such as your kid sister being on the phone all evening! The unavoidable fact is that current technology simply cannot provide a fast and inexpensive Internet connection to most people's homes.

Improvements are on the way, and some new technologies are already in use in limited areas. A digital phone line, called Integrated Services Digital Network or ISDN, provides a 2–4 fold speed improvement over standard modems.

Internets Versus Intranets

You might have heard the term *intranet*, and if so, you're probably wondering how an intranet is different from the Internet. An intranet is essentially identical to the larger Internet in the technology and protocols used. The difference is that the intranet is partially isolated from the Internet, so access to the computers on the Internet is limited.

A typical use for an intranet would be a company that wants its employees to have access to the Internet, but doesn't want the outside world to have access to its computers. The network inside the company is connected to the Internet through a firewall. A *firewall* is simply a computer with specialized software installed on it to prevent unauthorized access between the Internet and the intranet.

People outside the company can access the intranet only if they know the proper password or other authorization procedures. A travelling sales representative, for example, can connect to the company database to retrieve needed information. People inside the company can have unrestricted access to the Internet at large, or in some cases, the firewall might also restrict their access to prevent them from wasting time on non–business-related activities. The relationship between an intranet and the Internet is illustrated in Figure 1.2.

From the point of view of the programmer, writing applications for an intranet is no different than programming for the Internet. There are occasional minor differences, to be sure; in fact, some Visual Basic technologies are designed specifically for use on an intranet. For the most part, however, anything you learn about programming for the Internet can also be applied to intranet programming, and vice versa.

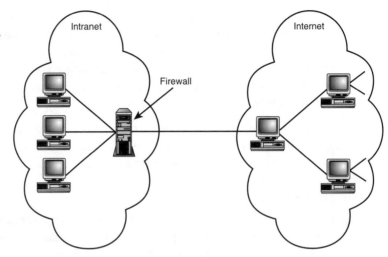

FIGURE 1.2

An intranet is partially isolated from the Internet.

Hypertext Markup Language

Hypertext Markup Language (HTML) is the language of the World Wide Web. It is the standard that is used to create all Web documents. That's right, every Web page you view is written in HTML. There are many details to HTML, but the concept is quite simple.

HTML documents contain only text, that is, the letters, numbers, and symbols you see on your keyboard. The text in an HTML file can be divided into two categories:

- *Content* is the subject matter of the document, the text that a user sees and reads when the document is displayed.
- *Tags* are special codes that control how the content is formatted, define hyperlinks, display images, and do other tasks.

It's easy to tell hypertext tags from content because tags are always enclosed in angle brackets <like this>. Anything inside angle brackets is a tag; everything else is content. It's also the case that many, but not all, HTML tags come in pairs. The first tag in the pair turns something on, and the second tag turns it off. For paired tags, the "off" tag is the same as the "on" tag but with a leading slash (/). For example, to display text in boldface, the on tag is <B> and the off tag is </B>. Here is a fragment of HTML:

```
The next <B>annual meeting</B> will be in Chicago.
```

And here is how it will be displayed:

```
The next annual meeting will be in Chicago.
```

In addition to controlling the formatting of the content text, HTML tags are used to display images in the document. Images are kept in their own separate disk files and then linked from the HTML document with an IMG tag. Here is an example:

```
<img src="birds.jpg">
```

This tag will display the image contained in the file birds.jpg, at the location in the document where the tag is located.

Perhaps the most important HTML tag is the one that defines a hyperlink. After all, the whole purpose of HTML is to permit users to quickly link, or jump, from one document to another. A link tag has the following form:

```
<a href="destination">Link text</a>
```

Here, destination specifies where the link points to, which could be another document on the Web or a different location within the same document. When specifying a different document, you use its uniform resource locator (URL). You'll learn more about URLs later in the chapter. Link text is the text displayed as a hyperlink in the document, with some special indication such as underlining or a different color to indicate that it is a hyperlink and not just regular text.

There are dozens if not hundreds more HTML tags, but I am going to stop here. This is not a book about HTML programming, after all! I will be introducing a few more tags throughout the book, but only as needed for the programming topics that I will be discussing. There are many good books on HTML, and you can refer to one of them for additional information.

Browsers

For anyone who wants to make use of the Web, a browser is the one essential piece of software. One fundamental job of a browser is to load an HTML file and display its contents with the formatting that is specified by the HTML tags in the document. The other fundamental task is to enable hyperlinks—in other words, when the user selects a hyperlink, to retrieve the HTML document specified in the hyperlink and display it onscreen.

Modern browsers have gone much further than these basics. They can display animations, execute Web-based software programs, and provide encryption-based security schemes. In fact, soon I expect to see a browser that will shine your shoes and scratch your back! Well, perhaps not, but the intense competition between Internet software companies has resulted in browsers with many features beyond the basics of displaying hypertext documents and enabling hyperlinks.

For users who are running the Windows operating system, the choice of browsers boils down to two: Netscape Navigator or Microsoft Internet Explorer. Both are excellent programs, and better yet, you can download them for free. You'll find Netscape Navigator downloads at `http://www.netscape.com/download/index.html` and Internet Explorer downloads at Microsoft's Web site at `http://www.microsoft.com/ie/ad/ieufront.asp`. These links were working at the time this was written, but remember that the Web is always changing. If you cannot connect to either of these sites, go to the company's main site (www.microsoft.com or www.netscape.com) and look for the new location of the downloads.

Which browser should you use? For your personal Web browsing, it doesn't matter, and you can use whichever suits your preferences. As a Web programmer, however, you need to have both Netscape Navigator and Internet Explorer. Testing is an essential part of developing applications for the Internet, and you need to ensure that your applications work properly in both the popular browsers.

Images on the Web

Images are an important part of the Web experience. Although dozens of different image file formats are available, only two of them are widely supported on the Web, with a third format just beginning to gain acceptance. Whatever format your images start out in, you will need to convert them to one of these formats before using them on the Web. A wide selection of "paint" programs are available, ranging from expensive commercial programs to inexpensive shareware offerings, and almost any one of them will perform the needed conversions. You need to know the details of these two supported graphics file formats in order to select the one that is best for your situation.

Graphical Interchange Format

Graphical Interchange Format files are identified by filenames with the `.GIF` extension. GIF files are *compressed*, which means that the image information is processed to result in the smallest size file for a given image. This small file size is an advantage for the Web because many people still use a relatively slow modem connection. The one significant limitation of GIF images is that they can display a maximum of 256 different colors. This means that although GIF format is fine for icons, clip art, and drawings, it does not work well for photographs or other images that attempt to present color in a realistic manner.

The GIF format has been significantly enhanced over the years, including capability to display simple animations and to create transparent images. This latter technique is particularly useful. One of the image's 256 colors, typically the background color, is designated as *transparent*. When the image is displayed in a browser, the transparent color does not display but rather permits the Web page background to show through.

Joint Photographic Expert Group Format

The full name of this format is almost never used. Rather, these images are referred to as JPEG (pronounced "jay-peg") images. Files in this format are given the extension .JPG or, occasionally, .JPEG. This file format is also compressed, but unlike the GIF format, in which the compression is always at a fixed level that maintains full image quality, JPEG images offer variable compression. This means that when saving a JPEG file, you specify the level of compression, with greater compression giving a lower quality image and a smaller file size. The JPEG format supports display of more than 16 million colors (sometimes called *true color*) and is therefore suitable for color photographs and similar images.

Portable Network Graphics Format

The PNG format is the new kid on the block and is only starting to receive support among software publishers. It was designed as a successor to the GIF format, keeping the benefits of that format while providing a superior compression technique and the capability to display true color images. I think that you'll be seeing much more use of the PNG format in the near future.

Internet Protocols

Don't be frightened by the term *protocol*. It simply means an agreed method of doing something. At a diplomatic dinner, for example, the questions of who sits where and with whom are decided by an elaborate set of rules, or protocol. If you and your spouse both speak multiple languages and agree to use English when speaking to each other on the telephone, that's a protocol.

Likewise, when two computers need to exchange information over the Internet, they need to agree on how it will be done. What size chunks of data will be sent? How will the address of the recipient be indicated? What should be done if something goes wrong? These are just a few of the many things that the sending and receiving computers must "agree" on if communication is to be successful. During the early days of the Internet, several flexible protocols were developed that permitted intercomputer and internetwork communication regardless of what types of machines were on the two ends of the line. Back then, it might have been an IBM mainframe talking to a Sperry-Univac mainframe. These days, it's more likely to be a PC talking to a Macintosh.

TCP/IP

TCP/IP is the acronym for Transmission Control Protocol/Internet Protocol. As the name indicates, it is actually two protocols, but because they work together to provide the backbone of Internet connectivity, they are almost always referred to as a unit. IP provides an addressing mechanism (the IP addresses that are explained later in this chapter) and a means for transmitting chunks of data, which are called *datagrams* or *packets*, from one computer to another. By itself, IP does not guarantee the delivery of the data, nor does it provide for error correction. That's the job of TCP. Working together, TCP and IP provide the means for one computer to reliably and accurately transmit data to another computer.

An important aspect of the TCP/IP protocol is the way that it breaks data into datagrams. Except when the data to be transmitted is very small in size, TCP/IP will break the data down into a number of smaller datagrams and transmit each individual datagram independently. Each datagram contains the address of the recipient computer, the address of the sending computer, and information that identifies the location of this chunk of data in the overall message. The datagrams are sent independently, and the way the Internet works means that they might not all take the same route to the destination computer and might not even arrive in the same order they were sent. The receiving computer reassembles all the datagrams into the correct order to re-create the original data. Figure 1.3 illustrates this process. If one or more datagrams are lost or become corrupted in transmission, they can be re-sent without having to re-send the entire message.

FIGURE 1.3

TCP/IP breaks data into packets, or datagrams, for transmission.

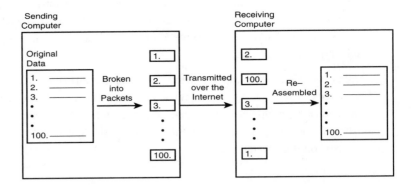

As an analogy, think about writing a book chapter, printing it out, numbering the pages, and then mailing each page in its own envelope. When the recipient has received all the envelopes, he can use the page numbers to put the pages in the proper order and in this way reconstruct the entire chapter. If one or more envelopes are lost in the mail, you only need to print and send those specific pages again.

HTTP

Hypertext Transfer Protocol is the protocol of the World Wide Web. This makes perfect sense, of course, because HTML is the language of the Web, as explained earlier in this chapter. HTTP, therefore, is the protocol by which HTML documents are moved over the Internet. It's important to note that TCP/IP is at work behind the scenes; HTTP is an additional protocol layer that makes use of TCP/IP specifically for transmitting hypertext documents.

An important aspect of HTTP is that it is a *stateless* protocol. This rather technical-sounding term means simply that during an HTTP session, no discrete connection is established between the client and the server. HTTP provides for a simple request/response interaction, as shown in Figure 1.4.

FIGURE 1.4

The request/response nature of HTTP.

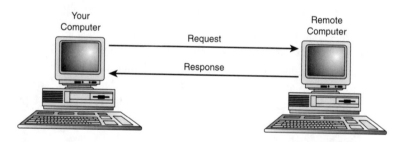

Suppose you sit down at your computer, fire up your browser, and connect to the Microsoft Web site. For the next hour, you browse through various pages on the Microsoft site, and then you quit. That's an HTTP session, but your computer is not really connected to the Microsoft Web server during this period. Instead, what is happening is that your computer is sending requests to the Web server, and the Web server is sending responses back to your computer.

Whenever you request a Web page, by selecting it from your favorites list or by clicking a hyperlink on another Web page, this is exactly what's happening. A request for that page is sent, using HTTP, to the computer that is specified in the link. That computer locates the document on its hard disk and uses HTTP to send it to your computer, which receives it and displays it in the browser. If you click another hyperlink, the process is repeated. The important thing is that, from the user's perspective, it doesn't matter where each document is located or how it is delivered.

Again, the postal system provides a perfect analogy. You could write a request for a document and mail it to your local library. They would make a copy of the document and mail it back to you. You might then request another document, this time from the New York City Public Library, and it, too, would be delivered to you.

FTP

File Transfer Protocol can do quite a bit more than its name suggests. It is indeed used for transferring files between computers, but by using FTP, you can sit at one computer and perform the following tasks on a remote computer connected over the Internet:

- Transfer files between computers in both directions.
- Obtain a directory listing of files on the remote computer.
- Delete, move, and rename files on the remote computer.
- Navigate the folder or directory structure on the remote computer.
- Create and delete new folders on the remote computer.

The extent to which you can perform FTP commands on a remote computer depends, of course, on your privileges. Only with full privileges would you be able to perform potentially dangerous actions such as deleting files. For this reason, it's always necessary to log in to an FTP server with a username and password. The administrator of the FTP server will decide on the level of access you have. If you have partial access privileges, for example, you might be able to a load and download files and obtain directory listings, but not delete or rename files.

Perhaps the most common type of FTP access is called *anonymous* log on. Typically, anonymous log on permits you to download files from the FTP server and nothing more. Anonymous FTP is very useful when you want to make files available to the general public. Most commonly, you log on as an anonymous user, using "anonymous" as your username and your email address as a password.

Unlike HTTP, FTP is not a stateless protocol. FTP involves two connections between the local and remote computer, and they are maintained throughout the FTP session. One of the connections is called the *control connection*, and it is used to send commands and responses to commands between the computers. The second connection is the *data connection*, which is used for the actual file transfers. When I talk about there being two connections in FTP session, I am referring to logical connections, not to physical connections. Of course, only a single physical connection exists between the two computers, but it is used for two distinct purposes: commands and data. This is somewhat analogous to using a single telephone line for both voice and fax communication.

Other Protocols

Although HTTP and FTP are the most important Internet services, you might run into several others that are not used as often. I will not be covering these further in the book, but you should know at least the basics.

Usenet

The Usenet protocol is used for sending messages to newsgroups. Rather than being sent to specific recipients, Usenet messages are *posted* to a specific news group. These groups are organized by subject matter and cover anything you can imagine and a few things you can't. Anyone who is interested can visit a news group, read posted messages, and post their own messages. You need a news reader program to access newsgroups, as well as access to a news server. When you *subscribe* to a news group, it means that your news reader program will automatically download a list of that news group's new messages each time you log on to the news server.

News groups are named to reflect their topic. Like domain names, news group names are hierarchical, but they work in left-to-right order. For example, the news group rec.food.recipes is in the broadest category of rec (for *recreation*), the narrower category of food, and the final category of recipes. There are thousands of newsgroups, some moderated and others pretty much a free-for-all.

Telnet

The Telnet protocol is used to log on to a remote computer and use it as if you were sitting in front of it. An engineer at a small college, for example, could use Telnet to log on to a supercomputer at Cal Tech and use it for calculations. To use Telnet, you generally need permission from the managers of the remote system. A few systems have set up anonymous Telnet accounts that permit anyone to log in and use a restricted set of the system's capabilities.

Gopher

Gopher has certain similarities to the World Wide Web, and with the widespread use of the Web, Gopher is rarely used anymore. With Gopher, you use a client program to locate and view information located on Gopher servers across the Internet. The difference between Gopher and the Web is in the way the information is organized. The sum of all information available via Gopher is referred to as *gopherspace*.

The Web uses hypertext to organize information, but gopherspace uses a system of hierarchical menus. Each Gopher server (a computer that is part of gopherspace) has a main menu. Each item on the main menu can lead to a submenu, to a menu on another server, or to a resource. Resources include text, pictures, and so on. When you select a menu item, your Gopher client will fetch the resource and display it for you.

Veronica and Jughead are tools that help you locate information in gopherspace. Veronica searches all the menus it can find, and Jughead searches a specified subgroup of menus.

Archie

Archie is a tool that helps you locate files on FTP servers. Specifically, Archie helps you to locate an FTP server that contains a copy of a particular file. An Archie client, located on your computer, works in conjunction with a remote Archie server. Each Archie server contains a regularly updated database of files available by anonymous FTP. After the Archie server has identified one or more FTP sites with the desired files, it's a simple matter to fetch it.

Talk and Chat

Talk lets you communicate in real time with other people on the Internet. You type something, and they see it on their screen almost immediately, and vice versa. Until recently, all talk consisted of this sort of typed message, but hardware advances have made it possible to actually talk and listen. For this sort of capability, both systems must have a sound card and microphone, as well as special software. All sorts of variations on talk are possible: private one-on-one conversations, restricted group meetings, or public free-for-alls.

Chat, or more precisely, Internet Relay Chat, is a talk facility that can be used by anyone, any time. Chat provides several simultaneous channels, with each channel carrying a conversation related to a specific topic. You can join existing channels at will and create your own channel if desired.

Muds and More

You have probably heard of the multiplayer role-playing game called Dungeons and Dragons. The first Mud was an online version of D & D, and that's where its name came from: *Multiple User Dungeon*. The idea is that you interact with other players in an imaginary setting, with each player adopting a fictional identity. Since the original D & D–based Mud, a whole slew of similar games have been developed. Variations have arisen, too, with names such as *Mushes*, *Moos*, *Mucks*, and *Muses*. I can't tell you how to find or use Muds because I've never been tempted myself.

Internet Addresses

1

If computers are going to communicate with each other across the Internet, or any network for that matter, they need some way to locate a specific target computer. Like a residence or a business in a town or a city, computers on the Internet are located by means of their addresses. Internet addresses operate at two different levels.

IP Addresses

Each and every computer on the Internet is assigned an IP address (IP stands for *Internet protocol*, something I will explain soon). An IP address consists of four numbers, each ranging from 0 to 255, separated by periods. Here's an example:

```
123.4.32.223
```

The total number of possible IP addresses is equal to 4,228,250,625, so there is plenty of room for future growth of the Internet. A particular computer's IP address uniquely identifies that computer and its location. When a message is sent to that computer, this ensures that the message reaches the proper destination.

The job of seeing that the message arrives at the proper destination is the job of the routers, specialized computers on the Internet that I mentioned earlier. The message reaches a router, the destination IP address is examined, and the message is sent on the next stage of its journey toward its destination. A message might travel through several routers between being sent and being received.

IP addresses are fine as far as they go, but they have two important limitations. First, being composed entirely of numbers, they are difficult to remember and to associate with the person or company that they belong to. More important, IP addresses are not portable. Because of the way IP addresses are assigned, a business could not move from New York to, say, Atlanta and retain the same IP addresses for its Internet computers. These problems were solved by the second level of the Internet address scheme, domain names.

> If you connect to the Internet via a modem or other dial-in connection, your computer is assigned a temporary IP address by your internet service provider (ISP). This IP address is valid only for the duration of the session, and you will be assigned a different IP address for subsequent sessions. Some ISPs offer the option of a permanent IP address, so you will have the same address each time you dial in. This is the exception to the rule, though.

Domain Names

The concept of *domain names* was developed to solve the problems inherent in using IP addresses by themselves. If you have used the Web at all, I am sure you have seen and used domain names. Table 1.1 shows a few examples.

TABLE 1.1   EXAMPLES OF DOMAIN NAMES

Domain Name	Belongs to
www.microsoft.com	Microsoft Corporation
www.duke.edu	Duke University
www.army.mil	U.S. Army
www.nih.gov	National Institutes of Health
ourworld.compuserve.com	CompuServe online service
www.npr.org	National Public Radio

Obviously, domain names make much more sense and are easier to remember than IP addresses. You might have noticed that domain names seem to consist of three parts, called *subdomains*. That's usually true, and each subdomain has a different meaning. Let's see what those meanings are, working from right to left.

Within the United States, the last part of the domain name identifies the type of organization to which the domain belongs. Five of the most common ones are all represented in Table 1.1; they are commercial enterprise (com), educational institution (edu), military (mil), governmental organization (gov), and nonprofit organization (org). The sixth common domain name suffix is net and is used primarily by organizations that provide network services. Some new domain name suffixes have been proposed to relieve the shortage of desirable names, and you might start to see some of these soon.

Outside the United States, the domain name suffix usually identifies the country: uk for United Kingdom, jp for Japan, es for Spain, and so on. There is even a suffix for the United States—us, of course—but it is rarely used. You'll see it used most frequently by states and local governments, along with a subdomain identifying the state. For example, www.state.nc.us is the State of North Carolina's Web page.

The second subdomain from the right usually identifies the organization that owns the domain name. Outside the United States, it sometimes identifies the type of organization. In the United Kingdom, for example, ac identifies an academic institution, and www.ruskin.ac.uk is the domain name for Ruskin College.

The first, or far left, subdomain identifies a particular computer within the domain. You'll see the letters www used frequently, as a convention for identifying a World Wide Web server, but there is no requirement to do so. Likewise, FTP (File Transfer Protocol) servers typically use ftp for the first subdomain. You could use nearly anything you like, however, so the Whoopie company could have servers named www1.whoopie.com, sales.whoopie.com, catalog.whoopie.com, and so on.

Domain Name Service

If the Internet uses IP addresses, and people use domain names, how are the two connected? The answer is the Internet's *domain name service*. When you register a domain name, you must also provide information about the IP address of the associated computer. This information is placed in the Internet address registry, which is maintained on computers known as *domain name servers* scattered around the Internet. When reference is made to a particular domain name, the associated IP address is automatically obtained from a domain name server. If you try to connect to an invalid domain name (one that is not registered) you will receive an error message from your browser.

Uniform Resource Locators

More commonly known as URL, a uniform resource locator identifies a specific resource on the Internet or Web. The term *resource* generally means a file or document. Here's an example of a URL:

```
http://www.microsoft.com/ie40.htm
```

A URL has three parts that provide all the information required to locate and retrieve the file. Let's dissect the preceding URL to see what these parts are.

- First is the protocol specification, in this case http://. This part of the URL specifies the communication protocol (Hypertext Transfer Protocol) to be used to retrieve the file. You learned about Internet protocols earlier in the chapter. The other protocol you will commonly see in URLs is ftp:// for File Transfer Protocol.

- Second is the domain name (www.microsoft.com) which identifies the computer where the file is located.

- Third is the name of the file (ie40.htm) to be retrieved.

The third part of a URL, the filename, is optional. If you use a URL without a filename, the remote computer returns a default file that is specified by the system administrator. For Web sites, the default file is often INDEX.HTM.

Email Addresses

If you have used email at all, I am sure you have noticed that email addresses are similar to domain names, such as mike@somewhere.com. The part of the address to the right of the @ sign is, in fact, a domain name and identifies the computer where the mailbox is located. The mailbox, which is nothing more than a software program, accepts incoming mail messages and identifies the recipient by the part of the address to the left of the @ sign. When the user logs on to the mail server, he or she sees a list of messages that have been received.

The New Dynamic Web

In the beginning, the Web was static. It consisted solely of static content made up of HTML pages, or files, located on server computers around the Internet. The user could retrieve these pages and view them in a browser, but that was all. There was no other interaction between the client and server, and the only way the content of the pages could be updated was for the Web site administrator to manually edit them.

It was soon realized that the Web would be greatly improved if it could offer dynamic, as well as static, content. Dynamic content permits the user to send a request for specific information to the server. The server responds to the request by running a script or application to generate a customized HTML page based on the user's request. It is this custom page, with up-to-date information, that is returned to the user. Figure 1.5 shows how this works.

Custom information can also flow from the user to the server. For instance, the user can enter his or her name and mailing address on a form displayed in the browser. This information is sent to the server, where it is saved for future use in a mailing list. In more sophisticated applications, ordering and credit card information can be sent to the server.

SECURITY ON THE WEB

In the early days of the Internet, security was not a concern. Sensitive information was rarely transmitted, and in any case, access to the Internet was limited, so unauthorized prying was not a concern. In fact, the open architecture of the Internet was one of the important reasons for its success. Today, however, everyone and her grandmother has Internet access, and there is a need to transmit confidential information, such as credit card numbers, in a secure manner. Most Web servers and browsers now have encryption features built in so that data can be transmitted securely when and if required.

Figure 1.5

The old static Web compared with the new dynamic Web.

The old static Web

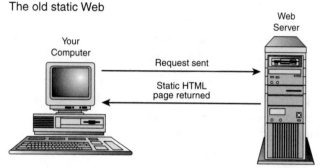

The new dynamic Web

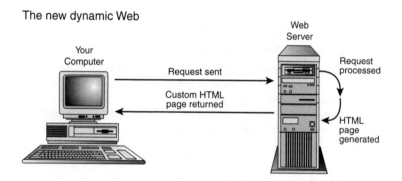

Types of Dynamic Content

What sorts of dynamic content are possible? It's difficult to answer this question because there is almost no limit to what you can do with dynamic Web pages. The possibilities range from the extremely simple to the very complex. Take a look at some examples.

On the simple end of the scale, suppose that you work for a professional graphics design house and are in charge of programming its Web page. Because presenting a graphically sophisticated design is a top priority, you do not want visitors to see the same pictures each time they visit the page. With dynamic programming, you could automatically display a different picture each day, or you could keep track of individual visitors and ensure that no one sees the same picture twice.

A somewhat more complicated dynamic Web site might be appropriate for an automobile manufacturer. You want to provide potential customers with an exciting experience that will tempt them away from their computers and down to the showroom. Your Web page lets them select a car model, add accessories, and select options such as interior and exterior color. As they make selections, a picture of the car changes to show how it will look with the selected options, and the price information is updated as well. Visitors can see what their dream car will look like and cost before setting foot in the showroom.

At the high end of the complexity scale would be a clothing retailer's online catalog and ordering Web site. Users can browse your products; check sizes, colors, and availability; and search for specific items. Selected items are added to an electronic "shopping cart." When the user is finished shopping, credit card and shipping information is processed and the order details are sent to your warehouse for processing.

I hope that you can see the wide possibilities of dynamic Web content. The flexibility and power of a dynamic Web site are limited only by the imagination and skills of the Web site developer.

> **DYNAMIC IS NOT ALWAYS THE WAY TO GO**
>
> Although dynamic content is suitable for many types of Web sites, you need to remember that this is not always the best way to go. Some types of Web sites work perfectly well with purely static content or perhaps only a small touch of dynamic content. You should not use dynamic techniques simply because they are available, but because they best suit the needs of your project.

Databases and the Web

One of the most exciting and powerful aspects of dynamic Web content is the ability to connect a Web page to a database. In the preceding dynamic Web site examples, the clothing retailer's online catalog was a case that would use database connectivity. Information about the products, such as price, available colors, and sizes, would be maintained in a database. This and other information would be extracted from the database and incorporated in the dynamic Web pages, depending on requests made by the user. Programming database connectivity into your dynamic Web pages is one of the things you'll learn in this book. As you will see, the Active Server Pages technology is an essential element of database connectivity.

Visual Basic and Web Programming

Now that you have learned the basics of the Internet and the Web, you might wonder about the tools and capabilities Visual Basic provides for Internet programming. There are many different ways to approach Web development, and I think you'll be glad to know that Visual Basic is one of the best. What exactly does Visual Basic offer to you, the Web site developer, that will help you to efficiently create exciting and functional Web sites? Here's a brief overview of the major topics that I will cover in this book:

- ActiveX control technology enables you to create powerful software components that can be used on a Web page in much the same way that a regular Visual Basic control is used on a Visual Basic form.

- ActiveX documents are created in essentially the same way as you program a Visual Basic form, but they are deployed on the Web and display in a browser window.

- Dynamic HTML provides sophisticated Web programming capabilities specifically for intranets.

- The Internet transfer control and the WebBrowser control make it simple to create Visual Basic applications that communicate over the Internet.

- Active Server Pages and the Visual Basic scripting language permit programming of dynamic Web content and database connectivity.

Summary

After reading this chapter, you should have a good fundamental understanding of how the Internet and World Wide Web function. You have also had a glimpse of the programming power that Visual Basic can bring to your Internet projects. Visual Basic might be the only Internet programming tool you'll ever need.

This chapter explains the origins of the Internet and Web and shows how these two terms, although related, refer to different things. You learned about the distinction between the Internet and intranets, had an introduction to Hypertext Markup Language, and learned about the most important protocols used on the Internet. You discovered the details of Internet addresses and uniform resource locators, or URLs. This basic understanding of how the Internet and Web operate is important for anyone who develops Web sites.

This chapter also showed you how the Web has been changing, moving from the older static content model to the newer and more flexible dynamic content model. Database connectivity is an important aspect of the new Web. Finally, I introduced you to the powerful tools that Visual Basic provides for your Internet programming needs. In the remaining 20 lessons, you learn everything you need to know in order to use these tools to accomplish your Internet programming needs.

Q&A

Q **What is the distinction between the Internet and the World Wide Web?**

A The term *Internet* refers to the computers and connections between them. The Web consists of information located on the Internet, linked by hyperlinks. One way to look at this is that the Internet is interconnected computers, whereas the Web is interconnected information.

Q **What are the three parts of a uniform resource locator, or URL? Which of the three parts is optional?**

A The first part of a URL specifies the transfer protocol, typically either Hypertext Transfer Protocol (`http://`) or File Transfer Protocol (`ftp://`). The second part of a URL specifies the domain name of the remote computer, for example, `www.microsoft.com`. The third part of a URL specifies the name of a specific file. The filename is the optional part; if it's omitted, the remote computer will return a default file.

Q **How does a dynamic Web page differ from a static Web page?**

A A static Web page can be changed only by someone sitting down and editing it. Every visitor to the page sees exactly the same thing. A dynamic Web page is "custom-made" for each and every visitor. The contents of a dynamic Web page depend on requests or information received from the individual viewing the page.

Q **What are the main differences between the GIF and JPG image formats?**

A The GIF format can display nearly 256 different colors, whereas the JPG format can display more than 16 million different colors. In addition, the JPG format offers a variable compression level that can be selected by the user, permitting you to select the ideal trade-off between image quality and file size.

Q **What are the two components of a Hypertext Markup Language document?**

A One component is contents, which will be displayed when someone views the document. The other component is tags, which are not displayed but rather control the document formatting and other functions.

Workshop

Quiz

1. What is the function of a domain name server?

2. How can you identify an HTML tag in a hypertext document?

3. What is a hyperlink?

4. Describe three important functions of the tags in an HTML document.

5. What is the function of a browser program?

6. What is TCP/IP?

7. What does the last part of a domain name mean?

DAY 2

Making Sense of ActiveX

One of the most powerful technologies available to Windows programmers is ActiveX. Almost any program you create with Visual Basic will use ActiveX, and that includes Internet programs. In fact, ActiveX has some features that seem to be specifically designed for the Internet. This is the first of several lessons that I devote to ActiveX. Today you will learn

- The importance of software components
- The history and terminology of ActiveX
- Ways to use ActiveX in your Visual Basic projects
- Details of ActiveX security and distribution concerns

The Software Component Revolution

Like anybody else, software programmers prefer to work efficiently. Among other things, this means never doing the same thing twice if it can be avoided. After you have written the code to perform a certain task, why waste time writing the same code again? It's much more efficient to reuse the same code.

The first method for reusing code was the *procedure*. I'll bet that you have used procedures in some of your Visual Basic projects. By putting code inside a procedure in order to perform a particular task and by assigning the procedure a name, you can call that code from anywhere in your project—in essence, reusing the code. Even greater flexibility is obtained by placing the procedure inside a separate Basic module. This way, the module can be included in other Visual Basic projects, making the procedures available to them as well. In a simple way, such procedures can be thought of as software components. You can see how this works in Figure 2.1.

FIGURE 2.1

*A procedure inside a
Basic module can be
reused in multiple
projects.*

Basic module

Project 1   Project 2

Procedure

Tip

> Place potentially reusable procedures in a separate Basic module. You can then reuse the code in other Visual Basic projects by adding the module to the project. Use the Add Module command on the Project menu for both these tasks.

A Giant Step Forward

When the original Visual Basic was introduced about ten years ago, it marked a giant step forward for software components. No longer were software components limited to code only; they could contain visual screen elements as well. I am, of course, talking about Visual Basic controls. If you were not involved in programming back then, it's probably impossible for you to imagine the excitement that this development caused. Commonly needed visual interface elements, such as text boxes and option buttons, had become available to simply drop into your project. Software components had graduated from doing a task, such as performing mathematical calculations, to providing the visual element, as well as all the required underlying functionality. The text box, for example, does not only display on the screen, but also accepts user input, permits editing, detects user events such as mouse clicks, and so on.

Object-Oriented Programming

The increased interest in the use of software components was paralleled by the development of a new programming technology, object-oriented programming (OOP). The impetus for the development of OOP came from programs growing larger and more complex all the time and, as a result, becoming more difficult to debug and maintain. Most of the problems with debugging and maintenance resulted from unforeseen interactions between different parts of the program. Make a modification or correction in one part of the program, and you might cause problems in another part of the program that you never could have predicted.

The way around this problem was to encapsulate different parts of the program into independent units called *objects*. The inner workings of each object are completely hidden from the rest of the program and therefore cannot have unexpected effects on its operation.

An object cannot be completely isolated from the rest of the program, of course, or it would be no use. An object interacts with other objects and other parts of the program by means of its *interface*. An object's interface consists of its properties and methods, which represent data and code, respectively, that are part of the object. Figure 2.2 illustrates the relationship between an object, its interface, and the rest of the program.

Interface Versus *Interface*

You might have noticed that the term *interface* is used in two different ways. It can refer to the visual elements that a program displays onscreen, or it can refer to the properties and methods of an object. You can usually deduce the correct meaning from the context in which the word is used.

Encapsulation

The manner in which objects hide, or isolate, their inner workings from the rest of the program is called *encapsulation*.

If you have worked with Visual Basic, you are already familiar with the idea of objects and their interfaces, even though you might not have used these terms. A Visual Basic control is an object, and its properties and methods are its interface. The inner workings of the control are completely hidden from you and the program. In fact, the programmers at Microsoft could change the way a control operates internally, and you and your programs would never know the difference, as long as the interface remained the same.

FIGURE 2.2

An object exposes only its interface to the rest of the program.

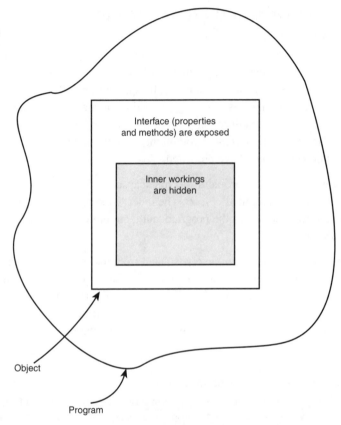

Interface (properties and methods) are exposed

Inner workings are hidden

Object

Program

IS VISUAL BASIC OOP?

Strictly speaking, Visual Basic does not offer real object-oriented programming. Languages that were specifically designed to be object-oriented have a few capabilities that are not present in Visual Basic. Don't let this worry you. Visual Basic's object-oriented features are more than sufficient for almost every programming need.

Objects in Visual Basic

We have seen that Visual Basic lets you use objects in your projects—but is that all? No, there's more. A very important capability of Visual Basic is that of enabling you to create your own objects from scratch. That's right. When the need arises, you can enclose code and/or visual interface elements within an object wrapper, so to speak, obtaining all the benefits of reusability and encapsulation that the object model offers.

Visual Basic offers the capability of creating two types of objects. The first type, which doesn't really have a name of its own, is created within a Visual Basic class module. You add a class module to a Visual Basic project by selecting Add Class Module from the Project menu. The objects you create in this way can be very useful, but they have one major limitation: They can be used and reused only within Visual Basic projects. For some situations, this is not a limitation at all, and you'll find these "regular" Visual Basic class modules to be a powerful tool when used appropriately.

2

OBJECTS AND CLASSES

You'll see the terms *object* and *class* used in discussions of OOP and software components, so you need to understand the distinction between them. A class is a plan for an object; a class is like a blueprint, and an object is something created from that blueprint. The relationship between a class and an object is like the one between a blueprint for a chair and an actual chair built from the blueprint. When you program a class module, you are defining a class; code in your program will then use the class to create one or more objects for use in the program. An object is sometimes called an *instance* of its class, and creating an object is sometimes referred to as *instantiating* a class.

The second type of object is called *ActiveX*. From a certain perspective, an ActiveX object is the same as a regular object: It is encapsulated, it has methods and properties, and so on. Because it uses ActiveX technology, however, it is much more flexible. Here are some of the ways that ActiveX technology adds power and flexibility to objects:

- ActiveX objects are not limited to use in Visual Basic projects.
- ActiveX objects come in several different types, so you can choose the "flavor" best suited to your current needs.
- Certain ActiveX objects can be deployed and used on the Web.
- ActiveX objects can have code-only functionality and visual interface elements as well.
- ActiveX objects automatically register themselves with Windows (by placing information in the Windows registry), enabling other programs to determine their availability and capabilities.

I think you can see that ActiveX is a powerful tool. You'll be learning a lot about this technology throughout the book, but first take a brief look at some history and terminology.

A Brief History of ActiveX

The promise of software components has been on people's minds for a long time. In fact, reusable and sharable components were one of the primary motivations behind the development of the Windows operating system (others include the ability to run multiple programs at once and to easily share data between programs).

The first attempt to implement software components was a technology called *Object Linking and Embedding* (OLE). The primary goal of OLE was to permit the creation of compound documents in which two or more specialized applications worked in tandem to create different portions of the document. For example, a document that contained both text and charts could be created using a word processor and a charting program. The word processor, with all its specialized text-editing features, would be active while you were working on text, and the charting program, with specialized graphics tools, would be active while you were working on a chart. This early OLE worked, after a fashion, but was slow and inconvenient. It was, however, a first step in the right direction.

OLE was based on a broader standard called the *Component Object Model* (COM). COM soon spread beyond the creation of compound documents, and the term *OLE* went with it. Soon, *OLE* was the term for anything that used the COM technology, including but not limited to compound documents. For example, in earlier releases of Visual Basic, some of the controls used the COM model and were referred to as *OLE controls*.

A few years ago, when Microsoft became seriously committed to the Internet, the term *ActiveX* was introduced. At first, it referred specifically to Internet- and Web-related things, but this usage didn't last long. Now, *ActiveX* refers to a range of COM-based technologies by which one piece of software makes its capabilities available to other software. Part of the ActiveX promise, one that is of particular interest to Internet programmers, is support for distributed computing. In other words, an ActiveX component can be available even if it is located on a computer half a continent away.

What about *OLE*? This term has returned to its original and more limited meaning having to do with the creation of compound documents.

ActiveX Pros and Cons

For providing active content on the Web, ActiveX is, in my opinion, the best technology available. It is not the only way to create active content, and some people will not agree that it is the best way to go. Let's take a look at the plusses and minuses of ActiveX.

On the Plus Side

One of the major selling points of the ActiveX technology is its power. There are very few limitations on what an ActiveX component can do; in other words, an ActiveX component can perform just about any task that a regular standalone program can. From the Web developer's perspective, this flexibility makes it that much easier to create dynamic and functional Web pages. Other technologies for active contents, most notably Java and common gateway interface (CGI) programming, are more limited in their capabilities.

Another plus, at least for many people, is the potential to leverage existing programming skills into ActiveX component creation. Visual Basic is the most popular programming language in the world, and it's much easier to expand your Visual Basic skills to meet your Web programming needs than it is to learn a whole new programming language.

The way that ActiveX handles downloads is also an advantage. When a user visits a Web page that uses one or more ActiveX components (assuming he or she is using an ActiveX-enabled browser), here's what happens:

1. A brief description of the component and its version number are downloaded.
2. The browser checks whether the component is already installed on the user's system.
3. If it is not installed, or if the installed version is older than the one specified by the Web page, the component is downloaded, installed, and run.
4. If the component is already installed, it doesn't need to be downloaded, but is simply run from the local copy.

I think you can see the advantage of this system; any given component needs to be downloaded only once. On the second and subsequent uses of the component, no download is required, and the response time is much faster. Other active content technologies, such as Java, require a component to be downloaded each and every time it is required, and the response time from the end user's perspective is correspondingly slower.

THE INTERNET DOWNLOAD SERVICE

An ActiveX-enabled browser makes use of the Internet Download Service to access ActiveX components on the Web. This service, part of the Windows API, performs download, verification, and installation of ActiveX components. When the browser encounters a component that is not already installed, it calls the API function `GoGetClassObjectFromURL`, passing it the identity of the ActiveX component. This function then takes care of the rest of the task of downloading, and so on.

Nothing Is Perfect

In the minus column for ActiveX is perhaps the most important item: security concerns. This problem is a seemingly unavoidable consequence of one of ActiveX's advantages, namely, its power and flexibility. An ActiveX component written by a malicious programmer could erase files on your hard disk or cause other serious problems. Should you feel safe downloading ActiveX components from the Web? The short answer is yes, and later in the lesson I will explain how Microsoft has implemented ActiveX security. Even so, any security system is theoretically breakable, so such concerns should not be totally ignored.

WHAT ABOUT JAVA?

Java is another important technology for creating active content. A Java *applet* is a small program that is downloaded and executed in the user's browser, providing many of the same capabilities as ActiveX. However, Java applets lack certain abilities, such as file access, that could potentially cause problems. In theory, therefore, a Java applet simply cannot be used maliciously, and security is not a problem.

Another problem with ActiveX technology is that only some browsers support it. If the functionality of your Web site depends on ActiveX components, visitors with a browser that is not ActiveX-enabled will be out of luck. Fortunately, this problem is not as serious as it might be. The two most popular browsers, Microsoft Internet Explorer and Netscape Navigator, both support ActiveX—Internet Explorer directly and Navigator through use of a plug-in. In any case, browser incompatibility is a potential problem only when programming for the Internet. In the case of an intranet, you have control over which browser is being used.

A final potential downside to ActiveX arises from components being downloaded and permanently installed on the user's machine, using up hard disk space. To be honest, I don't see this as a problem. Most components are relatively small in size, and today's hard disks are so huge that a few megabytes taken up by downloaded ActiveX components is unlikely to cause anyone a headache.

The Many Faces of ActiveX

ActiveX is a very flexible technology, and Visual Basic offers you several different ways to use ActiveX in your projects. I am not talking about using existing ActiveX components, although that is important, too. Rather, I am talking about the different kinds of ActiveX components you can create using Visual Basic. You see these different types listed when you start Visual Basic or start a new project, when the New Project dialog box is displayed (see Figure 2.3). You can see that several of the project types have ActiveX in their name.

FIGURE 2.3

The New Project dialog box offers several types of ActiveX projects.

ARE YOU EXPOSED?

The term *exposed* is used to refer to a software component being made available for use by other programs. If a Visual Basic program contained an ActiveX component that it makes available for use by other programs, you would say that the program exposes the component, or the component is exposed by the program.

Take a brief look at these various types of ActiveX projects. You'll learn more details later.

- ActiveX EXE—A Visual Basic program that exposes one or more ActiveX components. The term *component* in this context refers to functionality in code without a visual interface.

- ActiveX DLL—Exposes one or more components but has no other functionality other than to expose the components.

- ActiveX Document Exe—A complete Visual Basic program, in effect, that can be installed on a Web site and then downloaded and run in a Web browser.

- ActiveX Document Dll—Contains supporting code for an ActiveX Document Exe.

- ActiveX Control—A self-contained unit that includes both code and a visual interface. Many of Visual Basic's built-in controls are ActiveX controls. An ActiveX control can be used in Visual Basic projects and in Web pages.

THE ACTIVEX DOCUMENT MIGRATION WIZARD

Visual Basic provides a tool, the ActiveX Document Migration Wizard, that helps you in converting standard Visual Basic applications to ActiveX document projects. You will see how to use this tool on Day 8, "Migrating Regular Visual Basic Applications to ActiveX."

ActiveX and Security

I am sure that you have heard of viruses, programs that get onto your system and cause problems. A virus infection can range from a minor annoyance to a major catastrophe, and people put a lot of effort into ensuring that their computers remain virus-free. What about the possibility of downloading a virus or other harmful software from the Web?

In the early days of the Web, this was not a concern. The only types of files you downloaded were HTML documents and image files for display in your browser. A corrupted HTML or image file might display as garbage on your screen, but in no way could it cause any virus-like problems on your system.

With the emergence of the new dynamic Web technologies, things have become more complicated. What you might download from the Web is no longer limited to HTML and image files, but includes executable programs that actually run on your computer. There's no end to the potential problems that an executable program can cause, ranging from deleting files, to corrupting the operating system, to uploading sensitive data from your hard disk, to who-knows-where.

The people at Microsoft, Netscape, and other companies, who were developing Web programming tools, recognized the need for some form of security. When surfing the Web, you need reasonable assurance that a code element downloaded from one site or another will not mess up your system! Two basic approaches have been taken to this question of security.

One method is to simply make it impossible for a downloaded program to cause mischief. This was the approach taken with the Java language, which is used to write *applets*, downloadable Web applications. A Java applet does not have the capability to perform those actions, such as file access, that could be used by a malicious programmer to cause problems on your computer. You know that any Java applet you download is safe, just as you know that a rubber knife is safe for your child to play with.

The second method is the one adapted by Microsoft for ActiveX components. Rather than limit the capabilities of the technology, a technology called *Authenticode* permits users to verify the source and integrity of each and every component. The idea here is that if you know where a component came from (who created it), and you know that it has not been modified, you will feel safe in assuming that the component will cause no harm; you trust the source. This process is referred to as *digital signing*.

Digital Signing from the End User's Perspective

When you are browsing the Web using an ActiveX-enabled browser, you automatically have at your disposal several levels of security. You select the level that you feel is appropriate for your activities: lax, medium, or strict. With Microsoft Internet Explorer, select Internet Options from the View menu and select the Security tab in the dialog box (see Figure 2.4). In the top part of the dialog box, you assign Web sites to different zones, and then in the lower part of the dialog box, you specify the security settings for each zone. Web sites that you are sure about, such as your own company's sites or the sites of well-known software publishers such as Microsoft, can be put in the "trusted" zone with a low-level security. Likewise, you can specify that unknown sites automatically be assigned to the "restricted" zone to which you assign high security.

FIGURE 2.4

Setting active content security levels in Internet Explorer.

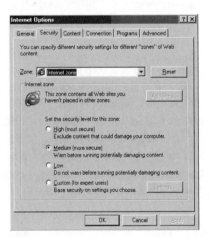

Tip | All Web sites that you have not specifically placed in other zones are included in the Internet zone.

Next, you assign one of four security levels to each zone; the security levels are described here:

- High—Potentially damaging active content is never downloaded; you are, however, notified of attempts to download such active content.
- Medium—You are warned of attempts to download active content and then given the choice to download it or not, based on the identity of the digital signature.
- Low—All active content is downloaded without notification.
- Custom—You can individually specify to always download, never download, or prompt for different types of active content. I suggest that you do not use this security option until you are thoroughly familiar with the various types of active content that you might encounter on the Web.

Do	Don't
DO assign Medium or High security level to the Internet zone.	DON'T assign Low security to any sites unless you are sure they can be trusted.

Here, then, is how it works. When you visit a Web page that attempts to download active content, your browser checks each item for a digital signature, or *certificate*. If there is no certificate, the content is downloaded only if low security is in effect. Otherwise, the source of the component is extracted from the certificate, and other information in the certificate is used to verify that the component has not been modified because the certificate was attached. This latter procedure is to guard against the possibility of someone obtaining a digitally signed component, modifying it, and then making it available for download with the original certificate still intact.

If you have the medium level of security in effect, the name of the component publisher is checked against a list of sources that you have indicated as okay. If the name is not on this list, you will see a dialog box that identifies the source of the component and asks you whether to download it. You also have the option of adding this publisher's name to your approved list.

Digital Signing from the Developer's Perspective

A digital signature contains three pieces of information: the identity of the software publisher (the person or company that created the active component), the identity of the certifying authority (the organization that issued the certificate), and an encrypted *hash total* that is used to verify that the component has not been altered. The first step in signing your components is obtaining a certificate.

> **YOU CAN FORGET ABOUT SIGNING FOR NOW**
>
> If you are just getting started creating ActiveX controls, you are probably anxious to get to work and might not want to worry about the admittedly complex details of digital signing. That's fine—go right ahead! You can create and test ActiveX controls as much as you want without signing them. Only later, when you want to deploy your controls on the Web, is it necessary to sign them. Skip this part of the lesson, if you like, and come back to it later.

If you are going to be developing active content for the Web, you will probably need to obtain an Authenticode certificate so that you will be able to digitally sign the components that you publish. One exception to this might be if you are developing for a company intranet only, in which case you could publish unsigned components and then have your users assign low security to the intranet sites.

If you work for a company, they might already have an Authenticode certificate that you can use. Otherwise, you will need to obtain your own. Although several organizations issue Authenticode certificates, Microsoft recommends the VeriSign Company. You can visit its Web site at `www.verisign.com/developers/index.html` for information on obtaining a personal certificate. The cost is currently $20 per year, and the procedure is painless. Here's how it works:

1. You fill out an online form with the information required for the certificate, as well as credit card information.
2. VeriSign sends you an email with a verification code.
3. You go to VeriSign's certificate installation page and enter the verification code that you were sent in the email message. You must do this from the same computer that was used for step 1.
4. The certificate is downloaded to your computer.

When downloading the certificate, you have the option of saving it in a file or in the registry. I suggest that you use the file option and keep the files on a diskette. This permits you to keep the files in a safe place, which prevents any unauthorized users of your computer from using your certificate to sign software. You'll actually receive two files: one containing the certificate itself, with the `.SPC` extension, and the other containing your encryption key, with the `.PVK` extension.

Do	Don't
DO keep your digital software certificate files on a diskette and keep the diskette in a safe place when not in use.	DON'T give anyone else access to your certificate files.

Software for Signing Components

After you have obtained an Authenticode certificate and encryption key, you are ready to sign your components. Well, almost! Unfortunately, Visual Basic does not include the capability to sign software components; you will need additional software. The software is part of the ActiveX Software Development Kit (SDK), which can be downloaded for free from Microsoft. You do not need the entire SDK (although you might find some other useful things in it). You need only these files:

- MakeCert—Creates a X.509 certificate for testing purposes.
- Cert2SPC—Creates a test software publishing certificate.
- SignCode—Signs an active component file.
- ChkTrust—Checks the validity of a component file, performing the same checks that a browser would if you tried to download the file.
- MakeCTL—Creates a certificate trust list.
- CertMgr—Manages certificates, certificate trust lists, and certificate revocation lists.
- SetReg—Sets registry keys that control the certificate verification process.

Be forewarned that all these are DOS programs and must be run in an MS-DOS window under the Windows operating system. To download the SDK, point your browser at msdn.microsoft.com/developer/sdk/inetsdk/asetup/default.htm; after reading the introductory material on this page, click the download link to go to the download page. You should use Internet Explorer to do this, not another browser, because the download page contains some active elements that determine which, if any, parts of the SDK you already have and that permit you to select which parts of the SDK to download. I do not recommend downloading the entire SDK unless you have a fast Internet connection, because it is more than 100MB. Rather, the download page, shown in Figure 2.5, lets you select which parts you want.

FIGURE 2.5

Microsoft's download page for the ActiveX SDK.

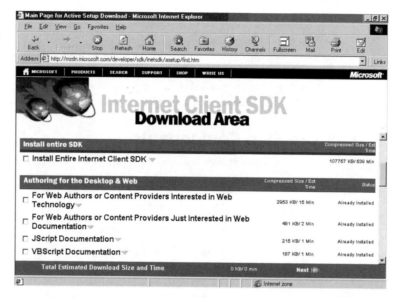

2

THINGS CHANGE

The one thing that is certain on the Web is change. By the time you read this, the URL and appearance of Microsoft's download page may have changed. If the preceding URL does not work, use the Microsoft Web site's search facility to locate the new URL for the Internet Client SDK.

You'll note that no selection for the Authenticode programs exists on the download page. That is because these programs are considered part of the core of the SDK and are always downloaded, no matter what you select. If you don't know what to select, choose the VBScript Documentation because this is something you will be able to use later. After the download and installation are complete, you'll find the SDK listed on your Windows Start menu, under Programs. The Authenticode programs will be located in \InetSDK\bin (assuming you used the default installation folder).

MORE AUTHENTICODE INFORMATION

You can find detailed information on the Authenticode technology, along with detailed instructions for signing components, at
www.microsoft.com/workshop/c-frame.htm#/workshop/security/default.asp.

> **X.509?**
>
> If you see the term *X.509*, don't worry. This is simply the technical name for the certificate specification used by Authenticode; you'll sometimes see Authenticode certificates referred to in this way.

Steps to Sign Components

Exactly what component files will you be signing? Here are the possibilities:

- .EXE files (an ActiveX document Exe)
- .DLL files (an ActiveX document Dll)
- .CAB files (compressed program installation files)
- .VBD files (part of an ActiveX document project)
- .OCX files (ActiveX controls)

The procedure for signing a file is the same, regardless of the type of file. Here are the steps to follow:

1. Be sure you have your certificate and personal key files available. For these examples, I will assume these files are named MYCRED.SPC and MYKEY.PVK, respectively, and that they are located on a diskette in drive a:.

2. Locate the file to be signed. This must be the final compiled and tested version, ready to be distributed to your Web site. If you recompile the project after signing the file, the digital signature will be lost and must be reapplied. For this example, assume you are signing MYCTRL.OCX in the current folder.

3. Open an MS-DOS window and move to the folder where the SIGNCODE.EXE program is located. Alternatively, you can have the program located in a folder that is part of the current path (see the next sidebar).

4. At the MS-DOS prompt, type in the required command. This is the general form of the command (type it all on the same line; it is placed on two lines here to fit the page width):

   ```
   signcode -spc CredentialFile -v
    PrivateKeyFile -n ControlName FileToSign
   ```

   This is the specific command for the example, assuming you want to assign the descriptive name "My Control":

   ```
   signcode -spc a:\mycred.spc -v a:\mykey.pvk -n "My Control"
   myctrl.ocx
   ```

5. Enter the password for your private key.

When finished, the program will display a message indicating whether it succeeded or there was a problem.

LONG FILENAMES

If your component file or the certificate and key files use long names, you may see them represented by shortened names in the MS-DOS box. For example, MYCONTROL.OCX would be MYCONT~1.OCX. You must use these short names when working with the SIGNCODE program.

What is this descriptive name that you can include in a digital signature? It is simply a name that will be displayed to users when they attempt to download the component (depending on their security settings). It is purely optional, but I think it's a good idea to include it.

TimeStamping Your Files

When you sign a file, you have the option of including a timestamp in the digital signature. This is an encoded representation of the date on which the component was signed. You can also add a timestamp to a previously signed file.

Why should you timestamp your components? The reason has to do with certificates expiring. Even though your Authenticode certificate has expired, components that you signed might still be in use on the Web. A component signed with an expired certificate might not be trustworthy, but if the component were timestamped, the browser's security software would distinguish between the following:

- A component that was signed with an expired certificate, which should not be trusted.

- A component that was signed with a certificate that was valid at the time of the signing but has since expired, which can be trusted.

A timestamp is obtained from a timestamp server, usually provided by the same organization that issued your certificate. The timestamp server will have a Web address such as the following:

```
http://timestamp.verisign.com/scripts/timstamp.dll
```

To timestamp a file at the same time you sign it, include the -t option in the SIGNCODE command line followed by the address of the timestamp server—for example:

```
signcode -spc a:\mycred.spc -v a:\mykey.pvk -n "My Control" -t
    http://timestamp.verisign.com/scripts/timstamp.dll myctrl.ocx
```

To timestamp a file that has already been signed, use the -x option:

```
signcode -t http://timestamp.verisign.com/scripts/timstamp.dll
 -x myctrl.ocx
```

Checking a File's Validity

You can use the program CHKTRUST to examine the signature of a component file. This program is part of the ActiveX SDK. The syntax is simple:

```
chktrust filename
```

For example:

```
chktrust myctrl.ocx
```

The program displays a dialog box with details of the component's signature, or if there is no signature, that fact is noted. Figure 2.6 shows a typical display.

FIGURE 2.6

Using CHKTRUST to verify a component's signature.

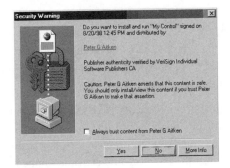

Note the following in the figure:

The component was distributed by Peter G Aitken.

It was given the description "My Control" when it was signed.

It was timestamped on 8/20/98 at 12:45 p.m.

The publisher's authenticity is verified by VeriSign.

This is the same dialog box that would be displayed to a user who is trying to download this component in Internet Explorer, if the security level was set to medium. Clicking the More Info button will display additional information about how security works. Click the publisher's name to view additional details about this certificate.

Publishing ActiveX Components

After you have created an ActiveX component for use on a dynamic Web site, how do you publish it? In other words, how do you make the component's file or files available on the Web site? Fortunately, Visual Basic comes to the rescue for this task. One of the tools provided with Visual Basic is the Package and Deployment Wizard, an add-in that walks you through all the required steps. This tool works for all types of program deployment, including making diskettes for distributing a standalone program to uploading ActiveX components to a Web site.

There are two parts to the process. The first is *packaging*, which consists of identifying all the required distribution files and putting them in a form suitable for deployment. In some cases, this is a simple process; deployment of an ActiveX control, for example, will usually require only a single OCX file. A complex dynamic HTML application, on the other hand, might require dozens of files. Packaging might involve combining and compressing the distribution files into a CAB (for *cabinet*) file.

The second part of the process is deployment, which means taking the packaged files and deploying them, getting them to where they need to be. This might involve copying the files to diskettes, to a specific folder on a network drive, or in the case of Web components, uploading the files to your Web site.

On Day 3, "Creating and Using an ActiveX Control," you will see more details of how the Package and Deployment Wizard works.

Summary

This has been an information-packed lesson, introducing you to ActiveX technology. If you will be using Visual Basic for your Web programming, it's essential that you understand ActiveX and what it can do for you. I know that you are anxious to start doing some real programming, and you will get to that in the next lesson on Day 3.

You have seen that ActiveX is a central part of Microsoft's software component strategy. Based on the Component Object Model, ActiveX provides several different ways for you to create reusable software components for Web programming. You have seen that although ActiveX is not perfect, it offers significant advantages and is likely to be one of the most important Web programming technologies for the foreseeable future. Visual Basic has the capability to create several types of ActiveX components.

You have also learned that security is an important consideration when using ActiveX components on the Web. Microsoft's Authenticode technology provides a method by which component publishers can digitally sign their files. This permits the end user to verify the identity of the component publisher and that the file has not been tampered with.

At the close of the day, you were shown how the Package and Deployment Wizard can simplify the task of distributing your components. This is in keeping with the general Visual Basic philosophy of making the programmer's job as easy as possible.

Q&A

Q What is the main purpose of the ActiveX technology?

A To provide a method for creating self-contained, reusable software components that can be used either locally or on a remote computer.

Q What is required by the end user to make full use of ActiveX controls that are used on a Web page?

A To make use of ActiveX components on a Web page, the end user must have an ActiveX-enabled Web browser. The two most popular browsers, Microsoft Internet Explorer and Netscape Navigator, both support ActiveX.

Q Suppose that you have a regular standalone Visual Basic project that you would like to convert for use on the Web. How would you accomplish this?

A An ActiveX document is the type of project that is designed specifically for placing the functionality of a complete Visual Basic program on the Web. You could use the ActiveX Document Migration Wizard to help you convert your regular Visual Basic program to an ActiveX document project.

Q What tools do you need to add a digital signature to an ActiveX component that you are planning to distribute?

A First, you need a digital certificate. Your employer might already have such a certificate, or you can obtain one of your own for a modest fee from a certificate authority such as VeriSign. Second, you need Microsoft's certificate tools, several programs that are part of the ActiveX Software Development Kit. You can obtain these programs free from Microsoft.

Quiz

1. What is the simplest way to reuse code in a Visual Basic program?
2. What are the five types of ActiveX projects available in Visual Basic?
3. What is the name of Microsoft's security system for ActiveX components?
4. How does the end user control whether active components are downloaded?
5. What is the advantage of including a timestamp when you apply a digital signature to a component?

2

DAY **3**

Creating and Using an ActiveX Control

Now that you have an understanding of the fundamentals of ActiveX technology, it's finally time to roll up your sleeves and do some programming. This lesson teaches some of the background you'll need to create ActiveX controls and then shows you all the steps required to create a simple ActiveX control and use it in a Web page. Today you will learn

- How to start an ActiveX control project
- How to work with the UserControl object
- The ways ActiveX controls respond to events
- Methods for testing your ActiveX control during development
- How to add properties to an ActiveX control
- How to use the control in a Web page

This is the first of three lessons on ActiveX controls. Because ActiveX controls are such a crucial topic, I felt that it was particularly important to present the material clearly and completely. In this lesson, you'll learn the fundamentals, and in the next lessons you will move on to some more advanced ActiveX control topics.

ActiveX Controls and Containers

One of the most important ways that Visual Basic makes ActiveX technology available to the programmer is by means of ActiveX controls. In many ways, an ActiveX control is very much like the standard controls provided with Visual Basic for using your programs. In fact, some of Visual Basic's intrinsic controls are ActiveX controls. Now, you can not only use ActiveX controls in your projects, but also create your own ActiveX controls from scratch, designing them to perform exactly the tasks that you require.

It's important to realize that an ActiveX control can do nothing on its own. To function, an ActiveX control must be contained within something else. The most common example of this is when a control is placed on a Visual Basic form; the form serves as the container. What makes an ActiveX control special is that it can be contained in a variety of different things. For the purposes of this book, the most relevant containers are Visual Basic forms and Web pages (or to be more precise, Web browsers). Figures 3.1 and 3.2 show an ActiveX control—in this case, the Calendar control—being contained in a Visual Basic form and in a Web browser (the Calendar control is provided with Visual Basic). The control looks and behaves the same, regardless of its container.

FIGURE 3.1

An ActiveX control can be contained in a Visual Basic form.

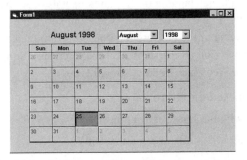

OTHER USES FOR ACTIVEX CONTROLS

ActiveX controls can be used also in programs developed using other tools, such as Delphi, Visual C++, and PowerBuilder.

FIGURE 3.2

An ActiveX control also can be contained in a Web browser.

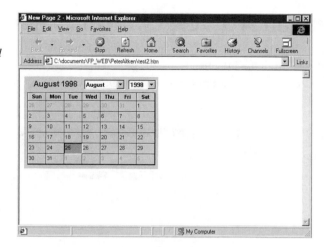

Programming an ActiveX Control

Many aspects of programming an ActiveX control are similar or identical to programming a standard Visual Basic executable. The visual interface part of the control is created on a form, and although the form is not the same as a standard Visual Basic form, most of the procedures are the same. There are two ways to create the visual interface of an ActiveX control. You can use other controls, including other ActiveX controls, or you can draw the interface by using Visual Basic's graphics statements. These two approaches to visual interface creation can be used individually or in combination.

An ActiveX control also contains code that provides its functionality. Code exists in procedures, or methods, that can be called by the ActiveX control's container. Code can also exist in event procedures to respond to events detected by the control. One special feature of ActiveX controls is the way events are handled. An event detected by the control, such as a mouse click, can be handled by code within the control, and it can also be "passed up" to the container object for handling there.

Finally, ActiveX controls can have properties. As with regular Visual Basic controls, properties can be used to determine how the control operates and also to hold data. Properties can be programmed to be read/write or read-only.

Starting an ActiveX Control Project

To begin creating an ActiveX control, start Visual Basic, or if it is already running, select New Project from the File menu. Visual Basic will display the New Project dialog box; click the ActiveX Control Project icon and then click OK. Your screen will look like Figure 3.3.

FIGURE 3.3

Starting an ActiveX control project.

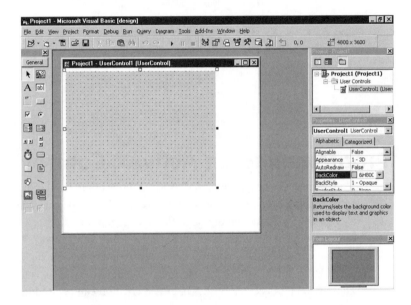

In many ways, this screen is the same as the one you see when starting a Standard EXE project, but you need to be aware of a few differences. Most important, an ActiveX control is based on something called a UserControl and not on a form. You can see this on the screen where the design area says UserControl1 in its title bar, not Form1. In many ways, a UserControl is like a regular Visual Basic form, but it provides the "wrapping" required to create an ActiveX control. Put another way, a UserControl has the same relationship with an ActiveX control as a regular form does with a window. A UserControl can hold other controls, can contain code, has properties and methods, and can respond to events. In other words, it is very much like a standard Visual Basic form.

You'll also note that the UserControl is not displayed in the Form Layout window in the lower right corner of the screen. This is because the screen position of an ActiveX control is determined by its container and cannot be set by the programmer during development.

Finally, look at the Project Explorer window. A UserControl category is listed there, with the project's one UserControl object listed. You can add other objects to an ActiveX control project, but for now you will concentrate on a simple case in which the project contains only one UserControl.

An ActiveX control, therefore, consists of the following main elements:

- A UserControl object with its properties, events, and methods.
- One or more constituent controls with their properties, events, and methods. Strictly speaking, an ActiveX control does not require constituent controls, but they are almost always present.
- Properties, methods, and events that you, the control developer, create in code.

You can see this relationship schematically in Figure 3.4.

FIGURE 3.4

The primary elements of an ActiveX control.

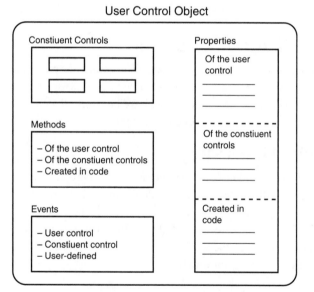

ActiveX Control Project Properties

Like any type of Visual Basic project, an ActiveX control project has properties that are accessed by selecting Project, Properties to display the Project Properties dialog box. Many project properties, such as Project Name and Project Description, are the same for an ActiveX project as for any other kind of Visual Basic project. I won't explain these, but instead will limit myself to those properties specifically relevant to an ActiveX control project. Some of these properties are found on the General tab in the Project Properties dialog box (see Figure 3.5).

FIGURE 3.5

The General tab of the Project Properties dialog box.

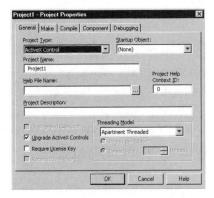

Upgrade ActiveX Controls

This option refers to the ActiveX controls used in your project and not to the ActiveX control that you are creating. If selected, your project is automatically updated to use new versions of ActiveX controls that have been installed since the last time you ran the project. Leave this option checked unless you have a specific reason to turn it off.

Require License Key

This option enables licensing for ActiveX control projects. When this option is selected, Visual Basic will generate a license file (*.vbl) when you build the project. The license file must be registered on the users' system for them to be able to use the ActiveX control in their own projects created with Visual Basic or another ActiveX-enabled development tool. See the section "Licensing Considerations for ActiveX Controls" later in this lesson for more information.

Threading Model

This property determines how the operating system and CPU execute the code in your component. The two options for this property are Apartment Threaded and Single Threaded. You should always use the Apartment Threaded setting.

Other properties that you need to be concerned with are found on the Debugging tab of the Project Properties dialog box (see Figure 3.6).

FIGURE 3.6

Setting debug properties for an ActiveX control project.

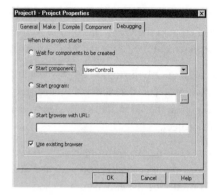

To understand how debugging properties work, you must remember how an ActiveX control runs. An ActiveX control must run inside a container and cannot run by itself. The setting that you make on the Debugging tab of the Project Properties dialog box determines what happens when you "execute" an ActiveX control project inside the Visual Basic development environment. Your options are

- Wait for Components to Be Created—Your project is compiled, but no container object is started in which to run the control. Use this option to test your project for syntax and compilation errors without actually running it.
- Start Component—This lets the component decide what happens. In the case of an ActiveX control, your default Web browser will be started as the container for the control, and the control will be run inside the browser. If your project contains more than one component, you select the one to run from the drop-down list. This is the default property setting and is suitable for most ActiveX control development.
- Start Program—Use this option when you want to start a specific local program to serve as the container for the ActiveX control. For example, you might have created and compiled a standard Visual Basic EXE program that uses the control.
- Start Browser with URL—This option permits you to start your browser and load a specific URL. Most often, the URL will point to a local HTML file that uses the control. If the Use Existing Browser option is turned on, and if a copy of your browser is already running, Visual Basic will use that copy rather than start a new copy.

You can also test an ActiveX control by placing it on a form in a Visual Basic project. There are two ways to do this.

You can start a second copy of Visual Basic and create the test project there (a Standard EXE project). After you have created the OCX file for the ActiveX control, the control will be available in the Components dialog box and can be instantiated for testing.

The other method involves running only a single copy of Visual Basic and creating a project group that contains two projects: the ActiveX control project and a Standard EXE project for testing. When you close the UserControl designer, the ActiveX control will be available for use in the other project.

Although these methods are useful in some circumstances, I advise against using them if you are creating an ActiveX control specifically for Web use. It's better to test the control in the container where it will finally be used, a Web browser.

The Extender Object

Before you get to the properties of the UserControl object, it's necessary to understand the Extender object, which is an essential part of ActiveX control programming. You have learned that an ActiveX control always runs within a container object, such as a Web browser. The Extender object is part of the container and provides a way for certain properties that are actually part of the container to appear as if they are part of the UserControl (that is, the ActiveX control). These properties are called *extender properties*.

A good example of extender properties are Top, Left, Height, and Width—the four properties that determine the position and size of a control within its container. A UserControl object does not possess these properties because the position and size of an ActiveX control are determined by its container object. These four properties are made available by the container through its Extender object and appear to the user to be properties of the ActiveX control.

When thinking about extender properties, it's important to remember that you will be working with ActiveX controls in two stages.

First is the stage when you are programming the control: creating its visual interface and writing its code. At this time, you have access to the properties of the UserControl object, which are displayed in the Properties window, and also to properties that you have added to the control, which are not displayed in the Properties window but are accessible in code. Extender properties do not exist at this time.

Second is the stage when you have completed and compiled the control and are using it in a project, for example, a Visual Basic program or a Web page. At this point, the control will have been placed into a container (a Visual Basic form or a browser). The properties of the UserControl object will no longer be available, but the properties that you added to the control, as well as the extender properties, will be available. If the control has been placed on a Visual Basic form, both the properties that you gave the control and the extender properties will be displayed in the Properties window. Figure 3.7 illustrates how this works.

FIGURE 3.7

The developer sees a single interface containing both control and extender properties.

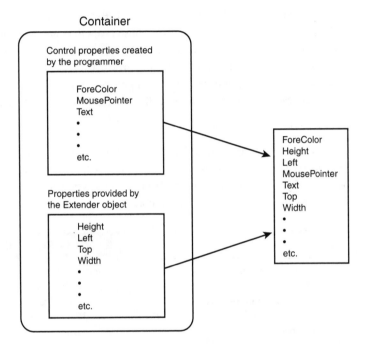

Standard Extender Properties

The ActiveX specification requires that all container objects provide a minimum set of extender properties (shown in Table 3.1). This is not a strict requirement, so you might run into container objects that do not provide all these extender properties.

TABLE 3.1 REQUIRED EXTENDER PROPERTIES

Property	Data Type	Read/Write	Description
Name	String	R	The name the user assigns to the control instance
Visible	Boolean	RW	Specifies whether the control is visible
Parent	Object	R	Returns the control's container object (for example, a Visual Basic form)

continues

TABLE 3.1 CONTINUED

Property	Data Type	Read/Write	Description
Cancel	Boolean	R	True if the control is the container's Cancel button
Default	Boolean	R	True if the control is the container's default button

Most container objects also provide Top, Left, Height, and Width extender properties to set the position and size of the control. These properties are not required, however. Extender properties are provided for the developer who uses the control; therefore, code in your control should never set these properties. You can, however, read extender properties as needed. For example, you might want your control's Caption property (which you must program) to initially display the Name property of the Extender object:

```
Caption = Extender.Name
```

As you can see from this example, extender properties are accessed in code by prefixing the property name with the Extender keyword. Because you cannot be sure that the container object will always have a given property, you should always use error trapping when accessing extender properties in code.

Do	Don't
DO remember that the extender properties that will be available depend on the type of container used. Always use error trapping when reading extender properties.	DON'T set extender properties with code in the UserControl, even if you are sure that a particular property will be available in the container object.

When a control is used, its Extender object is not available until the control has been placed in its container. This means that code cannot access extender properties in a control's initialize event procedure, which is fired before the Extender object is available. You can, however, access extender properties in the control's InitProperties and ReadProperties event procedures. You'll learn more about these and other ActiveX control events later in the next two lessons.

Extender and Control Property Collisions

The situation might arise in which the Extender object has a property with the same name as a property of the ActiveX control; this situation is called a *collision*. In this case, an ordinary reference to the property will access the extender property. Suppose that your control and its container have a property named Tag. Also suppose that your control is called `MyControl`, and there is an instance of it named `MyControl1`. The user writes the following code:

```
MyControl1.Tag = "Visual Basic"
```

This will set the value of the extender `Tag` property. To bypass the extender property and access the control's property, you must use the `Object` reference:

```
MyControl1.Object.Tag = "Visual Basic"
```

`Object` is a property of the Extender and returns a reference to the control associated with the Extender. To be more specific, it references the control's own interface without any extender properties. If the Extender does not have a `Tag` property, both the preceding lines will reference the control's `Tag` property.

MAKING YOUR CONTROL INVISIBLE AT RUNTIME

If you do not want your control to ever be visible at runtime, set the UserControl's `InvisibleAtRuntime` property to `True`. This is preferred to using the Extender object's `Visible` property, which should be used to make the control temporarily invisible. Setting `Visible` to `False` will indeed hide the control, but it will still have the overhead associated with a visible control, which is avoided by setting `InvisibleAtRuntime` to `True`. Note, however, that the functionality of an ActiveX control that never displays onscreen can usually be obtained, with greater efficiency, in an ActiveX DLL. The only reason to use an invisible ActiveX control would be if you need a feature that is available in a control and not in a DLL. Be aware that some containers do not support `InvisibleAtRuntime`, in which case the control will be displayed regardless of the property setting.

3

UserControl Properties

The UserControl object itself has a number of properties that affect the behavior and appearance of the final ActiveX control. It's essential that you become familiar with these properties because you'll be using them frequently every time you work on an ActiveX control project.

Many of the UserControl object's properties will be familiar to you because they are shared by other Visual Basic controls that you have worked with. Examples include `Font`, `DrawStyle`, and `FillColor`. There are also a few more advanced UserControl properties, mostly dealing with event detection, that I will cover on Day 5, "Real-World ActiveX."

AccessKeys

AccessKeys defines the keys that the user can press (with Alt) to move the focus to the control. For example, to make Alt+G the access key, set this property to "g". Access keys for the constituent controls (as set by including an ampersand in their Caption property string) are implicitly active but will not be returned by the AccessKeys property. Movement of the focus to a UserControl is regulated by the CanGetFocus and ForwardFocus properties.

CanGetFocus

If CanGetFocus is True (the default), the UserControl can have the focus, but only if none of its constituent controls can have the focus. If False, the UserControl cannot have the focus under any conditions.

ContainedControls

ContainedControls returns a collection of all the controls that were placed on the UserControl by the developer or end user. It is valid only if the ControlContainer property is True. This collection does not include the constituent controls used by the programmer to create the ActiveX control's visual interface.

ContainerHWnd

ContainerHWnd returns the hWnd, or window handle, of the control's container. You need this value for certain API calls.

ControlContainer

If ControlContainer is False (the default), the UserControl cannot be used as a container for other controls placed there by the developer. If True, the UserControl can contain other controls. This property determines the behavior of the finished control when it is being used in a project by a developer; it has nothing to do with whether you can use other controls to create the ActiveX control's interface. Of the intrinsic Visual Basic controls, for example, the Frame and PictureBox controls can serve as control containers.

> **WHERE IS THE CONTROL?**
>
> If an ActiveX control has `ControlContainer` set to `True` and `BackStyle` set to `Transparent`, a contained control placed on it will be visible and able to receive mouse events only where the contained control overlaps a constituent control (see the `BackStyle` property on Day 5).

ForwardFocus

If `ForwardFocus` is `True`, when the control's access keys are pressed, the focus moves to the next control in the tab order. If `False` (the default) and if the `CanGetFocus` property is `True`, the focus moves to the control itself.

Hyperlink

`Hyperlink` returns a reference to the `Hyperlink` object associated with the UserControl. See the section on the `Hyperlink` object later in this lesson.

Parent

`Parent` returns a reference to the ActiveX control's container object.

ParentControls

`ParentControls` returns a collection containing references to all the other controls contained in the same container as the UserControl, as well as the container object itself. The contents of this collection are determined entirely by the container object and might not be supported in all cases. Normally, the references to the controls include the container's Extender object; see the `ParentControlsType` property.

ParentControlsType

`ParentControlsType` determines whether control references in the `ParentControls` collection include the container's Extender object. The default is `vbExtender` (value = 1), which includes the Extender object. The other setting is `vbNoExtender` (value = 0), in which case the `ParentControls` collection returns controls without the container's Extender object. This property is used when an incompatibility exists between an Extender object and Visual Basic. For example, the Extender object of Microsoft Internet Explorer cannot be used by Visual Basic, and trying to use it will raise an error. Setting `ParentControlsType` to `vbNoExtender` prevents these problems.

Windowless

If Windowless is False (the default), the UserControl is assigned a window handle that can be referenced by its hWnd property. If True, no window handle is assigned, thus saving system resources. A UserControl needs a window handle only if it will make API calls that require such a handle or will serve as a control container (see the ControlContainer property).

Licensing Considerations for ActiveX Controls

One of the main advantages of ActiveX controls is that they can be easily distributed over a network. This has the potential to be a disadvantage, too. Although you want your end users to have easy access to your components, you do *not* necessarily want other developers to be able to use your components in their projects without your permission. Maybe they will even pay you for using your component! This is why a licensing feature was included in the ActiveX specification.

Let me make the distinction clear between an end user and a developer. If someone visits your ActiveX-enabled Web page, your ActiveX components will be downloaded to their local computer, installed, and executed, enabling them to experience the advantages of your carefully programmed active content. This is what I call an *end user*. If, however, the user is also a Visual Basic programmer—a developer—you might not want him to be able to use the ActiveX component in his own projects. This is when a license comes into play.

Earlier in the lesson, in the section "ActiveX Control Project Properties," I briefly explained the Require License Key option. If you select this option, a Visual Basic license file (*.vbl) will be created when the project is built. End users do not require this file, but a developer will have to register the license file on her machine in order to use the component in program design.

Here is how it works. To make your ActiveX control available to end users, say, as part of your Web page, you would publish the OCX file without the VBL file. If, however, you want to make your control available to other developers, you would also include the VBL file. The Package and Deployment Wizard will build a setup program that properly registers the *.vbl file on the end user's machine when the setup program is run.

> **USING OTHER LICENSED CONTROLS**
>
> If your ActiveX control contains one or more constituent controls that require licenses, the licensing files for those controls will be needed as well in order for another developer to use your control. You'll need to refer to the licensing agreements for the specific controls to determine what, if any, rights you have to further distribute the control.

If you do not select the Require License Key option, anyone will be able to use your ActiveX control in his own projects without restrictions.

The HyperLink Object

Every UserControl has a Hyperlink object associated with it. You access this object via the UserControl's `Hyperlink` property. The Hyperlink object can be very useful; as its name implies, it works with hyperlinks. You can use it in conjunction with a hyperlink-aware container, such as Internet Explorer, to link to a specified URL. The Hyperlink object has no properties and only three methods.

The most important method is `NavigateTo`. The syntax is as follows:

```
object.NavigateTo(Target [, Location [, FrameName]])
```

The elements of the call to the `NavigateTo` method are

`object` is a reference to a Hyperlink object.

`Target` is the destination location and can be either a document or a URL.

`Location` specifies the location within the target to navigate to. If the location is omitted, the default location will be displayed.

`FrameName` specifies the name of the frame within the target URL to jump to. If omitted, the default frame is used.

> **HYPERLINKING NOT SUPPORTED?**
>
> If the Hyperlink object is in a container that supports OLE hyperlinking (such as Microsoft Internet Explorer), the container will jump to the location specified in the call to the `NavigateTo` method. Otherwise, the system will start whatever application is registered as supporting hyperlinking to make the jump.

Here's an example. Suppose you have created an ActiveX control in which the UserControl is named UC1. The following code will navigate to Microsoft's home page:

```
UC1.Hyperlink.NavigateTo http://www.microsoft.com
```

Likewise, the following code will link to the indicated file on the local disk:

```
UC1.Hyperlink.NavigateTo "c:\webpages\opening.html"
```

If the destination location is invalid, an error occurs (which should, of course, always be trapped).

The other two methods of the Hyperlink object are GoForward and GoBack. These methods work only if the container object maintains a history list (a list of recently visited locations), and just because a container supports hyperlinking does not necessarily mean it maintains a history list. For this reason, code that uses either GoForward or GoBack should always use error trapping as shown here (again assuming a UserControl named UC1):

```
Private Sub cmdBack_Click()
    On Error GoTo noHistory
    UC1.Hyperlink.GoBack
    Exit Sub
noHistory:
    Resume Next
End Sub
```

Your First ActiveX Control

You have learned a lot about ActiveX controls already, but as the old saying goes, there is no teacher like experience! Now it is time to put some of this knowledge to work and create a working ActiveX control. You will be starting out simple, so you can get the hang of things. Then you will tackle a more complex ActiveX control project on Day 5.

Planning the Project

As with any Visual Basic project, it's a really good idea to plan ahead as much as possible. If you know exactly what you want the finished product to do and how it should appear, your programming will go much more quickly. Plans that you make are not written in stone, of course. One of Visual Basic's strong points is how easily it lets you modify an ongoing project. Even so, planning is a good idea.

The ActiveX control you will create is designed to display a rotating series of banners on a Web page. By *rotating*, I mean that the displayed banner changes at a regular interval: Banner A is displayed for 5 seconds, banner B for 5 seconds, and so on. This way, visitors to your page do not have to view the same banner all the time.

Creating the Banners

First, of course, you need to have the banners that the control will display. I used a paint program to create two banners, each 468 pixels wide by 60 pixels high. You can use whatever dimensions you want, but the preceding values seem to be common for Web banners. I saved the banners as BANNER1.BMP and BANNER2.BMP. You can use any file format you like, as long as it is supported by the Image control (this includes BMP, WMF, JGP, and GIF files).

BITMAPS ON THE WEB

Why did I save my banners as bitmap files if JPG and GIF are the only file formats supported by the Web? The reason is that these files will not be downloaded and displayed directly in a browser, but rather will be displayed in a Visual Basic Image control that is part of the ActiveX control. Therefore, any file format supported by the Image control will suit your purposes.

3

Starting the Project

To begin this project, start Visual Basic (or if it is already running, select File, New Project. Select ActiveX Control as the project type and then click OK. Visual Basic starts and displays a blank UserControl, as you saw earlier in Figure 3.3. Perform the following initial steps:

1. Change the Name property of the UserControl to UC1.

2. Open the Project Properties dialog box (select Project, Properties) and on the General tab, enter RotateBanners for the project name and Rotate Banners for the project description. Then click OK.

3. Save the UserControl to disk (File, Save) under the name RotateBanners.

4. Save the project to disk under the same name.

Adding the Constituent Controls

The ActiveX control will contain three constituent controls: two Image controls and one Timer control. The two Image controls will display the two banners, and the program will determine which one is visible by toggling their Visible properties between True and False. The Timer control will provide the toggle interval.

Add two Image controls and one Timer control to the UserControl. You can leave all the control properties at their default values, except for the Timer control's Interval property, which should be set to the desired default interval. I used a value of 3000 to get a 3-second interval.

Next, load the banner images into each of the Image controls. You do this by means of the Picture property, which permits you to browse your disk for the proper image files. Because the Image controls' Stretch property has been left at its default value of False, the controls will automatically resize themselves to fit the image.

Don't worry about the exact positions of the Image controls because they will be set later in code. Don't worry if they overlap one another, either. At this stage, your Visual Basic screen will look like Figure 3.8.

FIGURE 3.8

Designing the Rotate Banners ActiveX control.

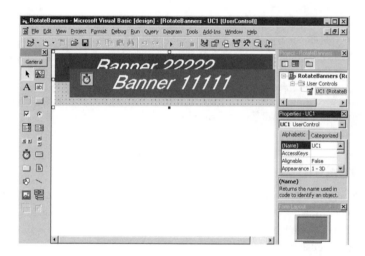

The final visual design step is to adjust the size of the UserControl. You want to make it exactly the same size as one of the Image controls so that the banner will display without a border. After you have done this, you are ready to start adding code.

Code for the ActiveX Control

Two tasks must be performed by code in the ActiveX control. One is to initialize the control, which requires the following:

1. Set the Visible property of one Image control to True and the other to False.

2. Move both Image controls to the top right corner of the UserControl. Because you have already set the UserControl to be the same size as the Image controls, this results in each image completely filling the UserControl.

3. Set the Timer control's Enabled property to True so that the Timer will start running.

The second task is to toggle the Visible properties of the two Image controls each time the Timer counts down, which will hide one banner and display the next.

The initialization code should be placed in the UserControl's initialize event procedure. This event is fired when an instance of the control is created. The toggling code should go, of course, in the Timer control's Timer event. Listing 3.1 shows the code for both these procedures.

LISTING 3.1 CODE IN THE ROTATE BANNER ACTIVEX CONTROL

```
Private Sub Timer1_Timer()

' Toggle the Visible properties of
' the two Image controls.
Image1.Visible = Not Image1.Visible
Image2.Visible = Not Image2.Visible

End Sub

Private Sub UserControl_Initialize()

' Set position and Visible states of
' the two Image controls.

With Image1
    .Visible = True
    .Top = 0
    .Left = 0
End With

With Image2
    .Visible = False
    .Top = 0
    .Left = 0
End With

' Start the Timer running.
Timer1.Enabled = True

End Sub
```

Testing the Control

To test the control, all that is required is to press F5 or click the Start button on the Visual Basic toolbar. The project will be compiled, and a browser window will be opened to display the control. You should use Internet Explorer 4 for testing your ActiveX controls, because it has the highest level of ActiveX support. In Figure 3 9, you can see the control executing in Internet Explorer. Of course, you cannot see the banners switching in the figure, but they really do!

FIGURE 3.9

Testing the ActiveX control in Internet Explorer.

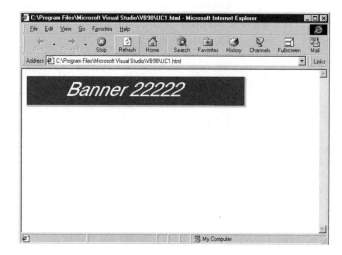

BROWSER DOESN'T START?

If Internet Explorer does not start when you run the ActiveX control project, and you are sure it is installed, check the project properties. On the Debugging tab, be sure that the Start Component option is selected with UC1 entered in the adjacent text box.

Compiling Your ActiveX Control

After your ActiveX control is working to your satisfaction, you need to compile it. The compilation process creates the final OCX file that is the final form of the control: what users must have on their system in order to use the control. The compilation process is easy. Select Make XXXX.OCX on the Visual Basic File menu, in which XXXX represents the name of the project. In this case, it will be RotateBanners.ocx.

When you select the command, Visual Basic will offer you the opportunity to select a different name for the OCX file and to select the folder where it will be placed. You are also warned if you try to overwrite an existing file, but that will happen only if you are recompiling the control after having made changes.

Using the ActiveX Control in a Visual Basic Project

After you have compiled the ActiveX control, it will be available for use in other projects, both regular Visual Basic projects and Web publishing projects. From this perspective, your control will be no different from ActiveX controls that are provided with Visual Basic or that you purchase.

To see what I mean, close the RotateBanners project and start a new Standard EXE project in Visual Basic. Press Ctrl+T to display the Components dialog box. Scroll down, and you'll see that Rotate Banners is listed as an available component, as shown in Figure 3.10. Click it to put a check mark in the adjacent box; then close the dialog box. An icon representing the control will appear in the Visual Basic toolbox (see Figure 3.11).

3

FIGURE 3.10

After compiling, an ActiveX control is available in the Visual Basic Components dialog box.

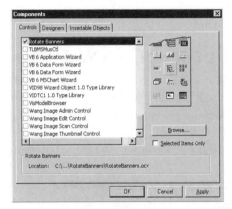

FIGURE 3.11

Your ActiveX control is represented by this icon in the toolbox.

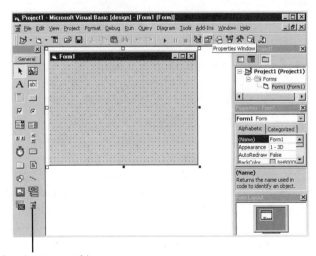

User-defined ActiveX control icon

> **CHANGING THE CONTROL'S ICON**
>
> By default, all user-created ActiveX controls are assigned the generic icon shown in Figure 3.11. To give your control its own icon for display in the toolbox, set the UserControl object's `ToolbarBitmap` property. You can use almost any image you like; it will automatically be scaled to the final 16×15 pixel dimension. You shouldn't use an icon file, because icon files do not scale well to the 16×15 size.

If you place an instance of the RotateBanners control on a standard Visual Basic form, you'll see that it has a whole set of properties displayed in the Properties window. This is true even though you have not given the component any properties. Remember, these are the properties of the Extender object (in this case, provided by the Visual Basic form), and they are automatically available, in addition to any custom properties that you might have programmed for the control.

Using the ActiveX Control in a Web Page

After compiling the control, it will also be available for use in Web projects. If your Web authoring tool supports ActiveX controls, the RotateBanners control will be on the list of available controls. In the Microsoft FrontPage Web editor, for example, you select Insert, Advanced, ActiveX Control to insert an ActiveX control onto the current Web page. As Figure 3.12 shows, the RotateBanners control is on the list of available controls.

FIGURE 3.12

A compiled control is available for insertion on a Web page.

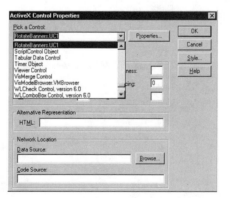

How exactly is an ActiveX control "inserted" on a Web page? After all, Web pages are HTML documents, and HTML is a text-only format. The answer lies in HTML tags. Just as there are tags for inserting images and controlling formatting, there are also tags for inserting an object, specifically, the `<OBJECT>` tag. When an ActiveX-enabled browser reads these tags, it takes the required action to run the control.

An <OBJECT> tag has the following form:

```
<object
codebase="download location"
id="name"
classid="Class ID"
width="w"
height="h">
Alternate
</object>
```

The various parts of the tag are explained here:

download location specifies where the object's installation files can be downloaded from if the component is not already installed on the user's system.

name is the identifier by which code in the HTML page will refer to the object.

Class ID is a unique identifier that identifies the object in the Windows registry.

W and *h* give the display size of the object, in pixels.

Alternate is the text that is displayed in place of the object if for some reason it cannot be loaded.

Here, for example, is the complete <OBJECT> tag for inserting the RotateBanners control in a Web page. Of course, the exact download location will depend on where on your Web site you install the component files.

```
<object codebase="ax.controls/rotatebanners.cab" id="RB1"
classid="clsid:D8DD67F4-3B40-11D2-BBC6-02608CACCADB"
width="468" height="60">Rotate banner</object>
```

The only difficult part of the <OBJECT> tag is the class ID. For this reason, the best way to insert ActiveX controls onto Web pages is to use an ActiveX-aware Web page editor, such as Microsoft FrontPage. This automates the task and makes it unnecessary for you to look up the class ID.

Distributing ActiveX Controls

After you have created an ActiveX control, you will probably want to distribute it. This can mean one of two things:

- Making the control available to other developers for use in their projects
- Placing the control on your Web site so that it will be available for download and installation by visitors to the site

Of course, you might want to distribute some controls both ways. I will be explaining only Internet distribution because that is the subject of the book. The Package and Deployment Wizard makes your task relatively easy. First, however, you need to understand exactly what goes into a deployment package.

Other Required Files

Most Visual Basic projects seem to result in only a single final file: an OCX file in the case of an ActiveX control, for example, or an EXE file for a standard executable. Is this one file all you need to distribute? In almost all cases, the answer is no.

Any compiled Visual Basic project depends on *Visual Basic runtime files*, which contain the compiled code for most of Visual Basic's built-in functionality. When your Visual Basic program uses the Open statement to open a file, for example, it is actually calling code in one of the runtime files. For a program or component created with Visual Basic to run, these runtime files must be present on the system. If you have Visual Basic itself installed, you already have these files. An end user, however, probably does not. Therefore, these files must be included in the distribution package that you create. Fortunately, the Package and Deployment Wizard performs the task of determining which files to include.

Packaging Your Component

The first step in distributing your ActiveX control is to package it: to gather the required files into the proper format. Only after packaging your files can you deploy them.

Before even starting the packaging and deployment procedure, be sure to thoroughly test your control. When you are convinced that it is working properly, compile it to create an OCX file. Only at this point are you ready to start the Package and Deployment Wizard by selecting it from the Visual Basic Add-Ins menu. You can also run it as a standalone by selecting Package and Deployment Wizard from the Start menu (its exact location on the menu will depend on the details of your Visual Basic installation).

CAN'T FIND THE WIZARD?

If the Package and Deployment Wizard is not listed on your Add-Ins menu, you need to use the Add-Ins Manager to load it. Select Add-In Manager from the Add-Ins menu and click on the Package and Deployment Wizard entry in the list. Select the Loaded/Unloaded option to load it now or select Load on Startup to load it automatically each time Visual Basic starts.

When you start the Wizard, it displays the screen shown in Figure 3.13. If you start it from within Visual Basic, the current project will be listed at the top of the dialog box. If you start the wizard from the command line, you will be able to use this box to specify the project to be packaged. Next, click the Package button.

FIGURE 3.13

The Package and Deployment Wizard's opening screen.

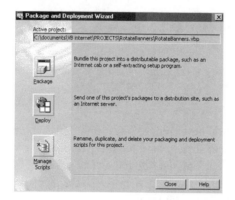

3

The next screen lets you select a packaging script (this screen is not displayed the first time you run the wizard). If you have packaged this project before and saved a script (as described later), you can load the script with the previously set options. Otherwise, select (none). Then click Next.

On the next screen, you select the type of package you want to create. For an Internet deployment, select Internet Package. Click Next when ready.

The next screen lets you select the folder where the package files will be placed. The default is to use a folder named Package located off the folder where the original project files are located. Unless you have a specific reason to change the folder, I suggest you accept this default location; then click Next.

On the next page, you are asked whether the package should include the property page DLL. Select Yes if your control will be used in a development environment other than Visual Basic. If you are not sure, again select Yes; including this file makes only a small difference in the size of the package files.

The next screen, shown in Figure 3.14, is the Included Files dialog box. Here you select the files to be included in the package. The wizard will list those files that it has determined should be included. In the figure, for example, you can see that the package for the RotateBanners ActiveX control will include the OCX file, as you would expect, as well as the Visual Basic runtime files and one additional DLL.

Selecting files to include in the distribution package.

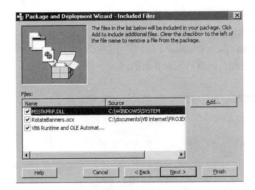

In my experience, you should never remove files from this list unless you are absolutely certain that all your end users already have the files. You might want to add files, however, which you do by clicking the Add button and selecting files. What would you need to add? A readme.txt file, for example, or perhaps a supplementary Help file. If you have created such extra files, you will know about them; otherwise, you can trust that the list created by the wizard is complete.

After selecting the files to include and clicking Next, you will see the File Source dialog box shown in Figure 3.15. Here you specify where each file will be downloaded from. Most of the Visual Basic runtime files are available on Microsoft's Web site, and by specifying that these files be downloaded from there rather than be included in your distribution package, you can drastically reduce the final size of the distribution file. A third choice is to specify an alternate download site for a file, on your own Web server perhaps. This would permit you to maintain a single set of runtime files on your intranet rather than include them in every distribution package you create. By maintaining the runtime files on your intranet, they will be available more quickly than if you specified the Microsoft site as the download location.

Figure 3.15

Selecting download locations for the package files.

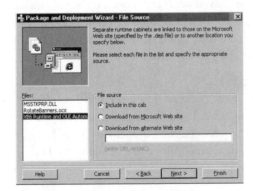

In the File Source dialog box, select a file in the file list and then specify the download source. If you specify the Download from Alternate Web Site option, you must enter the URL of the site, as well as the name of the CAB file. After all options are set, click Next.

CREATING A RUNTIME FILE'S CAB

To create a CAB containing only the Visual Basic runtime files, run the Package and Deployment Wizard for one of your projects. In the Included Files dialog box, deselect all files *except* the Visual Basic runtime files. Create the CAB with a name such as VBRUNTIME and upload it to your Web site.

The next dialog box (see Figure 3.16) is where you enter safety settings for the component(s) in this package. In the left column are listed all the components in this package—for this example, only one UserControl, named UC1. You can see that you have the option of marking the component as safe for scripting and for initialization. What does this mean?

FIGURE 3.16

Entering safety settings for the distribution package.

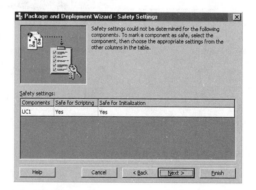

The rationale behind these settings comes from the possibility that your component might be used in a Web page that you did not create, in conjunction with scripting code and other components that you have no control over. Suppose that you created a component with a method that can delete files on the user's computer. Your component might use this method in a perfectly responsible manner, but if someone else uses your component, he could write a script that uses your file-deletion method to cause mischief. Safe for Scripting means that the component can be accessed from a scripting language such as VBScript without causing harm, and Safe for Initialization means that someone can create an instance of the component without causing harm. In this case, *harm* means the ability to delete or modify arbitrary files or system settings. These safety settings work in conjunction with digital signing to certify a component's safety.

WHAT IS VBSCRIPT?

VBScript is a scripting language designed for use in HTML documents. You will learn more about it on Day 17, "Client-Side Scripting with VBScript," and Day 18, "Creating Dynamic Content with Active Server Pages."

After setting the safety options, clicking Next opens the last wizard dialog box. Here you can save the Package options that you entered in a script, which can then be recalled if you need to package the component again. Click Finish to create the CAB files. At the end, the wizard displays a brief report summarizing the actions it performed.

Do	Don't
DO remember to mark your components as safe for scripting and initialization, unless they contain potentially dangerous code.	DON'T forget to apply your digital signature after creating your distribution files. The procedure for doing this is explained on Day 2, "Making Sense of ActiveX." You must sign each and every CAB file in the distribution package.

Deploying Your Component

After creating your package, the next step is to deploy your component. Although this might sound complicated, it means nothing more than copying the distribution file(s) to a location where it will be available for download over the Web. There are several possible scenarios for this.

In the easiest case, the computer you are using to develop components is also the Web server where you want to deploy the distribution files. Deploying your component requires only that you copy the file(s) to the proper folder—one that is accessible via the Web, based on the settings of your Web server software. For example, the root folder for my Web server is \INETPUB\WWWROOT, and I have created a folder called AX_CONTROLS, where I put all the deployment files for my components.

Another case is when you are on the same local area network (LAN) as the Web server. All you need to do is copy the files over the LAN to the proper folder on the Web server.

Use the Windows Network Neighborhood to locate the server and folder; you might need to talk to your network administrator about permissions and other matters.

Perhaps the most common case is when you must connect to the destination Web server over the Internet or an intranet. In this situation, you can use the Deployment part of the Package and Deployment Wizard to copy your files to the destination. You must create an Internet deployment package, as just described, before you can do this. The following describes what to do.

Start the Package and Deployment Wizard and on the opening screen click the Deploy button. The next screen lets you select a deployment script. If you are redeploying a component, you can select the associated script; otherwise, select (none) and then click Next.

The next dialog box is titled Package to Deploy. From the drop-down list, select the package that you want to deploy, and click Next. In the following dialog box, select Web Publishing as the type of deployment to be performed.

The next dialog box lets you select the files to deploy, as shown for the RotateBanners package in Figure 3.17. In this example are two files. RotateBanners.Cab is the required file, which contains the installation for the component. There is also a file named RotateBanners.Htm. This is a basic HTML document that contains the basic tags required to use the component. You can deploy this file to your Web site if you will find it useful in testing the component (it will require some editing before use). Otherwise, deselect it so that only the CAB file is deployed.

FIGURE 3.17

Selecting which package files to deploy.

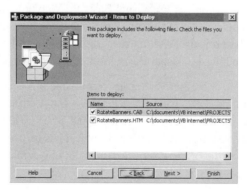

The next dialog box lets you specify additional files or folders to deploy. Generally, the Package Wizard will have included all the required files in the CAB file, but in special circumstances you might need to add other files, such as images, to the deployment.

The next dialog box lets you specify the URL for the deployment and the Web publishing protocol. For the URL, enter the complete address, including the folder name, for example, http://www.yoursite.com/ActiveX_controls/. For the protocol, you can select either HTTP Post or FTP, depending on the requirements of your Web server. Most servers support both methods, but check with the Webmaster if you are not sure. If you select FTP, be sure to edit the URL accordingly.

After you click Next, the final dialog box gives you the option of saving this deployment setup in a script. Finally, click Finish, and the deployment procedure will begin. Depending on the size of the package and the speed of your Internet connection, the procedure could take anywhere from a few seconds to an hour or longer.

TESTING THE DEPLOYMENT

It's a good idea to test your deployments, particularly if you are new at it. This, of course, requires creating and publishing a Web page that uses the component. The problem is that your components are already installed on your computer, so if you load that Web page, there will be no need to download and install the component, therefore precluding a test of the deployment. The only solution I have found is to use another computer where the component has not already been installed.

Summary

This is the first of several lessons devoted to an important topic, ActiveX controls. One of the most powerful ways you can use Visual Basic for Web programming is to create ActiveX controls, independent software components that can be used not only on Web pages but also in regular projects. What makes an ActiveX control special is its capability to be contained in something—a Visual Basic form or a Web browser, for example.

A control is just one type of the ActiveX projects available in Visual Basic. When you start an ActiveX control project, Visual Basic creates a UserControl object that serves as the basis for your control. You place other controls and Basic code in the UserControl to obtain the functionality you need. A UserControl object has its own properties and methods and also reflects the properties of the Extender object that is part of the container that the control runs in.

The last part of the lesson walks you through the process of creating a working ActiveX control. Although the control you programmed is simple, it provides a good introduction to the various steps involved in creating an ActiveX control. You also learned how to package an ActiveX control for distribution on the Web and how to upload the distribution files to your Web site.

Q&A

Q What is the purpose of the UserControl object?

A The UserControl serves as the foundation for any ActiveX control that you create in Visual Basic. You add other controls and Basic code to the UserControl to provide the functionality that you want in the control. The UserControl provides the ActiveX "wrapper" that lets the final control run in a container object.

Q What is the Extender object?

A The Extender object is not part of an ActiveX control but rather is provided by the container that the control is running in. The Extender provides properties that actually belong to the container but appear to be control properties.

Q When you are creating a deployment package for an ActiveX control, what files need to be included and how can you identify them?

A You must include the control's compiled OCX file, of course. The Visual Basic runtime files need to be included as well, unless you are certain that all your end users will already have them installed. The Package and Deployment Wizard will provide you with a list of the required files.

Workshop

Using the code for the RotateBanners ActiveX control presented in the lesson as a starting point, create a control that displays banners in a different manner. One possibility is to modify the control so that it rotates among more than two banners in a random sequence. Another potentially useful modification is to have the control display a different banner each time it is loaded. Remember that most of the Visual Basic programming that you already know can be applied to ActiveX control development.

When you have the new control working to your satisfaction, create an Internet deployment package and put it on your Web site. Create a Web page that uses the control and try it out.

Quiz

1. Name two containers that ActiveX controls can run in.

2. Can you access a control's Extender properties in its initialize event procedure?

3. What are the required Extender properties?

4. What happens when your ActiveX control has a property with the same name as an Extender property? How do you access the two properties?

5. If you deploy your ActiveX control to your Web page, how can you prevent other developers from downloading it and using it in their own projects?

6. How do you include an ActiveX control on a Web page?

DAY 4

Advanced ActiveX Control Techniques

You have had your first look at creating ActiveX controls, but we've just scratched the surface. There's much more to learn, now that you have mastered the basics from Day 3, "Creating and Using an ActiveX Control." Today you will learn

- How to create and use ActiveX control properties
- How to specify ActiveX control properties in an HTML page
- The ways that ActiveX controls handle events
- How to create and use custom events
- The basics of using VBScript
- How to use Ambient properties

Adding Properties to an ActiveX Control

You learned in Day 3 that an ActiveX control that you create automatically has a number of properties—the properties of the underlying UserControl object, as well as the `Extender` properties provided by the container object. As essential as these are, they are not enough. In almost every case, an ActiveX control also requires programmer-defined properties in order to be useful. You add properties to an ActiveX control by means of property procedures.

ActiveX control properties are accessed using the standard *ObjectName.PropertyName* syntax. This is true regardless of whether the property is one you have created or an Extender property.

Property Procedures

Property procedures are used to define procedures for an ActiveX control. There are two main types of property procedure: `Property Get` and `Property Let`. You use a `Property Get` procedure to read the value of a property, and you use a `Property Let` procedure to set the value of a property. A third variant is the `Property Set` procedure, which is used in place of `Property Let` for properties that are object references.

Let's look at an example. Suppose you want to define a property named `BorderColor` for an ActiveX control and that the data type `Integer` is appropriate for this property. First, you would define a private variable in the ActiveX control to hold the property value; for this example, it's called `pBorderColor`. Then, you would need the following two property procedures:

```
Property Get BorderColor() As Integer
    BorderColor = pBorderColor
End Property

Property Let BorderColor(ByVal NewBorderColor As Integer)
    pBorderColor = NewBorderColor
End Property
```

Note that the `Property Get` procedure is really a function, because it has a return value type. Here's how it works. Code in the container object can read the value of this property as follows (assume the instance of the ActiveX control is named `MyControl`):

```
X = MyControl.BorderColor
```

PRIVATE VARIABLE NAMES

The names you choose for the private variables used inside an ActiveX control to store properties are entirely arbitrary, as long as you follow Visual Basic's usual variable name rules. I have developed the convention of naming such variables the same as the property name, with a *p* prefix (for *property*). This makes it easy to identify these variables in code and determine what they are used for.

This statement causes the corresponding `Property Get` procedure to be called. Code in the procedure retrieves the value of the property from the internal storage variable (pBorderColor) and assigns it as the return value of the procedure. This return value is passed back to the calling program. To set the value of the property, the container would reference the property on the left side of an assignment statement, such as this statement:

```
MyControl.BorderColor = vbRED
```

This causes the corresponding `Property Let` procedure to be called, with the new property value passed as the procedure's argument. Code in the procedure assigns this value to the property's internal storage variable. The way this works is illustrated in Figure 4.1.

FIGURE 4.1

Property procedures are called when a property is referenced.

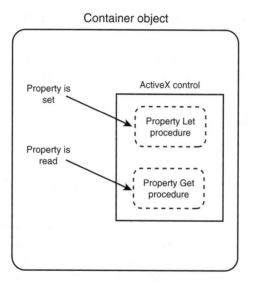

Container object

Property is set → ActiveX control

Property Let procedure

Property is read →

Property Get procedure

4

PROPERTY PROCEDURE RULES

You must follow two rules when creating property procedures:

1. The name of the `Property Get` procedure must be exactly the same as the corresponding `Property Let` (or `Set`) procedure (this is the name you'll use to refer to the property).

2. The return data type of the `Property Get` procedure must be the same as the type of the `Property Let` procedure's argument.

You might be wondering why you cannot simply declare a `Public` variable in the ActiveX module for each property. Such variables will be available outside the control and would remove the need for property procedures. Here are several good reasons why not to declare these variables:

- Good programming practice discourages the use of public variables for any reason, because they open the possibility of unintended interactions with the world outside the control.

- The use of property procedures gives you the chance to validate property values before accepting them.

- With property procedures, you can create read-only or write-only properties, something that would not be possible with `Public` variables.

Creating Read-Only or Write-Only Properties

In some situations, you will want to create an ActiveX control property that is read-only or write-only. Doing so is a simple matter of omitting one of the property procedures. To create a read-only property, create the `Property Get` procedure but not the `Property Let` procedure. For a write-only property, do the opposite.

Storing the Property Value

The method that the control uses to store the property internally is up to you, the programmer. Often you'll declare a private variable in the control module, making sure it's of an appropriate data type for the property. Sometimes you will not need to create a variable, because the property will be linked to a property of a constituent control.

Let me give an example of the latter case. Suppose your ActiveX control contains a Text Box control, and you want the container object to be able to change the color of the text displayed in the text box. For this example, suppose that the ActiveX control is named `MyControl` and the constituent Text Box control is named `Text1`. Your property procedures would look like this:

```
Property Let ForeColor(ByVal NewColor As Integer)
    Text1.ForeColor = NewColor
End Property

Property Get ForeColor() As Integer
    ForeColor = Text1.ForeColor
End Property
```

PROPERTY NAMES

Property names follow the same rules as regular Visual Basic variables. You can use the same names as the properties of constituent controls, and they will remain completely independent unless they are linked by code in the property procedures.

Other Uses for Property Procedures

Because of the way that property procedures operate, they can be used for much more than simply setting and retrieving property values. One of the most common uses is to validate the value of a property—to check that it falls within the allowed range before accepting it. This code would, of course, be placed in the Property Let procedure.

Here's an example. Suppose your ActiveX control has a property named BorderWidth that can take values only between 1 and 5. You could verify the passed value as follows:

```
Property Let BorderWidth(ByVal NewWidth As Integer)
    ' If out of range, exit sub without saving new value.
    If NewWidth > 5 Or New Width < 1 then Exit Sub
    pBorderWidth = NewWidth
End Property
```

Another use for property procedures is to carry out some action whenever a property value is set or read. Which action? It all depends on your control and what it needs to do. However, you have a great deal of flexibility because you are not limited as to the Basic code you can put in a property procedure.

EASY PROPERTY PROCEDURES

Use the Add Procedure command on the Visual Basic Tools menu to quickly add property procedures to your ActiveX control project. In the Add Procedure dialog box, enter the property name and select Property from the Type options. Visual Basic creates Get and Let procedures, using the Variant data type.

Adding a Property to the RotateBanners Control

Now that you understand the basics of adding properties to ActiveX controls, let's add a property to the RotateBanners control that was started in Day 3. What will be useful? Letting the developer specify the interval at which the banners are switched seems like a good idea. You will call this property Interval (what else?).

In the control, you don't need to create a variable to hold this property, because it will be stored in the Timer control's own Interval property. Remember that the Timer's Interval property specifies the interval, in milliseconds (1/1000 of a second) between "ticks" of the timer. It's probably inappropriate to have the banners rotate any faster than once a second, so you will also place code in the Property Let procedure to prevent settings less than 1000.

In Visual Basic, load the RotateBanners project and display the code editing window. Select Tools, Add Procedure to display the Add Procedure dialog box (see Figure 4.2).

FIGURE 4.2

Using the Add Procedure dialog box to add property procedures.

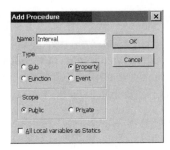

Enter `Interval` as the procedure name and select Property as the type; then click OK. The following code is added to your control:

```
Public Property Get Interval() As Variant

End Property

Public Property Let Interval(ByVal vNewValue As Variant)

End Property
```

Note that the default data type for the procedures is `Variant`. This is okay because type variant can hold any kind of data. The code for the `Property Get` procedure is simple, requiring only that the current value of the Timer's `Interval` property be retrieved. The `Property Let` procedure is a bit more complex because you need to verify that the new property value is not less than 1000. If it is less than 1000, the code should simply leave the `Interval` property unchanged and exit the procedure. Listing 4.1 shows the final code for these two property procedures.

LISTING 4.1   PROPERTY PROCEDURES FOR THE INTERVAL PROPERTY

```
Public Property Get Interval() As Variant

    Interval = Timer1.Interval

End Property


Public Property Let Interval(ByVal vNewValue As Variant)

    If vNewValue >= 1000 Then
            Timer1.Interval = vNewValue
    End If

End Property
```

After adding this code to the project, recompile it (select Make RotateBanners.ocx from the File menu) to update the OCX file. You can now use the control with its new property.

Using the `Interval` Property

Now that the RotateButtons control has an `Interval` property, how is it accessed? It depends on how you are using the control.

If you are using the control in a Visual Basic project, the `Interval` property will display in the Properties window when the `UserControl` object `UC1` is selected. This is shown in Figure 4.3. What are the other properties listed for the `UserControl` object? You'll remember from an earlier chapter that these are `Extender` properties, which are actually provided by the container object (a Visual Basic form in this case) and made available to the `UserControl` by means of the `Extender` object.

FIGURE 4.3

The user-defined `Interval` *property displays in the Visual Basic Properties window, along with the ActiveX control's other properties.*

When using the control in Visual Basic, any property that you defined for the control is accessed just like any other property: in the Properties window or in code. For example, if the instance of the RotateBanners control is named `RB1`, the following code will set the display interval to three seconds:

```
RB1.Interval = 3000
```

What about when you are using the control in a Web page? Then you use the `<PARAM>` tag to include settings for the properties that you want to change from their default values. The `<PARAM>` tag has the following form:

```
<param name="PropertyName" value = "PropertyValue">
```

You place as many `<PARAM>` tags as needed within the `<OBJECT>` tag. For example, here is an `<OBJECT>` tag that will insert a RotateBanners control on a Web page and set its `Interval` property to 2500:

```
<object codebase="ax_controls/rotatebanners.cab"
```

```
id="RB1"
classid="clsid:D8DD67F4-3B40-11D2-BBC6-02608CACCADB"
width="468"
height="60">
<param name="Interval" value="2500">
</object>
```

Note that numerical property values must be enclosed in double quotes, just like string values.

TAG FORMATTING

Browsers do not care one whit about the formatting of HTML tags. An <OBJECT> tag and any enclosed <PARAM> tags can all be on one line, separated by a number of lines, or whatever you like. I prefer to place one tag element per line, as in the preceding example, simply to make the tag more readable. Note also that the case of the tags doesn't matter; <OBJECT> and <object> mean exactly the same thing to the browser.

There's more to learn about ActiveX controls and properties, and you will get to that later in the chapter.

Events and ActiveX Controls

You are not going to get very far without understanding how ActiveX control events work. After all, in most cases, a control needs to respond to events in order to be useful. However, that's not the only area of ActiveX events that you need to know about; you also need to understand that events that occur as instances of an ActiveX control are created and destroyed.

Events in an ActiveX Control's Life

To understand the various events that occur during the lifetime of an ActiveX control, you must also understand the ephemeral nature of an ActiveX control. You might think that when you place an instance of an ActiveX control on a Web page, it is created and that is that. The same might go for lacing an ActiveX control on a Visual Basic form. Things are not nearly this simple.

Remember that an ActiveX control you design is really a class—a blueprint for something. When you place an instance of the control in a container and then test it, an instance of the control is created. When you terminate the test application, that instance is destroyed. When a user views the Web page that uses the control, an instance is created by his or her browser and then later destroyed. As you can see, ActiveX control instances seem to be coming and going all the time. Several events are associated with this process, and you will often need to use these events. Still more events are associated with size changes and other display-related happenings. Take a look at these events:

- The Initialize event is the very first event to fire when an instance of the control is created. It occurs each and every time the control is instantiated.

- The Terminate event is the last event to occur when an instance of the control is destroyed.

- The InitProperties event occurs the first time an instance of the control is created. This occurs when you first place the control in a container, such as a Visual Basic form or a browser.

- The ReadProperties event occurs the second and subsequent times an instance of the control is created—in other words, every time except the first time (when InitProperties is fired).

- The WriteProperties event occurs only at design time when an instance of the control is destroyed and at least one of its properties has been changed.

- The Resize event is fired every time an instance of the control is created and also whenever its size is changed, either at design time or runtime.

Figure 4.4 shows the course of events in an ActiveX control.

FIGURE 4.4

Events in the lifetime of an ActiveX control.

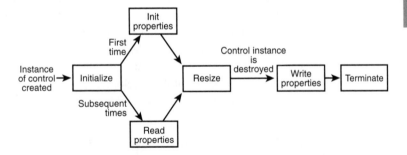

THE INITIALIZE EVENT AND EXTENDER PROPERTIES

The Initialize event occurs before the control's container object has made the Extender object available. Therefore, you cannot access Extender properties in a control's initialize event procedure.

The InitProperties, ReadProperties, and WriteProperties events are used when working with control properties, and I will discuss them in more detail later today. You will also use ReadProperties to perform initialization steps that require access to Extender object properties, because these are not available during the Initialize event. Use the Initialize event for all initialization that doesn't require access to Extender properties.

Do	Don't
DO place control initialization code in the initialize event procedure, *unless* it requires access to Extender properties. Then, place it in the ReadProperties event procedure.	DON'T try to access Extender properties in a control's initialize event procedure.

Responding to User Events

Separate from the internal events discussed in the preceding section are user events (mouse clicks and the like) to which many ActiveX controls need to respond. One of Visual Basic's strong points is simple event handling, and you might hope this simplicity extends to the programming of ActiveX controls. Unfortunately, it does not, because of some unavoidable, added complexity.

To understand, think about the RotateBanners control that you have been developing. It consists of an Image control that was placed on a UserControl object. The final ActiveX control will be executing within a container object, such as a form or a browser window. What happens, then, when a user clicks the control that is displaying in his or her browser? Is the click detected by the Image control, by the UserControl, or by the container object? Depending on the needs of the developer, any one of these might be desirable. Perhaps you can see now why event detection in ActiveX controls is not quite as simple as you might like!

The way that Visual Basic handles this apparent dilemma is to permit events to be "passed" from one object to another. In other words, the object that initially receives the event—the Image control in the preceding example—not only can respond to the event itself but can also pass it to the container object so that it, too, can respond. Figure 4.5 illustrates this.

The process is actually called *raising* an event and is accomplished using the RaiseEvent statement. The syntax is as follows:

```
RaiseEvent EventName [(ArgumentList)]
```

FIGURE 4.5

A constituent control or a UserControl *can "pass" an event up to its container object.*

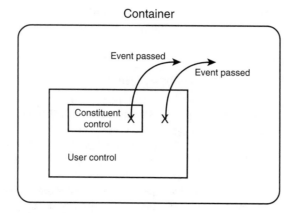

EventName is the name of the event, and the optional *ArgumentList* contains any arguments required by the event. To use RaiseEvent, it's necessary to declare the event procedure for the event that will be raised. The declaration takes this form:

```
[Public] Event EventName [(ArgumentList)]
```

This declaration must be placed at the module level in the module where the event will be raised. *EventName* and the optional *ArgumentList* are the same as for the RaiseEvent statement. Use the optional Public keyword if the event needs to be detected in another module. If Public is omitted, the event can be detected only in the module where it is raised.

What events are available to you? Pretty much the entire collection of Visual Basic events can be raised. Any event that a constituent control can detect on its own can be raised.

You can also raise custom events that have no relation to regular Visual Basic events. Suppose, for example, that one of the tasks that your ActiveX control performs involves downloading a large amount of data and that you want to inform the container object when the download is complete. You could define an event as follows:

```
Public Event DownloadComplete
```

Then, you could raise the event whenever the download process is complete:

```
Sub DownloadData()
    ' Code to perform the download goes here.
    RaiseEvent DownloadComplete
End Sub
```

When a custom event is raised, the container object will be able to respond to it, just like a Click or other standard Visual Basic event. Remember that raising an event does not in itself mean the container object will respond; it only makes the event available. As you will see later today, you must put code in the container to respond to the events.

THE USERCONTROL OBJECT AND MOUSE EVENTS

The UserControl object will sometimes respond directly to mouse events. This will occur when the event occurs on a constituent control, such as a Shape control, that does not itself detect mouse events. In this case, the events are automatically passed through to the underlying UserControl without any need for you to use the RaiseEvent statement. The UserControl will also directly detect mouse events when they occur on areas of the control where no constituent control is covering the UserControl.

Be aware that the UserControl itself doesn't respond to events raised from constituent controls. Raised events are always passed to the container object.

Using an Event in the RotateBanners Control

To demonstrate using events in an ActiveX control, I will first show you how to use an event internally without raising it to the container object. Then you will see how to raise an event and respond to it in the container.

What can be added to the RotateBanners control that will be really useful? Banners are usually used to advertise on Web sites, and clicking a banner typically takes you to that advertiser's own Web site. I will add code to the control that navigates to a particular Web site whenever the control is clicked by the user, with the destination Web site determined by which banner is displayed at the time of the click. This demonstration will also show you how to use the Hyperlink object.

The code is really very simple. There are two Image controls, one of which is visible at any given moment. All you need to do is place the necessary code in each Image control's Click event procedure. By using the Hyperlink object's NavigateTo method, it's a simple matter to go to another URL. Listing 4.2 shows the code for the two Click event procedures.

LISTING 4.2   CODE FOR THE TWO IMAGE CONTROLS' CLICK EVENT PROCEDURES

```
Private Sub Image1_Click()

    UserControl.Hyperlink.NavigateTo "http://www.microsoft.com"

End Sub

Private Sub Image2_Click()
```

```
UserControl.Hyperlink.NavigateTo "http://www.yahoo.com"

End Sub
```

I have chosen the Microsoft and Yahoo Web sites as the destinations for the two banners, but, of course, you can use any URLs you like.

INCLUDE THE PROTOCOL!

When specifying a target for the Hyperlink object's NavigateTo method, be sure to include the http:// protocol for remote URLs. If you omit it—for example, using www.microsoft.com alone—the Hyperlink object will think you are referring to a local file.

After adding this code to the RotateBanners ActiveX project, run it, and when the control displays in Internet Explorer, click the banners. Assuming that your Internet connection is operating, you'll navigate to one of the specified Web sites.

Raising an Event to the Container

Now that you have seen how an ActiveX control can use an event internally, let's see how to raise an event and respond to it in the container. You will use the Click event again, deleting the code from the preceding example and adding new code. The first step is to declare the event at the module level. At the top of the code editing window, select (General) and (Declarations) in the two boxes; then add this single line of code:

```
Public Event Click(Message As String)
```

This line declares an event that takes a single type String argument. You might be thinking that Visual Basic's normal Click event doesn't take any arguments, and you are correct—but it doesn't matter. When you declare an event to be raised, you can give it as many arguments as the program needs, even if it has the same name as a regular Visual Basic event.

Next, locate the Click event procedures for the two Image controls. Delete or comment out the calls to the Hyperlink object and add the code shown in Listing 4.3.

4

LISTING 4.3   RAISING EVENTS WHEN THE IMAGE CONTROLS ARE CLICKED

```
Private Sub Image1_Click()

    RaiseEvent Click("You clicked banner 1")

End Sub

Private Sub Image2_Click()

    RaiseEvent Click("You clicked banner 2")

End Sub
```

After entering this code, execute the component, and you'll see it displayed in Internet Explorer, as before. Click the banner, and what happens? Nothing! This is because you have not yet added the code to the HTML page that will cause the container to respond to the event that was raised.

How can you add code to an HTML page? That's the next topic. When we explore it, I'll return to the demonstration control and show how to use it and its events in a Web page. The control itself is complete, and the full code listing for the RotateBanners project is presented in Listing 4.4.

LISTING 4.4   THE COMPLETED CODE FOR THE ROTATEBANNERS ACTIVEX CONTROL

```
Public Event Click(Message As String)

Private Sub Image1_Click()

    RaiseEvent Click("You clicked banner 1")

End Sub

Private Sub Image2_Click()

    RaiseEvent Click("You clicked banner 2")

End Sub

Private Sub Timer1_Timer()

    ' Toggle the Visible properties of
    ' the two Image controls.
    Image1.Visible = Not Image1.Visible
    Image2.Visible = Not Image2.Visible
```

```
End Sub

Private Sub UserControl_Initialize()

    ' Set position and Visible states of
    ' the two Image controls.

    With Image1
        .Visible = True
        .Top = 0
        .Left = 0
    End With

    With Image2
        .Visible = False
        .Top = 0
        .Left = 0
    End With

    ' Start the Timer running.
    Timer1.Enabled = True

End Sub

Public Property Get Interval() As Long

    Interval = Timer1.Interval

End Property

Public Property Let Interval(ByVal vNewValue As Long)

    If vNewValue >= 1000 And vNewValue < 65535 Then
        Timer1.Interval = vNewValue

    End If

End Property
```

Introduction to VBScript

The original language of the Web was HTML, which could do little more than specify content and formatting. As the need for dynamic Web content became clear, people began to think that Web pages would be much more flexible if some sort of a programming language could be incorporated into the pages. This led to the development of *scripting languages*, which are designed specifically for use in Web pages.

Here's how this works. Scripting language commands are placed in a Web page, just like the regular HTML elements. All scripting commands are enclosed in special tags that identify them as script. When a browser loads the page, one of two things happens, depending on the browser:

- If the browser supports the scripting language, the scripting code is loaded into the browser's script interpreter and executed (as diagrammed in Figure 4.6).

- If the browser doesn't support the scripting language, the script code is ignored.

FIGURE 4.6

The browser executes scripting language commands in an HTML page.

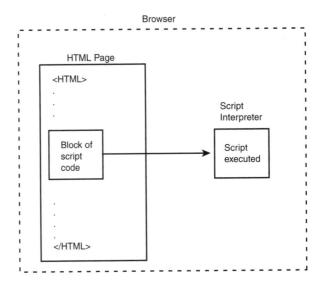

The first Web scripting language was JavaScript, a somewhat distant relative of Java that was developed by the Netscape Corporation. As soon as Microsoft realized the potential of Web scripting, it introduced its own scripting language, called Visual Basic Scripting Edition or VBScript. As the name implies, some similarities exist between Visual Basic and VBScript, but keep in mind that they are very different tools, designed for different jobs.

VISUAL BASIC AND VBSCRIPT

VBScript has some syntax in common with Visual Basic, so if you know Visual Basic, you will be able to pick up VBScript relatively quickly. You don't use the Visual Basic development environment to write VBScript, however; in fact, you can use VBScript on your Web pages without even owning Visual Basic. Some Web development tools, such as Microsoft FrontPage, include tools that simplify the task of adding VBScript to your pages. Lacking

> such tools, you can simply type the VBScript into your HTML pages by using your usual HTML editor.
>
> VBScript is a subset of Visual Basic designed specifically for Web scripting. It lacks certain language features such as file input/output, intrinsic constants, intrinsic data types, and graphics statements.

Adding VBScript to a Web Page

You place your VBScript code in a Web page like this:

```
<script language="VBScript">
<!--
VBScript code goes here
-->
</script>
```

Let's look at this a line at a time. The first line is the `<script>` tag that identifies the start of a section of VBScript code. It includes the language specification; this would be `"javascript"` if you were using that scripting language, but for your needs, of course, you use `"VBScript"`.

The second line (`<!--`) is the standard HTML comment tag. It's not part of VBScript, but part of HTML. When a Web browser sees this tag, anything following, up to an end comment tag, is ignored. It's included so that browsers that are not script-enabled will not treat the script code as content but will ignore it.

The fourth line (`-->`) is the HTML end comment code, and the fifth line (`</script>`) marks the end of the script block.

Where does the VBScript go? That depends. VBScript code can be used in two ways. First, you can create procedures that are executed only when called by other VBScript code or in response to events. Second, you can create VBScript code that is not in a procedure but is simply meant to be executed immediately when the page is loaded by the browser. VBScript procedures are placed in the HTML page's HEAD section, whereas nonprocedure code is placed in the BODY section. Here's an example (which omits the various other HTML elements that a real page would have):

```
<HTML>
<HEAD>
<script language = "VBScript">
<!--
VBScript procedures go here.
-->
</script>
</HEAD>
```

4

```
<BODY>
<script language = "VBScript">
<!--
VBScript nonprocedure code goes here.
-->
</script>
</BODY>
</HTML>
```

Detecting Events in VBScript

VBScript code reacts to events in the same way as Visual Basic code—by means of event procedures. The syntax is even the same:

```
Sub ObjectName_EventName()
...
End Sub
```

ObjectName is the name of the object receiving the event, and *EventName* is (you guessed it!) the name of the event. If the event has any arguments associated with it, they must be declared within the parentheses following *EventName*. To detect a click event on an object named MyObject, you would write

```
Sub MyObject_Click()
...
End Sub
```

Likewise, if you had declared an event in your ActiveX control as follows:

```
Public Event DownloadFinished(Result As Boolean)
```

the VBScript event procedure to respond to that event would be raised (assuming the control instance is named MyAx1):

```
Sub MyAx1_DownloadFinished(Result As Boolean)
...
End Sub
```

You can see that responding to an event in VBScript is fairly simple, and you can apply your existing Visual Basic knowledge to the task.

But Wait, There's More (Lots More)

There is a lot more to learn about VBScript, but I am going to leave that for later. At this point, it's important for you to have a fundamental understanding of what VBScript is and how it works, but you don't need all the details yet.

Completing the RotateBanners Control Project

Actually, the heading of this section is misleading because the RotateBanners project is complete. What you have not done is see how to use the event that the control raises, along with VBScript, to create an integrated Web page that responds to the user. This requires that you create a Web page that contains not only the <OBJECT> code to display the RotateBanners control but also the VBScript to respond when the control is clicked by the user.

What do you want to happen when the control is clicked? Because this is a demonstration, let's simply display a message to the user, indicating which banner was clicked. You will use VBScript's MsgBox statement, which works very much like Visual Basic's statement of the same name.

You need to create an HTML page that includes an <OBJECT> tag to load an instance of the RotateBanners control and includes the VBScript event procedure that will be called when the Click event is raised. I created a more complete Web page to show the control, and the HTML code for this page appears in Listing 4.5. Some additional elements here were placed by FrontPage, the HTML editor that I use.

4

LISTING 4.5   HTML AND VBSCRIPT IN THE PAGE THAT DEMONSTRATES THE ROTATEBANNERS ACTIVEX CONTROL

```
<html>

<head>
<title>Testing the RotateBanners AX control</title>
<script language="VBScript">
<!--
Sub RB1_Click(Message)
    MsgBox Message
end sub
-->
</script>
</head>

<body background="../IMAGES/PAPER1.GIF">

<p>This page demonstrates the RotateBanner ActiveX control
    that was developed in the book</p>

<p><br>
```

continues

LISTING 4.5   CONTINUED

```
<big><em>Teach Yourself Internet Programming
        with Visual Basic 6 in 21 Days</em></big></p>

<p>Written by Peter G. Aitken</p>

<p>Published by Macmillan Computer Publishing</p>
<p align="center">Click the banner!</p>
<p> </p>

<p align="center"> 
<object classid="clsid:D8DD67F4-3B40-11D2-BBC6-02608CACCADB" width="468"
height="60"
id="RB1"
codebase="/ax_controls/rotatebanners.cab">
  <param name="_ExtentX" value="12488">
  <param name="_ExtentY" value="1693">
Rotate Banners ActiveX Control
</object>
</p>

<hr>

<p> </p>
</body>
</html>
```

Figure 4.7 shows what this page looks like when viewed in Microsoft Internet Explorer, after you click the banner.

TRY IT ON THE WEB

You can view this page, as well as download and install the ActiveX control if necessary, at http://www.pgacon.com/ipbook/rotatebanners.htm.

TESTING METHODS

To test an ActiveX control in a Web page that contains VBScript code and/or <PARAM> tags, you cannot use the Start Component option on the Debugging tab of the Project Properties dialog box. This option runs the control in a bare-bones Web page that contains nothing more than the required <OBJECT> reference. Rather, you must create a Web page that contains not only the <OBJECT> tag but also other tags and the VBScript that you want to test.

To use the page you created for testing, select the Start Browser with URL option on the Debugging tab of the Project Properties dialog box. Enter the URL of the HTML file you created, making sure to include the `file://` specification so that the browser will know it's a local file (for example, `file://c:\testpages\test.htm`). Then, when you click the Run button in Visual Basic, it will start your browser and load the specified page.

FIGURE 4.7

Viewing the RotateBanners demonstration Web page.

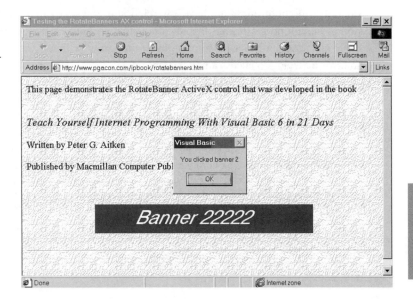

Using the Ambient Properties

You have learned that ActiveX controls display within containers. To provide for the smoothest possible integration between control and container, it's sometimes desirable for the control to be able to find out certain things about its container. For example, to blend in with the appearance of the container object, a control might want to set its BackColor property to the same background color used by the container.

A control can access certain relevant information about its container by means of the AmbientProperties object. This object is provided by the UserControl object, via its Ambient property. For example, BackColor is one of the standard Ambient properties. A UserControl can set its own BackColor property to match the container's BackColor as follows:

```
BackColor = Ambient.BackColor
```

Important Ambient Properties

The ActiveX specification requires that all container objects expose a minimum set of ambient properties. Certain container objects may expose additional ambient properties. In addition, the UserControl object provides a wider set of ambient properties than the minimum required by the standard. If your program reads one of the ambient properties that is not exposed by the current container object, the UserControl returns a default value that might or might not have any relation to the state of the container. This provision of default properties has the advantage that an ActiveX control written in Visual Basic can access a wider range of ambient properties without worrying about triggering an error by trying to access a nonexistent one.

EXTRA AMBIENT PROPERTIES PROVIDED BY CONTAINERS

If a specific type of container object exposes additional ambient properties, you can find out about them from the container's documentation. However, these properties will not be in the Visual Basic type library and will not display in the object browser. As a result, Visual Basic cannot verify their existence at compile time, and attempts to access nonexistent ambient properties will not cause an error until runtime. Therefore, you should always be sure to use error handling when working with ambient properties.

The Ambient properties that you are most likely to use in your projects are described in this section:

- DisplayAsDefault returns True if the control has been chosen by the container to act as the default button. The designer of the control should include code that, when this property is True, will draw a heavy border on the control to visually indicate that it's the default control. You can ignore this property if you did not set up the control to be the default control.

- DisplayName returns the name of this particular instance of the control. This can be useful in error trapping, because it permits the program to identify the particular control that generated the error.

- ForeColor, BackColor, and Font provide information about the display colors and font being used by the container object. The ActiveX control can adopt the same settings as the container to blend in visually.

- TextAlign informs the control how the container would like text to be displayed. By convention, if this property is 0, the control should set its text to the general format, with text aligned to the left and numbers aligned to the right. Property values of 1–4 specify left, centered, right, and justified alignment, respectively.

- `LocaleID` specifies the locale (language and country) of the user.
- `Palette` returns a `Picture` object whose palette is the one suggested by the container for the control to use.
- `UserMode` returns `False` if the control is running in a design environment and `True` if it's a runtime instance. You can use this property in your control if you want certain other properties to be available only at design time or only at runtime.

There are a number of other ambient properties, but the ones in this list are those you'll be most likely to need in your Visual Basic projects. You can obtain information about the other ambient properties in the Visual Basic help system.

How does your control use the ambient properties? Much depends, of course, on the control itself. For instance, a control that doesn't display text is unlikely to need to pay attention to the `Font` ambient property. Therefore, your first step is to determine which, if any, of the ambient properties your control needs to take into account.

After this is done, the next step is to write the code that reads the values of the ambient properties and copies them into control properties. There are two times when you might need to do this. The first is when the control is initially situated on the container object. This code should go in either the `InitProperties` or `ReadProperties` event procedure. You cannot use the `Initialize` event because the `AmbientProperties` object is not yet available when that event is fired.

The second time when you might need to read ambient properties is when the control is executing and one or more of the container object's properties changes. Whenever one of the ambient properties changes, the `UserControl` object's `AmbientChanged` event is fired. The associated event procedure is passed a single string argument containing the name of the property that changed:

```
Private Sub UserControl_AmbientChanged(PropertyName As String
...
End Sub
```

If you want the control to react to ambient property changes while it's executing, put the required code in the `AmbientChanged` event procedure.

Do	Don't
DO use the Ambient properties to adjust the display characteristics of your ActiveX control to match those of its container object.	DON'T try to access Ambient properties in a control's initialize event procedure.

Summary

This chapter shows you some of the more advanced tasks you can accomplish with ActiveX controls. Among the most important things you learned is how to add custom properties to an ActiveX control, something that will be required in almost every ActiveX control project you undertake. In addition to setting and reading property values, property procedures can be used for other tasks, such as verifying property values.

You also learned about the complex ways that events work in ActiveX controls. A number of events are associated with the creation and destruction of controls, and you will use these events to initialize data and perform other essential tasks. ActiveX controls can also detect user events, such as mouse clicks. Visual Basic provides tools that enable you to specify where user events are available and which components respond to them. It's also possible to define custom events that can be raised for detection by the container object.

VBScript, you also learned today, is a scripting language that can be embedded in a Web page and used to respond to events generated by ActiveX controls. You also saw how Ambient properties can be used to obtain information about the container object.

You are not finished with ActiveX controls yet. In Day 5, "Real-World ActiveX," the final chapter on this topic, you will learn about some more advanced ActiveX control properties and events and will see how to give your controls a property page. You will tie all this material together by developing a sophisticated ActiveX control.

Q&A

Q What are the two main advantages of using property procedures instead of Public variables to create custom properties in an ActiveX control?

A Property procedures let you validate property values and create read-only and write-only properties.

Q What are the rules for formatting text and tags in an HTML document?

A There are no rules. In an HTML document, whitespace, line breaks, and other formatting are ignored. Only the content and the tags are relevant to the final appearance of the document.

Q You want the container object to be able to respond when the user clicks one of an ActiveX control's constituent controls. How is this done?

A You must declare an event of the desired name in the ActiveX control module by using the Event keyword. Then, when the user clicks the constituent control, code in the control must raise the event, by using RaiseEvent, so that it will be passed to the container object.

Q Does the container object, such as a Web browser, automatically respond to events raised by an ActiveX control?

A No. Raising an event in an ActiveX control only makes it available. The container will respond only if it contains an event procedure for the specific event. For Web browsers, such procedures are usually written in VBScript.

Q What is the syntax for naming event procedures in VBScript? How does it differ from the syntax used in Visual Basic?

A Event procedure syntax is the same for both VBScript and Visual Basic. An event procedure name consists of the object name, followed by an underscore and the event name.

Workshop

Quiz

1. How would you create a read-only property in an ActiveX control?
2. What is the first event to fire when an instance of an ActiveX control is created?
3. When does the ReadProperties event fire?
4. Does the UserControl object ever receive mouse events?
5. How does a browser identify VBScript code and tell it apart from other elements of the page?
6. What are ambient properties, and what are they used for?

Exercise

Create a mini-calculator ActiveX control that enables the user to enter two numbers and then add, subtract, multiply, or divide them. The answer should be displayed in the control, as well as be made available to the container object. Make sure the control uses the same background color and font as the container object.

Day 5

Real-World ActiveX

You have learned a lot about ActiveX controls, enough to already start doing some useful programming. It's a complex and powerful technology, however, and there are a few more advanced topics that I have yet to cover. When you have these under your belt, you'll be ready to tackle just about any ActiveX control programming challenge that comes your way. Today you will learn

- How to add a property page to your controls
- How to use a property bag to create persistent properties
- How to use some advanced ActiveX control display techniques
- How to develop a complete ActiveX control, using some of these techniques

Adding a Property Page to an ActiveX Control

You have already learned how to add custom properties to an ActiveX control. The properties that you define are displayed in the Visual Basic (VB) properties window, just like other properties. There's another way to present a control's properties, called a *property page*. When a property page has been defined, the developer has the option of viewing and manipulating the object's properties in a dialog box instead of the properties window.

Many of Visual Basic's regular controls have property pages associated with them. You can display the property page by right-clicking the control and selecting Properties from the pop-up menu. For example, the Treeview control's property pages are shown in Figure 5.1.

NO PROPERTY PAGE?

If a control doesn't have a property page, selecting Properties from its pop-up menu simply activates the regular properties window.

FIGURE 5.1

The Treeview control's property pages.

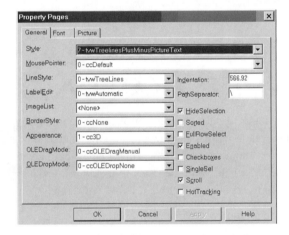

In Figure 5.1, there are actually three property pages—in other words, each tab in the Property Pages dialog box represents a separate property page.

Property pages offer several advantages over the regular properties window. They are particularly useful when several of the object's properties interact in a complex manner. Several related properties can be grouped together on a property page, which makes it easier for the developer to set them properly. Property pages also enable controls to be used in development environments that don't have a properties window. Finally, property pages are ideal for controls that you plan to distribute internationally, because the page captions can be easily changed to reflect the local language.

Your ActiveX control project should be well along before you add a property page to it. It doesn't make any sense to add a property page if the control doesn't yet have any custom properties defined! You can define additional properties after creating a property page and optionally add them to the page as well.

Creating a Property Page

To add a property page to an ActiveX control, open the control project in Visual Basic and select Add Property Page from the Project menu. Visual Basic displays the Add Property Page dialog box, as shown in Figure 5.2. You have three choices in this dialog box.

FIGURE 5.2

The Add Property Page dialog box.

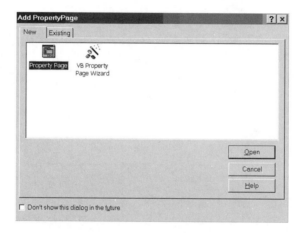

1. To create a new property page from scratch, select the Property Page icon.
2. To have the Property Page Wizard help create your property page, select the VB Property Page Wizard icon.
3. To use an existing property page, click the Existing tab and then locate the property page file.

USING AN EXISTING PROPERTY PAGE

When would you use an existing property page in your project? Only when the existing page is very similar to the page you need. Otherwise, the needed modifications will be more work than creating a new page from scratch. This situation is most likely to arise when you are creating a new control based on an existing control. After modifying an existing property page, be sure to save it under a new name.

Creating a Property Page from Scratch

When you select the Property Page icon in the Property Page dialog box, Visual Basic opens a new blank property page designer, as shown in Figure 5.3. You can tell that the blank form on the screen is indeed a property page because the title bar says `PropertyPage1 (PropertyPage)`. Note also that the Property Pages category has been added to the Project window with the new property page listed underneath.

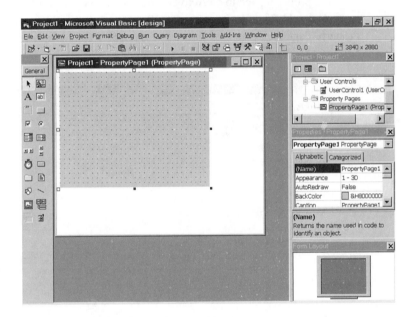

After starting the property page, you should assign a caption to it. The Caption property is the text that displays on the page's tab in the Property Pages dialog box. For projects that use only one property page, it's standard practice (although not required) to use the caption `General`. Projects that use multiple property pages usually have a General page, as well, and some other pages that are for specialized properties and have corresponding captions, such as Display or Security.

Each property page also has a Name property. You can use any name you want, but I have found it useful to name property pages by combining the page's Caption property with a prefix that identifies the control it is associated with. For example, when I created an ActiveX control named Fancy Command Button, I assigned the name `FCBGeneral` to its General property page.

Designing a property page is very similar to creating a regular Visual Basic form. You place controls on the page, add labels to identify them, and so on. For each property that you want represented on the page, you need an appropriate control to hold and display its value. The type of control to use depends on the nature of the property data:

- If the property holds arbitrary string data, a Text Box control is usually appropriate.
- If the property is selected from a subset of possibilities (an `Enum`, for example), a List Box or Combo Box might work well.
- If the property is a `True/False` value, you can use a Check Box.
- If the property holds a numerical value, a Text Box or an UpDown control might be used.

These are just some examples—you can use your full range of Visual Basic programming knowledge to design property pages. Just remember the purpose of the page: to present the control's properties to the developer in a clear and understandable manner. Figure 5.4 shows an example of a simple property page in the process of being designed. This page has elements for three properties; a type `String` named `Caption`, a type `Integer` named `NumOfTries`, and a type Boolean named `Verify`. You can see that each property is associated with a control that is appropriate for its data type.

FIGURE 5.4

A property page during design.

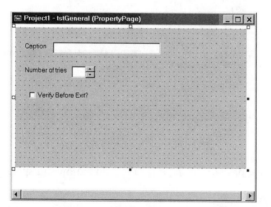

5

NAMING CONTROLS ON A PROPERTY PAGE

There are no special rules for naming the controls on a property page. It makes things easier, however, if each control is named according to the property it will hold. For example, the Text Box that holds the Caption property would be named `txtCaption`.

You can add controls to a property page for properties that don't yet exist in the control. Designing the page is only the first step. You must write code to connect the property page to the control and to copy values of the properties from the control to the page and back again. I'll show you how to do this soon.

Using the Property Page Wizard

The quickest way to create a property page for your ActiveX control is to use the Property Page Wizard. As explained earlier, this is one of the options available to you when you select the Project, Add Property Page command. For the wizard to work, your project must have its properties defined—that is, you must have already created the Property procedures for the control properties. This is because the wizard creates a page based on existing properties.

When you start the Property Page Wizard, the first dialog box you see is used to select the property pages the wizard works with, as shown in Figure 5.5. If the project has any existing property pages, they will be listed in the dialog box. Here's what you can do in this dialog box:

FIGURE 5.5

Selecting the property page(s) for the wizard to use.

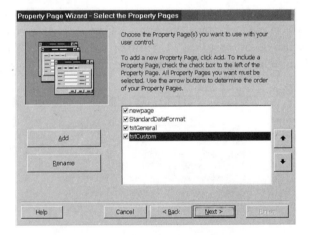

- To add a new property page, click the Add button and specify the name for the new page.
- To use one or more existing property pages with the wizard, click the page name to place a checkmark in the adjacent box.
- To rename an existing property page, select it in the list and click the Rename button.

After you have added or specified the property page or pages for the wizard to use, click the Next button to display the Add properties dialog box, which is shown in Figure 5.6.

On the left side of this dialog box is a list of all the available properties—those properties that are defined in the project but haven't been added to a property page yet. On the right side are the property page or pages that you specified in the previous step. If you specified more than one page, each one is represented by a tab with the page name on it.

FIGURE 5.6

The Add Properties dialog box.

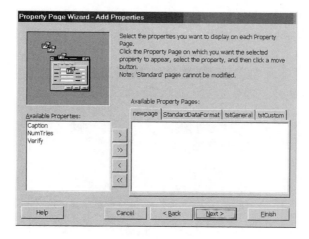

Here are the steps to take in this dialog box:

- To add a property to a page, click the page's tab, select the property name in the Available Properties list and click the > button.

- To add all available properties to a page, click the page's tab and click the >> button.

- To remove a property from a page, select the property name on the page and click the < button.

- To remove all properties from a page, click the page's tab and click the << button.

EASY DRAGGING

In the Add Properties dialog box you can also add a property to a page by dragging it from the Available Properties list to the page's tab. You can also remove a property from a page by dragging it back to the Available Properties list.

After you have placed the properties as desired, click Next and then Finish. The wizard creates the pages with controls for the specified properties. Each property is given a control with an adjacent label. The label's caption and the control's name are created based on the property name.

Figure 5.7 shows the property page created by the wizard for a control with the following three properties:

A type `String` named `Caption`

5

A type `Integer` named `NumTries`

A type `Boolean` named `Verify`

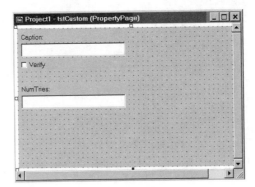

FIGURE 5.7

A property page created by the Property Page Wizard.

Looking at this property page, you might want to make some changes. One problem is that the name of a property does not always make the most descriptive caption for the property page. You are completely free to modify the property page after the wizard has created it. Particularly for control projects that have many properties, the wizard can save a lot of time. This time saving is even more evident when you realize that the wizard adds much of the code that is necessary to connect the property page to the control. Creating this connection is the next topic.

Connecting the Property Page to the Control

After creating one or more property pages for your control, you still need to connect the pages to the control, which is comprised of two parts. The first requires setting the UserControl's `PropertyPages` property to point at the page or pages you want to use. Here are the steps to follow:

1. Select the `UserControl` object in your project.

2. In the Properties window, scroll down to the `PropertyPages` entry and click the button with the ellipses (...). Visual Basic displays the Connect Property Pages dialog box, as shown in Figure 5.8.

This dialog box lists all the property pages that are part of the project, plus several standard pages. Put a checkmark next to each page that you want to associate with the UserControl. To change the order in which multiple pages are displayed, use the Page Order buttons to move a page up or down in the list.

FIGURE 5.8

Selecting property pages for the UserControl *object.*

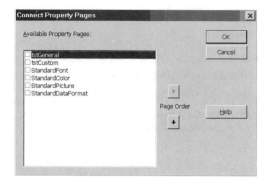

THE STANDARD PROPERTY PAGES

Visual Basic provides four standard property pages that are designed for setting these commonly needed properties: Font, Color, Picture, and DataFormat. These standard property pages cannot be edited. When you create a property with the data type Font, OLE_COLOR, Picture, or stdDataFormat, the corresponding standard property page will automatically be associated with the property.

Note that stdDataFormat is an object type, and it will not be available in your project unless you select the Microsoft Data Formatting Object Library in the References list.

The second part of connecting property pages to a control is writing the code that performs the following actions:

1. Copies property values from the UserControl to the property page(s) when the property page is displayed.

2. Registers whether the developer has made any changes to the property values displayed on the property page.

3. Copies the new property values from the property page back to the control when the property page is closed (or when the Apply button is clicked.

The first step is done in the property page's SelectionChanged event procedure. This event is fired whenever the developer changes the selected control on the container object that the ActiveX control has been placed on. It is also fired when the property page for a control is first displayed. Code in this event procedure should copy the property values from the ActiveX control to the individual controls on the property page.

How do you know which control is selected on the container? Use the SelectedControls collection. This is a 0-based collection of all the controls that are currently selected on the container by the developer. Because there is usually only one

5

control selected, a reference to `SelectedControls(0)` reliably returns a reference to whatever control is selected.

Suppose that your ActiveX control has a property named `Caption`, and on the property page there is a Text Box named `txtCaption` associated with this property. Then the `SelectionChanged` event procedure will look like this:

```
Private Sub PropertyPage_SelectionChanged()
    txtCaption.Text = SelectedControls(0).Caption
End Sub
```

The event procedure will have to contain one line for each property, using the previous format to copy each and every property value from the control to the property page. If your project uses more than one property page, you'll have to do this in each property page's `SelectionChanged` event procedure.

The next step is letting the property page know when one or more properties have been changed. Every property page has a `Changed` property, which is set to `False` when the page first displays. Setting the `Changed` property to `True` is how you notify the property page that one or more properties have been modified. The effect of setting this property to `True` is to make the property page's Apply button available.

DIRTY PAGES

A property page that has had one or more property values changed is sometimes referred to as being *dirty*. A *clean* page, on the other hand, is one on which no properties have been changed.

The `Changed` property must be set to `True` if any property on the page is changed. The best way to do this is to use each individual control's `Change` event procedure. Therefore, for the `Caption` property previously described, you would write the following:

```
Private Sub txtCaption_Change()
    Changed = True
End Sub
```

You must do this in the `Change` event procedure for every control on the property page that is used to display a property value.

The final coding step is to copy all the property values from the property page back to the ActiveX control. This is done in the property page's `ApplyChanges` event procedure. This event is fired when the developer clicks either the Apply or the OK button in the Property Pages dialog box.

This procedure is the reverse of what you did in the `SelectionChanged` event procedure—values are copied from controls on the property page to the ActiveX control. Continuing with my example, the code is as follows:

```
Private Sub PropertyPage_ApplyChanges()
 SelectedControls(0).Caption = txtCaption.Text
End Sub
```

Remember that the value of every property on the property page must be transferred back to the control. For properties that have not been modified this will have no effect, of course, but copying all the properties is a lot easier than trying to keep track of which ones have been changed and copying only those.

Dealing with Multiple Selected Controls

When creating property pages, you should take into account the possibility that the developer has selected more than one control in the container. Some design tools don't permit the selection of multiple controls—the Microsoft FrontPage editor is one example—but others, such as Visual Basic, do permit it.

You can detect when multiple controls are selected by means of the `SelectedControls` collection. This collection's `Count` property indicates the number of controls currently selected. If `Count` is 1 only a single control is selected.

What should you do if multiple controls are selected? Take your hint from Visual Basic itself. If you select two or more controls on a Visual Basic form, the properties window displays only those properties that all the selected controls have in common. If you change one of these properties, the new value is applied to all the selected controls.

In a property page, use the `SelectionChanged` event procedure to see if multiple controls are selected. If so, disable those controls on the property page that correspond to properties you don't want the developer to be able to change when multiple controls are selected.

Return to the example of a control with a `Caption` property. Because you would probably not want two or more controls to have the same caption, you would want this property to be unavailable for change when multiple controls are selected. Here is the code for the `SelectionChanged` event procedure:

```
Private Sub PropertyPage_SelectionChanged()

If SelectedControls.Count > 1 Then
    txtCaption.Enabled = False
Else
    txtCaption.Enabled = True
    txtCaption.Text = SelectedControls(0).Caption
```

5

```
End If

End Sub
```

You also have to copy the new value back to all the selected controls. This can be accomplished by looping through all the controls in the `SelectedControls` collection. Here is the code you would place in the `ApplyChanges` event procedure:

```
Private Sub PropertyPage_ApplyChanges

    Dim c As Variant
        For Each c In SelectedControls
        c.Caption = txtCaption.Text
        Next

End Sub
```

Do	**Don't**
DO take the possibility of multiple selected controls into account, even if you use the simplest approach of disabling all property page controls.	DON'T allow changes to a property for multiple selected controls unless the property is appropriate for such a change. BackColor, ForeColor, and Font are examples of properties that are usually appropriate for multiple simultaneous change.

Using a Property Bag to Make Properties Persistent

Suppose that a Web page developer uses an ActiveX control that has been created with the techniques presented so far. She places an instance of the control on a Web page and changes some of the custom properties. Then, she saves the project and shuts the system down for the night. The next day when she opens the project, guess what will have happened to those properties whose values she changed? They will be back at their default values—the changes will be lost.

Clearly, this inability to save properties is not acceptable. There must be a way to make property values persistent between instantiations of an object. The way this is done is with a *Property Bag*, a rather descriptive term for the way ActiveX control properties can be saved and reloaded. Property bags are used in conjunction with the `ReadProperties` and `WriteProperties` events.

The Property Bag is actually provided by the container object, and most of what goes on is done behind the scenes with no need for your attention. If you want a property value to be persistent, write it to the property bag when the control is destroyed and read it back into the control when the control is created again. These actions are carried out in the `ReadProperties` and `WriteProperties` event procedures, which have the following declarations:

```
Private Sub UserControl_ReadProperties(PropBag As PropertyBag)
...
End Sub

Private Sub UserControl_WriteProperties(PropBag As PropertyBag)
...
End Sub
```

You can see that both of these event procedures are automatically passed a `PropertyBag` object, courtesy of the container object. Within each procedure, use the methods of the `PropertyBag` object to save and retrieve properties. There are only two methods for the `PropertyBag` object:

```
PropBag.ReadProperty(PropertyName[, DefaultValue])

PropBag.WriteProperty(PropertyName, Value[, DefaultValue])
```

In both cases, *PropertyName* is the name of the property that you are reading or writing, and the optional *DefaultValue* is the property's default value. For the `WriteProperty` method, *value* is the property value to be saved.

WHY HAVE DEFAULT VALUES?

The *DefaultValue* arguments work differently for the `ReadProperties` and `WriteProperties` methods. For `ReadProperty`, *DefaultValue* is the value returned by the method if *PropertyName* is not found in the property bag. For `WriteProperty`, defining a *DefaultValue* can save time because *value* is not actually written to the file where the property bag is kept unless it is different from the default value already stored there.

In the `WriteProperties` event procedure, place one call to `WriteProperty` for each of the object's properties that you want to make persistent. For the `Caption` property, you would write:

```
Private Sub UserControl_WriteProperties(PropBag As PropertyBag)

    PropBag.WriteProperty "Caption", Caption, Extender.Name

End Sub
```

5

This code uses the `Name` of the `Extender` object as the default value for the `Caption` property. Then, to retrieve the property value add the following code in the `ReadProperties` event procedure:

```
Private Sub UserControl_ReadProperties(PropBag As PropertyBag)

    Caption = PropBag.ReadProperty("Caption", Extender.Name)

End Sub
```

Now that you understand how property bags work, the way that property-related event procedures are fired will make sense. The `ReadProperties` event is not only fired the first time an instance of the control is created, but also the second and subsequent times. This makes sense because the first time an instance is created—when the developer first puts the control on its container—there can in fact be no modified properties that require saving. It is the `InitProperties` event that fires the first time and instance in which the control is created, and never again. You place code in `InitProperties` to set the initial default values of the properties.

The `WriteProperties` event is fired each and every time an instance of the control is destroyed, including the first time. Thus, modified properties can be saved each and every time it might be needed. The second and subsequent times an instance of the control is created, `ReadProperties` is fired to enable saved property values to be read in.

Do	Don't
DO use the `InitProperties` event procedure to set the initial default values for your control's properties.	DON'T neglect to save the values of your control's custom properties in a property bag.

Advanced ActiveX Display Techniques

So far you have learned a lot about creating functional ActiveX controls. What about their appearance? Although creating controls that operate properly should be your first concern, today's competitive world demands controls that look great too.

The Basic Control

A basic ActiveX control, with all its appearance-related properties at their default value, displays as a solid rectangle of whatever color is specified by the `BackColor` property (the default being the standard medium gray that you see in Windows so much). Constituent controls and the output of any graphics methods are displayed "floating" over the background color. It can have a border or not, as set by its `BorderStyle` property.

You can "fancy-up" an ActiveX control by displaying an image in the background instead of a solid color. Use the Picture property to select the image; you can use any of several graphics formats, including BMP, GIF, and JPG. Images aren't stretched or shrunk to fill the control, so you must custom size the image to make it fit.

Custom Fitting an Image

You can custom fit an image to fill the UserControl by first loading the image into a PictureBox control and then using the `PaintPicture` method to copy it to fill the UserControl. Place a PictureBox on the UserControl, load it with the desired image by settings its `Picture` property, and then set its `AutoSize` property to `True` so it will automatically size itself to match the image. Also, set the `Visible` property to `False` so that it will not be seen. Then, place the following code in the UserControl's `Paint` event procedure (assume the PictureBox's name is `Pic1`):

```
Private Sub UserControl_Paint()

PaintPicture Pic1.Picture, 0, 0, _
    Width, Height, 0, 0, _
    Pic1.Width, Pic1.Height

End Sub
```

Figure 5.9 shows an ActiveX control where this technique has been used to display an image behind the constituent controls.

FIGURE 5.9

Displaying an image as the background in an ActiveX control.

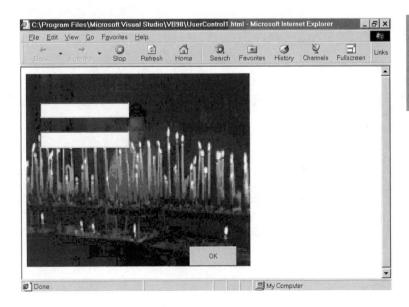

Using a Transparent Background

The UserControl object has a property called BackStyle that has two possible settings: Opaque (value = 1) or Transparent (value = 0). The default setting is Opaque, which lets you determine the background of the control by setting the BackColor or Picture properties. Anything that is behind the UserControl in the container object is hidden.

If you set BackStyle to Transparent, many interesting possibilities are opened up. The Picture and BackColor properties are ignored, and the background of the UserControl isn't visible but enables whatever is behind it in the container to show through behind the constituent controls. Figure 5.10 shows two instances of an ActiveX control, with BackStyle set to Opaque (left) and Transparent (right).

FIGURE 5.10

The effects of setting a UserControl's BackStyle *property to* Opaque *(left) and* Transparent *(right).*

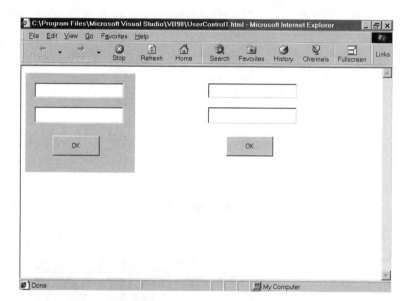

MOUSE EVENTS AND A TRANSPARENT BACKSTYLE

If a UserControl's BackStyle property is set to Transparent, the control won't detect mouse events in the transparent areas. That is to say, the constituent controls will still detect mouse events but the UserControl will not. Such events will be detected by whatever is behind the control.

Using a Picture Mask

The idea of a transparent background can be taken a step further by using a *mask*. To define a mask you must do two things:

1. Create or locate a bitmap image that contains the desired mask pattern. This image is specified in the UserControl's MaskPicture property.

2. Specify a mask color in the UserControl's MaskColor property.

Here's how it works. Wherever the color in the MaskPicture image is the same as the color specified by MaskColor, the background of the UserControl will be transparent. Where the MaskColor image is another color, the background will be opaque. Note that the bitmap MaskPicture image is never actually displayed; it only defines the mask pattern. In the areas of the background that are opaque the UserControl displays the color specified by the BackColor property.

An example will make things more clear. I first created the mask image that is shown in Figure 5.11. It is a simple white cross on a black background. I specified this image as the UserControl's MaskImage property. While designing the ActiveX control, the MaskImage is not visible.

FIGURE 5.11

The original mask image.

Next, I set the BackStyle property of the UserControl to Transparent, and the MaskColor property to White (&H00FFFFFF). The BackColor property was left at its default value of gray. Finally, I added a Text Box control to the UserControl. The

UserControl was made approximately the same size as the mask image. When I execute the ActiveX control it appears as shown in Figure 5.12.

FIGURE 5.12

Demonstrating the use of a mask image.

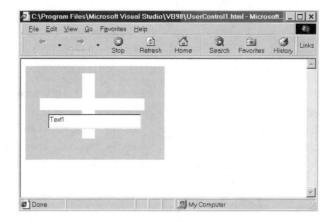

When looking at Figure 5.12 it's important to realize that the cross in the middle of the control isn't white because the mask image was white in those areas—it's white because the white background of the container is showing through. If I had created a mask image with a green cross, the result would be exactly the same as long as I specified Green as the UserControl's MaskColor.

Now look at Figure 5.13. The only difference here is that I changed the UserControl's MaskColor property to Black. Now the UserControl's background is transparent where the mask image is black.

FIGURE 5.13

Using the same mask image with a different MaskColor *property.*

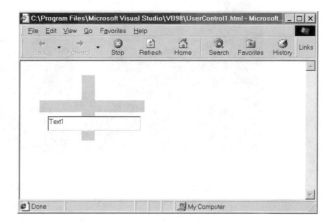

When you use a mask image, the transparent portions of the background don't detect mouse events, just as when the entire background is made transparent. Also, graphics methods are clipped and appear only on the opaque areas. This can be illustrated by drawing two diagonal lines on the control. Place the following code in the UserControl's Paint event procedure:

```
Private Sub UserControl_Paint()

    Line (0, 0)-(Width, Height)
    Line (0, Height)-(Width, 0)

End Sub
```

The results are shown in Figure 5.14 (with the MaskColor property set back to White). You can see that the lines appear only on those parts of the control background that are opaque.

FIGURE 5.14

Drawing methods are clipped to the opaque parts of the background.

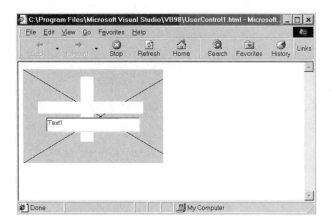

A Demonstration

Before leaving the topic of ActiveX controls, I think it will be valuable for you to see a more complete demonstration. The RotateBanners control that you developed in previous days was fine as far as it went, but it didn't make use of some of the ActiveX techniques you have learned today.

For the demonstration I have created an ActiveX control that calculates loan payments. The user enters the loan amount, interest rate, and length of the loan, and the monthly payment is calculated and displayed. The control uses a property page (created with the Property Page Wizard) and also uses a property bag to make its properties persistent. Figure 5.15 shows what the control looks like.

5

FIGURE 5.15

The Loan Calculator control.

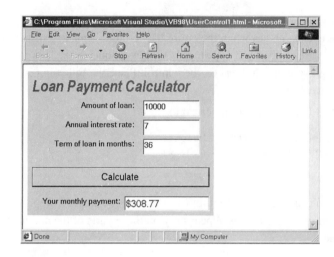

The UserControl has all its properties left at their default values. There are 10 constituent controls placed on the UserControl; they are listed, along with non-default property values, in Table 5.1. You can get a feel for how the controls are arranged by looking at the figure (or, you can arrange them differently if you prefer).

TABLE 5.1   CONSTITUENT CONTROLS IN THE LOANPAYMENTS CONTROL PROJECT

Control Type	Property	Value
Label	Name	Label1
	Caption	Loan Payment Calculator
	Font	Roman Bold Italics 20 points
	BackStyle	Transparent
	ForeColor	Dark red (&H000000C0)
Command Button	Caption	Calculate
	Name	cmdCalculate
	Font	MS Sans Serif 12 point
Text Box	Name	txtPayment
	Locked	True
	Font	MS Sans Serif 12 point
	ForeColor	Dark Blue (&H00C00000)
Label	Name	Label2
	Caption	Your monthly payment
	Font	MS Sans Serif 10 point
	Alignment	1 - Right Justify

Control Type	Property	Value
Label	Name	Label3
	Caption	Amount of loan:
	Font	MS Sans Serif 10 point
	Alignment	1 - Right Justify
Label	Name	Label4
	Caption	Annual interest rate:
	Font	MS Sans Serif 10 point
	Alignment	1 - Right Justify
Label	Name	Label5
	Caption	Term of loan in months:
	Font	MS Sans Serif 10 point
	Alignment	1 - Right Justify
Text Box	Name	txtAmount
	Font	MS Sans Serif 10 point
Text Box	Name	txtInterest
	Font	MS Sans Serif 10 point
Text Box	Name	txtTerm
	Font	MS Sans Serif 10 point

The control's code is shown in Listing 5.1. Most of this code you should understand perfectly well based on material in the last three days, so I will mention only a couple of things.

Note that the Change event procedure for all three input Text Box controls is used. Any time the user changes the value in one of these Text Boxes, the result of the previous calculation is erased. This prevents the possibility of misreading an incorrect answer.

It is in the cmdCalculate event procedure where the actual calculations are done. First, code verifies that all three input boxes contain data, if not, a warning message displays. If all the input data is available, the calculations are performed. The formula for calculating a payment on a loan is:

```
Payment = (amount * rate) / (1 - (1 + rate) ^ -term)
```

For this formula to work correctly, it is necessary for the interest rate to be expressed as a decimal value. Thus, 7 percent would be 0.07. Also, the period used must be the same for rate, term, and payment. In other words, if you want to calculate a monthly payment you must express the loan term in months, so a 3 year loan would be 36 months. Likewise, the interest rate must be the per month rate, so the annual interest rate entered by the user must be divided by 12.

5

In addition to displaying the results of the calculation in a Text Box, the control also raises an event named `Calculate` with the result passed as an argument. This is done so that the container object has access to the result if it needs it.

LISTING 5.1   CODE FOR THE LOANPAYMENTS CONTROL PROJECT

```
Option Explicit
Public Event Calculate(Payment As Variant)

Public Property Get InterestRate() As Variant

    InterestRate = txtInterest.Text

End Property

Public Property Let InterestRate(ByVal vNewValue As Variant)

    txtInterest.Text = vNewValue

End Property

Public Property Get Term() As Variant

    Term = txtTerm.Text

End Property

Public Property Let Term(ByVal vNewValue As Variant)

    txtTerm.Text = vNewValue

End Property

Public Property Get amount() As Currency

    amount = txtAmount.Text

End Property

Public Property Let amount(ByVal vNewValue As Currency)

    txtAmount.Text = vNewValue

End Property

Private Sub cmdCalculate_Click()

    Dim LoanPayment
    Dim rate As Single
```

```
        Dim months As Integer
        Dim amount As Currency

        If txtAmount.Text = "" Or _
            txtInterest.Text = "" _
            Or txtTerm.Text = "" Then
              MsgBox "Please enter values in all three boxes."
              Exit Sub
        End If

        ' Convert to monthly interest rate.
        rate = Val(txtInterest.Text / 12)
        ' Convert to decimal.
        rate = rate / 100
        amount = Val(txtAmount.Text)
        months = Val(txtTerm.Text)

        LoanPayment = (amount * rate) / (1 - (1 + rate) ^ -months)
        txtPayment.Text = Format(LoanPayment, "Currency")
        RaiseEvent Calculate(LoanPayment)

End Sub


Private Sub txtAmount_Change()

    txtPayment.Text = ""

End Sub

Private Sub txtInterest_Change()

    txtPayment.Text = ""

End Sub

Private Sub txtTerm_Change()

    txtPayment.Text = ""

End Sub

Private Sub UserControl_Initialize()

    txtPayment.Text = ""

End Sub

Private Sub UserControl_InitProperties()
```

continues

LISTING 5.1 CONTINUED

```
        txtInterest.Text = "7"
        txtTerm.Text = "36"
        txtAmount.Text = "10000"

End Sub

Private Sub UserControl_ReadProperties(PropBag As PropertyBag)

        txtInterest.Text = PropBag.ReadProperty("Interest", "7")
        txtAmount.Text = PropBag.ReadProperty("Amount", "10000")
        txtTerm.Text = PropBag.ReadProperty("Term", "36")

End Sub

Private Sub UserControl_WriteProperties(PropBag As PropertyBag)

        PropBag.WriteProperty "Interest", txtInterest.Text, "7"
        PropBag.WriteProperty "Amount", txtAmount.Text, "10000"
        PropBag.WriteProperty "Term", txtTerm.Text, "36"

End Sub
```

The project's property page was created using the Property Page Wizard and is shown in Figure 5.16. The three properties enable the developer to change the default values for the amount, rate, and term to suit their particular needs. The code in the property page is presented in Listing 5.2.

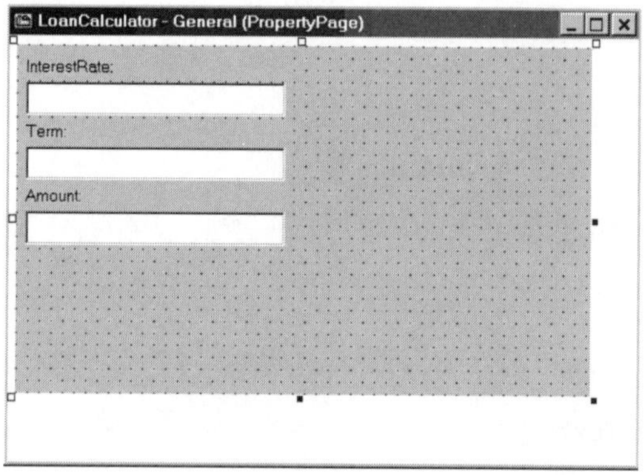

FIGURE 5.16

The LoanPayment control's property page.

LISTING 5.2   PROPERTY PAGE CODE IN THE LOANPAYMENT ACTIVEX CONTROL PROJECT

```
Option Explicit

Private Sub txtAmount_Change()

    Changed = True

End Sub

Private Sub txtTerm_Change()

    Changed = True

End Sub

Private Sub txtInterestRate_Change()

    Changed = True

End Sub

Private Sub PropertyPage_ApplyChanges()

    SelectedControls(0).amount = txtAmount.Text
    SelectedControls(0).Term = txtTerm.Text
    SelectedControls(0).InterestRate = txtInterestRate.Text

End Sub

Private Sub PropertyPage_SelectionChanged()

    txtAmount.Text = SelectedControls(0).amount
    txtTerm.Text = SelectedControls(0).Term
    txtInterestRate.Text = SelectedControls(0).InterestRate

End Sub
```

5

TRY IT ON THE WEB

You can try out the Loan Payment ActiveX control at
http://www.pgacon.com/ipbook/loanpayments.htm.

Summary

The ActiveX control specification permits you to put a lot of power in the controls
you create. With Visual Basic, programming your own custom ActiveX controls is a

relatively easy task. Many of the capabilities that are needed on Web pages can be encapsulated in an ActiveX control and then reused as many times as needed.

Today you learned some advanced ActiveX control programming techniques, including the very important ones of giving an ActiveX control a property page and making its custom properties persistent with a property bag. You also mastered some sophisticated display techniques that can be used to provide your controls with great-looking visual interfaces. Finally, you created a complete ActiveX control using some of these techniques. You should be ready to start working on some sophisticated ActiveX control projects of your own.

In the next lesson we leave ActiveX controls and turn our attention to another powerful ActiveX technology: ActiveX documents.

Q&A

Q What is the main advantage of giving your ActiveX control a property page rather that making do with the default properties window display?

A A property page enables you to group related properties together, making it easier for the developer to make settings properly. Interactions between properties can also be dealt with by code in a property page. Finally, property page captions can be easily changed, which simplifies international distribution issues.

Q How do you connect a property page to an ActiveX control?

A There are two steps. First, you must associate the property page with the control by setting the UserControl's PropertyPage property. Then you must add code to the property page that transfers property values back and forth between the control and the property page.

Q How does a control author make properties persistent? Where are the values stored?

A Properties are made persistent by writing them to a Property Bag when the control is destroyed, and then reading them back from the property bag when an instance is created again. The container object manages storage of the property bag.

Q What are two important results of setting a UserControl's BackStyle property to Transparent?

A In the areas between the constituent controls, the UserControl is not visible and whatever is behind the control in the container shows through. Also, mouse events on the transparent areas are not detected by the UserControl.

Q How would you make part of a UserControl's background transparent while leaving the rest of it opaque?

A Create a mask image the same size as the UserControl in which the areas you want to be transparent are all a certain color. Other parts of the image can be any other colors. Set the UserControl's `MaskImage` property to this image, it's `BackStyle` property to `Transparent`, and its `MaskColor` property to the "transparent" color used in the image.

Workshop

Quiz

1. Can you use the Property Page Wizard to add properties to an ActiveX control?

2. In property page code, how can you determine if the developer has selected more than one control?

3. Where should you place code that writes to and reads from a property bag?

4. How would you display a bitmap image as the background of a UserControl?

Exercises

You now know enough about ActiveX control programming to start working on your own projects. Think of something you can really use in your own Web programming, then get to work. It might be best to start simple, but there's no teacher like experience. If you cannot come up with an idea, here are a few:

- A clock that displays the current time in analog or digital format

- A "fancy" command button that displays different bitmaps in the clicked and unclicked states

- A chart that can receive data from code on the Web page and display a bar graph of the data

5

DAY **6**

Understanding ActiveX Documents

ActiveX technology goes well beyond control creation. One of the most powerful ways that Visual Basic leverages ActiveX for the Web is by means of ActiveX documents. An ActiveX document can be thought of as an entire Visual Basic application wrapped up in an Internet package. This is the first of three lessons on this topic. Today you will learn

- What an ActiveX document is
- How ActiveX documents can be used for dynamic Web programming
- How to create a basic ActiveX document
- How to add public properties and methods to an ActiveX document
- How to create an ActiveX document project that uses multiple documents and secondary forms

What Are ActiveX Documents?

I think that ActiveX documents are poorly named, and I think that when you learn what they can do, you will agree with me. In a nutshell, an *ActiveX document* is a complete Visual Basic application that can be downloaded over the Internet and executed in a Web browser. Precisely, an ActiveX document is analogous to a single Visual Basic form. You know how flexible Visual Basic forms are, so I hope you are excited about ActiveX documents.

In effect, ActiveX documents enable you to utilize the power and flexibility of Visual Basic to create "Web pages." I put Web pages in quotes because an ActiveX document is not a regular Web page: It doesn't consist of an HTML document with embedded content and tags. From the perspective of end-users, this doesn't matter. They just want Web content and applications that meet their needs. ActiveX documents are a great way to give it to them.

ActiveX EXE Versus ActiveX DLL

In the New Project dialog box, you will note the two types of ActiveX document projects: EXE and DLL. Functionally, they are essentially identical—the difference is that a DLL runs in-process, whereas an EXE runs out-of-process. What does this mean?

An *in-process component* runs in the same memory space as its container object. Communication between the two is fast, but crash protection is minimal, which means that a bug in the ActiveX document can crash not only itself but also the container. Soon you'll learn more details about DLL versus EXE.

An *out-of-process component* runs in its own memory space, separate from the container object's memory space. Communication is slowed down significantly, but crash protection is much better because the ActiveX document can crash without bringing down the container.

A Cross Between a Document and an Application

Perhaps the ActiveX document name comes from the fact that an ActiveX document is a cross between a document and an application. To understand, think about the relationship between a word processor and a document. I'll use Microsoft Word as an example.

A Word document and the Word application are related but distinct. The document, stored in a DOC file, contains the content, whereas the application, in an EXE file, contains the tools to create and manipulate the document. The Word application also exposes a set of classes that can be used by other applications to view or edit a Word document.

You can see this at work in a Visual Basic project. If you place an OLE Container control on a form, you can insert various kinds of objects in it, including a Microsoft Word document. The power of OLE enables you to use a Visual Basic form as a container for some of the objects, or classes, exposed by the Word application. As a result, the user of your Visual Basic application can view and manipulate Word documents.

An ActiveX document takes this concept one step further. An ActiveX project consists of a document, which contains whatever data is being used, and a server, which provides the tools and functionality to work with that data. The document is contained in a Visual Basic document file with the VBD extension, and the server is contained in either an EXE or a DLL file. Together, these two parts make up an ActiveX document, which can be executed in any one of several different containers. For Internet programmers, the container of most interest is Internet Explorer.

During development, an ActiveX document is kept in a *DOB file*. This is a plain text file that defines the controls, properties, and source code of the document. DOB files are analogous to the FRM files used to store the source information for Visual Basic forms. If a UserControl contains graphical elements that cannot be stored as text, these are stored in DOX files, which are parallel to the FRX files used to store graphical elements of forms.

Advantages of ActiveX Documents

From the perspective of the experienced Visual Basic programmer, a number of advantages are derived by using ActiveX documents. Some of these plusses will apply even if you are not an experienced Visual Basic programmer!

- You can make use of your existing Visual Basic programming knowledge. Most of the things you know about creating standard forms in Visual Basic also apply to creating ActiveX documents. You don't face a steep learning curve before you can accomplish anything useful.

- ActiveX document applications are created in the Visual Basic development environment with all its advantages, such as syntax checking and the debugger.

- Your projects will have the benefit of a consistent interface. An ActiveX document looks and behaves just like a regular Visual Basic application or most any other Windows program, even though it's deployed on the Internet and executed in a browser. No longer will your Internet applications have a different look and feel.

- Because ActiveX documents support the Hyperlink object, they can be integrated seamlessly into the structure of the Web.

6

- ActiveX documents support menu negotiation, which means that your document's menus replace the container's menus when the document is executing. This results in a simpler interface.

- ActiveX documents permit *viewport scrolling*, which enables you to control what part of the document is visible in the container.

- ActiveX documents execute locally, on the client machine. This lessens the server workload and provides much faster response for most operations.

- If you are programming for an intranet, an ActiveX document application can provide sophisticated data access, using all of Visual Basic's data tools, including ADO, RDO, and DAO.

CONTAINERS FOR ACTIVEX DOCUMENTS

Various container objects can be used with ActiveX documents, increasing their flexibility. For example, the Microsoft Office Binder can serve as a container for ActiveX documents, as can the Visual Basic development environment. Because this is a book on Internet programming, I will limit discussion to using Internet Explorer as a container.

The ActiveX document picture isn't all roses. Perhaps the most important caution to keep in mind is the question of browser support. Until recently, Microsoft Internet Explorer was the only browser that supports ActiveX documents, which made them poorly suited for general Internet use. Netscape Navigator has some ActiveX support, but whether full ActiveX document support will be available by the time you read this is an open question. Until more widespread browser support is a sure thing, you might want to limit ActiveX documents to intranet distribution.

ActiveX Documents Versus ActiveX Controls

As you read through this chapter, you will surely notice that many similarities exist between ActiveX documents and ActiveX controls. Perhaps the most important similarity is that both types of object cannot exist on their own but must run inside a container. There are other similarities: Both are downloaded from an Internet site and are locally installed and run; both have properties, share some of the same events, and support persistent data with the PropertyBag object. How are they different? Perhaps more important, how do you decide which type of project to use for a given task? The answer is fairly simple.

- ActiveX controls are ideal for encapsulating relatively small chunks of functionality that involve little or no user data.

- ActiveX documents are better suited for more complex applications that involve significant amounts of data.

When you are starting a project, it might not always be clear to you which to use. That's okay. Developing that kind of judgement takes a lot of experience. Some projects can be accomplished as either an ActiveX control or an ActiveX document. If you find that your ActiveX control project is becoming unwieldy, perhaps it would be better accomplished as an ActiveX document.

Here's the rule of thumb that I use. First, forget about the Internet temporarily and assume you are creating an application that will run only locally. Would you create a regular Visual Basic project? If your answer is yes, and you do in fact need Internet access for your application, you need an ActiveX document project.

An Overview of Creating an ActiveX Document

Before getting to the details, I think it would be useful to have an overview of the process of creating an ActiveX document. In general, the procedure is much like designing a standard Visual Basic form. An ActiveX document project can contain more than one ActiveX document, and each ActiveX document application can also display secondary forms. There are a few limitations. For example, you cannot place an OLE Container control on an ActiveX document, nor can you place embedded objects such as a Word or Excel document. You can, however, use almost all the controls available in Visual Basic.

The major steps involved in creating an ActiveX document are as follows:

1. Plan the project, at least in broad outline. Decide how many UserDocuments it will require, how many secondary forms, and what properties, events, and methods the project's interface will expose.
2. Start an ActiveX document project.
3. Place controls on the UserDocument to create the application's visual interface.
4. Create additional UserDocuments and secondary forms as needed.
5. Write the code to define the interface of the application—its properties, events, and methods.
6. Test the project in the appropriate container object.
7. Package and deploy the application to the Internet.

6

This procedure doesn't sound too different from creating a regular Visual Basic project—and that's the point!

The UserDocument Object

An ActiveX document is based on a UserDocument object. You can see a parallel here with the way an ActiveX control is based on a UserControl object. Just as the UserControl object provides an ActiveX "wrapper" for a control, the UserDocument object provides the wrapper for a document. Also, just as you need to be aware of the UserControl's properties, events, and methods to effectively create an ActiveX control, you need to know the details of the UserDocument's interface before working on an ActiveX document project.

In some ways, the UserDocument object is similar to a standard Visual Basic form, so much of what you know about forms can be applied here as well. You also need to be aware of some important differences.

UserDocument Properties

The UserDocument object has an extensive set of properties. Although some similarities exist between a UserDocument and a Form, there are also many differences. As a result, some overlap exists in the property lists, but also the UserDocument has many properties that you have never seen on a form.

AutoRedraw   Set to True to make the output of graphics methods on the UserDocument persistent so that they don't have to be explicitly redrawn each time they are uncovered (the redrawing is done automatically). Set to False to make the output of graphics methods nonpersistent; the drawing statement will have to be placed in the Paint event procedure so that these methods are executed each time the UserDocument needs to be redrawn.

ClipControls   Set to True if you want graphics methods in the Paint event procedure to repaint the entire UserDocument when all or part of it is uncovered. Set to False to have only the newly uncovered regions repainted. Setting this property to False usually results in faster loading and repainting of complex UserDocuments.

ContinuousScroll   Set to True for continuous scrolling, which means that the UserDocument appears to move smoothly during scrolling. If False, the UserDocument is redrawn only when the scrollbar thumb is released.

Controls   Returns a reference to a collection containing all the controls that are on the UserDocument.

HScrollSmallChange and VscrollSmallChange   The distance the UserDocument will scroll when the user clicks the container's scroll arrows on the vertical or horizontal scrollbars.

WHAT ABOUT LARGECHANGE?

Unlike a ScrollBar object, the UserDocument doesn't have VLargeChange and HLargeChange properties to control movement when the user clicks on a scrollbar between the thumb and an arrow. The amount of movement in this situation is determined by the Viewport object's ViewPortHeight and ViewPortWidth properties.

Hyperlink   Returns a reference to a Hyperlink object (if supported by the container). The Hyperlink can be used to navigate to other ActiveX documents and URLs.

Parent   Returns a reference to the UserControl's container object.

Picture   Specifies a bitmap image to be displayed in the UserDocument's background. You can use BMP, GIF, or JPG files, as well as icons and metafiles.

ScaleLeft and ScaleTop   Specify the coordinates of the left and top edges of the UserDocument. Useful for creating a user-defined coordinate system for placement of controls and output of graphics methods on the UserDocument. Used in conjunction with ScaleHeight and ScaleWidth. Setting any of these properties automatically sets ScaleMode to 0-vbUser.

ScaleHeight and ScaleWidth   Specify the height and width of a UserDocument for a user-defined coordinate system. See ScaleTop and ScaleLeft.

ScaleMode   Specifies the units used for the output of graphics methods and control placement on the UserDocument. The possible settings are the same as for the Form object and other Visual Basic objects that support this property. Set to 0 - vbUser to define your own coordinate system, using the ScaleLeft, ScaleTop, ScaleHeight, and ScaleWidth properties.

6

SITING AN ACTIVEX DOCUMENT

An ActiveX document can run only within a container, and the process of hooking up an ActiveX document with its container is called *siting*—assigning the document a site in the container. Certain UserDocument properties, such as Parent and Hyperlink, are not available until siting is complete.

The Initialize event occurs before siting is complete, but Show occurs afterwards. Use the Show event procedure to access container properties that aren't available before siting.

Events in a UserDocument

Most events detected by a Form object are available on a UserDocument as well. Form events not present on a UserDocument include Activate, Deactivate, LinkClose, LinkError, LinkExecute, LinkOpen, Load, QueryUnload, and Unload.

The UserDocument object has several events that are not found on a Form. These include AsyncReadComplete, EnterFocus, ExitFocus, InitProperties, ReadProperties, Scroll, Show, and WriteProperties. Table 6.1 briefly explains these events, which are covered in more detail as the need arises.

TABLE 6.1 USERCONTROL EVENTS NOT PRESENT IN FORM OBJECTS

Event Name	Description
AsyncReadComplete	Occurs when the container has completed retrieving data in response to an asynchronous read request.
AsynchReadProgress	Occurs when more data is available from an asynchronous read request.
EnterFocus	Occurs when either the UserDocument or one of its constituent controls receives the focus.
ExitFocus	Occurs when the focus leaves the UserDocument. The UserDocument itself or one of its constituent controls could be losing the focus.
Hide	Occurs each time the user navigates away from the UserDocument.
InitProperties	Occurs each time an instance of the UserDocument is created, if no properties have been saved to a PropertyBag object.
ReadProperties	Occurs each time an instance of the UserDocument is created, if one or more properties have been saved to a PropertyBag object.
Resize	Occurs when the container is resized.
Scroll	Occurs when one of the container's scrollbars is moved.
Show	Occurs each time the UserDocument is displayed in the browser, that is, each time the user navigates to the document from another document or URL.
Terminate	Occurs just before the ActiveX document is destroyed.
WriteProperties	Occurs before an instance of the UserDocument is destroyed, if the user has saved a property.

THE INITPROPERTIES, READPROPERTIES, AND WRITEPROPERTIES EVENTS

These three properties should sound familiar to you because the UserControl object, the basis of ActiveX controls (which were covered in the preceding three chapters), has the same events. You'll be glad to know that these properties work in much the same way for a `UserDocument` object as they do for a `UserControl` object.

There is one important difference. In a `UserControl`, `InitProperties` occurs *only* the first time the object is instantiated, and `ReadProperties` occurs each subsequent time. In a `UserDocument`, `InitProperties` continues to occur each time the object is instantiated, as long as no properties have been saved. When data has been saved, `ReadProperties` occurs each time the object is instantiated.

ACTIVEX DOCUMENT TERMINATION

In Internet Explorer versions 4 and later, an ActiveX document is terminated as soon as the user navigates away from it. Internet Explorer version 3 maintains a cache of four documents, so a given ActiveX document isn't destroyed until the user navigates to a fifth document.

Figure 6.1 diagrams the sequence of important events for an ActiveX document.

FIGURE 6.1

Events in the life of an ActiveX document.

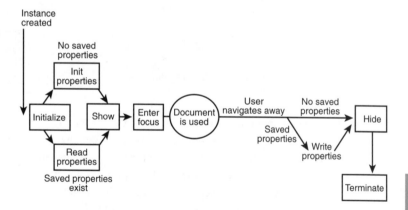

Your First ActiveX Document

Now is a good time to walk through the steps of creating an ActiveX document. You can use this simple document to get a first-hand look at how the UserDocument events work. It will also give you some experience at the procedures involved.

Creating the Document

1. Start a new Visual Basic project, selecting ActiveX Document EXE as the project type. Select UserControl1 in the Project window and change its `Name` property to `TestEvents`. Then select Project1 in the Project window and change its name to `AXEvents`. Save the UserDocument and the project under the default names suggested by Visual Basic. Your screen will look like Figure 6.2.

FIGURE 6.2

After starting the project and assigning UserDocument and Project names.

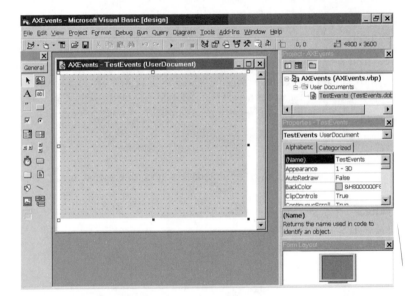

2. Place a Label control and a ComboBox control on the form. Change the Label control's caption to `Select Destination:` and change the ComboBox's `Name` property to `cmbURLs` and its `Text` property to a blank string. Add a CommandButton and change its `Name` property to `cmdGo` and its `Caption` property to `Go`. Your `UserDocument` will now look like Figure 6.3.

3. Open the code editing window and select the UserDocument's initialize event procedure. Add the code shown in Listing 6.1. You can use other URLs if you like; these are to the well-known Microsoft and Yahoo sites and to my own less well-known site. Be sure to include the `http://` protocol part of each URL.

FIGURE 6.3

The UserDocument after adding the controls.

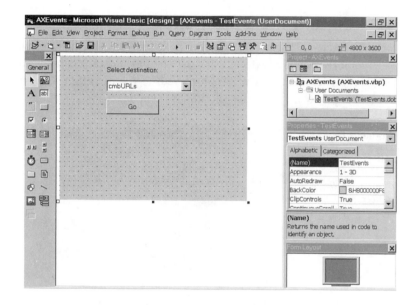

LISTING 6.1   CODE IN THE USERCONTROL'S INITIALIZE EVENT PROCEDURE LOADS THE COMBOBOX WITH URLs

```
Private Sub UserDocument_Initialize()

' Load the combo box with some URLs

cmbURLs.AddItem "http://www.microsoft.com"
cmbURLs.AddItem "http://www.pgacon.com"
cmbURLs.AddItem "http://www.yahoo.com"

End Sub
```

4. Still in the code editing window, open the click event procedure for the cmdGo CommandButton. Add the code shown in Listing 6.2.

LISTING 6.2   THE CLICK EVENT PROCEDURE FOR THE CMDGO BUTTON

```
Private Sub cmdGo_Click()

    Hyperlink.NavigateTo cmbURLs.Text

End Sub
```

5. Save the modified project.

6

Running the Document

The ActiveX document is ready to be executed. Click the Run button on the Visual Basic toolbar or press F5. Because it's the first time the project has been run, the Project Properties dialog box will be displayed, so you can select debugging options. As shown in Figure 6.4, you should select Start Component.

FIGURE 6.4

Selecting debugging properties for the ActiveX document project.

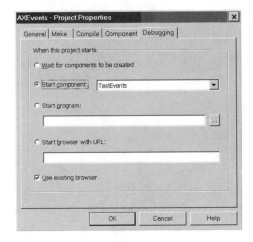

When the project runs, here's what happens:

1. Visual Basic creates the actual document file, which has the name assigned to the project and the VBD extension. This file is placed in the same directory as the Visual Basic program.

WHAT'S IN A VBD FILE

Initially, the VBD file associated with an ActiveX document contains the class ID of the document—or more precisely, the class ID of the EXE or DLL file that is created when you compile the project. If you elect to permit users to save data, the data is stored in the VBD file as well.

---

2. Internet Explorer is started and loads the VBD file.

3. The ActiveX document is displayed in Internet Explorer.

Figure 6.5 shows your test document executing in Internet Explorer. The controls that you placed on the ActiveX document appear exactly as if they were executing in a regular Visual Basic program. The Internet Explorer address bar indicates the name of the file that is loaded, in this case, TESTEVENTS.VBD.

FIGURE 6.5

Executing the test ActiveX document.

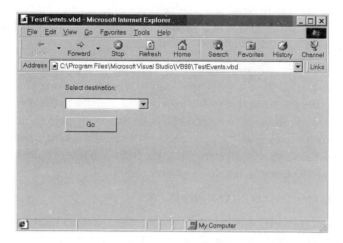

When you execute the document, pull down the Combo Box and select one of the URLs; then click the Go button. Internet Explorer opens the specified URL. If you click Internet Explorer's Back button, you will return to the ActiveX document.

YOUR INTERNET CONNECTION

To try this project, you must be connected to the Internet so that Internet Explorer can navigate to the remote URLs. If you use a modem and are not currently connected, the DialUp Networking service will ask you whether you want to dial your remote service.

To terminate the document, switch back to Visual Basic and click the End button or select End from the Run menu. Visual Basic will display a dialog box asking whether you want to end the program at this time. Select Yes.

6

QUITTING MORE GRACEFULLY

When you want to terminate an ActiveX document application, you can quit Internet Explorer first and then switch back to Visual Basic and select End. Because Internet Explorer is no longer using the ActiveX document, Visual Basic will not ask you whether you really want to end it.

Looking at Events

So far, I think you'll agree that creating an ActiveX document is fairly simple and not all that different from creating a regular Visual Basic application. One of the purposes of this first ActiveX document is to illustrate some of the events that occur in an ActiveX document's lifetime, so that's the next goal.

The approach I will use also illustrates an important aspect of creating ActiveX documents: You still have all of Visual Basic's debugging tools at your disposal. This permits you to use the Debug.Print statement. By placing the Debug.Print statement, with appropriate messages, in several of the UserDocument object's event procedures, it will be possible to monitor the occurrence of these events in the Immediate window while the ActiveX document is executing. Add the following line of code to the existing code in the UserDocument's initialize event procedure:

```
Debug.Print "Initialize event"
```

Then add the code shown in Listing 6.3 to the UserDocument. This code includes a Debug.Print statement for all the other UserDocument events we are interested in.

LISTING 6.3   CODE TO PERMIT EVENT TRACKING IN THE USERDOCUMENT

```
Private Sub UserDocument_Hide()

    Debug.Print "Hide event"

End Sub

Private Sub UserDocument_InitProperties()

    Debug.Print "InitProperties event"

End Sub

Private Sub UserDocument_ReadProperties(PropBag As PropertyBag)

    Debug.Print "ReadProperties event"

End Sub

Private Sub UserDocument_Show()

    Debug.Print "Show event"

End Sub

Private Sub UserDocument_Terminate()
```

```
      Debug.Print "Terminate event"

End Sub

Private Sub UserDocument_WriteProperties(PropBag As PropertyBag)

      Debug.Print "WriteProperties event"

End Sub
```

After adding this code, execute the project again. Arrange your screen so that you can see the Visual Basic Immediate window behind the Internet Explorer window, as shown in Figure 6.6. This figure shows the Immediate window after starting the document, navigating to one of the other URLs, and then using the browser's Back button to return to the ActiveX document.

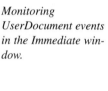

FIGURE 6.6

Monitoring UserDocument events in the Immediate window.

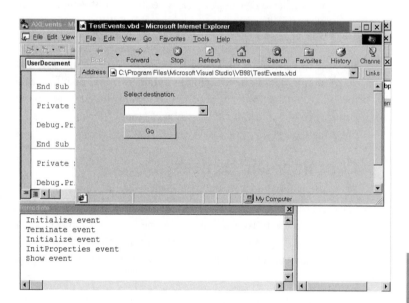

By understanding when and in what order these events occur, you will be better able to make good use of them in your ActiveX document projects.

6

Writing ActiveX Documents for Different Containers

An ActiveX document must be run in a container, and you have at least three different container objects available:

- Microsoft Internet Explorer version 3 and later. Internet Explorer provides an ActiveX document with some added Internet capabilities (such as the Hyperlink object) and also the capability of deploying the application over the Internet.
- Microsoft Office Binder versions 1 and later. The Binder is used to hold related documents from different sources, such as Word documents and Excel worksheets. An ActiveX document can provide a Binder with database or multimedia capabilities unavailable in other document types.
- Visual Basic Development Environment Tool Window. You can create an ActiveX document that provides additional capabilities within the Visual Basic development environment and then make it available for use by placing it in the Tool Window.

Because this is a book on Visual Basic Internet programming, I will be limiting detailed discussion to the Internet Explorer container. If you plan to create ActiveX documents for other container objects, you'll need to refer to their documentation or use the Object Browser to obtain details of their object models. I will provide information on only a few important basics.

Container Differences

The various possible ActiveX document containers have differing capabilities and different ways of doing things. For example, Internet Explorer has the capability to display frames, with an ActiveX document in one frame and an HTML document in another. The Visual Basic Tool Window, however, does not. Similarly, to move from one ActiveX document to another in Internet Explorer, you use the Hyperlink object's NavigateTo method:

```
UserDocument.HyperLink.NavigateTo "file://c:\salesdocs\sales1998.vbd"
```

In contrast, the Binder requires you to add a section to the Binder, and the code is completely different.

The bottom line is that you must be aware of which container(s) your ActiveX documents will be used with and to what extent your application will or will not take advantage of capabilities that are container-specific.

Identifying the Container Object

An ActiveX document can identify the container it's running in by using the `TypeName` statement as follows:

```
ContainerType = TypeName(UserDocument.Parent)
```

You can identify the container by the return value, which is one of the strings listed in Table 6.2.

TABLE 6.2 USING THE TYPENAME STATEMENT TO IDENTIFY AN ACTIVEX DOCUMENT'S CONTAINER

Return Value	Container Type
IwebBrowserApp	Internet Explorer
Section	Microsoft Binder
Window	Tool Window

TYPENAME RETURN VALUES

The `TypeName` returned when the container is Internet Explorer seems to vary slightly, depending on the exact version of the browser you have. For example, some versions return IWebBrowser2. Although the Microsoft documentation is silent on this inconsistency, it seems safe to assume that if the `TypeName` value includes the string `"browser"`, you are dealing with some version of Internet Explorer.

Adding a Form to an ActiveX Document

An ActiveX document project can have one or more forms associated with it. These are standard Visual Basic forms and are added in the same way as you would for a standard Visual Basic project (select Project, Add Form). Of course, it will have the same events and properties as a `Form` object, not the events and properties of a `UserDocument` object.

Because a secondary form is not a UserDocument, it cannot be displayed in the same way as a UserDocument. In other words, you don't navigate to a secondary form, but rather display it by using the `Show` method. Likewise, use the `Hide` method to remove the form from the screen.

6

MODELESS SECONDARY FORMS

Some containers, including Internet Explorer, don't permit a modeless form to be displayed by an in-process component (a DLL). If your application needs to show modeless forms, you will have to create it as an ActiveX document EXE.

To see exactly how it works, add a secondary form to the project that you started earlier. Open the project and display the UserDocument. Then follow these steps:

1. Select Project, Add Form. When the Add Form dialog box displays, select the Form icon and click OK. You could also use any of the predefined forms as a starting point for your form.

2. Be sure the new form is displayed in the Visual Basic environment. Change its Name property to frmAux (for auxiliary form) and its Caption property to Secondary Form.

3. Place a CommandButton on the form. Change the CommandButton's Caption property to OK and its Name property to cmdOK. Add the line of code shown in Listing 6.4 to the click event procedure for the CommandButton.

LISTING 6.4   THE EVENT PROCEDURE FOR THE SECONDARY FORM'S COMMANDBUTTON

```
Private Sub cmdOK_Click()

Hide

End Sub
```

4. Save the form as frmAux.frm. Your Visual Basic screen will look like Figure 6.7.

FIGURE 6.7

After designing the secondary form.

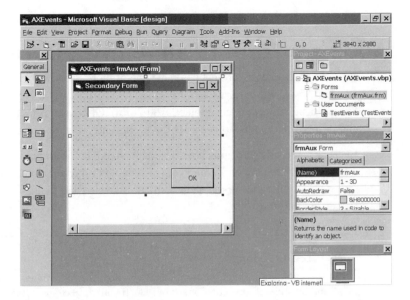

5. In the Project window, select the UserDocument object TestEvents and click the View Object button. Add two CommandButtons to the UserDocument. Assign Name and Caption properties of cmdShowForm and Show Form to the first button and cmdHideForm and Hide Form to the second button. The UserDocument should now look like Figure 6.8.

FIGURE 6.8

After adding two CommandButtons to the UserDocument.

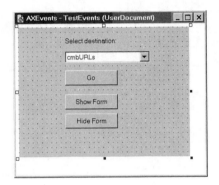

6. Open the code editing window for the UserDocument. Add code to the click event procedures for the two newly added CommandButtons, as shown in Listing 6.5.

LISTING 6.5 THE CLICK EVENT PROCEDURE FOR THE TWO COMMAND BUTTONS

```
Private Sub cmdHideForm_Click()

    frmAux.Hide

End Sub

Private Sub cmdShowForm_Click()

    frmAux.Show

End Sub
```

6

You are now ready to try the project. Click the Run button, and Internet Explorer will start and display the ActiveX document. The Go button will work just as it did before, because you did not change any of that code. Click the Show Form button, and the form will be displayed over the browser window, as shown in Figure 6.9. To close the form, you can click either the Hide Form button on the ActiveX document or the OK button on the form.

Figure 6.9

Showing the secondary form of an ActiveX document.

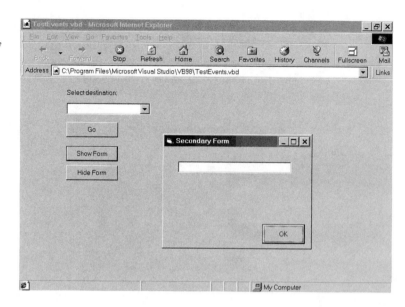

Communication between the UserDocument and any secondary forms is accomplished using the regular Visual Basic statements and syntax (referring to public properties, global variables, and so on).

Using Multiple ActiveX Documents in a Project

An ActiveX document project can contain more than one document, just as a standard Visual Basic project can have more than one form. To add an ActiveX document to an open project, select Project, Add User Document. Visual Basic displays the Add User Document dialog box, as shown in Figure 6.10. You have three choices in this dialog box:

- Select the UserDocument icon to create a blank user document.
- Select the Visual Basic ActiveX Document Wizard if you want to migrate a regular Visual Basic form to an ActiveX document (migrating forms to ActiveX documents is explained on Day 8).
- Click the Existing tab if you want to add an existing UserDocument to the project.

When you have two or more ActiveX documents in your project, for the most part you program each one individually. Some special considerations, however, are covered in this section. Then you will add a second UserDocument to the demo project.

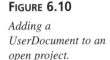

FIGURE 6.10

Adding a UserDocument to an open project.

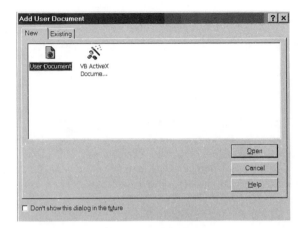

Code Modules in ActiveX Document Projects

You can add a code module to an ActiveX document project by using the Project, Add Module command. Code modules are used for most of the same purposes in an ActiveX document project that you are accustomed to using them for in a standard Visual Basic project: declaring global variables and constants, defining ENUMs, and creating public sub and function procedures. The special requirements of ActiveX document projects make code modules essential for one additional purpose: making object references available globally. You will see why and how this is done later in the chapter.

Public Properties and Methods in ActiveX Documents

Like the ActiveX controls that you learned about on Days 2–5, an ActiveX document can have public properties and methods. In many ways, creating such properties and methods is the same as you learned for ActiveX controls. As you will see, some additional tricks are required to make these items available.

Creating Properties and Methods

The techniques for creating public properties and methods in an ActiveX document are essentially the same as for an ActiveX control. Because this was covered on Day 4, I will mention only the broad outline here.

To create a public method, write a procedure in the UserDocument, being sure to use the Public keyword. For example, the code in The following piece of code creates a public method named MyMethod.

6

```
Public Sub MyMethod()

    ' Code goes here.

End Sub
```

USING PUBLIC METHODS

In my experience, public methods are rarely used in ActiveX document projects. The reason is that if you want some code to be generally available in the project, you are better off creating a sub or function in a code module where it will be available to all the ActiveX documents in the project without the trouble of requiring a reference to the ActiveX document where the method is defined.

To create a public property in an ActiveX document, you use the exact same techniques that you learned for an ActiveX control. These were explained in detail on Day 4, so I will provide only a brief review.

1. Provide an internal storage location for the property. This could be a variable declared at the module level within the UserDocument, or it could be a property of one of the constituent controls.

2. Used the Tools, Add Procedure command to add property procedures. Property procedures come in pairs; Property Get to read the property value and Property Let to set the value (or Property Set, if the property is an object reference). The procedure names must be the same as the property name.

3. Put code in the property procedures to transfer the value to or from the property's internal storage location. Listing 6.6 shows examples of Property Get and Let procedures.

4. Access the property by using the standard Object.Property syntax.

LISTING 6.6 THE VARIABLE DECLARATION AND PROPERTY PROCEDURES TO CREATE A PUBLIC PROPERTY NAMED BACKCOLOR

```
Dim gBackColor

Public Property Get BackColor() As Variant

    BackColor = gBackColor

End Property

Public Property Let BackColor(ByVal vNewValue As Variant)
```

```
    gBackColor = vNewValue

End Property
```

Refer to Day 4 if you want to learn about property procedures in more detail.

Accessing Public Methods and Properties

Although creating public properties and methods is the same for an ActiveX document as for an ActiveX control, accessing them is more involved. This is an unavoidable consequence of the way ActiveX projects work.

The whole point of making a method or property public is so that it will be available outside the module (UserDocument) in which it's defined. In the case of an ActiveX document project, this means that you want the property or method to be available to code in other ActiveX documents in the same suite or project.

With ActiveX documents, when do public items become available? When an instance of the document is created—and that happens only when the document is loaded into a container. Perhaps you can see the potential for problems. Suppose a project includes three ActiveX documents: Doc1, Doc2, and Doc3. Doc1 exposes some public properties and methods used by Doc3. What happens if the user loads Doc3 without having previously loaded Doc1? Or, even if Doc1 were previously loaded, its instance might be destroyed when it's unloaded (depending on the container). When code in Doc3 tries to access a property or method in Doc1, it will not be available.

The solution to this apparent dilemma is to save a reference to Doc1 when it's instantiated. This object reference must, of course, be saved somewhere outside Doc1 so that it will be preserved when Doc1 is unloaded. If a reference to an object exists, the instance will not be destroyed when it's unloaded, and it will be available for use by code in other parts of the project.

The place to keep this object reference is in a global variable declared in a code module. This has the added advantage of making the reference available to other documents in the project, which is just what you need. Here is what you do. Assume that the ActiveX documents are named Doc1 and Doc2 and that Doc1 has a public property named BackColor that code in Doc2 needs to access.

1. In the project's code module, declare a global variable to hold a reference to Doc1:

   Dim gDoc1 As Doc1

2. In the code in Doc1, place code to set the object reference to Doc1. This code should go in a location where it will be executed when the user is navigating from Doc1 to Doc2—for example,

6

```
Private Sub cmdLoadDoc2_Click()
    Set gDoc1 = Me
    HyperLink.NavigateTo "c:\...\Doc2.vbd"
End Sub
```

3. In Doc2, put code in the Show event procedure that verifies that the reference to Doc1 is set and, if so, uses the reference to access the public properties as needed. For example, this code sets Doc2's BackColor to the same as Doc1's BackColor (Doc1 must have a public property named BackColor for this to work, of course).

```
Private Sub UserDocument_Show()
    If Not gDoc1 Is Nothing Then
        gBackColor = gDoc1.BackColor
        Set gDoc1 = Nothing
    End If
End Sub
```

DESTROYING OBJECT REFERENCES

After using this technique, be sure to set the reference to the first document to Nothing. You can see I did this in the code in the second document. If the object reference isn't explicitly destroyed in this way, the object (Doc1) will continue to exist and consume system resources, even though it's never loaded again. Of course, do not set the object reference to Nothing unless you are finished using it.

The preceding code is foolproof in that it doesn't depend on Doc1 having been loaded before Doc2. If it was not, Doc2 just uses its default BackColor setting. At times, however, ActiveX documents must be loaded in a certain order. You can extend the technique of global object references to deal with this situation, as covered next.

Communication Between ActiveX Documents

How can ActiveX documents communicate between themselves? If you have written a suite of ActiveX documents (a set of documents that are all part of the same Visual Basic project), communication of some sort might be required at times. I am not talking about exchanging data *per se*, although these techniques can be used for this. Data exchange is generally accomplished by means of file transfers.

The type of communication I am talking about is made necessary at times by the very nature of ActiveX documents. In a regular Visual Basic application, you can control access to the various forms. If the nature of the application is such that the user has to make choices on Form 1 before ever seeing Form 2, you can design the project so that seeing Form 2 without having seen Form 1 first is impossible.

ActiveX documents do not permit this level of control. Each document can be navigated to independently, and there is no direct way you can force users to load Document 1 before loading Document 2. There is, however, a way that Document 1 can leave a record of whether it has been loaded. Document 2 can check this record, and if Document 1 has not been loaded, it can display a message to the user and perhaps navigate directly to Document 1.

The technique involves using a global variable that is accessible to both UserDocuments. As mentioned earlier, global variables are placed in a code module that is part of the ActiveX document project. The data in global variables is accessible to all the project's UserDocuments.

CODE MODULES IN ACTIVEX DOCUMENT PROJECTS

Just like a regular Visual Basic project, an ActiveX document project can contain a code module. It can contain code procedures that are used by two or more of the UserDocuments in the project, as well as global variables such as the one used here. Code modules were covered in greater detail earlier in this chapter.

First, declare a global variable in a code module, giving it the data type of the first UserDocument—the one that must be opened first. If the two UserDocuments are FirstDoc and SecondDoc, for example, you could put the following in the code module:

```
Public gFirstDocOpened As FirstDoc
```

Then, in FirstDoc you would place code that sets the global variable if, and only if, FirstDoc has been opened. This might be done in the same section of code that navigates from FirstDoc to SecondDoc. Note that the global variable is loaded with a reference to the FirstDoc, using the Me keyword:

```
Private Sub cmdNext_Click()
    Set gFirstDocOpened = Me
    Hyperlink.NavigateTo "c:\...\SecondDoc.vbd"
End Sub
```

Next, in SecondDoc place code that checks to see whether the global variable contains the proper reference; in other words, it's not Nothing. This should be done in the Show event procedure:

```
Private Sub UserDocument_Show()
    If Not gFirstDocOpened Is Nothing Then
        ' FirstDoc was loaded - can go ahead.
        ' Other code here can use the reference to
        ' FirstDoc to access properties, etc.
```

6

```
        Set gFirstDocOpened = Nothing
    Else
        ' FirstDoc was not loaded. Display a
        ' message then navigate to FirstDoc.
        MsgBox "You must open FirstDoc before using this document"
        Hyperlink.NavigateTo "c:\...\FirstDoc.vbd
    End If
End Sub
```

Why did I use a global variable that contained a reference to the first UserDocument rather than simply use a type Boolean? The advantage of this approach is that by making a reference to the first document available in the second document, that reference can be used to refer to properties in the first document. This technique is covered earlier in this chapter.

Navigating Between ActiveX Documents

If a project contains more than one ActiveX document, you will usually want to make it possible for the user to navigate between them. When you are targeting Internet Explorer as the target container, you will use the Hyperlink object and its three methods (NavigateTo, GoBack, and GoForward) to move from one document to another. You must provide the NavigateTo method with a complete path to the VBD files.

While you are developing an ActiveX document project, you can predict where the VBD files will be placed. When you run the project from within Visual Basic, the VBD files are written to the Visual Basic directory. When you compile the project to create the EXE or DLL file, the VBD files are written to the same location as the compiled files. However, when you deploy the application on the Internet, you have no way of knowing where the user will put the VBD files. How, then, can you know the proper path to use?

The answer lies in the fact that all of a suite's VBD files should be downloaded to the same folder. When the user loads the first document, you can use the container's LocationURL property to determine the full path to the currently loaded document. By stripping off the name of the current document, you obtain the path, which can be combined with the name of the target document (the one you want to load) to create a full path for passing to the NavigateTo method.

To simplify this task, I have developed a function called GetCurrentPath, which can be placed in the project's code module. Passed the full path of the current document, it returns the path. Listing 6.7 shows the code.

LISTING 6.7   GETCURRENTPATH RETURNS THE CURRENT DOCUMENT'S PATH

```
Public Function GetCurrentPath(CurrentDocPath As String) As String

' Passed the full path and filename of a document,
' strips off the filename and returns the path.

Dim i As Integer

' Get rid of any leading or trailing spaces.
CurrentDocPath = Trim$(CurrentDocPath)

' Find last slash.
For i = Len(CurrentDocPath) To 1 Step -1
    If Mid$(CurrentDocPath, i, 1) = "\" Or _
        Mid$(CurrentDocPath, i, 1) = "/" Then Exit For
Next i

' Strip the name.
GetCurrentPath = Left$(CurrentDocPath, i)

End Function
```

After you have the proper path, you can combine it with the name of a specific ActiveX document to pass to the NavigateTo method. Listing 6.8 shows an example.

LISTING 6.8   AN EXAMPLE OF PASSING A PATH TO THE NAVIGATETO METHOD

```
Private Sub cmdGoToNextDoc_Click()

    Dim x As String

    x = GetCurrentPath(UserDocument.Parent.LocationURL)
    HyperLink.NavigateTo x & "Doc2.vbd"

End Sub
```

6

Adding a Second Document to the Demo Project

Now that you have learned some of the techniques involved in multiple document projects, it's time to give them a try. You will modify the project created earlier as follows:

- It will have a second ActiveX document.

- The first ActiveX document will have a public property that is accessed by the second document.

- Code will determine the absolute path for navigation.

- The second document will check whether the first document has been displayed and, if not, will display a message and navigate to it.

Start by opening the project begun earlier in this chapter. Then, follow these steps to make the modifications:

1. Display the `Initialize` procedure for the `TestEvents` UserDocument. Remove the line of code that adds the path to SecondDoc to the ComboBox. The ComboBox should be loaded only with the URLs of the remote locations.

2. Display the `TestEvents` UserDocument. Add a TextBox and set its `Name` property to `txtMessage` and its `Text` property to `This is the message`. Also, add a CommandButton and set its `Name` to `cmdDoc2` and its `Caption` to `Next Doc`. The document will now look like Figure 6.11.

FIGURE 6.11

After adding the new controls to the `TestEvents` *UserDocument.*

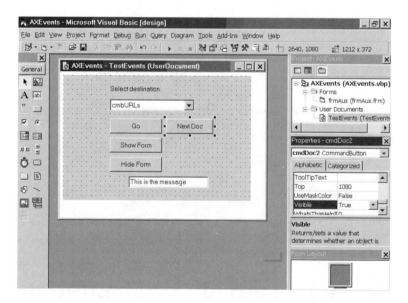

3. Select Tools, Add Procedure and add a property procedure named `Message`. Edit the procedures as shown in Listing 6.9.

LISTING 6.9 THE PROPERTY PROCEDURES FOR THE MESSAGE PROPERTY

```
Public Property Get Message() As String

    Message = txtMessage.Text

End Property

Public Property Let Message(ByVal vNewValue As String)

    txtMessage.Text = vNewValue

End Property
```

4. Edit the click event procedure for the cmdDoc2 button as shown in Listing 6.10.

LISTING 6.10 THE CLICK EVENT PROCEDURE FOR THE CMDDOC2 BUTTON

```
Private Sub cmdDoc2_Click()

' Navigate to SecondDoc.

Dim x

Set gFirstDoc = Me
x = GetCurrentPath(UserDocument.Parent.LocationURL)
Hyperlink.NavigateTo x & "SecondDoc.vbd"

End Sub
```

5. Add a code module to the project. Enter the code shown in Listing 6.11 into the module.

LISTING 6.11 THE CODE IN THE PROJECT'S CODE MODULE

```
Public gFirstDoc As TestEvents

Public Function GetCurrentPath(CurrentDocPath As String) As String

' Passed the full path and file name of a document,
' strips off the file name and returns the path.

Dim i As Integer

' Get rid of any leading or trailing spaces.
CurrentDocPath = Trim$(CurrentDocPath)
```

6

continues

LISTING 6.11   CONTINUED

```
' Find last slash.
For i = Len(CurrentDocPath) To 1 Step -1
    If Mid$(CurrentDocPath, i, 1) = "\" Or _
        Mid$(CurrentDocPath, i, 1) = "/" Then Exit For
Next i

' Strip the name.
GetCurrentPath = Left$(CurrentDocPath, i)

End Function
```

6. Use the Project, Add UserDocument command to add a second UserDocument to the project. Assign the new UserDocument the Name property SecondDoc and save it as SecondDoc.dob.

7. Place one TextBox and one CommandButton on the new UserDocument. Assign the Name property cmdGoBack and the Caption property Go Back to the CommandButton. Assign the Name txtMessage to the TextBox. The document will look like Figure 6.12.

FIGURE 6.12

Designing the visual interface of the second UserDocument.

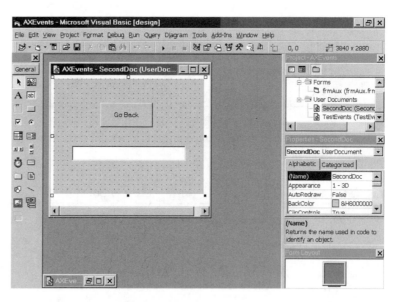

8. Open the code window for SecondDoc and add the code shown in Listing 6.12.

LISTING 6.12 THE CODE IN SECONDDOC

```
Private Sub cmdGoBack_Click()

Hyperlink.GoBack

End Sub

Private Sub UserDocument_Show()

Dim x
If Not gFirstDoc Is Nothing Then
    txtMessage.Text = gFirstDoc.Message
Else
    MsgBox "You must open the TestEvents document first"
    x = GetCurrentPath(UserDocument.Parent.LocationURL)
    Hyperlink.NavigateTo x & "TestEvents.vbd"
End If

End Sub
```

The project is now complete. Be sure to save your files; then run the project. You'll see the first document, TestEvents, display first. You can use the ComboBox and the Go button to navigate to remote URLs, as before. Type a message in the text box, if you want, and then click the Next Doc button. The second document will be displayed, with the message you typed displayed in its text box. You can see this in Figure 6.13. Click Go Back, or the browser's own Back button, to return to the first document.

FIGURE 6.13

The second document displays the Message *property of the first document.*

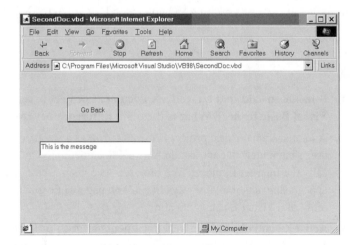

6

After seeing how the project works, exit and return to Visual Basic. Select AXEvents Properties from the Project menu and click the Debugging tab. Note that the Start Component option is selected with TestEvents in the adjacent box. Pull down the box and select SecondDoc, which tells Visual Basic to display SecondDoc first in the browser when the project is run. Now when you run the project, SecondDoc loads, but because there is no reference to the first document in the global variable gFirstDoc, the program displays a message box and then navigates to the TestEvents document.

Summary

This chapter introduces you to one of Visual Basic's most powerful Internet technologies, ActiveX documents. You have seen how an ActiveX document is, in effect, a complete Visual Basic application packaged in a manner that enables it to be deployed on the Internet and downloaded by users.

Like ActiveX controls, ActiveX documents must run in a container. Although a variety of containers are available, Internet programmers will be most interested in writing ActiveX document applications for the Internet Explorer container.

ActiveX document project can contain multiple documents, and each document can have secondary forms associated with it. Public properties and methods can be defined, but because of the way ActiveX document projects work, it's necessary to use a global object reference to access one document's properties and methods from another.

Given their power, it's not surprising that ActiveX documents are a complex topic. You will further explore this exciting technology on Day 7, "ActiveX Documents—Beyond the Basics."

Q&A

Q It has been said that an ActiveX document project is very similar to a regular Visual Basic project. What is the main difference between them?

A A regular Visual Basic project is meant to run as a standalone program on the user's computer. In contrast, an ActiveX document project runs in a container, typically the Internet Explorer Web browser. As a result, the ActiveX document project appears and acts in many ways like a Web page while having the power and flexibility of a Visual Basic application.

Q ActiveX controls and ActiveX documents are two project types supported by Visual Basic. When beginning a new project, how do you decide which of these types is appropriate?

A Basically, simpler tasks are better handled by ActiveX controls, and more complex tasks are better accomplished with an ActiveX document. An ActiveX control encapsulates a small amount of functionality that can be used on a Web page. An ActiveX document can provide much more sophisticated functionality in a form that appears to be a Web page.

Q **Although Internet Explorer supports the `Hyperlink` object, not all available containers for ActiveX documents do. What happens if an ActiveX document tries to execute the `NavigateTo` method in a container that doesn't support it (such as the Microsoft Office Binder)?**

A If the ActiveX document's container doesn't support the `Hyperlink` object, it will open another application (typically Internet Explorer) to handle the request.

Q **How does the process of creating and accessing public properties and methods differ between an ActiveX document and other Visual Basic classes?**

A The process of creating the properties and methods is no different for an ActiveX document, but the procedure for accessing them is different in that it requires the availability of a global object reference.

Workshop

Quiz

1. Which type of ActiveX document project runs faster, a DLL or an EXE?

2. Which Visual Basic control *cannot* be placed on a UserDocument in an ActiveX document project?

3. How many individual ActiveX documents can an ActiveX document project have?

4. Where would you declare a global variable that needs to be visible to all ActiveX documents in a project?

5. When does a UserDocument's `Activate` event occur?

6. How can an ActiveX document determine what type of container it's executing in?

6

DAY 7

ActiveX Documents— Beyond the Basics

By packaging an entire Visual Basic application in an Internet-capable wrapper, ActiveX documents provide a lot of power and flexibility to the Web developer. When you can write a sophisticated application that seems to the user to be just another Web page, the task of integrating your application with other Web technologies is much easier. More advanced aspects of ActiveX document design are the focus of this lesson. Today you will learn

- How to give your document a menu
- How container viewports work
- How to save ActiveX document properties and data between sessions
- How to use asynchronous data transfer to obtain remote data
- How to package and deploy an ActiveX document

Creating a UserDocument Menu

When you run an ActiveX document in Internet Explorer, the menu that is displayed is defined by Internet Explorer, not by your application. Many ActiveX documents would benefit from having their own menu, and you can indeed add a menu to any UserDocument by using the same menu editor as you use for regular Visual Basic forms.

If you design a menu for your ActiveX document, where is it displayed? It will be combined with the Internet Explorer menu so that while the ActiveX document is executing, the menus will contain both the regular Internet Explorer commands and the commands in the ActiveX document menu. This process is called *menu negotiation*.

The placement of ActiveX document menu items on a container's menu bar is controlled by the NegotiatePosition property. You set this property in the Menu Editor dialog box, as shown in Figure 7.1.

FIGURE 7.1

The Menu Editor dialog box.

THE NegotiatePosition PROPERTY

The NegotiatePosition property is applicable to top-level menu items only. For lower-level menu items, you cannot change this property from its default value of 0.

For each top-level menu item, you can set NegotiatePosition to one of the following four values:

- 0 - None   The menu is not displayed in the container object.
- 1 - Left   The menu is displayed at the left end of the container's menu bar.
- 2 - Middle   The menu is displayed in the middle of the container's menu bar.
- 3 - Right   The menu is displayed at the right end of the container's menu bar.

Menu display in the container depends on both the top-level menu caption and the setting of the `Negotiate` position. Suppose you give your ActiveX document a Help menu. Internet Explorer already has its own Help menu, so will the container display two Help menus when your document is loaded?

If `NegotiatePosition` is set to `3 - Right`, the two Help menus will be merged because the normal position of the Internet Explorer Help menu is on the right. The sub-items on your Help menu will be integrated into the Internet Explorer Help menu. To be more precise, the Internet Explorer Help menu will contain an item called *XXX* Help, where *XXX* is the name of the ActiveX document. Selecting this item displays another menu with your Help menu commands on it.

If, however, your Help menu's `NegotiatePosition` property is set to `1 - Left` or `2 - Middle`, it will display as a separate menu because Internet Explorer does not have a matching menu in either of those positions.

Finally, if the top-level menu caption doesn't conflict with an existing Internet Explorer menu, your menu will have its own place on the menu bar.

FIGURE 7.2

The UserDocument menu is merged with the Internet Explorer menu.

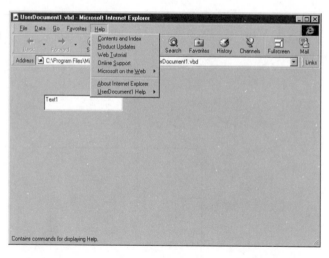

Figure 7.2 shows an example, using the menu defined in the Menu Editor in Figure 7.1. Note that this UserDocument menu has a Help menu (with `NegotiatePosition` set to `3 - Right`) and a Data menu (with `NegotiatePosition` set to `2 - Middle`). The ActiveX document's Help menu is merged with the Internet Explorer Help menu (UserDocument1 Help), whereas the Data menu has its own spot on the menu bar.

7

ALWAYS PROVIDE AN ABOUT BOX

It's highly recommended that you provide an About box, accessed from the Help menu, for all your ActiveX documents. When they load your document, users might not immediately realize what they are seeing or that it's somewhat different from a regular Web page.

Working with Viewports

What happens if an ActiveX document is larger than its container object? This is a distinct possibility, given that users can resize the container's window and that monitor sizes range from 14 inches to 21 inches and even larger. To handle this possibility, container objects have the capability of scrolling to bring different areas of the ActiveX document into view. The display area of the container is the *viewport*. You can think of it as a window through which you view all or part of the UserDocument. Figure 7.3 shows the relationship between a UserDocument and the container viewport.

FIGURE 7.3

The container's viewport provides a window onto the UserDocument.

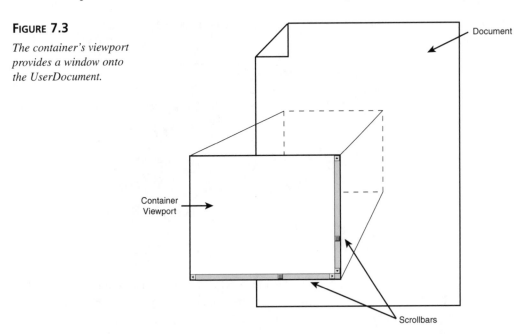

The default viewport/scrolling behavior is suitable for most situations. When the viewport is smaller than the document (as shown in Figure 7.3), the container displays a vertical or horizontal scrollbar. The user can use the scrollbars to bring other parts of the document into view. This all happens automatically. For example, if the user resizes the container, the scrollbars appear and disappear as needed.

The display of scrollbars by the container is controlled by the UserDocument's `ScrollBars` property. Possible settings are

```
0 - None
1 - Horizontal
2 - Vertical
3 - Both
```

The default setting for this property is `3 - Both`, and it's difficult for me to conceive of a situation in which you might want to change it. By disabling one or both scrollbars, you would make it impossible for users to view parts of the document that are outside the viewport. Their only option would be to increase the size of the container window, something that might not be possible if they're working with a small screen. Of course, special situations might occur in which you would want to disable one or both scrollbars, but I have yet to run across them.

Two properties determine the viewport size at which scrollbars appear. `MinHeight` determines the threshold for the vertical scrollbar, and `MinWidth` determines the threshold for the horizontal scrollbar. The default settings for these properties are determined by the height and width of the UserDocument. In other words, scrollbars appear whenever the viewport dimension is smaller than the size of the UserDocument. If you want to change these properties from their default values, you must do so in code—they are not available at design time.

Determining the Viewport Coordinates

Although the size and position of the viewport are determined by the container object, the UserDocument has four properties that permit your document to determine the current viewport coordinates. These coordinates are expressed relative to the UserDocument, in the units specified by the UserDocument's `ScaleMode` property. These properties are

`ViewportLeft`   The coordinates of the left edge of the viewport, relative to the UserDocument.

`ViewportTop`   The coordinates of the top edge of the viewport, relative to the UserDocument.

`ViewportWidth`   The width of the viewport.

`ViewportHeight`   The height of the viewport.

7

All these properties are read-only at runtime. This means that you cannot set these properties to change the viewport; you can only read them to determine its current size and location. With some UserDocuments, for example, it might be desirable to set the document size to match the viewport size.

When a UserDocument is first loaded into a container, the top left corner of the document is positioned in the top left corner of the viewport. Hence, the ViewportLeft and ViewportTop properties will both be 0. If the user scrolls down or to the right, the ViewportLeft and ViewportTop properties will change to reflect the new position of the viewport's top left corner with respect to the document. The ViewportHeight and ViewportWidth properties change only if the size of the container object changes.

SCROLLING SPEED AND STYLE

Set the UserDocument's VScrollSmallChange and HScrollSmallChange properties to control the speed at which the document scrolls within the viewport. Set the ContinuousScroll property to True or False for smooth or "all-at-once" scrolling.

Saving Data from an ActiveX Document

In many ActiveX document applications, you need a way to save user data between sessions. In other words, data that the user enters into the document during one session should be available during subsequent sessions. The technique for saving data involves the use of the PropertyBag object, which you were introduced to in the previous chapters on ActiveX controls.

Why would you use the property bag object to save user data? Isn't it intended for saving properties? Yes, that's true, but the nature of ActiveX documents means that data entered by the user is most efficiently handled by treating it as a property.

For instance, suppose you wrote an ActiveX application that lets users type reminders to themselves, which are entered into a Text Box. The text property of this Text Box could be associated with a public property called RemindersText. The value of this property (along with any others) could be saved in the property bag. This is illustrated in Figure 7.4.

Why not save user data in a regular disk file? After all, ActiveX documents provide all the file reading-and-writing capabilities of Visual Basic. It would be a simple matter to keep user data separate from document properties, using disk files for the former and reserving the property bag for the latter.

FIGURE 7.4

Saving user data in the property bag.

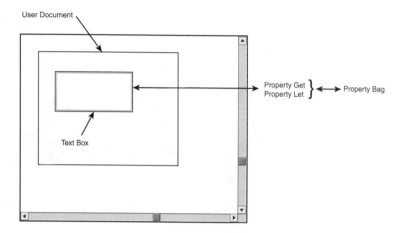

Although using disk files to store data is certainly possible, it's advisable to use the property bag for data whenever possible. There are several reasons for this. First, by keeping all data and properties together in a single storage location, the application is simplified. Furthermore, writing to and reading from the property bag is handled more or less automatically by the container object. Finally, general principles of design for Internet applications dictate minimal access of the user's file system.

The procedures for saving data and properties are outlined here.

1. Write the property procedures to define the required public properties.

2. Call the UserDocument's `PropertyChanged` method whenever a property value is changed, passing the property name as an argument.

3. Put code in the UserDocument's `WriteProperties` event procedure to save each property to the property bag. You use the `PropertyBag` object's `WriteProperty` method to write each property.

4. Put code in the UserDocument's `ReadProperties` event procedure to read the property values from the property bag. This is done with the `PropertyBag` object's `ReadProperty` method.

A Demonstration

For a hands-on experience of how saving data and properties works, you will create a simple ActiveX document that saves the text the user enters in a Text Box.

1. Start a new ActiveX document project (you can use either a DLL or EXE). Set the `Name` property of the UserDocument to `SaveData`.

7

2. Place a Text Box on the UserDocument, sizing it to almost fill the document area. Set the Text Box properties as follows: Name: `txtUserData`; Multiline: `True`; Text: (nothing). Save the UserDocument and project, using the name `SaveData` for both. Your Visual Basic screen should look like Figure 7.5.

FIGURE 7.5

The UserDocument to demonstrate saving data in the property bag.

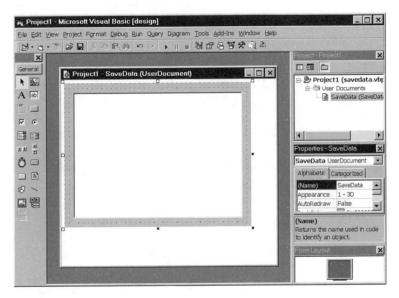

3. Display the code window for the UserDocument. Use the Tools, Add Procedure command to add property procedures named `UserData`. Edit the procedures as shown in Listing 7.1.

LISTING 7.1 PROPERTY PROCEDURES FOR THE `UserData` PROPERTY

```
Public Property Get UserData() As Variant

    UserData = txtUserData.Text

End Property

Public Property Let UserData(ByVal vNewValue As Variant)

    TxtUserData.Text = vNewValue

End Property
```

4. Display the Change event procedure for the txtUserData Text Box. Add the following single line of code:

```
PropertyChanged "UserData"
```

THE PropertyChanged METHOD

Passing a property name to the PropertyChanged method is optional. You can call the method without any arguments, and it will work the same way. As long as the PropertyChanged method has been called at least once, with or without arguments, the container will "know" that one or more properties have changed and need to be saved. Which properties are saved is determined by code in the WriteProperties event procedure.

---

5. Continue to edit the UserDocument code, creating ReadProperties and WriteProperties procedures as shown in Listing 7.2.

LISTING 7.2 THE USERCONTROL'S ReadProperties AND WriteProperties EVENT PROCEDURES

```
Private Sub UserDocument_ReadProperties(PropBag As PropertyBag)

TxtUserData.Text = PropBag.ReadProperty("UserData", "")

End Sub

Private Sub UserDocument_WriteProperties(PropBag As PropertyBag)

PropBag.WriteProperty "UserData", txtUserData.Text

End Sub
```

After the code and interface are complete, compile the ActiveX document to an EXE or DLL by selecting the appropriate command from the File menu. Next, start Internet Explorer and navigate to the SaveData.vbd file. Open the document and enter some text in the Text Box. When you try to navigate away from the document, Internet Explorer displays the dialog box shown in Figure 7.6. You have the option of saving the changes, discarding them, or keeping the document open.

7

Figure 7.6

Internet Explorer's Save Data dialog box.

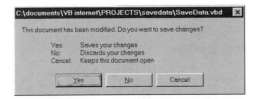

> **Why Not Run the Demo in Visual Basic?**
>
> You might be wondering why I directed you to compile the demonstration document rather than simply use Visual Basic's Run command. The reason is that the property bag doesn't function properly when an ActiveX document project is run from within Visual Basic. Internet Explorer will prompt you to save changes, but the changes are not retained the next time you open the document.

After exiting the document and saving the changes, navigate back to the document. You'll see that the text you entered in the Text Box is still there, courtesy of the property bag.

Where is this data saved? To be honest, I don't know and I don't care. It's taken care of by the container object—in this case, Internet Explorer—so you can feel comfortable making use of the service without being concerned with the details.

Asynchronous Data Transfer

A powerful aspect of the UserDocument object is the capability to asynchronously read data from a file or URL. The important thing is the term *asynchronous*. This means that the UserControl submits a request for the data but does *not* have to sit around waiting for it. The download process is done in the background while the UserDocument continues doing other tasks. When the download is complete, an event is fired, notifying the UserDocument so that it can access the data. The retrieved data is saved in a local file, which the ActiveX document can then open and read using Visual Basic's regular file access statements.

At the heart of asynchronous data transfer is the `AsyncRead` method. It has the following syntax:

```
object.AsyncRead Target, AsyncType [, PropertyName], [AsyncReadOptions]
```

Target is a string specifying the location of the data. It can be a path to a file or a URL.

AsyncType is an integer that specifies the format of the data. There are three possible settings, shown in Table 7.1.

TABLE 7.1 SETTINGS FOR THE AsyncType ARGUMENT

Constant	Meaning
VbAsyncTypeFile	The data is in a file created by Visual Basic.
VbAsyncTypeByteArray	The data is in a byte array with no assumptions about its structure.
VbAsyncTypePicture	The data is a Picture object.

PropertyName is an optional arbitrary string identifying the specific download. It is not related at all to the UserDocument's properties. If two or more downloads are in progress at the same time, their PropertyName arguments are used to differentiate them (if, for example, an error occurs in one).

AsyncReadOptions is an optional specification of download options having to do with server versus local copies of the data (see the sidebar). Table 7.2 lists the possible settings. To combine options, use the Or operator.

SERVER VERSUS LOCAL CACHE COPIES

In many Internet data transfers, including those performed with the AsyncRead method, the data being retrieved is typically located on a remote server. When a file is retrieved, a copy is usually saved on the local hard disk; this is called a *cached copy*. If the data is needed again, the cached copy can be used to avoid the overhead of a network transfer.

If the data is being accessed for the first time, then of course, there can be no cached copy, and a network transfer is unavoidable. If a cached copy does exist, there are several options:

- Use the cached copy, regardless of whether it is older than the server copy.
- Compare the dates and use the cached copy only if it is not older than the server copy; otherwise, download the data from the server and update the cache.
- Download the server copy, regardless of whether it is newer than the cached copy.

7

TABLE 7.2 OPTIONS FOR THE AsyncRead METHOD'S AsyncReadOptions ARGUMENT

Constant	Value	Meaning
VbAsyncReadSynchronousDownload	1	The download is performed synchronously, meaning that execution does not return from the AsyncRead method until the download is complete.
VbAsyncReadOfflineOperation	8	Only the locally cached resource is used.
VbAsyncReadForceUpdate	16	The resource is downloaded from the server even if a locally cached copy is available.
VbAsyncReadResynchronize	512	The locally cached copy of the resource is updated only if the version on the server is newer.
VbAsyncReadGetFromCacheIfNetFail	524288	The local cached copy is used if there is a problem with the network connection.

Asynchronous Data Transfer Events

Two events are central to using asynchronous data transfer: AsyncReadProgress is fired whenever more data is available from the transfer, and AsyncReadComplete is fired when an AsyncRead request has completed. The syntax is

```
Sub UserControl_AsyncReadProgress(AsyncProp As AsyncProperty)
...
End Sub
Sub UserControl_AsyncReadComplete(AsyncProp As AsyncProperty)
...
End Sub
```

Both these event procedures receive a single argument, a type AsyncProperty object that contains the current or final status of the data transfer. By examining its properties, the program can determine whether the download was successful, among other things. Use AsyncReadProgress to keep track of the progress of a download or to react to error conditions, and use AsyncReadComplete to respond to the completion of the download. The AsyncProperty object's properties are explained here.

AsyncType   The type of the data returned. The possible values are the same as for the AsyncRead method's AsyncType argument, as explained in Table 7.1.

BytesMax   A type Long giving the estimated number of bytes to be read. Use this property in the AsyncReadProgress event procedure to estimate download time remaining.

BytesRead   A type Long giving the total number of bytes that have been read.

PropertyName   The value passed to the PropertyName argument when the AsyncRead method was invoked.

Status   Returns a string that describes or is related to the code in the StatusCode property.

StatusCode   Returns a code specifying the current status of an AsyncRead operation. Table 7.3 lists the possible values of this property.

Target   The Target argument that was passed to the AsyncRead method.

Value   Contains the filename of the local file in which the downloaded data has been placed.

TABLE 7.3   POSSIBLE VALUES FOR THE AsyncProperty OBJECT'S StatusCode PROPERTY

Constant	Value	Meaning
VbAsyncStatusCodeError	0	An error occurred during the download. The Value property contains information about the error.
VbAsyncStatusCodeFindingResource	1	The resource is being located.
VbAsyncStatusCodeConnecting	2	A connection is being established with the resource.
VbAsyncStatusCodeRedirecting	3	AsyncRead has been redirected to another location for the resource.
VbAsyncStatusCodeBeginDownloadData	4	Data download has begun.
VbAsyncStatusCodeUsingCachedCopy	10	A local cached copy of the resource is being used.
VbAsyncStatusCodeSendingRequest	11	AsyncRead is requesting the resource.
VbAsyncStatusCodeMIMETypeAvailable	13	The MIME type of the resource is specified in the Status property.

7

continues

TABLE 7.3   CONTINUED

Constant	Value	Meaning
VbAsyncStatusCodeCacheFileNameAvailable	14	The filename of the local cached copy of the resource is specified in the Status property.
VbAsyncStatusCodeBeginSyncOperation	15	The download is being performed synchronously.
VbAsyncStatusCodeEndSyncOperation	16	A synchronous download has completed.

Demonstrating Asynchronous Data Transfer

Creating an ActiveX document that uses asynchronous data transfer is relatively simple, as you will see in this section. Things become more complicated in a real-world program, which must deal with possible error conditions, handle multiple transfers simultaneously, and so on. Even so, this simple demonstration will help you understand the basic procedures. It uses the AsyncRead method to retrieve a local or remote file that you specify, and then it displays the file contents in a Text Box. Obviously you should not try to retrieve a binary file, or the result will be gibberish.

1. Start an ActiveX document project, selecting either the DLL or EXE type of project.

2. On the UserDocument, place two Text Box controls and one Command Button. Make one of the Text Boxes large, filling most of the form. Set its properties as follows: Name: txtData; MultiLine: True; Text: (nothing). Place the other Text Box at the bottom of the form and set its Name property to txtStatus and its Text to a blank string. Position the Command Button in the lower right corner; its Name should be changed to cmdGo and its Caption to Go. At this stage, your screen will look like Figure 7.7.

3. Open the UserDocument's code window and add the code shown in Listing 7.3. This listing includes several event procedures.

FIGURE 7.7

Designing the asynchronous transfer demonstration program.

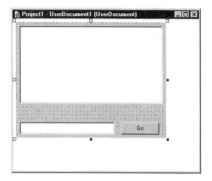

LISTING 7.3 CODE FOR THE ASYNCHRONOUS DATA TRANSFER DEMONSTRATION

```
Option Explicit

Const SOURCE = "http://www.pgacon.com/welcome.htm"
Dim AsyncReadInProgress As Boolean

Private Sub cmdGo_Click()

If Not AsyncReadInProgress Then
    UserDocument.AsyncRead SOURCE, vbAsyncTypeFile, "MyRead"
    AsyncReadInProgress = True
End If

End Sub

Private Sub UserDocument_AsyncReadComplete(AsyncProp As AsyncProperty)

Dim FileNum As Integer

If AsyncProp.PropertyName = "MyRead" Then
    FileNum = FreeFile
    Open AsyncProp.Value For Input As FileNum
    txtData.Text = Input(LOF(FileNum), FileNum)
    Close FileNum
    AsyncReadInProgress = False
End If

End Sub

Private Sub UserDocument_AsyncReadProgress(AsyncProp As AsyncProperty)

txtStatus.Text = AsyncProp.Status

End Sub
```

7

continues

LISTING 7.3   CONTINUED

```
Private Sub UserDocument_Initialize()

AsyncReadInProgress = False

End Sub
```

4. Edit the code so that the constant SOURCE is set to the resource you want to retrieve. In the listing, it points to the HTML file for my home page, but you can load it with anything you want. For a local file, use the full path, for example, C:\DATA\README.TXT. For a remote file, be sure to include the http:// protocol specification.

At this point, the project is ready to run. Give it a try and see how asynchronous transfer works. I think you'll agree that it has some advantages over synchronous transfer.

Deploying and Downloading an ActiveX Document

The procedure for deploying an ActiveX document is almost identical to that for ActiveX controls, which you learned about on Day 4, "Advanced ActiveX Control Techniques." You can turn back to that chapter for the details, if necessary. Here I will provide only a brief overview of the procedure.

1. Compile your project to an EXE or DLL and thoroughly test it.

2. Use the Package and Deployment Wizard to create a set of Internet distribution files for the project. Be sure to mark each of your documents as safe for scripting and safe for initialization, as appropriate.

KEEP YOUR FILES SMALL

To keep the size of your distribution files to a minimum, select the option in the Package and Deployment Wizard to have the Visual Basic runtime files downloaded from the Microsoft Web site rather than included in your files. This does not decrease the total amount the user must download, however.

---

3. Apply your digital signature and a timestamp to the resulting CAB file.

4. Use the Package and Deployment Wizard to deploy the distribution files to your Internet site. You can also use a standard FTP program to upload the files.

What files are created by the Package and Deployment Wizard for an ActiveX document project? Here's the list:

- A compressed CAB file containing the compiled EXE or DLL file and, if you did not elect to have them downloaded from the Microsoft Web site, the Visual Basic runtime and support files
- One VBD file for each ActiveX document in the project
- An HTML document containing links to each ActiveX document

LINKING TO AN ACTIVEX DOCUMENT

Linking from an HTML document to an ActiveX document is very easy and much simpler than using an ActiveX control in a Web page. This is because the VBD file itself contains the class ID and other information about the ActiveX application. Therefore, all you need in an HTML document is a simple hyperlink:

```
<a href=MYAXDOX.VBD>Click for MyAXDoc</a>
```

This technique works for Internet Explorer versions 4 and later, but navigating to an ActiveX document in Internet Explorer 3 requires much more complicated HTML. The sample HTML document created by the Package and Deployment Wizard includes this code, in comments, so you can see what it looks like. Believe me, it's much easier to upgrade your users to Internet Explorer 4!

When a user links to an ActiveX document, the browser takes care of the job of downloading and installing the components. This task has two aspects. First is the executable part of the project, the DLL or EXE that was created when you compiled the application. Downloading and installation depend on the browser's security settings and on the digital signature, if any, embedded in the CAB file. This is the same ActiveX Internet security system that you learned about on Day 4. The result, if the download is accepted, is that the ActiveX component is downloaded and installed on the user's system.

The second part of the download task is obtaining the documents themselves—the VBD files. There are no security concerns with VBD files because by themselves, they are inherently harmless. The user must decide whether to download the files or to open them from the remote location. The latter option is the more frequent choice.

7

Choosing Between In-Process and Out-of-Process Components

Like most ActiveX components, an ActiveX document can be created to run either in-process or out-of-process, represented by an ActiveX DLL or an ActiveX EXE, respectively. An *out-of-process* component runs in its own process with its own independent execution thread. An *in-process component* runs in the client's process and shares the client's execution thread. Choosing which approach to use for your project is an important decision.

ACTIVEX CONTROLS?

All ActiveX controls (OCX files) run as in-process components.

A major advantage of DLLs is superior performance—they just run faster. This is because communication between two separate processes (the case with an out-of-process component and its container) is inherently much slower.

One disadvantage of EXEs is that global data is exposed to potentially dangerous changes. If an ActiveX document EXE is being accessed by two instances of Internet Explorer, both clients will have access to the ActiveX document's global data. If one client changes a global variable, the other client will "see" the new value without any warning. This sort of unexpected interaction is a recipe for disaster.

A potential disadvantage can sometimes be turned into an advantage. With careful planning, global variables can be used as a means of communication between clients. By maintaining a local copy of each global variable, it's possible to detect changes and react accordingly.

One advantage of an out-of-process component is that it is isolated from the container by virtue of being in its own thread, and a crash or other unrecoverable error in the component will not crash the container. Ideally, proper programming practices and thorough debugging should eliminate the chance of such crashes, but you must operate in the real world, where things are usually not ideal.

Returning to the original question, should you use an ActiveX document DLL project or an ActiveX document project EXE? Here is my advice. Use a DLL unless one or more of the following factors come into play to make an EXE more appropriate:

- The nature of the application is such that component-client communication is minimal, negating the speed advantage of a DLL.

- The possibility of alterations to global data does not exist or will be used for a specific programming task.

- The component is inherently unstable, making the crash protection provided by an EXE worth the other trade-offs.

Summary

Today you learned how the flexibility of an ActiveX document is increased even further when it has its own menu. Using the technique called *menu negotiation*, the document's menu is integrated with the container's menu so that both sets of commands are available to the user. You learned how to work with the container object's viewport to control the way the document is seen by the user.

You also saw how an ActiveX document can save properties and data in the property bag. By assigning user data to properties, the data can be made persistent and will be available the next time the application is run.

Asynchronous data transfer is a very important tool, permitting an ActiveX document to retrieve data from any source, either local or remote. Because the data transfer is performed asynchronously, the program doesn't have to sit around and wait for the data.

ActiveX documents are an impressive technology. Certainly, they are the easiest way for an experienced Visual Basic developer to create applications that can be deployed on the Internet. What about regular Visual Basic applications that already exist? Can they be ported to the ActiveX document format? Yes, they can, and that's the topic of tomorrow's lesson.

Q&A

Q What happens if your UserDocument has a menu with the same title as a menu in the container object?

A It depends on the setting of the menu item's NegotiatePosition property. If the two menus are set to display at the same position on the container object's menu bar, the UserDocument menu is merged with the container's menu. If they are set to display at different positions on the menu bar, each will display independently.

7

Q **What is the normal behavior of a container object when displaying an ActiveX document that is too large to see all at once?**

A If the container's viewport is smaller than the ActiveX document, the container will automatically display vertical or horizontal scrollbars to permit the user to scroll other parts of the document into view.

Q **What is the best way for an ActiveX document to save user data so that it will be available the next time the document is opened?**

A Rather than write user data directly to a file, it's better to store the data in a property and then save it in the property bag, along with other data and properties. This way the container object handles most of the details of saving and retrieving the data.

Q **In an asynchronous data transfer, what does *asynchronous* mean? What is its advantage over synchronous data transfer?**

A In an asynchronous data transfer, the data is retrieved in the background while the program is free to do other things. Synchronous transfer, on the other hands, requires that the program sit and wait until the transfer is complete.

Workshop

Quiz

1. Suppose that your ActiveX document has a menu and you want to temporarily disable its display in the container object without actually deleting the menu from the project. How could this be done?

2. To have your ActiveX document automatically resize itself to fit the container's viewport, what property values do you need to obtain?

3. Are all of an ActiveX document's properties automatically saved in the property bag?

4. How does the container object know that one or more property values have changed and might need saving?

5. Do all the distribution files for an ActiveX document project require digital signing?

6. When an `AsyncRead` request has been completed, where is the retrieved data located?

Exercises

Now that you have finished learning about ActiveX documents, you are all set to start writing your own. If you have a pet project that you have been waiting to tackle, now might be the time to start. If not, here are some ideas for applications that could be written using an ActiveX document project.

- An "appointment book" that lets the user enter information about meetings and other scheduled appointments and then reminds him or her of each day's schedule.

- A "note taker" application that is used to enter and organize information. By running the note taker in one browser window and using another browser window to surf the Web, the user can cut and paste useful data into the application.

- A database application that downloads a remote database file and then permits the user to search for and view information.

7

WEEK 1

In Review

I hope you enjoyed your first week of learning how to use Visual Basic for Web programming. You covered a lot of material, including Web and Internet basics, and learned many details about ActiveX technology. You created your first ActiveX control and ActiveX document and should be ready to start using these techniques in your own Web projects.

Where You Have Been

At the beginning of the week, you learned many details about the Web and Internet: how they work, what they can do, and what special terminology is used when talking about them. The remainder of the week was devoted to ActiveX technology. It might seem like a lot of time to spend on one topic, but ActiveX is a central component of many of the Web-related things you can do with Visual Basic. You learned how ActiveX controls are self-contained software components that can be used in regular Visual Basic projects, as well as on Web pages. You also saw the power of ActiveX documents, which permit you, in effect, to package a complete Visual Basic application for use and deployment on the Internet.

WEEK 2

At a Glance

In week 2, you will cover a wide range of topics. First, you complete the ActiveX technology topic. Then you tackle Dynamic Hypertext Markup Language (DHTML), a powerful method for creating dynamic Web pages. The remainder of the week explains how to use Visual Basic's Internet-related controls to add Internet and Web functionality to your Visual Basic applications. By the time you finish this week, you will have a powerful array of Web programming tools at your disposal.

Where You Are Going

This week's first lesson finishes the ActiveX topic started last week, showing you how existing Visual Basic applications can be migrated to the ActiveX document format. The next two days focus on DHTML, a flexible technology that combines HTML—the language of the Web—with Visual Basic programming to create dynamic and powerful Web applications. You will create and run your own DHTML programs. The remainder of the week deals with the Internet-specific controls provided with Visual Basic. The Internet transfer control makes it easy to transfer data across the Internet, and the email controls enable you to integrate your Visual Basic applications with sending and receiving email messages. Along the way, you will create fully functional applications for checking the integrity of Web links and for searching the Web.

WEEK 2

DAY 8

Migrating Regular Visual Basic Applications to ActiveX

Over the past two days, you have learned how to create ActiveX documents, an impressive technique that provides all the power of a regular Visual Basic application in an Internet-capable package. Suppose, however, that you had an existing Visual Basic application, created as a standard EXE project, that you would like to move to the Internet. Would you have to start from scratch and rewrite the application as an ActiveX document? Fortunately, no. It's possible to migrate standard Visual Basic applications to ActiveX document format. Today you'll learn

- The advantages of migrating an existing Visual Basic project to ActiveX document format

- The important differences between a standard project and an ActiveX document project

- How to use the ActiveX Document Migration Wizard

Why Migrate?

Why would you want to migrate an existing Visual Basic application to ActiveX document format? If you have been a Visual Basic programmer for a while, you already know the answer. You have put a lot of work into creating a variety of applications. You should get as much use as possible out of your past efforts, and if some of those existing applications could have a second life on the Internet, there are many potential benefits.

Let's look at an example. A few years ago I wrote a Visual Basic program called Retirement Planner, which, as its name suggests, helps people do financial planning for retirement. It was a moderate-size application and took perhaps a month of my time from start to finish. Figure 8.1 shows it executing in its original standard EXE form.

FIGURE 8.1

Retirement Planner started out as a standard EXE Visual Basic program.

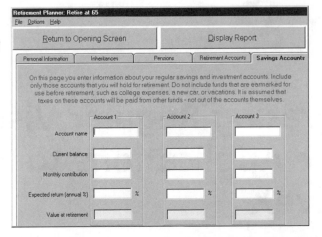

When ActiveX document technology became available, it occurred to me that Retirement Planner might also have some success as an Internet application. It took me less than 4 hours to migrate it to an ActiveX document project—a small investment of time to expose my program to a huge new audience. You can see the ActiveX document version of the program in Figure 8.2.

Not all migrations proceed so easily, of course, but you will always save significant time and effort compared with starting from scratch.

FIGURE 8.2

Migrating Retirement Planner to an ActiveX document was a fairly easy task.

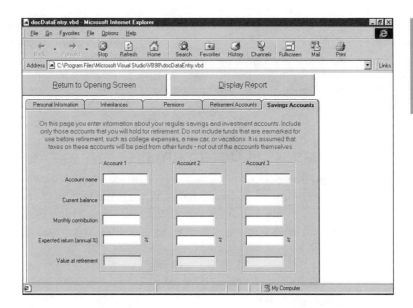

General Considerations

When you need to migrate a regular Visual Basic project to an ActiveX document project, there is both good and bad news. The good news is that just about everything in a standard Visual Basic project—controls, events, code—will migrate smoothly to the ActiveX document format. The bad news is that the process is not seamless; it can be tricky. Areas where the migration will take some effort fall into three categories:

- Some things that are possible in regular Visual Basic projects are simply not supported in ActiveX documents. For example, the OLE Container control is not permitted in an ActiveX document.

- Some things that are done in a standard project can also be done in an ActiveX document, but syntax or naming conventions might differ. For example, the role of the Form object in a standard project is taken over by the UserDocument object in an ActiveX document.

- Some things that need attention in an ActiveX document are never required in a standard project. For example, identifying its container object can be essential for an ActiveX document but is meaningless for a standard project.

Do	DON'T
DO have a thorough understanding of ActiveX documents and how they work, before trying to migrate a standard Visual Basic project.	**DON'T** try to migrate a project that depends on embedded OLE objects, because they are not supported in ActiveX documents.

Forms Versus Documents

The most important part of migrating a standard Visual Basic program to ActiveX document format is the conversion of Visual Basic forms to UserDocuments. It is the UserDocument object that has the special capability to run within a Web browser container. Does this mean that every form in your project must be converted to a UserDocument?

MODELESS FORMS

Recall from Day 7 that an ActiveX document DLL cannot display modeless forms. If your project requires the use of modeless forms, you must create it as an ActiveX document EXE.

Fortunately, the answer is no. As you have learned, a UserDocument can have one or more secondary forms associated with it. A secondary form is a regular Visual Basic form, not a UserDocument, and as such, the migration tasks are lessened. You might be able to convert only some of your forms, or perhaps only one, to a UserDocument; the other forms can stay as forms.

Remember, however, that Forms and UserDocuments are not exactly equivalent from the end user's point of view. Depending on its settings, a Form can be resized, minimized, and maximized by the user, whereas a UserDocument cannot (although it might be possible to resize the container). Also, a UserDocument has access to the capabilities of its container, such as the Hyperlink object and the property bag.

Another important difference is the way you move to and from Forms and UserDocuments. You can display only a single UserDocument at a time (unless you have two containers open, which is unlikely), but you can display as many Forms as needed. The UserDocument is always visible onscreen until the user navigates away from it; any secondary forms are displayed "on top" of the UserDocument. Moving from one UserDocument to another is always done with the Hyperlink object's NavigateTo method. In contrast, displaying a secondary Form is done with the Show method, and hiding it requires the Hide method. Figure 8.3 illustrates some of these differences.

FIGURE 8.3

How the end user moves between Forms and UserDocuments.

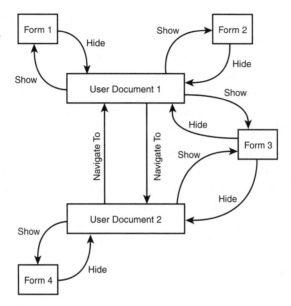

You need to keep all these factors in mind when deciding which of your project's forms need to be converted to UserDocuments and which can remain as Forms.

Controls

All Visual Basic controls can be used on an ActiveX document, with one exception: the OLE Container control. Also, although not strictly controls, embedded objects such as Word documents or Excel spreadsheets are not permitted.

Few, if any, modifications are required to control-related parts of a project being migrated. The individual controls will still have their own properties, methods, and events, and the originally assigned names can be kept as well.

Events

When migrating a regular Visual Basic project to an ActiveX document project, your main concerns with events will have to do with UserDocument objects not having all the same events as Form objects. These differences are due in part to UserDocument objects always existing within a container object.

Form events that are not present on a UserDocument include `Activate`, `Deactivate`, `LinkClose`, `LinkError`, `LinkExecute`, `LinkOpen`, `Load`, `QueryUnload`, and `Unload`. The three `Link...` events are related to OLE and have no counterpart in a UserDocument. Now look at the others and see how they relate to events that are available on a UserDocument.

The `Activate` and `Deactivate` events occur when a Form becomes or stops being the active window, respectively. Because a UserDocument itself is not a window (the container is), these events do not make sense for this object. The closest counterparts are `EnterFocus` and `ExitFocus`, which occur when the UserDocument or one of its constituent controls either receives or loses the focus.

The `QueryUnload` and `Unload` events occur, in that order, when a Form is closed. As you know from programming regular Visual Basic projects, you can use the `QueryUnload` event procedure to cancel the unload process if desired. Because UserDocuments operate differently from Forms, they do not have these events. They do, however, have the `Terminate` event (which Form objects also have; it occurs after `Unload`). The `Terminate` event is fired when all references to the object are destroyed.

WAITING TO TERMINATE

The `Terminate` event for UserDocuments can be difficult to predict. Its occurrence is not directly related to anything the user does or sees on the screen, such as navigating away from a UserDocument. Instead, it is related to what is happening internally—specifically, to whether a reference to the UserDocument object still exists in memory.

Even if the user navigates away from a UserDocument, there are two situations in which a reference will be retained, at least briefly. Internet Explorer 3 retains cached copies of the most recent documents, so a given document's reference will continue to exist until the user has navigated three or four steps away. Also, the programming technique of storing a reference to a UserDocument in a global variable, as covered on Day 7, will delay the occurrence of `Terminate` until that reference (and all others) is set to `Nothing`.

The Form object's `Load` event is the one that requires the most attention during the migration process. `Load` occurs when a Form is first loaded into memory, and its closest counterparts in a UserDocument are `Initialize` and `Show`. Neither of these UserDocument events is an exact replacement for `Load`.

`Initialize` occurs whenever an instance of the object is created. Form objects have the `Initialize` event, too, and it occurs before `Load`. For a UserDocument, however,

Initialize is not a good replacement for Load because it occurs before the UserDocument is sited in the container and therefore before container-related properties are available.

Show occurs each time the UserDocument is displayed, in other words, each time the user navigates to it. If you simply move code from the Form's Load event procedure to the UserDocument's Show event procedure, it might be executed multiple times during a session when it should be executed only once.

CALL Form_Load FROM UserDocument_Show

When a Form is converted to a UserDocument, there is no longer any Form object. As a result, event procedures such as Form_Load become regular procedures not associated with any object or event. You can simply call them in code like any other procedure. To execute the code in Form_Load when the UserDocument's Show event is fired, you could write

```
Private Sub UserDocument_Show()
    Call Form_Load()
End Sub
```

Be sure to use a flag, as described in the text, to prevent the call from being made more than once.

You can maneuver around this problem by maintaining a global flag to indicate whether the code has been executed. Code in the Show event procedure checks the flag and executes the old Form_Load code only if the flag is False. Then the flag is set to True so that if Show is fired again, the code is not executed. Here's an example:

```
Private DocShown As Boolean

Private Sub UserDocument_Show()
    If Not DocShown Then
    ' Old Form_Load code here.
        DocShown = True
    End If
End Sub
```

Code

Certain code that can be present in a standard project is not permitted in an ActiveX document. This can be because the code refers to an unsupported method or because it is a statement that is illegal in an ActiveX document. The following code cannot be used in an ActiveX document:

```
Form.Show
Form.Hide
Me.Show
Me.Hide
Form.Load
Form.Unload
Me.Load
Me.Unload
End
```

To be precise, the form-related statements, such as Form.Load, can be used if the ActiveX document contains subsidiary forms, but cannot be used with the ActiveX document itself.

Other Basic code might be illegal in an ActiveX document, depending on the exact syntax and how it is used. Such code will be caught by the compiler when you build or execute the project.

Using the ActiveX Document Migration Wizard

Visual Basic is famous for making the programmer's life easier and does not let you down when it comes to migrating projects to ActiveX document format. The ActiveX Document Migration Wizard automates many of the tasks involved in performing a migration. It doesn't do everything, and it isn't perfect. You still need to carefully check the resulting ActiveX document project.

Before starting the migration wizard, you should give some thought to which of the forms in your project need to be converted to ActiveX documents. As discussed earlier in this chapter, you rarely need to convert all of a project's forms. Many forms can remain as forms and be displayed as secondary forms from an ActiveX document. The decisions you make at this point are not final, because when the wizard converts a form to an ActiveX document, the original form is retained. This makes it easy to experiment and determine whether the project is better served by converting the form to an ActiveX document or by leaving it as a form.

Do	Don't
DO use the ActiveX Document Migration Wizard to simplify the task of migrating standard Visual Basic applications to ActiveX document format.	**DON'T** expect the migration wizard to do everything. You still need to thoroughly review and test the new ActiveX document application after the wizard creates it.

8

When you have made your preliminary plans, here are the steps required to use the wizard:

1. Start Visual Basic and load the project that you want to migrate.

2. Start the ActiveX Documents Migration Wizard by selecting it from the Visual Basic add-ins toolbar. If the wizard is not listed on this toolbar, you'll have to use the Add-In Manager to load it. The wizard first displays its opening screen, shown in Figure 8.4. This screen presents general information only, and its display can be disabled by selecting the Skip This Screen option. Click the Next button to go to the next wizard screen.

FIGURE 8.4

The ActiveX Document Migration Wizard opening screen.

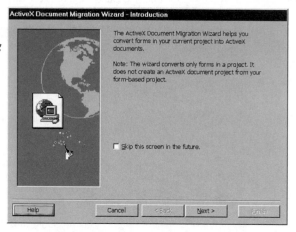

3. The next wizard screen, in Figure 8.5, lists all the forms in your project. Place a check mark next to each form that you want converted to an ActiveX document.

4. On the next screen (see Figure 8.6), the wizard presents several conversion options: Select the Comment Out Invalid Code option if you want the wizard to look for code that is illegal in an ActiveX document and to convert it to comments.

FIGURE 8.5

Selecting the forms to be converted.

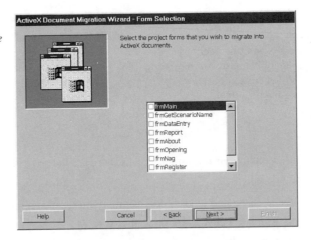

Select Remove Original Forms After Conversion if you want to have the original forms removed from the project. This option does not erase the form files; it only removes them from the new ActiveX document project.

Select the desired Convert To option, depending on whether you want the new project to be an ActiveX document DLL or an ActiveX document EXE.

FIGURE 8.6

Selecting ActiveX Document migration options.

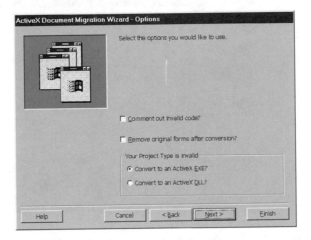

5. The final wizard screen (not illustrated) gives you the option of viewing a summary report of the actions taken by the wizard, which I recommend, and of saving your settings as the defaults for future sessions. Click the Finish button to begin the conversion process.

6. When finished, the wizard displays the summary report (if that option was selected). Your ActiveX document project is now ready for testing and further development.

What exactly does the ActiveX Document Migration Wizard do? For each form in the original project that is selected for conversion, here is what it does:

- Copies Form properties to a new UserDocument.

- Copies all controls from the Form to the UserDocument, retaining their names and positions.

- Copies all code from the Form to the UserDocument. Event procedures are converted as appropriate. For example, `Form_Click()` is converted to `UserDocument_Click()`. Where there is no corresponding event, the original name is maintained. Therefore, `Form_Load()` is not changed.

- Optionally, comments out all illegal code.

- Changes the project type to ActiveX EXE or DLL.

CONVERT A COPY

The ActiveX Document Migration Wizard converts the project you specify without saving a backup copy. I strongly advise you to make a copy of your project before conversion so that the original project will remain available.

Summary

Today's lesson has been a short one, but nonetheless important. You can save a lot of work by migrating your existing Visual Basic applications to ActiveX document format. Because an ActiveX document is, in effect, a Visual Basic form "wrapped" for the Internet, the conversion process is straightforward. By being aware of the differences between a Form and a UserDocument and by making use of the ActiveX Document Migration Wizard, the process of leveraging your existing applications for Internet deployment should be an easy one.

Q&A

Q What are the primary advantages of converting a standard Visual Basic application to an ActiveX document application?

A By converting an application to ActiveX document format, you gain the ability to deploy the application on the Internet, as well as the use of the normal distribution methods available for standard applications (for example, diskettes). Converting an existing application, even if significant modifications are required, is much more efficient than starting a new application from scratch.

Q What are the main differences between a standard Visual Basic application and an ActiveX document application?

A The main difference is that whereas a standard application consists of forms, an ActiveX document application contains UserDocuments and, optionally, one or more forms. A UserDocument differs from a form in that it runs inside a container and, as a result, has different events.

Q What should you do with the code in a form's Load event procedure when converting to a UserDocument?

A Place it in the UserDocument's Show event procedure, using a flag to prevent it from being executed more than once.

Workshop

Quiz

1. Is the End statement permitted in an ActiveX document?
2. When you convert a standard application to an ActiveX document application, do you always get one UserDocument for each form?
3. What is the UserDocument object's Show method used for?
4. After running the ActiveX Document Migration Wizard, can you immediately compile and deploy the new ActiveX document application?

WEEK 2

DAY 9

Understanding Dynamic HTML

One of the primary themes of this book is the importance of dynamic Web pages. Furthermore, we know that HTML is the language of the Web. The subject of this and the following days—dynamic HTML—should therefore be pretty interesting. Indeed, it is an important Visual Basic technology for creating Web pages that more closely meet the needs of you and your users. Today you will learn

- What dynamic HTML, or DHTML, is and how it works
- The advantages and limitations of DHTML
- The structure of a DHTML application
- What elements can be used on a DHTML page
- Techniques for designing DHTML page interfaces

DHTML Applications

For Internet programmers, one of the most powerful features in Visual Basic is what's called an *DHTML application*. This type of application is similar in many ways to a standard Visual Basic program, with the following two differences: it runs on the Internet, in the user's browser, and the user interface consists of HTML pages instead of forms.

This similarity to a standard Visual Basic application means that DHTML is an essential technology for experienced Visual Basic programmers who need to create dynamic Web-based applications. Most of what you already know about programming can be transferred and used. There are differences, to be sure, but trust me when I tell you that learning DHTML programming is a lot easier than learning one of the other tools, such as CGI programming. Furthermore, DHTML offers several advantages over the other available technologies. I'll explain these advantages soon.

DHTML VERSUS DHTML

The original Hypertext Markup Language (HTML) specification was developed to create World Wide Web pages. It was a static language, meaning that the only way to modify a Web page was to edit it. In the quest for greater power and flexibility, a new HTML specification was developed that permits a Web document to respond to user input and to modify itself on-the-fly, changing the content and formatting of its display as needed. This new specification is called dynamic HTML, or DHTML. Now, Microsoft has included a new type of application in Visual Basic called *DHTML Application*. Although this type of application can make use of dynamic HTML, there is more to it than that. As a result, the use of terms is confusing. Remember that when you see DHTML, it can refer either to the dynamic HTML specification or to a type of Visual Basic application.

Why would you want to create a DHTML application instead of using tried and true Web publishing techniques? The answer lies in the word *dynamic*. Although browsing static content might be fine at times, developers are finding more and more situations where it just won't cut the mustard. To provide the information needed by customers and employees in a timely and efficient manner, Web pages must react to the user. The nature of the information displayed, and the way it is displayed, must respond—and respond quickly—to user input. Here are just a few examples:

- A surgical equipment manufacturer wants to allow its field representatives to log on and obtain up-to-date information on product specifications, price, and availability.

- A travel agency wants to allow potential customers to visit its Web site and browse vacation cruise packages based on destination, cost, and time of year.

- A corporation wants to allow its employees to log on and view the latest version of the company policies handbook.

DHTML is very flexible, and can be used for a wide variety of tasks from the simple to the complex.

9

TWO WAYS TO BE DYNAMIC

The techniques for making Web pages dynamic can be divided into two general categories based on where the changes are made—on the client or on the server. DHTML represents the former technique because when a DHTML page changes in response to user actions, the changes are being performed on the local client computer. This is different from Active Server Pages (covered in a later day) in which custom Web pages are generated on the server in response to user input.

Advantages of DHTML Applications

DHTML is certainly not the only technology that can be used to create dynamic Web pages. Furthermore, because I am an admitted Visual Basic fan, I would naturally tend to prefer a Visual Basic-based technology over the competitors. Even so, consider some objective factors where DHTML seems to have the advantage. One that I have already mentioned is the ability to leverage your existing Visual Basic programming experience. Here are some more:

- More local processing—Compared with other technologies, a DHTML application performs more of its processing on the client computer without having to make a call to the server. This results in less load on the server and, more importantly, faster response time for the user.

- Improved state management—Traditional HTML pages are stateless, which means that when a client makes a request to a server, information about the request is lost once the response from the server has been received. This made it difficult to create integrated multipage applications without repeated server requests or clunky work-arounds such as cookies.

- Code security—Scripts embedded in an HTML page can be downloaded and read by anyone. Nothing stops people from adapting your code for their own pages. Code in a Visual Basic DHTML application is compiled and therefore hidden from prying eyes.

Disadvantages of DHTML Applications

With so many advantages to DHTML applications, there almost has to be a downside. There are, in fact, two—one less serious and the other more so.

The less serious problem with DHTML applications is the possibly annoying download requirement. For a DHTML application to run, the Visual Basic runtime must be present on the client system. This consists of a several hundred kilobyte file that has to be downloaded only once, the first time the client tries to run any DHTML Web application (if the client has Visual Basic 6 installed, or any other application created with Visual Basic 6, this file does not need to be downloaded at all). After this initial download, DHTML applications have relatively low requirements for communicating with the server (as discussed previously).

A download of this size, even if required only once, can be off-putting to users who connect by modem. This is why Microsoft states that DHTML applications run optimally on intranets, where connection speed is usually not a factor. Even so, these applications run perfectly well on the Internet, and after the initial large download is accomplished they should run better than traditional CGI applications.

INTRANET VERSUS INTERNET

We all know what the Internet is and that transmission speed can be a problem. With most users still connecting via a modem, Web developers need to consider download size when creating pages for general use. An *intranet*, on the other hand, is a network that uses Internet technology but has restricted access, such as the employees of a particular company. Because intranets rarely use modems, download speed is less of a concern.

The more serious problem is that, at the time I am writing this, DHTML applications require Microsoft Internet Explorer version 4.0 or later. You cannot view/execute a DHTML application created with Visual Basic in any other browsers. I expect this problem to vanish rather quickly, however, as the strong competition in the browser market will almost surely result in other products, most importantly Netscape Navigator, having DHTML support in the near future. Before embarking on a complex DHTML development project, you need to verify whether your potential users will have the required support.

If you are programming for an intranet, you might find that all potential users of your application are required to standardize on a specific browser. If this is Internet Explorer 4.x, you are all set. If a non-Microsoft browser is used, it's less likely that you would be using a Microsoft development tool in the first place. In any case, knowing that all your users have the same browser always makes Web development easier, whether you are using Visual Basic or some other tool.

If you are programming for a more diverse audience, and must create a Web site that can work with a variety of browsers, you face more difficult problems. Until DHTML becomes a universally accepted standard, you must accept that fact that someone might visit your site with a non-compatible browser. There are several approaches to take.

- Abandon DHTML and use an older technology, such as CGI programming, to create the application. Although this is in some ways a step backwards, the demands of compatibility sometimes outweigh the advantages of newer technology.

- Accept the loss of potential visitors who are using non-compatible browsers. This approach will be much more viable when the Netscape browser supports DHTML because well over 90% of users have either the Netscape or Microsoft browsers.

- Create parallel applications that use different technologies—for example, DHTML and CGI—to perform the needed tasks. When a user first logs on to your site, the software detects the type of browser he is using and steers him to the correct set of pages. This approach requires a lot of extra work, but is the only way to use the latest development technology for your site while making it accessible to all users.

- Inform visitors that Microsoft Internet Explorer is required to take full advantage of the site, and direct them to the free download location (currently `http://www.microsoft.com/ie/download/`).

With Web development technology in its current state of flux, there is unfortunately no getting away from these complications. Perhaps someday you will be able to create and publish a DHTML application without any compatibility worries, but not today.

Trying It Out

Because DHTML is admittedly a bit strange when you first start working with it, it will be helpful to create a simple (*very* simple!) DHTML application before we get into the details. With a little experience under your belt, the information presented later today will make more sense.

1. Start a new Visual Basic project and select DHTML as the project type. When the Visual Basic screen appears with the new project, note that the Project window has two entries under the main DHTMLProject1: Modules and Designers. Click the plus sign next to each of these, and your screen will look like Figure 9.1. Note that there is one Module (modDHTML) and one Designer (DHTMLPage1) in the project.

FIGURE 9.1

A new DHTML project contains one Designer and one Module.

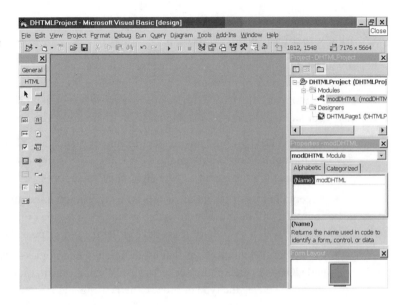

2. In the project window, click the DHTMLPage1 entry and then click the View Object button. Visual Basic displays the DHTML Designer window with a blank document, as shown in Figure 9.2.

FIGURE 9.2

A DHTML Designer initially displays a blank page.

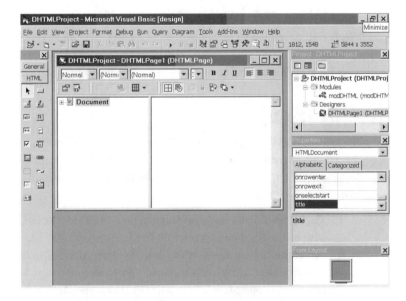

In Figure 9.2, note that the Designer displays two panels. The treeview panel on the left shows a hierarchical list of the objects, or elements, on the page. The detail panel on the right shows a visual representation of what the page will look like. At present your page contains only the base Document object.

3. In the Toolbox, Visual Basic displays icons for the various visual elements that you can place on the page. Find the icon for the TextField element (hint: it looks like a Text Box) and then double-click it. Visual Basic places a Field element on the page, as shown in Figure 9.3.

FIGURE 9.3

After placing a TextField element on the page.

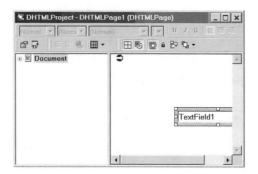

4. Use the mouse to point at the stippled border around the TextField element (the mouse cursor changes to a 4-headed arrow). Drag the element to the top-left corner of the page. Next, point inside the TextField so the mouse cursor displays as a vertical I-beam, and then click. Use the Del or Backspace key to delete the default text in the element.

5. Locate the Toolbox icon for the Button element, which looks like a regular Visual Basic Command Button. Double-click to place a Button on the page. Repeat the procedure in Step 4 to move the Button so that it is centered under the TextField element, and to change its caption to "Say Hello." At this point your screen will look like Figure 9.4.

FIGURE 9.4

After adding two elements to the DHTML page.

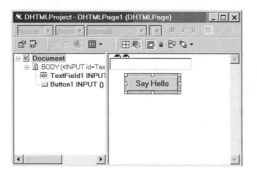

In the left panel of the Designer, you can click the plus sign next to the Document object to view the list of elements on the page. You can see in Figure 9.4 that the page you are creating has three elements: the Body element (present on all HTML pages) plus the two elements that you just added.

6. Double-click the Button element to open the code editing window for its OnClick event procedure. Add the code shown in Listing 9.1. This code assigns the return value of a function named MakeGreeting (which will be written next) to the InnerText property of the TextField element. As you can probably guess, the InnerText property specifies the text that the element displays.

LISTING 9.1   THE BUTTON'S ONCLICK EVENT PROCEDURE

```
Private Function Button1_onclick() As Boolean

TextField1.innerText = MakeGreeting()

End Function
```

7. In the Project window select the module modDHTML and click the View Code button. When the code window opens you will see that the module already contains some code, placed there by Visual Basic. Ignore this code for now, and add the function shown in Listing 9.2. This function is relatively simple. It generates a random number and then, based on its value, returns one of four greetings to the caller.

LISTING 9.2   THE MAKEGREETING FUNCTION

```
Public Function MakeGreeting() As String

' Returns a random greeting.
 Dim x As Single

 x = Rnd()

If x < 0.25 Then
    MakeGreeting = "Hello, there!"
    Exit Function
ElseIf x < 0.5 Then
    MakeGreeting = "Buenos Dias!"
    Exit Function
ElseIf x < 0.75 Then
    MakeGreeting = "Guten Tag!"
    Exit Function
Else
```

```
        MakeGreeting = "Buon Giorno!"
    End If

    End Function
```

The project is complete and ready to run. Don't forget to save it; I used the name DHTMLDEMO for all the various files but you can use any names you like. When you click the Run button in Visual Basic, Internet Explorer starts and loads the page. When you click the Say Hello button, a greeting is displayed in the TextField, as shown in Figure 9.5.

FIGURE 9.5

Running the demonstration DHTML application.

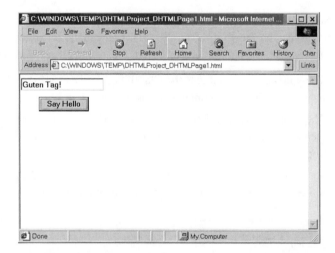

Although this is a really simple DHTML page, it demonstrates the most important feature of DHTML—it is dynamic! The information displayed by the page changes in response to user actions. Furthermore, the code that controls the changes is your old friend Basic. There's no need to learn a new language to create dynamic Web pages.

What's Inside?

Although a DHTML project contains several files, the finished application is refreshingly simple. It consists of a single DLL file that contains the project's code, plus one

HTML document for each document in the project. Each of the HTML documents includes an object reference to the DLL file, plus tags that specify the various element on the page.

OTHER APPLICATION FILES

When you compile a DHTML project, Visual Basic creates some additional files besides the DLL and the HTML documents. These include a VBW file, a LIB file, and an EXP file that don't need to be distributed with the application.

You can see what I mean by taking a look at the HTML page generated by the demonstration project, as shown in Listing 9.3. This is actually an edited version of the HTML file with some nonessential items removed. Please note three things:

1. The <object> tag that lists the ClassID of the DHTMLPage1 object—this links the page to the DLL that contains the associated code.
2. The <input> tag that defines the TextField1 element—You can see that the various elements of this tag specify the type and name of the element as well as its position and size.
3. Another <input> tag that defines the Button element—Again, the tag includes information about the object's position, caption, and so on.

THE <INPUT> TAG

In HTML, the <input> tag is used to define page elements that can interact with the user, such as fields for text entry and buttons for selecting actions.

LISTING 9.3   THE HTML DOCUMENT FROM THE DEMONSTRATION PROJECT

```
<object id="DHTMLPage1"
classid="clsid:9BF29644-47CD-11D2-BBC6-02608CACCADB"
width=0 height=0>
</object>

<body>

<input id="TextField1"
name="TextField1"
style="LEFT: 2px;
POSITION: absolute;
TOP: 8px" size="20">
```

```
<input id="Button1"
name="Button1"
style="LEFT: 40px;
POSITION: absolute;
TOP: 47px"
type="button"
value="Say Hello">
</body>
```

9

Now that you have seen a basic DHTML application in action, you can start learning the details.

The Structure of a DHTML Application

It always helps to know the details of what you are working with. Learning to create DHTML applications in Visual Basic will be much easier if you know the parts of a DHTML application.

The Internal Structure of a DHTML Application

A DHTML application has an internal structure that you need to understand. This structure can be looked at from two perspectives. First, there is the logical structure that determines how the various application objects relate to each other and how events are processed. At the top of the object hierarchy is the BaseWindow object, representing the browser in which the DHTML application is being viewed. Next is the Document object, corresponding to an HTML page displayed in the browser. A DHTML application can have more than one HTML page, and hence more than one Document object, but only one is displayed at a time.

Each Document object contains a DHTMLPage object. This is a runtime utility that serves to connect the page to its Visual Basic code, and also to provide certain events for the page. You don't interact with this object directly (other than with its events), or see it, but it's essential to much of what goes on in a DHTML application.

Each Document object also contains a variety of other objects, generically called *elements*, that make up the page's visual interface. Text, images, buttons, and hyperlinks are some of the elements you can use in a DHTML document. We will deal with elements later. Figure 9.6 illustrates the internal structure of a DHTML application.

The internal structure of a DHTML application.

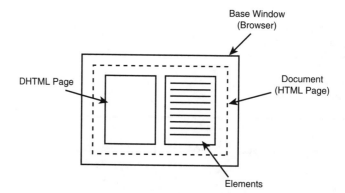

From the Developer's Point of View

The second way to look at a DHTML application's structure is from the perspective of the programmer. When you are working on a DHTML application, what are the parts you will be working with?

You'll have one or more HTML pages, each corresponding to the Document object described in the previous section. In your project, you will have one DHTML designer for each page. A page in a Visual Basic DHTML application is similar to a regular Visual Basic form in that it contains visual interface elements as well as code. You'll also have a code module that contains code that is used by the DHTML pages in the project.

Then, when the project is compiled and deployed, it consists of the following components:

- One or more HTML pages.
- Visual Basic code that handles the events generated from the HTML pages. The compiled code is placed in the project DLL, which is generated automatically.
- A runtime component that hosts the page in the Web browser or Web browser control.

Elements on a DHTML Page

With all this talk about elements, perhaps it's time to see exactly what's available. When you are working with a DHTML page, it might appear similar to placing controls on a Visual Basic form, but it isn't the same thing. The elements that are displayed in the Toolbox while you are designing a DHTML page are specifically HTML elements—in other words, they are part of the more general DHTML technology and not specifically part of Visual Basic's approach to DHTML. You could use these elements on a Web page even if you had never heard of Visual Basic.

> ### Editing a DHTML Page
>
> Although DHTML elements are different from Visual Basic controls, the process of designing a page is similar to the way you design a form. Double-click an element's icon to place a default-size copy on the page, or single-click and draw on the page to place an element at a specific location and size. Select an element on the page by clicking it, and then drag its handles to change its side or its border to change its position. The properties of the selected element display in the Properties window.
>
> Some things that you are used to doing on a Visual Basic form aren't possible in the DHTMLPage designer. You cannot select multiple objects on the page, nor can you use the Format menu commands to control the alignment and spacing of elements.

It's not possible to provide complete information on all the available DHTML elements and the details of their use. Entire books are devoted to this one subject, and you'll also find a lot of reference information in the Microsoft Internet Client Software Developer Kit. The next section gives you a brief rundown of the available DHTML elements and their most important details.

What Elements Are Available?

This section briefly describes the DHTML elements that are available in the page designer Toolbox. Figure 9.7 identifies the Toolbox icons.

Figure 9.7

The elements in the DHTML toolbox.

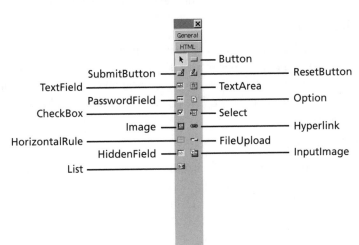

WHICH ELEMENT IS WHICH?

If you aren't sure which Toolbox icon goes with which element, rest the mouse cursor over an icon for a second and a ToolTip pops up, identifying the icon.

NAMES AND IDs

Like standard Visual Basic controls, DHTML elements have a Name property. They also have an ID property. In code, you use the ID property and not the Name property to refer to the element.

Button

Similar to a Visual Basic Command Button, the Button element is typically used to permit the user to carry out some action, such as closing the page or performing calculations. The Value property holds the text that is displayed on the Button.

SubmitButton

This element is similar to a Button element, but typically has the special function of sending information that the user entered on the page to a remote server. The `Value` property holds the text that is displayed on the SubmitButton.

ResetButton

The ResetButton element is also similar to a Button element but is traditionally used to clear all data from a page that is used for data entry. For example, if the user made an error, she can click the Reset button to clear all data rather than going back to individual elements and editing them. The `Value` property holds the text that is displayed on the ResetButton.

TextField

The TextField element is similar to a Visual Basic Text Box. It can display a single line of text, and receive input from the user. The `Value` property holds the text that is in the element. When the text in the element is selected, the `OnSelect` event is fired.

TextArea

The TextArea element can be thought of as a multi-line TextField. The TextArea element will display scroll bars if needed to access text that isn't in view. The `Value` property holds the text, and the `Rows` and `Columns` properties specify the height and width of the element. The `OnSelect` event fires when the text in the element is selected, and the `OnChange` event fires when the text is modified.

PasswordField

This element is almost identical to a TextField, but the main difference is the text that the user types in the field is displayed as asterisks (to keep sensitive passwords from prying eyes). The actual text is contained in the `Value` field. You can set the `Value` property in code or at design time to provide a default password for the element.

Option

The Option element is like a Visual Basic OptionButton. It's used to create a group of options where one and only one option can be selected at a time. To create a group, place two or more Option elements on the page then set their `Name` property to the same thing (being sure each retains a unique `ID` property). Use the `Checked` property to set or read the current option status.

Checkbox

A CheckBox is very similar to a regular Visual Basic CheckBox control except that it doesn't include a built-in label. The label is usually added by placing text directly on the HTML page. The `Checked` property is used to set or read the status of the element.

Select

The Select element is similar to a Visual Basic Combo Box control. It displays a list of items and the user clicks to select an item from the list. The `Size` property specifies the number of items visible at once. To add items to a Select element at design time, right-click the element and select Properties to display its Property Page. This is shown in Figure 9.8.

FIGURE 9.8

Adding items to a Select element at design time.

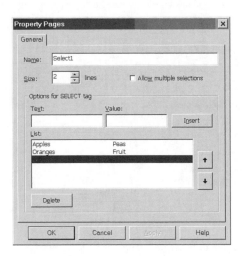

Each item in a Select element has two parts, Text and Value. Text is what is displayed in the list, and Value is what is returned in the element's Value property. In the figure, for example, the Select element's list will display "Apples" and "Oranges". If the user selects "Apples", the element's Value property will contain "Fruit".

Image

The Image element is used to display a graphic image on the DHTML page. Set the element's SRC property, either at design time or in code, to specify the image to be displayed. Set the Title property to define pop-up text that displays if the user clicks the image.

Hyperlink

The Hyperlink element creates a link to another page in your application or at another location on the Web. Set the element's HREF property to specify the target URL. The text that is displayed as the hyperlink isn't part of the Hyperlink element itself, but is regular HTML text on the page that you can edit. This text is initially the same as the element's Name property. Here is the HTML that is added to the document when you insert a Hyperlink element:

```
<A href="" id=Hyperlink1 name=Hyperlink1>Hyperlink1</A>
```

CANCELING A HYPERLINK

The default action when the user clicks a Hyperlink element is for the browser to navigate to the destination URL. You can cancel the default action by setting the return value of the event procedure to False. The following code displays a message box when the user clicks the Hyperlink, asking him to verify whether he really wants to jump away from the current page:

```
Private Function Hyperlink1_onclick() As Boolean

Dim answer

answer = MsgBox("Are you sure you want to navigate away?",
          ➥vbYesNo)

If answer <> vbYes Then
    Hyperlink1_onclick = False
Else
    Hyperlink1_onclick = True
End If

End Function
```

If the user selects Yes, the browser navigates to the URL specified in the Hyperlink object. If he selects No, the jump is cancelled.

WHERE IS THAT WINDOW?

If you are running your DHTML application from within Visual Basic and it displays a window or dialog box (such as with the MsgBox function), you might have to switch from the browser back to Visual Basic to see it. This problem doesn't occur when the application is running on its own.

HorizontalRule

This element displays as a horizontal line across the page. Use its Size and Color properties to set the line's thickness and color. Use its Width property to set the line's length.

FileUpload

This element consists of a text box with an adjacent Browse button. It permits the user to select a file on his system for upload to the server. The path and filename can be typed directly into the text box, or the user can click the Browse button to display a File Open dialog box and select the file. The Value property returns the path and name of the selected file. Note that this element doesn't actually perform the upload, but only permits specification of the filename.

HiddenField

A HiddenField element is, in essence, an invisible TextField. It cannot be seen by the user but can be accessed in code. It is typically used as a temporary storage location for data that the user doesn't need to see or change.

InputImage

This element displays a graphical image, like the Image element. Set the SRC property to specify the path or URL of the image to display. Unlike the Image element, an InputImage can be used for user input, responding to mouse clicks, for example.

List

The List elements displays as a scrolling list box, and is similar to the ListBox control in Visual Basic. Use the element's property page to add items to the list. In most ways the List element works the same way as the Select element, explained earlier.

Using ActiveX Controls on a DHTML Page

In addition to the standard DHTML elements, you can place ActiveX controls on a DHTML page. This includes ActiveX controls that are provided with Visual Basic, such as the Multimedia Control, as well as ActiveX controls that you created yourself.

For the most part, an ActiveX control on a DHTML page is programmed in the same way as on a standard Visual Basic form. There are a few exceptions; for example, the `Visible` property isn't used in the same way on a Web page as it is on a form. There will also be some additional attributes associated with each ActiveX control, required by the HTML specification. These include ClassID, CodeBase, and ID.

To add an ActiveX control to a DHTML page, you must first select it in the Components dialog box. Select Project, Components or press Ctrl+T to view this dialog box. Selected ActiveX controls are available in the General Visual Basic toolbox, which is displayed by clicking the General button in the toolbox. This toolbox also displays the icons for Visual Basic's intrinsic controls, but you'll see that when the DHTML page designer is open all the icons for the intrinsic controls are grayed out, and only those ActiveX controls that you selected in the Components dialog box are available.

Using an ActiveX control on a DHTML page is no different from using it on any other Web page. When you add an ActiveX control to the page, the page designer inserts the necessary `<object>` tag that includes the ClassID of the control and other required information. You learned about `<object>` tags on Day 3.

USING SINGLE-THREADED CONTROLS

The default threading model for DHTML applications is apartment threaded. Some ActiveX controls, however, are created using the single-threaded model. You cannot use a single-threaded control in an apartment-threaded application, and if you try to do so Visual Basic will display a message to that effect. You then have two options. The easiest one is to change the threading model of your DHTML application to single threaded; this is done on the General tab of the Project Properties dialog box. Your other option is to see if an updated version of the ActiveX control, using a multi-threading model, is available.

Page Text

One part of a DHTML page is not an element at all but just regular text. If you click on the page without first selecting an element from the Toolbox (be sure the arrow at the top of the Toolbox is selected), Visual Basic displays a blinking vertical cursor. Any text you type is inserted directly onto the document, using the font, size, and alignment as specified on the designer toolbar. This is regular HTML text, and you might notice that its position sometimes doesn't seem to respect other elements on the page, going behind them. You should use this type of text for document content that won't change and won't be manipulated programmatically.

TEXT SIZE IN HTML

Unlike a word processor, an HTML document doesn't specify text size in points. Instead there are seven sizes available, identified by the numbers 1 (smallest) through 7 (largest).

Formatting of this type of text is done in a manner similar to what you use in a word processor. You can control the font and size of the text; display it in any combination of boldface, italics, and underlined; and specify whether the text is left-justified, centered, or right-justified on the page. You have the option of specifying the formatting before you type the text, or entering the text first then highlighting it (by dragging over it with the mouse) and changing the formatting. Formatting is controlled by several items on the DHTML Page Designer toolbar, as shown in Figure 9.9. You can also assign predefined standard HTML styles to text using the Style box on the toolbar.

FIGURE 9.9

Text formatting tools in the page designer.

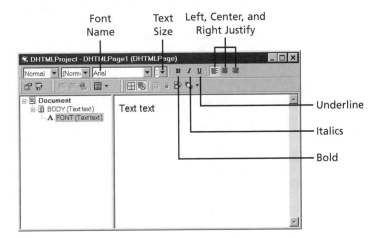

Regular text isn't positioned in the same way as elements. You cannot select text and drag it to a new location. Instead, the position of text on the page is determined by what comes before it in the HTML document. Here are some examples:

- To move a line of text down on the page, position the cursor at the start of the line and press Enter one or more times.

- To move a line of text up on the page, position the cursor at the start of the line and press Backspace one or more times.

EDITING HTML

Visual Basic gives you the option of using an external editor to edit your DHTML files. Given the limited design capabilities of the page designer, this might not be a bad idea. To specify the editor, select Tools, Options to display the Options dialog box, and click on the Advanced tab. Enter the full path and program name of the desired editor in the External HTML Editor box, or click the adjacent button to browse for the desired file. The default external editor is Notepad, which is simply a text editor. If you have Microsoft FrontPage or another specialized HTML editor installed on your system, you should use it rather than Notepad.

To use an external editor, you must tell Visual Basic to save the page's HTML in an external file. The default is to save the HTML inside the DHTMLPage designer file, where it cannot be edited except by the DHTML page designer. A regular HTML file is created only when the project is compiled. To save a page's HTML in a separate file, select the Save HTML In An External File option when first creating the page, or for an existing page enter the desired filename in the SourceFile property of the DHTMLPage object. Launch the editor by clicking the Launch Editor button in the DHTMLPage designer toolbar. After editing, quit the external editor and answer Yes when Visual Basic asks if you want to reload the edited HTML. The designed DHTML page then updates to reflect the changes you made.

Positioning Elements on the Page

When positioning elements on a DHTML page, you can use two modes: Absolute and Relative.

In Absolute mode (the default), each element is positioned exactly where you place it.

In Relative mode, each element is positioned at the next available cursor location (similar to text, as described in the previous section).

To see the difference, look at Figure 9.10. The three elements at the top of the page were positioned using Relative mode, whereas the other three elements were positioned using Absolute mode.

Absolute mode gives you more precise control over the placement of the elements on the page, but Relative mode results in a more flexible page that adjusts to different viewing conditions. If you create the page on a large, high-resolution monitor, the entire page might not fit on the screen of a user with a smaller screen. If you use Absolute mode, some elements will simply be off screen and the user will have to scroll to see them. With Relative mode, the browser automatically wraps the page elements so that they are all visible.

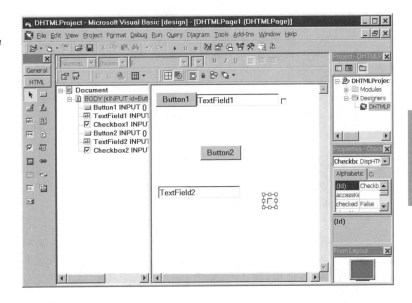

FIGURE 9.10

The difference between Absolute and Relative element positioning.

The DHTML Page Designer has two buttons on its Toolbar that control the positioning mode. Experiment with the different modes and then use the one that best suits your project.

SELECTING ELEMENTS

To work with an individual element on a page, you must select it. A selected element shows a wide gray border with small white boxes (called *sizing handles*) on it. You can select either the border or the body of an element. When the border is selected, the border displays gray fill, and you can delete the element or move it by dragging the border. When the body is selected, the border displays diagonal hatching and you can edit the contents of the element.

Summary

This has been an information-packed day, getting you started with the exciting and powerful techniques of creating DHTML applications in Visual Basic. A DHTML application combines traditional HTML with Visual Basic code. It's this latter element—the code—that puts the *dynamic* in DHTML, permitting the application to respond to user input and to manipulate page appearance and data on-the-fly. Because you are using the same Visual Basic code that you are familiar with, you have a leg up over other dynamic Web page technologies.

A DHTML page is made up of elements that provide the page's visual interface. These elements are similar in some ways to the controls that you use on a regular Visual Basic form, but there are important differences. You can place ActiveX controls on a DHTML page as well.

Tomorrow we will continue to explore DHTML technology, looking at events, state management, and other more advanced topics.

Q&A

Q What are two important differences between a DHTML page and a regular Visual Basic form?

A A Visual Basic form runs as a standalone application, while a DHTML page runs in Internet Explorer. Also, the elements that make up the visual interface of a DHTML page are DHTML elements and aren't regular Visual Basic controls.

Q What is the main disadvantage of DHTML applications?

A At present, DHTML applications can run only in the Microsoft Internet Explorer 4 browser. Although support for DHTML applications might be added to other browsers, this is a serious limitation at present.

Q What are my two positioning options when placing elements on a DHTML page?

A Absolute and relative positioning. Absolute mode lets you position elements at a specific location on the page, while relative mode positions elements based on their position in the HTML stream.

Q Would I want to do sophisticated page design using the Visual Basic DHTML page designer?

A No, because the page designer is a fairly simple HTML editor. You are much better off saving the HTML in an external file and using a specialized HTML editor, such as Microsoft FrontPage, for any complex page design.

Workshop

Quiz

1. Can you use regular Visual Basic controls on a DHTML page?

2. When adding text to a DHTML page, how do you start a new paragraph?

3. How many individual pages can a DHTML application contain?

4. How do you define a group of Option elements so that only one can be on at a time?

5. When placing text on an DHTML page, what point sizes are available?

Exercises

You have learned enough about DHTML applications to start creating your own simple projects. Here are a few relatively simple applications you should be able to try on your own.

1. A calculator that performs the four basic functions of addition, subtraction, division, and multiplication

2. A number guessing game in which the computer picks a random number and then gives the players higher and lower hints when they guess

3. A program that converts between metric and English units of measure

9

DAY **10**

Putting the *Dynamic* into DHTML

Yesterday you had a good start in mastering Visual Basic's Dynamic HTML technology. Today I will continue, providing the remaining information you need on this topic. The title of this chapter reflects that events are a central part of DHTML, and much of today's lesson is devoted to the details of using events. I'll finish the lesson with some more advanced DHTML topics. Today you will learn

- Events in a DHTML application's lifetime
- Responding to user input
- How to use the Event object
- Navigating in DHTML applications
- Advanced page design techniques
- State management
- Testing and deploying DHTML applications

DHTML Application Events

For the most part, the events you will work with in a DHTML application are the same events you are accustomed to using in a standard Visual Basic program. In most cases, however, the event names are different. Many DHTML event names start with on, so Click becomes OnClick, and so on. The syntax for naming event procedures follows the usual conventions. For example, if you have a button named Button1, its click event procedure is

```
Private Function Button1_onclick() As Boolean
```

EVENT FUNCTIONS?

As you can see from this example, some event procedures in DHTML are really event functions. You will soon learn the details.

As with all Visual Basic applications, some events are associated with user input, whereas others are part of the application's fundamental structure and lifetime.

Events in a DHTML Application's Lifetime

The events you'll use most often are received by the DHTMLPage object. The Initialize event is the first event that is fired for a DHTML page, and it occurs during the process of loading the page. When Initialize occurs, all the page's objects might not have been loaded. Therefore, this event procedure should not be used to set object properties.

Next, after the Initialize event is the Load event. The load event procedure is the preferred location for code that sets information on the page. The exact occurrence of Load depends on whether the page is being loaded synchronously or asynchronously.

SYNCHRONOUS VERSUS ASYNCHRONOUS PAGE LOADING

A DHTML page can be loaded synchronously or asynchronously, depending on whether its AsyncLoad property is set to True or False (the default). With asynchronous loading, the page's code will begin execution before all the page elements are loaded. Asynchronous load provides a page that is responsive sooner to the user, but can be used only if the page's code isn't dependent on elements that might not be loaded. With synchronous load the entire page is loaded before code starts executing.

The Unload event is fired when the user moves to another page or closes the application. All the page's objects still exist during the Unload event, so it can be used for removing unneeded object references and other cleanup tasks.

The final event, Terminate, occurs just before the HTML page is destroyed. Object references no longer exist at this time, so you cannot put cleanup code in the Terminate event procedure.

KEEPING YOUR EVENTS STRAIGHT

Because of the way DHTML applications are structured, it can be confusing trying to remember which events happen to which object and when. For example, the DHTMLPage object has the Load event, and the BaseWindow object has the OnLoad event. Both are related to the loading of a Document object, but the DHTMLPage object's Load event fires before the BaseWindow object's OnLoad event. Interestingly, the Document object itself—the thing that is actually being loaded—does not have an equivalent to the Load event.

10

User Events

Many of the events that you will be working with in your DHTML projects are closely related to the events that you are accustomed to using in Visual Basic. Because the DHTML model is different, however, there are also some differences in the events that are available and the way they work. In this section, I will examine these differences. First, however, you need to know about the Event object.

The Event Object

The Event object is an essential tool for using events in a DHTML application. It supplies information about recent events and also can be used to control event bubbling (a topic to be covered later). Strictly speaking, the Event object is a property of the BaseWindow object and is accessed by code in a DHTML Document as follows:

```
Document.parentWindow.event
```

However, a Visual Basic shortcut makes the Event object appear as the DHTMLEvent property of the DHTMLPage object. Suppose you wanted to determine the X and Y coordinates of a mouse click. The firing of the OnClick event procedure tells you that a click happened, but you must query the Event object to determine where.

```
MouseX = DHTMLPage.DHTMLEvent.x
MouseY = DHTMLPage.DHTMLEvent.y
```

The Event object is available only during events, that is, inside event procedures. Although all its properties are available regardless of the event that occurred, some of them will be meaningless during certain events. For example, the frmElement and toElement properties are meaningful only when processing onMouseOver and onMouseOut events.

Following are descriptions of the Event object's properties:

AltKey   True if the Alt key is down, False if not.

Button   Specifies which mouse button is clicked. 0 = no button, 1 = left button, 2 = right button, and 4 = middle button.

CancelBubble   Set to True to prevent the event from bubbling up in the object hierarchy.

ClientX and ClientY   Specify the position of a mouse click with respect to the window's client area.

CtrlKey   True if the Ctrl key is down, False if not.

FromElement   Specifies the page element being moved from during onMouseOver and onMouseOut events.

KeyCode   Gives the Unicode key code of the key that was pressed. Setting this property changes the value of the keystroke that is received farther up the event chain.

OffsetX and OffsetY   Specify the relative position of a mouse click.

Reason   Indicates the final disposition of a data transfer for a data source object. 0 = successful, 1 = aborted, and 2 = error.

ReturnValue   Set to False to cancel the default action of the element that received the event.

ScreenX and ScreenY   Specifies the position relative to the physical screen.

ShiftKey   True if the Shift key is down, False if not.

SrcElement   Specifies the element that fired the event.

SrcFilter   Identifies the element that caused the onFilterChange event to fire.

Type   Returns the name of the event that occurred. Names are without the On prefix, so if OnClick fires, this property will contain "click".

X and Y   Specify the position of a mouse click relative to the container. If the mouse is outside the window, these properties return -1.

READ-ONLY PROPERTIES

With the exception of `CancelBubble`, `KeyCode`, and `ReturnValue`, all the `Event` object's properties are read-only.

To demonstrate the use of the `Event` object and to help you develop a feel for how DHTML events work, you can create a simple application that tracks mouse movement. You can also use this application to get a feel for the differences between the four different ways that the `Event` object can report mouse coordinates.

Start a new DHTML project and display the page designer. Place four TextField elements on the page. Leave all the properties at their default values, but change the size of all the TextField elements to make them about twice as wide as the default.

Next, display the code window. Select Document in the Object drop-down list and onMouseMove in the `Event` drop-down list. Add the code in Listing 10.1 to the event procedure. This code does nothing more than display the `Event` object's mouse-related property values in the four TextFields.

LISTING 10.1 DISPLAYING MOUSE COORDINATES

```
Private Sub Document_onmousemove()

TextField1.innerText = "ClientX, ClientY = " & _
    DHTMLEvent.clientX & ", " & DHTMLEvent.clientY

TextField2.innerText = "OffsetX, OffsetY = " & _
    DHTMLEvent.offsetX & ", " & DHTMLEvent.offsetY

TextField3.innerText = "ScreenX, ScreenY = " & _
    DHTMLEvent.screenX & ", " & DHTMLEvent.screenY

TextField4.innerText = "X, Y = " & _
    DHTMLEvent.x & ", " & DHTMLEvent.y

End Sub
```

Run the application and move the mouse over the window. You'll see the values displayed in the window change as the mouse position changes, as shown in Figure 10.1. Note that the display is not updated when the mouse is outside the browser window.

Now that you know about the `Event` object, you can look at some of the specific user events available in DHTML applications.

10

FIGURE **10.1**

*Testing mouse events
in a DHTML applica-
tion.*

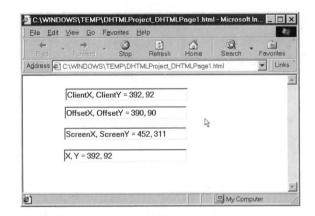

FIGURE 10.1

Testing mouse events in a DHTML application.

Keyboard Events

DHTML keyboard events are essentially direct counterparts to the Visual Basic events
KeyDown, KeyPress, and KeyUp; simply add the on prefix, and you are ready to use
onKeyDown, onKeyPress, and onKeyUp. The Event object's KeyCode property contains the
Unicode representation of the key that was pressed, and the AltKey, CtrlKey, and
ShiftKey properties indicate which of these keys were pressed at the same time.

Mouse Events

The DHTML mouse click events, onClick and onDblClick, work the same way as the
Visual Basic Click and DoubleClick events. The Event object has four pairs of properties that you can read to determine the location of the click or double-click in four different coordinate systems. Note that the onClick event also fires when the user presses
Enter on an element that can receive the focus.

Similarly, the DHTML events onMouseDown, onMouseUp, and onMouseMove operate in a
parallel fashion to the Visual Basic equivalents.

The onMouseOut and onMouseOver events have no direct Visual Basic counterparts.
OnMouseOut fires when the mouse leaves an element, and onMouseOver fires when the
mouse enters a new element (onMouseMove fires in between, as well). You can use these
events to create "hover button" effects in which a page element changes its appearance
when the mouse pointer is over it.

This technique is easy to demonstrate. Here's how to program a Button element whose
border color changes when the mouse pointer is hovering over it.

A Demonstration of the onMouseOver and onMouseOut Events   Create a new
DHTML project and place a single Button element on the page. Open the code window

and select (General) from the Object drop-down list. Enter the following line of code, which declares a global variable to hold the original border color:

```
Dim oldColor As String
```

The other remaining code goes in the Button element's `onMouseOver` and `onMouseOut` event procedures. The code is shown in Listing 10.2.

LISTING 10.2   CREATING A "HOVER" EFFECT ON A PAGE ELEMENT

```
Private Sub Button1_onmouseout()

Button1.Style. Color = oldColor

End Sub

Private Sub Button1_onmouseover()

oldColor = Button1.Style.Color
Button1.Style.Color = RGB(255,0,0)

End Sub
```

10

When you run the application, you'll see that the color of the Button text changes when the mouse pointer is over it and then changes back to the original color when the mouse moves away. Not bad for fewer than half a dozen lines of code!

THE STYLE COLLECTION

In this example, you changed the Button element's appearance by modifying its `Style` property. This property actually represents an *in-line style sheet* for a particular page element. When you refer to an element's `Style` property, you are actually referring to a collection of all the individual appearance-related properties that the element has. Remember that DHTML page elements are defined by tags in the HTML document; the in-line style sheet specifies any style settings that are different from the default. For example, if you added a `Button` object and changed its `Color` property to Red, the HTML tag for the element would look like this:

```
<input type="button" value="Button" name="B1"
style="color: rgb(255,0,0)">
```

The last part of this tag,

```
style="color: rgb(255,0,0)"
```

is the in-line style sheet, and it specifies that the `Color` property (or style setting) should be the indicated value. This style sheet contains all the individual style settings for the element. You can access individual Style settings in code by referring to the properties of an element's Style property, as we did in the preceding example. Of course, you need to know which style settings are available for each type of element. The Microsoft Internet Client Software Development Kit provides a complete reference for this information, which is too extensive to present in this book. You can download the SDK from the Microsoft Web site.

Be aware that the Visual Basic DHTML designer is limited, as far as HTML editors, and does not permit you to easily change the styles of page elements. More sophisticated editors, such as Microsoft FrontPage, do provide direct and convenient access to element style settings.

Focus and Selection Events

This is an area where DHTML events differ somewhat from what you are accustomed to in Visual Basic. Events related to the focus are available only with certain elements, and selection and dragging are handled differently. Let's take a look.

OnFocus and OnBlur are the DHTML equivalents of Visual Basic's GotFocus and LostFocus. OnFocus fires only when the focus moves to a page element capable of receiving user input, such as a TextField or Button. OnBlur fires when the focus moves away from such an element. These events occur regardless of where the focus is going to or coming from. If the user switches to a totally different application, OnBlur fires for the DHTML page element that had the focus when the switch was made. When the user switches back to the DHTML application, OnFocus fires for the same element.

Visual Basic's SelChange event has two related events in DHTML. OnSelectStart occurs when the process of making a selection is started, for example, when the user clicks something in the document. Then, OnSelect occurs when the selection is changed, for example, by dragging over part of the document.

For dragging actions, Visual Basic has the two events DragDrop and DragOver. In contrast, DHTML has the single event OnDragStart, which is fired when the user starts to drag a selection. The usual action taken in response to this event is to prepare the selection, whatever it may be, for copying to another page element.

Miscellaneous Events

The events described in Table 10.1 do not fall into one of the preceding categories, but are still important for developing DHTML pages.

TABLE 10.1 MISCELLANEOUS DHTMLPAGE EVENTS

DHTML Event	Visual Basic Equivalent	Description
OnChange	Change	Occurs when the user presses Enter or tabs away from an element whose contents have been changed. This is different from the corresponding event in Visual Basic, which is fired as soon as a change is made.
OnError	Error	Occurs when there is an error condition loading an image on processing a script.
OnLoad	Load	Fired by the BaseWindow object when a document and all its elements (images, and so on) have been completely downloaded.
OnResize	Resize	The event fires in a manner similar to the Visual Basic counterpart, but resizing of an HTML page does not need to be handled in the same way as resizing of a Visual Basic form.
OnScroll	Scroll	Fires whenever a scrollbar for the page or for any element within the page is moved.
OnAbort	*None*	Occurs when the user aborts the download of an image or other page element by clicking the browser's Stop button.
OnReset	*None*	Fires when the user selects a reset button on the page.
OnSubmit	*None*	Fires when the user selects a submit button on the page.

The best way to become familiar with events in a DHTML application is to work with them. Using the same techniques presented earlier in this chapter, you can use the `Debug.Print` statement and the Visual Basic Immediate window to see the occurrence of events as they happen.

Event Bubbling

DHTML applications have a characteristic called *event bubbling*, which is one of the ways in which they differ from standard Visual Basic applications. In a standard application, each object must have its own event handler. If a particular object—a text box, for instance—does not have a click event handler, any click events occurring on that object are lost.

With event bubbling, things work differently. If a given event is not handled by the element that received it, those events "bubble up" to the next object in hierarchy. Any event will bubble up until it is explicitly cancelled. An event is lost only if it reaches the top object in the hierarchy without finding a matching handler.

10

The DHTML object hierarchy through which events bubble is described earlier in the chapter. In the simplest situation, a Button element is subsidiary to the Document object. In a more complex page, the Button element might be subsidiary to a Table element, which in turn is subsidiary to a Body element. The Body element is contained within an HTML page, which is subsidiary to the Document object, always the top-level object.

> **WATCH THOSE EVENTS!**
>
> Because of event bubbling, you need to exercise care in writing event procedures. The Document, for example, will receive a Click event whenever one of its elements is clicked, *unless* the event bubbling is cancelled. If you don't plan carefully, event procedures in higher-level objects will be firing when you don't expect it.

To prevent an event from bubbling farther up, set the Event object's CancelBubble property to True. As you learned earlier in the chapter, the Event object is accessed by means of the DHTMLEvent property. Suppose you wrote code in a Button element's OnClick event procedure to handle the event and did not want the event to bubble farther up the chain. Here's the required code:

```
Private Function Button1_onclick() As Boolean

    ' Code to handle event here.
    DHTMLEvent.cancelBubble = True

End Function
```

Be aware that the order of objects in the hierarchy is largely dependent on the position of elements within the HTML stream, not necessarily on the way elements are displayed onscreen. In the preceding example, the Button element is subsidiary to the Table element because it comes later in the HTML stream and not simply because the button is displayed within the table. If you later change the position attributes of the Button so that it's displayed outside the table, it will still be subsidiary to the table because its position in the HTML stream has not been changed.

> **THE HTML STREAM**
>
> The term HTML stream refers to the order in which elements appear in the text within the HTML document. If the tag for a TextField element comes before the tag for a Button element in the HTML document, its position in the stream is "before," even though the TextField might display "after" the Button when the document is viewed (because of absolute positioning attributes). The treeview panel in the DHTML Page Designer always lists elements in their true order in the HTML stream.

Responding to Events

One of the strengths of Visual Basic's DHTML model is that individual page elements are programmable. You can write code that responds to events detected by the elements, and you can also write code that manipulates the elements and their data.

All DHTML page elements are not automatically programmable, however. To be accessed in code, an element must have an ID. An element's ID provides a unique identifier for the element, making it unique from all other elements on the page. Most elements are automatically assigned an ID when you place them on a page, but this is not always the case. For example, regular text is organized into paragraphs in an HTML page, but each paragraph is not automatically assigned an ID. If you want to manipulate paragraph text in a DHTML document, each paragraph must have a unique ID.

Do	Don't
DO assign unique ID properties to each page element that you want to be able to access in code.	DON'T try to access page elements in code by using their Name property, because it will not work.

You can tell whether an element has been assigned an ID by using the treeview pane. For example, look at Figure 10.2, which shows a DHTML page with three paragraphs on it. The treeview shows that only the first Paragraph element (Welcome) has an ID, in this case, para1. The other two Paragraph elements do not have IDs.

FIGURE 10.2

The treeview pane lists the IDs of page elements.

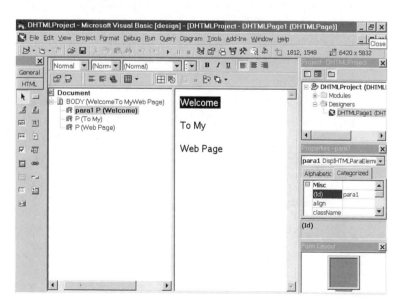

To assign an ID to an element or to change an existing ID, select the element in the tree-view pane. Then select the (Id) property in the Properties window and enter the desired ID.

THE PARAGRAPH ELEMENT

You can give your pages a lot of flexibility by programmatically manipulating the properties of Paragraph elements. A DHTML Paragraph element has a wide range of properties, including in-line styles, that can be manipulated in code. To see for yourself, create a DHTML application and insert a paragraph of text that says something like "This is the original text." Assign the ID para1 to the paragraph. Then, add a Button and put the following in its OnClick event procedure:

```
Private Function Button1_onclick() As Boolean

para1.Style.Color = RGB(0, 255, 0)
para1.innerText = "This is the new text"

End Function
```

When you run the application, click the Button, and you'll see both the color and content of the paragraph text change.

Coordinating Event Procedures with Default Actions

Many of the DHTML elements that you have at your disposal have a default action associated with them. In other words, the action occurs even without you putting any code in the associated event procedure. Suppose, however, that you want to put code in the event procedure and also have the default action occur. Then you must follow the procedures explained here.

Take a look at an example. When clicked, the Checkbox element has the default behavior of changing its state from checked to unchecked (or vice versa). If you want something else to happen when a Checkbox is clicked, you would put the code in the corresponding event procedure:

```
Private Function Checkbox1_onclick() As Boolean

' Your code here.

End Function
```

If you run the application, you will see that clicking the Checkbox causes your code to be executed, but the default behavior (changing between checked and unchecked) does not. What's going on?

Look at the event procedure definition, and you will see that it is actually a function with a type Boolean return value. Here's where the problem lies. Visual Basic type Boolean variables default to False, so, as written, this event procedure returns False to the system. This False value signals the system not to carry out the default action. Therefore, the solution is to rewrite the procedure as follows:

```
Private Function Checkbox1_onclick() As Boolean

' Your code here.
Checkbox1_onclick = True

End Function
```

With a return value of True, the system is instructed to carry out the element's default action. You have the ability to control whether the default action is carried out, based on the return value of the event procedure.

Navigating in DHTML Applications

Because a DHTML page is actually a Web page and is viewed in a browser, the possibility exists of navigating to other pages. The page you navigate to can be another DHTML page in your application or any other page on the Web. You have two options for navigation.

Navigating with the Hyperlink Element

The Hyperlink element is designed specifically for navigation and is often your best choice for adding this capability to your pages. You were introduced to the Hyperlink element earlier in this chapter. Here are the steps required to add a Hyperlink element to your page and link it to a destination page:

1. Select the Hyperlink icon in the DHTML toolbox and add it to your page.

2. Edit the element's HREF property to point at the destination page.

3. Edit the associated text so that it reads as desired.

CONVERTING TEXT TO A HYPERLINK

You can convert existing page text to a hyperlink by selecting the text and then clicking the Make Selection Into Link button on the page designer toolbar.

10

Navigating in Code

If you don't want to use a Hyperlink element for navigation, you can do it in code. You can associate the code with just about any page element by placing it in the associated event procedure. The actual navigation is done by the `BaseWindow` object's `Navigate` method—for example,

```
BaseWindow.Navigate "http://www.microsoft.com"

BaseWindow.Navigate "DHTMLPage2.html"
```

The first line navigates to an external Web page, and the second one navigates to another page that is part of your project.

> **GOING FORWARD AND BACKWARD**
>
> The `BaseWindow` object also has `GoForward` and `GoBack` methods that navigate forward and backward in the browser's history list.

You will usually want to use the Button element for programmatic navigation. Although other DHTML elements can be used, it might not be intuitive to your users that they are being used for navigation.

Grouping and Isolating Page Elements

You have seen how just about everything on a DHTML page is an element of one sort or another. As long as an element has a unique ID, it can be accessed and manipulated in code—the basis of much of the power of DHTML programming. You might find, however, that you sometimes need to access parts of the page in ways that do not neatly fall on the boundaries between elements. Here is an example:

- You want to change the formatting of several words in a paragraph of text without affecting the remainder of the paragraph.
- You want to modify the properties of several page elements in code without having to access each element individually.

DHTML provides two special tags for these tasks. The `<div>` tag lets you group two or more page elements so that they can be referred to as a unit. The `<span>` tag has the opposite effect, isolating a portion of a page element. Both the `<span>` and the `<div>` tag can be assigned IDs, permitting them to be manipulated in code.

To assign <span> or <div> tags to your document, select the text or elements to be included in the tag. Then, click either the Wrap Selection in <div>...</div> button or the Wrap Selection in <span>...</span> button on the page designer toolbar. The tags will be added to your document and will also display as elements in the treeview pane.

USING <SPAN> AND <DIV>

When you insert a <div> tag, a paragraph break is inserted immediately after the closing </div>. This means that anything following the <div> will start on a new line. Therefore, you cannot use <div> within a paragraph of text. In contrast, <span> does not modify the page formatting by adding paragraph breaks and is appropriate for use within paragraphs.

10

To see how <span> and <div> work, you can create a simple demonstration.

1. Start a new DHTML project and add two lines of text to the page, being sure to press Enter after the first line so that you will have two separate paragraphs.

2. Use the mouse to highlight all the text. Then click the Wrap Selection in <div>...</div> button on the toolbar.

3. Highlight a single word in the first line of text. Then click the Wrap Selection in <span>...</span> button.

4. Repeat step 3 for a single word in the second line of text.

5. In the treeview pane, select the DIV element. In the Properties window, assign the ID div1 to this element.

6. Repeat step 5 to assign the IDs span1 and span2 to the two SPAN elements. At this stage, your screen will look like Figure 10.3.

FIGURE 10.3

Demonstrating the use of <span> *and* <div>.

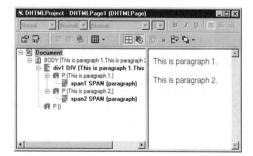

7. Add a Button element to the page. Add the code in Listing 10.3 to the OnClick
    event procedure for the button.

LISTING 10.3   USING <SPAN> AND <DIV> TAGS TO CONTROL FORMATTING CHANGES

```
Private Function Button1_onclick() As Boolean

div1.Style.Color = RGB(0, 0, 255)
span1.innerText = "XXXXXXX"
span2.innerText = "!!!!!!!"

End Function
```

After saving the project, you can run it. The original text displays at first, but see what
happens when you click the Button. The color of all the text changes, and the two individual words that you selected earlier are replaced by *X*'s and exclamation points. The
use of <span> and <div> tags let you define meaningful "chunks" of the document that
can be accessed as units.

Changing a Document's Style and Appearance

Much of the appeal of DHTML applications comes from the fact that their formatting
and appearance can be changed dynamically in code. You learned earlier that most elements have a Style object associated with them that contains a collection of the available properties. For example, to change a Button element's background color, you would
write the following:

```
Button1.style.BackgroundColor = "blue"
```

> **COLORS IN DHTML**
>
> Colors are specified differently in DHTML than in a regular Visual Basic application. You
> must use either a numeric RGB value or one of Internet Explorer's defined color names,
> such as "blue." You can find complete information on the available color names in the
> Microsoft Internet Client SDK.

Many different properties are available in the Style collection; the ones available depend
on the specific element in use, also. Table 10.2 describes some of the most frequently
used properties.

TABLE 10.2 SOME COMMONLY USED DHTML STYLE PROPERTIES

DHTML Style	Description
Backgroundcolor	Sets the background color of all elements except the Document object, which represents the body of the page.
Border	Controls the display of a border around an element. All elements, including text paragraphs, can have a border.
Color	Sets the foreground color of all elements except the Document object.
Font	Determines the font used for text. Several related properties, such as fontstyle, control individual aspects of the font's appearance.
Margin	Controls the amount of margin, or empty space, around an element. Related properties let you control individual margins (left, top, and so on).
Padding	Controls the spacing between the element's border and the text displayed inside it.
Textdecoration	Controls special aspects of text display, such as making it blink or displaying it underlined.

10

NO STYLE

Only one element within a DHTML page does not have a Style collection—the Document object. Properties of the Document object are referenced directly, which is similar to the way it is done for objects in Visual Basic. For example, to change the foreground color of the Document (which specifies the color of text), you would write:

```
Document.fgcolor = "slateblue"
```

Refer to the Visual Basic online help or the Internet Client SDK for reference information on the Document object's properties and methods.

Importing Existing HTML Pages

At times you might want to import an existing HTML page into the page designer. This will happen when you are converting an existing Web site into a DHTML application. It will also be necessary when you want to use an advanced HTML editor to create the page and then import it into Visual Basic to link it to the other parts of the DHTML application. Here's how to do it:

1. Open the DHTML application that you want to import the HTML page into.

2. Select Add DHTML Page from the Project menu. Visual Basic displays the property page for the new HTML page, as shown in Figure 10.4.

FIGURE **10.4**

*Importing an existing
HTML page into a
DHTML project.*

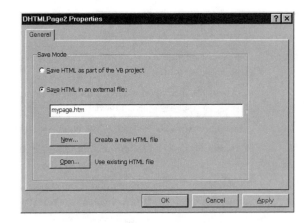

3. Select the Save HTML In An External File option.

4. Click the Open button to display the Open dialog box. Locate the HTML file that you want to import; then click Open.

5. Click OK.

After you have imported an existing HTML file, Visual Basic will continue to save it as a separate file. At any time, you can return to editing the page in the external editor. See "Editing HTML" for details.

EDITING HTML

As you know, an HTML document is a regular text file, and as such it can be modified in any text editor. You can use NotePad or WordPad, two text editing utilities that come with Windows. There are also dozens of specialized HTML editors available, some as shareware or freeware, others as part of Web publishing suites such as Microsoft FrontPage. These specialized programs are easier to use because they have custom features for HTML editing.

State Management in DHTML Applications

Like almost everything on the Web, DHTML applications rely on the Hypertext Transfer Protocol (HTTP). This is a *stateless* protocol, which means that no information is retained between requests. In practical terms, there is no way to "remember" what the user did on one page after navigating to another page. This is where the term *stateless* comes from—the state of the system is not retained between requests.

In many Web applications, the capability of retaining state information is extremely useful. If you have used the Web much, I'm sure that you have seen this in action. A Web site might permit you to customize the way it works, and if it remembers your individual settings each time you visit, it is saving state information. This is done using a technique called *cookies*.

A cookie is nothing more than a small tidbit of data stored on the local machine. A cookie includes the data itself, an identifying label, and information about the Web page that stored it. A cookie can be stored by one page in your application and retrieved by another page. This is the preferred method for the DHTML applications to preserve state from one page to another. Cookies are also retained between sessions, so you can store cookies to have data available the next time the applications runs.

ARE COOKIES DANGEROUS?

In a word, no. A lot of nonsense has spread around the Internet that cookies provide a means for hackers to break in to your system and cause damage or steal information. This is simply not true. The mechanism by which cookies are stored makes it impossible for these things to happen. Some browsers have an option that lets you either refuse all cookies or receive a warning whenever a Web page attempts to store a cookie. Don't waste your time. There has not been a single documented instance of cookies being used for any underhanded purpose.

10

Storing data in cookies is made easy by two procedures provided by Visual Basic. They are automatically inserted when you add a code module to your project. Clearly, then, your project must have a module to use these procedures. Listing 10.4 shows the code.

LISTING 10.4   PROCEDURES FOR SAVING AND RETRIEVING COOKIES

```
'PutProperty: Store information in a cookie by calling this function.
'             The required inputs are the named Property
'             and the value of the property you would like to store.
'
'             Optional inputs are:
'               expires : specifies a date that defines the valid life
'                         time of the property.  After the expiration
'                         date has been reached, the property will no
'                         longer be stored or given out.

Public Sub PutProperty(objDocument As HTMLDocument, strName As String, _
    vntValue As Variant, Optional Expires As Date)
```

continues

LISTING **10.4**   CONTINUED

```
        objDocument.cookie = strName & "=" & CStr(vntValue) & _
          IIf(CLng(Expires) = 0, "", "; expires=" & Format(CStr(Expires), _
            "ddd, dd-mmm-yy hh:mm:ss") & " GMT") ' & _

    End Sub

    'GetProperty: Retrieve the value of a property by calling this
    '             function.  The required input is the named Property,
    '             and the return value of the function is the current
    '             value of the property.  If the property cannot be
    '             found or has expired, the return value will
    '             be an empty string.
    '
    Public Function GetProperty(objDocument As HTMLDocument, _
        strName As String) As Variant

        Dim aryCookies() As String
        Dim strCookie As Variant
        On Local Error GoTo NextCookie

        'Split the document cookie object into an array of cookies.
        aryCookies = Split(objDocument.cookie, ";")
        For Each strCookie In aryCookies
            If Trim(VBA.Left(strCookie, InStr(strCookie, "=") - 1)) _
                = Trim(strName) Then
                GetProperty = Trim(Mid(strCookie, InStr(strCookie, _
                    "=") + 1))
                Exit Function
            End If
    NextCookie:
            Err = 0
        Next strCookie
    End Function
```

To save a cookie, call PutProperty. The declaration is

```
Public Sub PutProperty(objDocument As HTMLDocument, strName As String, _
    vntValue As Variant, Optional Expires As Date)
```

The arguments are as follows:

objDocument is the document from which the cookie is being saved.

strName is a string label identifying the cookie.

vntValue is the data to be saved.

Expires is an optional argument giving the cookie's expiration date.

STALE COOKIES

When you write a cookie, you have the option of specifying an expiration date. After a cookie's expiration date has passed, the cookie is no longer available. Use an expiration date to make cookies temporary and to ensure that old, invalid data is not maintained.

To save a cookie, you would write the following. In this case, suppose you want to store the data that is in `TextField1` and have it expire in 30 days:

```
PutProperty BaseWindow.Document, "TextField1", _
TextField1.Value, DateAdd("d", 30, Now)
```

In another page of your application, you would retrieve that data like this:

```
TextField2.Value = GetProperty(BaseWindow.Document, "TextField1")
```

If the specified property doesn't exist or has expired, `GetProperty` returns an empty string.

Testing and Compiling a DHTML Application

The full set of Visual Basic debugging tools are at your disposal when you test and debug a DHTML application. Breakpoints, watch variables, and debug statements are a few of the useful tools that make the job much easier.

Use the Debugging tab of the Project Properties dialog box to specify what Visual Basic does when you run the project: Wait for your input, automatically start a specific page designer in the browser, and so on. You can also indicate whether to open a new instance of Internet Explorer or use an existing instance.

When you compile the application to create a DLL, Visual Basic creates an HTML file for each page in the application. Each file contains an `<object>` tag that references the associated DLL, where the project's compiled code is located. The page also contains the text and HTML tags that define the page elements.

Packaging and Deploying a DHTML Application

The process of packaging and deploying a DHTML application is very similar to ActiveX controls and ActiveX documents, which are discussed on Days 2 and 3. You use the Package and Deployment wizard to create the project's distribution files first and then to deploy them to diskettes, Internet sites, and so on. The same security-related concerns of digitally signing your files, and marking them as safe for scripting and initialization, hold for DHTML applications as well. Please refer back to earlier chapters for details.

Summary

Today's lesson completes the coverage of DHTML, one of the most powerful technologies that Visual Basic provides for the Web programmer. Events are key to DHTML application programming, and you must understand the application's internal events, as well as how to respond to user events, if you are to be an effective programmer. You have seen how user events in a DHTML application differ from the events in a regular Visual Basic application, both in the way they are named and in that events bubble up the object hierarchy.

You also looked at several other areas, including the use of the <div> and <span> tags to group and isolate page elements. DHTML is a very flexible tool, one which I think you'll be using often.

Q&A

Q In the DHTML object hierarchy, which object's lifetime events are of most use to the programmer? What are the main events that occur in this object's lifetime?

A The DHTMLPage object generates the lifetime events that the programmer needs to be the most concerned with. These are Initialize, Load, Unload, and Terminate.

Q When responding to a mouse or keyboard event, how does a DHTML program obtain information about the details of the event, such as which key was pressed or which mouse button was clicked?

A Details about events are provided by the Event object. This is different from events in a standard Visual Basic project, where such details are usually passed as arguments to the corresponding event procedure.

Q What mouse events fire when the mouse cursor is moved around a DHTML page without clicking?

A OnMouseMove is fired whenever the mouse moves. OnMouseOver and OnMouseOut fire when the cursor enters and leaves, respectively, the area of a page element.

Q What is event bubbling, and why is it useful?

A Event bubbling refers to the way user events, such as mouse clicks, percolate up the object hierarchy. This means that many events can be detected not only by the immediate object that received the event, but also by its parent and so on, up the chain. Event bubbling simplifies the programmer's task because a single event procedure can be written to respond to events that have bubbled up from several elements.

Q How can you programmatically manipulate regular text on a DHTML page?

A First, you must assign a unique ID to the Paragraph element(s) that you want to manipulate. Then, in code, you can access members of the Paragraph element's `Style` collection to change its properties.

Q What are the `<div>` and `<span>` tags used for?

A You use `<div>` to group two or more page elements into a group that can be manipulated as a unit. `<span>` does the opposite; it defines a subsection of an element that can be manipulated separately from the rest of the element.

Q How can a DHTML application save information between sessions?

A To be available to another session, data must be saved in a cookie. The procedures `PutProperty` and `GetProperty` are used for this purpose.

10

Workshop

Quiz

1. How are DHTML event names different from standard Visual Basic event names?
2. Which of the `Event` object's properties are *not* read-only.
3. When does a DHTML element's `LostFocus` event fire?
4. How do you stop an event from bubbling farther up in the object hierarchy?
5. What is the HTML stream?
6. What is necessary if you want to be able to access and manipulate an element in code?
7. How do you access element properties that affect its appearance?
8. What are the two ways to provide navigation capabilities in a DHTML page?
9. Which element in a DHTML application does *not* use a Style collection?

WEEK 2

DAY 11

The Internet Transfer Control

In today's lesson you will have a change of pace. Rather than learn how to create applications that run on the Internet, you will learn how to create applications that use the Internet—in other words, a regular standalone Visual Basic program that has the capability to use the Internet for data transfer and similar tasks. As you will see, Visual Basic provides a handy control, with most of the needed capabilities built right in. Today you will learn

- What the Internet Transfer control is and what it can do
- All about Internet Transfer control properties and methods
- How to use the Internet Transfer control for HTTP data transfers

This chapter presents the basics of the Internet Transfer control, concentrating on using the control for Hypertext Transfer Protocol (HTTP) transfers. In tomorrow's lesson you will explore using this control for FTP transfers.

What Is the Internet Transfer Control?

We all know that the Internet is used for transferring data, so it's pretty easy to figure out what the Internet Transfer control (ITC) does. Inside this control, you'll find capabilities for data transfer using either the HTTP or the File Transfer Protocol (FTP). If your Visual Basic program needs to send data over the Internet, the ITC is surely the easiest way to do it.

IT'S NOT A BROWSER

The ITC does not perform the functions of a Web browser. This control transfers data only. It does not display Web pages, does not permit navigation of links, and so on. If you want to retrieve the text of a Web page without displaying it, the ITC is just what you need.

The ITC does not display onscreen when your program is running. Like Visual Basic's Timer control, it works behind the scenes without its own visual interface.

A Quick Demonstration

To give you a feel for the capabilities of the ITC, and for how easy it is to use, let's create a simple demonstration program. With very little effort, you'll create a program that can retrieve data from both HTP and FTP servers.

SELECT YOUR COMPONENTS

To create this project, you need to open the Components dialog box (press Ctrl+T) and select both of the following to controls: Microsoft Internet Transfer Control 6.0 and Microsoft Rich Textbox Control 6.0.

---

1. Start a new Standard EXE project. Add an Internet Transfer control to the form, leaving all its properties at their default values. Add a Rich Textbox control, sizing it to fill most of the form. Change its Text property to a blank string.

2. Add a TextBox control. Change its Name property to txtURL and its Text property to www.microsoft.com or whatever you want the default download location to be.

3. Add a control array of two Command Buttons. Change the Caption property of the button with Index 0 to Go and of the other button to Quit. Your project will now look similar to Figure 11.1.

FIGURE 11.1

Designing the ITC demonstration program.

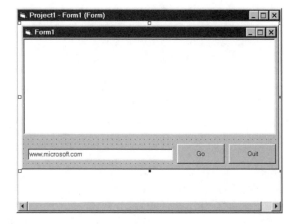

The program's only code goes in the Click event procedure for the command buttons. It is presented in Listing 11.1.

LISTING 11.1   CODE FOR THE ITC DEMONSTRATION PROGRAM

```
Private Sub Command1_Click(Index As Integer)

Select Case Index
    Case 0:
        If txtURL.Text <> "" Then
            RichTextBox1.Text = Inet1.OpenURL(txtURL.Text, _
                icString)
        End If
    Case 1:
        End
End Select

End Sub
```

11

After saving the project, you can run it. Be sure that you are connected to the Internet, first dialing your ISP (Internet service provider) if that's how you connect. When you run the program, enter the desired URL in the Text Box and then click the Go button. The program will retrieve the specified file and display its contents in the Rich Text Box. The data is displayed as unformatted text and not as you would see a Web page in a browser. Figure 11.2 shows the program running, with the Microsoft Web site's main page displayed.

FIGURE 11.2

Running the ITC demonstration program.

GETTING DEFAULT DATA

You can retrieve a specific file with the ITC by including its name as part of the URL. For example, the URL www.microsoft.com/billgates.htm would retrieve the file billgates.htm from the Microsoft Web site (assuming such a file exists). If you do not specify a particular file in the URL, the default data is returned. For Web sites, this is usually index.htm. For an FTP site, the default data is usually a listing of the default directory. To demonstrate this, enter ftp://ftp.microsoft.com as the URL and see what the program displays.

HTTP Transfers with the Internet Transfer Control

Hypertext Transfer Protocol (HTTP), is the fundamental data transfer protocol for the World Wide Web. Web pages are written in hypertext, and HTTP is the protocol used to transfer Web pages from server to client.

FOLLOWING PROTOCOL

Don't be frightened by the term *protocol*. A protocol is simply a set of rules about how to perform a task. HTTP is the universally accepted set of rules for transferring hypertext documents over a network. Although the inner workings of HTTP are complex, the ITC hides all the details.

HTTP is a relatively simple protocol. It is a *stateless* protocol, which means that a connection between the client and the server is not maintained throughout the session. The client sends a request to the server; when the server receives the request, it sends a response to the client. Although originally designed for transmission of text, HTTP can be used to transfer binary files as well.

The OpenURL Method

The easiest way to use the Internet Transfer control is with the OpenURL method (which is used in Listing 11.1). The syntax is as follows:

```
Inet1.OpenURL(URL, DataType)
```

URL is the full URL that you want to open; it can be either an HTTP server or an FTP server. DataType is the type of data being retrieved: text or binary. The two values are icString (the default, value = 0) and icByteArray (value = 1).

The return value of the OpenURL method is the data returned by the URL. This method operates synchronously, which means that the program pauses until the data transfer is complete. The synchronous nature of OpenURL is important, as I will explain soon.

When retrieving text, the data returned by the OpenURL method should be put in a string variable or the equivalent (such as a the Text property of a TextBox control). When retrieving binary data, it should be put in a byte array. You saw in the demonstration program how to retrieve a text file and display it in a Rich TextBox control. The following code fragment shows you how to use OpenURL to retrieve a binary file and save it to disk.

```
Dim b() As Byte
Dim strURL As String, fn As Integer

' Note: this is not a real URL!
strURL = "ftp://ftp.somewhere.com/Datafile.zip"

' Retrieve the file as a byte array.
b() = Inet1.OpenURL(strURL, icByteArray)

fn = Freefile
Open "C:\datafile.zip" For Binary Access Write As #fn
Put #fn, , b()
Close #fn
```

11

> **WATCH THOSE SLASHES!**
> Whereas the Windows operating system uses the backslash character (\) as a separator in paths, most Web servers use the forward slash (/). This can be confusing and is the source of many hard-to-find errors. No solution exists to the problem other than being careful.

The OpenURL method is certainly convenient and is a great example of how Visual Basic makes seemingly difficult tasks simple. Even so, I suggest you use it only for simple and noncritical tasks. There are two reasons for this recommendation. One is that OpenURL operates synchronously, so the program is effectively paused until the request is complete. The ITC's other methods can be used for *asynchronous* operation, which permits your program to perform other tasks while the data transfer is in progress. The other reason to avoid OpenURL is that the ITC's other methods provide greater flexibility. For example, you can retrieve only the header of a Web page and not the entire page.

These other methods operate using Visual Basic's event-driven programming model. When the program requests a data transfer, the ITC starts carrying out the request in the background while your program is free to continue performing other tasks. When some data has been received, an event is fired to notify the program. Code in the associated event procedure retrieves the data from the ITC's internal buffer. This process is repeated until all the data has been downloaded. To use these other methods, you need to understand the ITC's one event.

The StateChanged Event

The ITC has only one event, StateChanged. As the event name suggests, it fires whenever the state of the control changes. *State* refers to the connection status of the control, the receipt of some data, and similar occurrences—in other words, any communication event that your program might need to know about. The StateChanged event procedure has the following declaration:

Inet1_StateChanged(ByVal *NewState* As Integer)

NewState is a value identifying the new state of the control. The possible values for this argument are described in Table 11.1.

TABLE 11.1 STATE VALUES FOR THE STATECHANGED EVENT

Constant	Value	Control Status
IcNone	0	None to report
IcResolvingHost	1	Looking up the IP address of the specified host computer
IcHostResolved	2	Has found the IP address of the specified host computer
IcConnecting	3	Connecting to the host computer
IcConnected	4	Connected to the host computer
IcRequesting	5	Sending a request to the host computer
IcRequestSent	6	Successfully sent a request
IcReceivingResponse	7	Receiving a response from the host computer
IcResponseReceived	8	Received a response from the host computer
IcDisconnecting	9	Disconnecting from the host computer
IcDisconnected	10	Successfully disconnected from the host computer
IcError	11	An error occurred in communicating with the host computer
IcResponseCompleted	12	Request completed, all data received

When an error has occurred, StateChanged is passed icError. This is important because many things can go wrong when you are trying to transfer data over a network. The ITC has two properties, ResponseInfo and ResponseCode, that simplify the task of dealing with errors. ResponseCode provides a numerical code of the most recent error, and ResponseInfo provides a text description.

In your program, you will use the StateChanged event to respond to changes in communication status. You can also use this event to provide the user with status messages giving information on what tasks the ITC is doing or has completed. The code to do this is presented in Listing 11.2. This example uses a Text Box named txtStatus to display the status messages. You can also use other methods, such as a status bar, to display the messages. When an error occurs, as indicated by the value icError, this code uses the two properties ResponseCode and ResponseInfo to provide information on the nature of the error.

LISTING 11.2 USING THE STATECHANGED EVENT TO DISPLAY STATUS MESSAGES

```
Private Sub Inet1_StateChanged(ByVal State As Integer)

Select Case State
    Case icResolvingHost
        txtStatus.Text = "Looking up IP address of host computer"
    Case icHostResolved
        txtStatus.Text = "IP address found"
    Case icConnecting
        txtStatus.Text = "Connecting to host computer"
    Case icConnected
        txtStatus.Text = "Connected"
    Case icRequesting
        txtStatus.Text = "Sending a request to host computer"
    Case icRequestSent
        txtStatus.Text = "Request sent"
    Case icReceivingResponse
        txtStatus.Text = "Receiving a response from host computer"
    Case icResponseReceived
        txtStatus.Text = "Response received"
    Case icDisconnecting
        txtStatus.Text = "Disconnecting from host computer"
    Case icDisconnected
        txtStatus.Text = "Disconnected"
    Case icError
        txtStatus.Text = "Error " & Inet1.ResponseCode & _
            " " & Inet1.ResponseInfo
    Case icResponseCompleted
        txtStatus.Text = "Request completed - all data received"
End Select

End Sub
```

11

You can see this at work by making some easy modifications to the demonstration project created in Listing 11.1. Add another Text Box to the form, assigning it the Name of txtStatus. Put the code from Listing 11.2 in the Inet1_StateChanged event procedure and then run the program. As shown in Figure 11.3, the program will display messages in the status Text Box while it is transferring data.

FIGURE 11.3

Using the StateChanged *event to display status messages.*

As Listing 11.2 makes clear, StateChanged events are generated by the OpenURL method even though, given that this method operates synchronously, the events are not needed other than to provide status messages.

Retrieving Data Asynchronously

You have seen how the StateChanged event works, and now you can continue exploring how to perform asynchronous data transfer with the ITC. The specific methods that you use will be covered soon, but in any case, you will need to retrieve the data from the control's internal buffer after it has been received. This is done with the GetChunk method, which has the following syntax:

```
Inet1.GetChunk( datasize [,datatype] )
```

The *datasize* argument is a type Long that specifies how many bytes of data to retrieve from the buffer. The optional *datatype* argument specifies whether the data is binary or text. You use the constants icString and icByte for this argument (the same as you use with the OpenURL method). Trying to retrieve more bytes of data than are present in the buffer simply returns whatever data is available. If you retrieve only part of the available data, the remaining data remains in the buffer to be retrieved the next time GetChunk is called.

When should your program call GetChunk? When the StateChanged event fires, indicating that data has been received. The two events of interest are icResponseReceived and icResponseCompleted. Place the calls to GetChunk in the StateChanged event procedure, to be executed only if one of these two states has occurred.

Can you be sure that a single call to GetChunk will retrieve all the data in the ITC's buffer? No, so you need to use a loop to allow for the chance that more than one call to GetChunk will be necessary. As soon as the GetChunk method returns nothing, you know that the buffer has been emptied. This is illustrated in Listing 11.3, which shows code that will retrieve the entire contents of the ITC's buffer and display it in a Rich TextBox control named RTB1.

LISTING 11.3   USING THE GETCHUNK METHOD TO RETRIEVE DATA

```
Private Sub Inet1_StateChanged(ByVal State As Integer)

Dim temp1, temp2

Select Case State
    ' Other State cases not shown.
    Case icResponseCompleted
        temp1 = ""
        temp2 = ""
        Do
            temp1 = Inet1.GetChunk(512, icString)
            temp2 = temp2 & temp1
        Loop Until temp1 = ""
        RTB1.Text = temp2
End Select

End Sub
```

You might be wondering what size chunks of data you should get with each call to GetChunk. In one sense, it really does not matter, because if your code is written properly, you'll retrieve all the data regardless of the chunk size. For efficiency, however, you should not work in small chunks. I have used chunk sizes of 512 and 1024 with good results.

> **WHAT, NO DATA?**
>
> Occurrence of the icResponseReceived state does not always mean that data is in the buffer. Some other operations, such as handshaking with an FTP site, can result in this state without any data being placed in the buffer. A well-designed program takes this possibility into account. If, however, you wait for icResponseCompleted, you know that all data has been received.

11

The Execute Method

The most flexible of the ITC's methods is `Execute`. This method can be used to send commands to the remote computer. The syntax is

```
Inet1.Execute (url, command, data, requestHeaders)
```

The optional `url` argument specifies the remote computer to which the command will be sent. If the `url` argument is omitted, the control's `URL` property is used. The `command` argument is the command to be sent (explained next). The `data` and `requestHeaders` arguments are used for extra information required by certain commands.

What commands can you send with the `Execute` method? It depends on the connection protocol that is in use. FTP commands are covered later in the chapter. For an HTTP connection, you have these commands available:

- `GET`   Retrieves data from the server
- `HEAD`   Retrieves header information from the server
- `POST`   Sends information required to complete a request
- `PUT`   Uploads a file to the server

The `POST` and `PUT` commands are for advanced use and require a thorough knowledge of the details of the HTTP protocol, so I will not discuss these commands further. You use the `HEAD` command to retrieve the HTTP headers only. The headers are intercepted by the ITC and will not be placed in the buffer, so the header data itself is not available to you. The `HEAD` command is most commonly used to verify that a URL is working while avoiding the overhead of retrieving the URL's entire content with the `GET` command. When you execute the `HEAD` command, success is indicated by the `StateChanged` event firing with the `icResponseCompleted` code; you then know that the URL is functional.

By far, `GET` is the most common command sent with the `Execute` method. The `GET` command results in the data being placed in the ITC's internal buffer. You use the procedures explained earlier in this chapter to retrieve the data from the buffer, using the `GetChunk` method. Here are some illustrations of using `Execute` to send the `GET` command:

To download the default home page from the Ford Corporation:

```
Inet1.Execute "http://www.ford.com", "GET"
```

To retrieve the Visual Basic page from my personal Web site:

```
Inet1.Execute "http://www.pgacon.com/visualbasic.htm", "GET"
```

USING GET WITH CGI SCRIPTS

The GET command can be used to submit data to common gateway interface (CGI) scripts. One common example is the submittal of queries to Web search engines. Of course, you must know the correct query syntax for the particular search engine. The following code, for example, will connect to the Yahoo search engine and return references to Japan:

```
Inet1.Execute "http://search.yahoo.com/bin/search?p=japan" , "GET"
```

INTERNET TRANSFER CONTROL ERRORS

It's particularly important to be on the lookout for errors when using the ITC. Certain errors are easy to deal with because they trigger the StateChanged event with the icError argument. For example, this will occur if you try to connect to a nonfunctioning Web site or if your Internet connection is not functioning properly.

Other "errors" are trickier. They do not trigger a StateChanged event. In fact, they're not considered real errors in the usual sense because the program is still functioning properly. If you request a file and the Web site is functioning, but the file does not exist, no error occurs. Rather, the HTTP host returns an Object Not Found message. This is an error in the sense that the user is not able to retrieve the data requested. A program needs to be on the alert for messages returned from the server, indicating that something has gone wrong.

11

Properties of the Internet Transfer Control

You have learned about some of the ITC's properties, but there are a lot of other properties that I have not mentioned. Many of these other properties rarely need to be changed, but in some circumstances you might need to change some of them from their default values.

- AccessType specifies how the control will access the Internet. There are three possible settings:

    icUseDefault (the default; value = 0). The control uses the access settings that are specified in the Windows registry to access the Internet.

    icDirect (value = 1). The control has a direct connection to the Internet.

    icNamedProxy (value = 2). The control uses a proxy server. The proxy server must be specified in the control's Proxy property.

- Document specifies the name of the default document, the file that will be used with the Execute method if one is not specified in the method's arguments. If this property is left blank, the server's default document is returned.

- Password specifies the password used when the control is logging on to a remote server.

- Protocol specifies the Internet protocol to use with the Execute method. The possible settings for this property are shown in Table 11.2. This property interacts with ITC's URL property and also with the protocol specification (if any) included in the URL passed to the OpenURL and Execute methods. For instance, if Execute is called with a URL that includes the http:// specification (such as http://www.microsoft.com), the Protocol property updates to reflect the HTTP protocol.

TABLE 11.2 SETTINGS FOR THE INTERNET TRANSFER CONTROL'S PROTOCOL PROPERTY

Constant	Value	Protocol
IcUnknown	0	Unknown
IcDefault	1	Default protocol
IcFTP	2	File Transfer Protocol
IcReserved	3	Reserved for future use
IcHTTP	4	Hypertext Transfer Protocol
IcHTTPS	5	Secure Hypertext Transfer Protocol

- Proxy specifies the name of the proxy server used to communicate with the Internet. This property is used only if the AccessType property is set to icNamedProxy.

- RequestTimeout specifies the time, in seconds, that the control will wait for a response before a time-out expires. If no response occurs within the specified time, and if the request was made with the OpenURL method (synchronous), an error is generated. If the request was made with the Execute method, the StateChanged event will occur with an error code. Set RequestTimeout to zero to disable time-outs (the control will wait as long as needed).

- ResponseCode returns an error code when the StateChanged event occurs with the icError state.

- ResponseInfo returns a description of the most recent ITC error.

- StillExecuting returns True if the control is busy, False if not.

- URL specifies the URL, including protocol, that is used by the Execute or OpenURL methods. If a URL is specified as an argument to one of these method's argument, the URL property updates to reflect that URL.

- UserName specifies the username that will be sent as a logon name to remote computers. If this property is blank, anonymous is sent.

Some of these properties are used with FTP transfers, a topic covered in Chapter 5, "Real-World ActiveX."

An HTTP Demonstration

Now that you understand the fundamentals of how the ITC operates, it's time to see it at work in a real application. Sure, it's a simple matter to throw together a program that uses the control to download a Web page, as you saw earlier in the chapter. In the real world, however, such simple applications are rarely useful. You'll learn much more by trying something that performs a needed task. That's the aim of this section.

The application I will develop is a link checker. Given a list of Web page URLs, it checks each link to see whether it is functioning. My need for such an application grew out of my hobby, stamp collecting. On my Web page, I maintain an extensive list of Web links related to the hobby, and I find that many other collectors find this resource very useful. The problem is that Web pages often move around and disappear. A collector will put up his or her own stamp-related Web page, and I will link to it. Then he or she loses interest and removes the page or moves to a different URL, and all of a sudden my link is dead. Visitors to my site will be less than thrilled if a large proportion of my links do not work.

With more than 600 links, the idea of checking them manually on a regular basis was out of the question. I needed to automate the process. Because I keep the links database in a Microsoft Excel worksheet, it occurred to me that I might write a Visual Basic program that would interface with Excel. Specifically, the program would do the following:

1. Open the worksheet, using OLE Automation.

2. Use OLE Automation to read the first URL and see whether it's functioning.

3. Write data back to the worksheet, indicating the result for the URL.

4. Repeat the preceding steps for all URLs in the list.

5. Save and close the worksheet.

HOW DOES OLE AUTOMATION WORK?

OLE Automation is a Windows technology by which separate programs can send data and commands back and forth. A program must expose one or more objects that are related to the kind of data the program works with. For example, the Excel application exposes the Application and Workbook objects (among others). If a Visual Basic program creates an instance of such an object (which does not display onscreen), it has access to the object's data and commands. These commands and data are, of course, application-specific.

11

> This is a book on Internet programming, so I will not be covering OLE Automation any
> further. You can refer to the Visual Basic documentation for further information.

When the program has completed its task, each record in the Excel worksheet will contain an entry specifying the current status of the URL. Rather than simply mark URLs as okay or bad, I decided it would be more useful to save specific information about why a failed link failed.

With the help of the Internet Transfer control, this task was readily accomplished. I designed the program to run minimized in the background so that the user could continue using the computer for other tasks. The number of links already checked is displayed in the program's title bar and therefore also displayed on the taskbar icon when the program is minimized, enabling the user to keep track of progress. When all URLs have been checked, the program closes the worksheet and displays a summary report.

> **IDENTIFYING EXCEL COLUMNS**
> When you are using Excel, columns in a worksheet are identified by letters, starting with
> A for the farthest left column. In OLE Automation, however, columns are identified by
> number: A is 1, B is 2, and so on.

My links worksheet is arranged so that the URL is kept in column C, the third from the left, and the information as to whether the link is okay is kept in column E. Data begins in row 4. Your program must have this information so that it will know where to look for and put data. If you adopt this program to your own links database, you will have to adjust this information accordingly. It is placed in constants defined at the beginning of the code.

To create the project, start a Standard EXE project. On the form, place a TextBox control and set its Multiline property to True. Add a control array of two Command Buttons with the captions Start and Quit. Add four Label controls and finally an Internet Transfer control. At this stage, the form will look similar to Figure 11.4.

Listing 11.4 shows the program's complete code. I have included detailed comments in the code so that you can see how it works. If you do not understand the details of the OLE Automation statements, that's okay. Enter them as shown because, rest assured, they work. You must attach the Excel type library for this program to work. This is done in the References dialog (select Project, References and check the Microsoft Excel X.0 Object Library entry).

FIGURE 11.4

*Designing the link
checker application.*

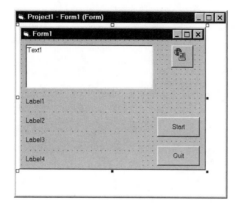

WHERE IS EXCEL?

You must have Microsoft Excel installed on your system for this program to work.

LISTING 11.4   CODE IN THE LINK CHECKER PROGRAM

11

```
Option Explicit

' Put the full filename and path to your file here.
Const FILENAME = "c:\documents\stamps\links.xls"

' Row and column locations for the data.
Const STARTROW = 4
Const URL_COLUMN = 3
Const LINKSTATUS_COLUMN = 5

' Declare a variable to hold the reference
' to the Excel worksheet.
Dim XLObj As Excel.Application

Private Sub Command1_Click(Index As Integer)

Select Case Index
    Case 0 'Start
        Command1(0).Enabled = False
        Call CheckLinks
        Command1(0).Enabled = True
    Case 1 ' Quit
        End
End Select
```

continues

LISTING 11.4 CONTINUED

```
End Sub

Private Sub Form_Load()

' Create the Excel object.
Set XLObj = CreateObject("Excel.Application")
' Open the specified worksheet
XLObj.Workbooks.Open FILENAME
' Set the transfer protocol.
Inet1.Protocol = icHTTP

End Sub

Public Sub CheckLinks()

Dim row As Integer, url As String
Dim buf As String, msg As String, fnf As Integer
Dim snf As Integer, tout As Integer, ok As Integer

' Necessary to catch time-out errors.
On Error Resume Next
' Make row equal to the Worksheet row where
' your data starts.
row = STARTROW

' Time-out total
tout = 0
' File not found total.
fnf = 0
' Link OK total.
ok = 0
' Server not found total.
snf = 0

' Minimize the program's form so that it will run
' in the background while the user performs other tasks.
' The taskbar icon will display its progress.

Form1.WindowState = 1

' Loop through all the URLs.
Do
    ' Get a URL
    url = XLObj.Cells(row, URL_COLUMN)
    ' If it's empty, we are done.
    If url = "" Then Exit Do
    ' Try to open the URL.
    Text1.Text = Inet1.OpenURL(url)
    ' Essential to avoid tying up the system.
```

```
    DoEvents
    ' If the URL returned any text, put the
    ' first 50 characters in a buffer. Error
    ' messages will be found here.
    If Len(Text1.Text) > 50 Then
        buf = Left(Text1.Text, 50)
    Else
        buf = Text1.Text
    End If
    ' Catch a time-out error.
    If Err = 35761 Then
        msg = "Timed out"
        tout = tout + 1
        Err.Clear
    ' If nothing is returned, it usually means
    ' that the server was not found.
    ElseIf Text1.Text = "" Then
        msg = "Server not found"
        snf = snf + 1
    ' If error 404 is returned from the URL,
    ' it means the server was found, but
    ' the requested file was not present.
    ElseIf InStr(1, buf, "404") Then
        msg = "File not found"
        fnf = fnf + 1
    ' Otherwise, the link is okay.
    Else
        msg = "OK"
        ok = ok + 1
    End If
    ' Put the result in the proper worksheet column.
    XLObj.Cells(row, LINKSTATUS_COLUMN) = msg
    ' Move to the next row.
    row = row + 1
    ' Display current status on form. The form
    ' caption shows the total of links checked.
    Form1.Caption = ok + fnf + snf + tout
    ' The individual labels show the totals
    ' for each result category.
    Label1.Caption = "OK: " & ok
    Label2.Caption = "File not found: " & fnf
    Label3.Caption = "Server not found: " & snf
    Label4.Caption = "Timed out: " & tout
Loop While True

' When all links have been checked,
' restore the form.
Form1.WindowState = 0
' Close the worksheet. Excel will prompt
```

11

continues

LISTING 11.4 CONTINUED

```
' the user to save changes.
XLObj.Workbooks.Close
' Delete the object.
Set XLObj = Nothing
' Display a summary of results.
buf = "OK: " & ok & vbCrLf
buf = buf & "Server not found: " & snf & vbCrLf
buf = buf + "File not found: " & fnf & vbCrLf
buf = buf & "Timed out: " & tout
MsgBox (buf)

End Sub
```

When you run the program, it will minimize itself and continue to work in the background while you do other things. The program's taskbar icon will display the number of links checked so far. At any time, you can restore the program to see detailed statistics, as well as the text returned by each URL displayed in the Text Box. After all links have been checked, the program will display a summary report and then terminate. With a slow Internet connection, this program can take 30 seconds or more to check each link. Figure 11.5 shows the program in operation.

FIGURE 11.5

Running the link checker program.

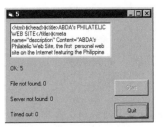

You might be asking yourself why I used the OpenURL method in this program instead of Execute. Wouldn't the latter method's asynchronous operation have been superior? Not in this case. Using asynchronous data retrieval lets your program do other tasks in the meanwhile, but there is nothing else for this program to be doing. Using synchronous transfer with OpenURL has no effect on the ability to use other programs, so it is not a problem.

Summary

I think you'll agree that the Internet Transfer control can be extremely useful. With relatively simple programming, it lets you retrieve text and binary files from Web sites. It is essential for programming tasks that require you to retrieve Web data for processing, as opposed to merely viewing it in a browser.

In tomorrow's lesson, you will continue the exploration of this control, seeing how it is used for FTP transfers.

Q&A

Q How does the Internet Transfer control differ from a Web browser?

A A browser is specialized to download Web pages and display them as intended, with images, functioning hyperlinks, and so on. The ITC downloads hypertext and other files and makes them available as raw data to your program.

Q What is the main difference between a synchronous transfer with OpenURL and an asynchronous transfer with Execute?

A With a synchronous transfer, the program cannot do anything else until the transfer is complete. Asynchronous transfer works in the background while the program does other things.

Workshop

Quiz

1. What transfer protocols can the ITC use?
2. What event is fired when the ITC completes a download?
3. How can your program know that an error has occurred in the ITC?
4. What method is used to get data from the ITC's buffer during an asynchronous data transfer?
5. Does the ITC's Execute method always use the URL in the control's URL property?

Exercise

Write a Visual Basic application that uses the ITC to retrieve the contents of an HTML document whose URL you specify, and then saves it to your local disk under a new name.

11

DAY 12

Using the ITC for FTP

Of the two transfer protocols that the Internet Transfer control can handle, FTP is undoubtedly the more flexible. Not only can you upload and download files, but you also have the power to perform file management functions such as deleting files and creating folders on the remote computer. The ITC hides most of the details of FTP from the programmer, but there are still quite a few things you need to know. Today you will learn

- What the FTP protocol can do
- Details of FTP logon procedures
- How to use FTP commands
- How to use FTP in a real-world Visual Basic program

You should read Day 11, "The Internet Transfer Control," before starting this chapter. ITC fundamentals that you need to know are explained there.

What Is FTP?

Why do you need another protocol for transferring files? Isn't HTTP sufficient? Indeed, the HTTP protocol is all you need in some situations, but other times you will need to use FTP. Although FTP is similar to HTTP in that it is a protocol for transferring files between computers, it is significantly more powerful. As is always the case, more power means more complexity, but nothing in life is free! Most of the complexities of FTP are hidden from you by the Internet Transfer control (ITC).

FTP is not a stateless protocol, because a control connection is maintained between client and server for the duration of an FTP session. In fact, the FTP protocol uses two distinct connections between client and server, one for control commands and the other for data. This is shown in Figure 12.1.

FIGURE 12.1

An FTP session uses two separate connections between the client and server.

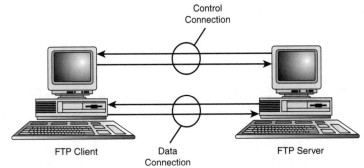

From the user's perspective, FTP is more powerful because it permits not only file downloads but also uploads, as well as file management capabilities on the remote computer, such as deleting files, creating folders, and so on. From the site administrator's point of view, FTP offers much more control over site access. Different people can be given various privileges, controlled by passwords.

CREATING AN FTP SITE

To create an FTP site, you need to run an FTP server on your computer. A server will let you set up one or more FTP folders; assign usernames, permissions, and passwords; and do other related tasks. The server will automatically respond to requests coming in over your Internet connection. Several good FTP servers are available as shareware.

Logging On with FTP

Unlike HTTP servers, FTP servers require that every user log on. There is an unrestricted access type of logon, called *anonymous logon*, as well as specific user logons assigned by the FTP site administrator. Even for anonymous logon, your program must send a username and password.

ANONYMOUS FTP LOGON

Anonymous logon is used to provide the general public with limited access to an FTP site. Most commonly, people who log on this way can do nothing except download files from a limited set of folders. Anonymous users cannot delete files or cause any other mischief. To log on as an anonymous user, the typical procedure is to send "anonymous" as the user name and your email address as the password.

You specify the username and password that are sent by the Internet Transfer control by setting its Username and Password properties. If the UserName property is null or blank, "anonymous" is sent. The Password property is more complicated because it works in conjunction with the UserName property. Table 12.1 gives the details.

TABLE 12.1   INTERACTIONS BETWEEN THE Password AND Username PROPERTIES OF THE INTERNET TRANSFER CONTROL

If the Username Property Is...	And the Password Property Is...	This Password Is Sent to the Server
Null or blank string	Null or blank string	User's email address
Non-null string	Null or blank string	Blank string
Null	Non-null string	Error
Non-null string	Non-null string	Password property

You can see that one Password/Username combination is not permitted: You cannot have a null Username property and a non-null Password property at the same time. If you leave both these properties blank, the ITC will attempt a standard anonymous FTP logon, which consists of sending "anonymous" as the UserName and your email address as the password.

> **NULL VERSUS BLANK**
>
> It's important to remember that in Visual Basic a blank string is not the same as null. Null is a special value, identified by the NULL keyword, that is used to indicate specifically that a variable does not contain valid data. Because a blank string may in fact be perfectly valid, the requirement for this distinction is obvious.

The ITC will sometimes not send "anonymous" as the username when the UserName property is blank. This is, I believe, a bug and might be fixed by the time you read this. In any case, you can easily work around it by assigning the string "anonymous" to the Username property.

> **IDENTIFYING FTP SERVERS**
>
> Most FTP servers have ftp as the first part of their URL, such as ftp.microsoft.com. This is not a requirement, however, and some URLs that do not start with ftp may have an operating server.

FTP with the OpenURL Method

The OpenURL method is the easiest way to perform some FTP tasks. The following obtains the directory of an FTP site (the directory is an FTP site's default file):

```
Text1.Text = Inet1.OpenURL("ftp://ftp.somesite.com", icString)
```

To download a file from an FTP site, you need to use binary mode, unless you are sure it is a text file (although binary mode works fine for text files, too):

```
Dim b() as Byte
b() = Inet1.OpenURL("ftp://ftp.somesite.com/program.exe" , _
    icByteArray)
```

Then you can save the downloaded file to disk as follows:

```
Open "c:\program.exe" For Binary as #1
Put #1,, b()
Close #1
```

As you will see, however, the FTP protocol includes specific commands for tasks such as downloading and saving a file, and they are easier to use.

FTP with the `Execute` Method

The `Execute` method provides many more capabilities than does `OpenURL`. You saw this method used for HTTP transfers in Day 11. Using `Execute` with FTP is simpler than using it for HTTP, because only two of the method's four arguments are required. For FTP tasks, the syntax of `Execute` is as follows:

```
Inet1.Execute (url, operation)
```

The *url* argument is the URL of the FTP site, including the directory, if desired. The *Operation* argument is a string containing the FTP command and any parameters needed by the command. FTP commands are always formatted this way: The command itself and any needed parameters are combined in a single string, separated by a single space. You will learn more about specific FTP commands later in the chapter.

FTP data retrieved by the ITC is handled in two different ways, depending on the specific FTP command. Some data, such as a returned response to a `DIR` command, is placed in the ITC's buffer and must be read using the `GetChunk` method. In Day 11, I provide a detailed explanation of using `GetChunk` for HTTP data transfers. It works the same way with FTP.

Other data, such as a file being transferred with `GET`, is transferred directly to disk without ever appearing in the ITC's buffer. There is no need to use `GetChunk`, and programming is simplified.

Do	Don't
DO remember that your FTP commands are carried out by the remote FTP server. Although FTP command syntax is reasonably well standardized, you cannot be sure that all FTP commands will be understood by all servers. If a command doesn't work, the problem might be with the server.	**DON'T** try to execute FTP commands that are not permitted with your logon privileges. If you do, the server will return an error message.

12

FTP Commands

FTP commands provide you with a lot of flexibility. You can transfer files in both directions, change to different folders on the remote computer, rename and delete files, and so on. Remember that the commands you may use depend on your logon privileges. If you have used anonymous logon, you will only be able to view directory listings and download files.

Table 12.2 lists the most commonly needed FTP commands and explains what they do. You will see some of the commands at work in the demonstration program later in the chapter.

TABLE 12.2 FTP COMMANDS YOU ARE MOST LIKELY TO NEED

Commands and Arguments	Description
CD path	Change to the remote directory path.
CDUP or CD..	Change to the parent directory.
CLOSE	Close the current FTP connection.
DELETE file1	Delete the remote file file1.
DIR file1 or LS file1	Search the current directory for the file specified in file1. Wildcards are permitted but must use the remote host's syntax. If file1 is not given, this command returns a listing of the current working directory. LS returns a less detailed listing than DIR.
MKDIR path	Create the remote directory path.
PUT file1 file2 or SEND file1 file2	Copy local file1 to remote file2.
PWD	Return the name of the current remote directory.
QUIT	Terminate the FTP connection.
RECV file1 file2 or GET file1 file2	Copy remote file1 to local file2.
RENAME file1 file2	Rename the remote file1 to file2.
RMDIR path	Delete the remote directory path.
SIZE file1	Return the size in bytes of the file or directory file1.

An FTP Demonstration

Knowing the details of how to perform FTP transfers with the Internet Transfer control is one thing, and actually getting it to work in a functioning program is quite another. The demonstration presented here shows you how the control is used to perform various tasks.

I called the program Simple FTP because that's what it is—a basic, no-frills FTP client. It lets you log on to an FTP server as a registered user or as an anonymous guest and view a listing of the default directory. Other capabilities include changing to different directories and downloading and uploading files (depending, of course, on your permission level at the FTP site).

THE StillExecuting PROPERTY

Any program that uses the ITC must keep track of the StillExecuting property. This is because the Execute method operates asynchronously; therefore, execution may return to your program when the control is still busy with the previous Execute command. If you try to call Execute again, an error will occur. It's necessary, therefore, to check the StillExecuting property and call Execute if, and only if, this property is False.

Listing 12.1 gives the program's objects and properties. Rather than walk you through all the steps of creating this program's interface, it will be quicker to provide an object and properties listing in this format (which is the exact format that Visual Basic itself uses inside FRM files). Each control is listed along with the values of its nondefault properties. By looking at the picture of the program's form (see Figure 12.2) and reading the listing, you will be able to create the program with no trouble.

FIGURE 12.2

The Simple FTP program.

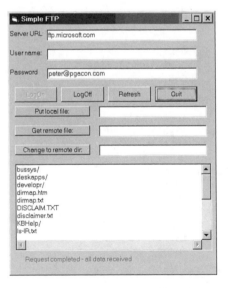

The Simple FTP demonstration program's code is presented in Listing 12.2. After reading this chapter, you will not have any trouble figuring out what's going on. Remember that Simple FTP is a no-frills program, and although it has basic error-handling capabilities, it has no provisions for user errors such as trying to GET a file that doesn't exist.

LISTING 12.1   OBJECTS AND PROPERTIES IN SIMPLE FTP

```
VERSION 5.00
Object = "{48E59290-9880-11CF-9754-00AA00C00908}#1.0#0"; "MSINET.OCX"
Begin VB.Form Form1
   BorderStyle     =   1  'Fixed Single
   Caption         =   "Simple FTP"
   ClientHeight    =   6216

   ClientLeft      =   48
   ClientTop       =   336
   ClientWidth     =   5244
   LinkTopic       =   "Form1"
   MaxButton       =   0   'False
   MinButton       =   0   'False
   ScaleHeight     =   6216
   ScaleWidth      =   5244
   StartUpPosition =   3  'Windows Default
   Begin VB.CommandButton Command2
      Caption      =     "Change to remote dir:"
      Height       =     255
      Index        =     2
      Left         =     120
      TabIndex     =     17
      Top          =     3000
      Width        =     1932
   End
   Begin VB.CommandButton Command2
      Caption      =     "Get remote file:"
      Height       =     255
      Index        =     1
      Left         =     120
      TabIndex     =     16
      Top          =     2520
      Width        =     1932
   End
   Begin VB.CommandButton Command2
      Caption      =     "Put local file:"
      Height       =     255
      Index        =     0
      Left         =     120
      TabIndex     =     15
      Top          =     2040
      Width        =     1932
   End
   Begin VB.TextBox txtRemoteDir
      Height       =     285
      Left         =     2280
      TabIndex     =     14
      Top          =     3000
```

```
         Width           =    2772
End
Begin InetCtlsObjects.Inet ITC1
   Left                  =    2160
   Top                   =    4680
   _ExtentX              =    995
   _ExtentY              =    995
   _Version              =    393216
End
Begin VB.TextBox txtRemoteFileName
   Height                =    285
   Left                  =    2280
   TabIndex              =    13
   Top                   =    2520
   Width                 =    2772
End
Begin VB.TextBox txtLocalFileName
   Height                =    285
   Left                  =    2280
   TabIndex              =    12
   Top                   =    2040
   Width                 =    2772
End
Begin VB.CommandButton Command1
   Caption               =    "Quit"
   Height                =    375
   Index                 =    3
   Left                  =    3720
   TabIndex              =    11
   Top                   =    1560
   Width                 =    1095
End
Begin VB.CommandButton Command1
   Caption               =    "LogOff"
   Height                =    375
   Index                 =    2
   Left                  =    1320
   TabIndex              =    10
   Top                   =    1560
   Width                 =    1095
End
Begin VB.CommandButton Command1
   Caption               =    "Refresh"
   Height                =    375
   Index                 =    1
   Left                  =    2520
   TabIndex              =    9
   Top                   =    1560
   Width                 =    1095
End
```

12

continues

LISTING 12.1 CONTINUED

```
Begin VB.CommandButton Command1
   Caption          =   "LogOn"
   Height           =   375
   Index            =   0
   Left             =   120
   TabIndex         =   8
   Top              =   1560
   Width            =   1095
End
Begin VB.TextBox txtDir
   Height           =   2175
   Left             =   120
   Locked           =   -1   'True
   MultiLine        =   -1   'True
   ScrollBars       =   3    'Both
   TabIndex         =   6
   Top              =   3480
   Width            =   5052
End
Begin VB.TextBox txtPassword
   Height           =   285
   Left             =   960
   TabIndex         =   2
   Top              =   1080
   Width            =   3855
End
Begin VB.TextBox txtUserName
   Height           =   285
   Left             =   960
   TabIndex         =   1
   Top              =   600
   Width            =   3855
End
Begin VB.TextBox txtURL
   Height           =   285
   Left             =   960
   TabIndex         =   0
   Top              =   120
   Width            =   3855
End
Begin VB.Label lblStatus
   ForeColor        =   &H000000FF&
   Height           =   252
   Left             =   360
   TabIndex         =   7
   Top              =   5760
   Width            =   4332
End
Begin VB.Label Label3
```

```
            Caption         =    "Password"
            Height          =    252
            Left            =    0
            TabIndex        =    5
            Top             =    1080
            Width           =    852
        End
        Begin VB.Label Label2
            Caption         =    "User name:"
            Height          =    252
            Left            =    0
            TabIndex        =    4
            Top             =    600
            Width           =    972
        End
        Begin VB.Label Label1
            Caption         =    "Server URL:"
            Height          =    252
            Left            =    0
            TabIndex        =    3
            Top             =    120
            Width           =    972
        End
    End
End
```

LISTING 12.2   CODE IN SIMPLE FTP

```
Option Explicit

Private Sub Command1_Click(Index As Integer)

Select Case Index
    Case 0 ' Logon button
        txtDir.Text = ""
        Call LogOn
    Case 1 ' Refresh button
        Call RefreshDirList
    Case 2 ' LogOff button
        txtDir.Text = ""
        ITC1.Cancel
        Call SetCmdButtonState(False)
        lblStatus.Caption = "Logged Off"
    Case 3 ' End button
        ITC1.Cancel
        End
End Select

End Sub
```

12

continues

LISTING 12.2   CONTINUED

```
Private Sub Command2_Click(Index As Integer)

Dim s As String

Select Case Index
    Case 0 ' Put a local file.
        If txtLocalFileName.Text = "" Then
            s = "You must enter the name of the " & vbCrLf
            s = s & "local filer to upload."
            MsgBox (s)
            Exit Sub
        End If
        Call PutLocalFile
    Case 1 ' Get a remote file
        If txtRemoteFileName.Text = "" Then
            s = "You must specify the name of the " & vbCrLf
            s = s & "remote file to download."
            MsgBox (s)
            Exit Sub
        End If
        Call GetRemoteFile
    Case 2 ' Change directory
        If txtRemoteDir.Text = "" Then
            s = "Please enter the name of the new directory."
            MsgBox (s)
            Exit Sub
        End If
        Call ChangeDir
End Select

End Sub

Private Sub Form_Load()

' Set buttons initially for logged off state.
Call SetCmdButtonState(False)

End Sub

Private Sub ITC1_StateChanged(ByVal State As Integer)

Dim Data1 As String, Data2 As String

Select Case State
    Case icResolvingHost
        lblStatus.Caption = _
            "Looking up host computer IP address"
    Case icHostResolved
        lblStatus.Caption = _
```

```
                "IP address found"
        Case icConnecting
            lblStatus.Caption = _
                "Connecting to host computer"
        Case icConnected
            lblStatus.Caption = "Connected to host computer"
        Case icRequesting
            lblStatus.Caption = _
                "Sending a request to host computer"
        Case icRequestSent
            lblStatus.Caption = "Request sent"
        Case icReceivingResponse
            lblStatus.Caption = _
                "Receiving a response from host computer"
        Case icResponseReceived
            lblStatus.Caption = "Response received"
        Case icDisconnecting
            lblStatus.Caption = _
                "Disconnecting from host computer"
        Case icDisconnected
            lblStatus.Caption = "Disconnected from host computer"
        Case icError
            lblStatus.Caption = "Error " _
                & ITC1.ResponseCode & _
                " " & ITC1.ResponseInfo
        Case icResponseCompleted
            lblStatus.Caption = _
                "Request completed successfully."
            ' Loop until you get all chunks.
            Do While True
                Data1 = ITC1.GetChunk(512, icString)
                If Len(Data1) = 0 Then Exit Do
                DoEvents
                Data2 = Data2 & Data1
            Loop
            txtDir.Text = Data2
End Select

End Sub

Public Sub LogOn()

' Logs on to the FTP host specified in the
' txtURL text box and displays the directory.

On Error GoTo GotError

If txtURL = "" Or txtPassword = "" Then
    MsgBox ("You must specify a URL and Password")
```

12

continues

LISTING 12.2   CONTINUED

```
        Exit Sub
    End If

    Command1(0).Enabled = False
    ITC1.Protocol = icFTP
    ITC1.URL = txtURL.Text
    If txtUserName.Text = "" Then
        ITC1.UserName = "anonymous"
    Else
        ITC1.UserName = txtUserName.Text
    End If

    ITC1.Password = txtPassword.Text
    ITC1.Execute , "DIR"
    Call SetCmdButtonState(True)

    Exit Sub

    GotError:

    If Err = 35754 Then
        MsgBox ("Cannot connect to remote host")
    Else
        MsgBox (Err.Description)
    End If
    Call SetCmdButtonState(False)
    ITC1.Cancel

    End Sub

    Public Sub PutLocalFile()

    ' Puts the local file specified in
    ' txtLocalFileName to the remote server.

    Dim RemoteFileName As String, cmd As String

    RemoteFileName = InputBox("Name for remote file?", _
        "Get", txtLocalFileName.Text)

    cmd = "PUT " & RemoteFileName & " " _
        & txtLocalFileName.Text
    If ITCReady(True) Then
        Call SendCommand(cmd)
    End If

    Exit Sub

    End Sub
```

```
Public Sub GetRemoteFile()

' Retrieves the remote file specified in
' the textbox txtRemoteFileName. Stores the
' downloaded file using user-specified name.

Dim LocalFileName As String, cmd As String

On Error GoTo GotError

LocalFileName = InputBox("Name for local file?", _
    "Get", txtRemoteFileName.Text)

cmd = "GET " & txtRemoteFileName.Text & " " & _
    LocalFileName
If ITCReady(True) Then
    Call SendCommand(cmd)
End If

Exit Sub

GotError:
MsgBox (Err.Description)

End Sub

Public Sub ChangeDir()

Dim cmd As String

' Changes to the remote directory specified
' in txtRemoteDir.Text; then displays its
' directory.

cmd = "CD " & txtRemoteDir.Text
If ITCReady(True) Then
    Call SendCommand(cmd)
    Do
        DoEvents
    Loop Until ITCReady(False)
    txtDir.Text = ""
    Call SendCommand("DIR")
End If

End Sub

Public Sub SetCmdButtonState(LoggedOn As Boolean)

Dim x As Integer
```

12

continues

LISTING 12.2   CONTINUED

```
' Enables and disables the program's command buttons
' for the logged on and logged off situations.

If LoggedOn Then
' Logged on state.
    Command1(0).Enabled = False ' Logon button
    Command1(1).Enabled = True ' Refresh button
    Command1(2).Enabled = True ' Logoff button
    For x = 0 To Command2.Count - 1
        Command2(x).Enabled = True
    Next
Else
' Logged off state.
    Command1(0).Enabled = True  ' Logon
    Command1(1).Enabled = False ' Refresh button
    Command1(2).Enabled = False ' Logoff button
    For x = 0 To Command2.Count - 1
        Command2(x).Enabled = False
    Next
End If

End Sub

Public Sub RefreshDirList()

' Refreshes the remote directory listing.

If ITCReady(True) Then
    txtDir.Text = ""
    Call SendCommand("DIR")
End If

End Sub

Public Sub SendCommand(cmd As String)

' Sends the specified command to the
' FTP server,

On Error GoTo GotError

ITC1.Execute , cmd
Exit Sub

GotError:

MsgBox (Err.Description)
Resume Next
```

```
End Sub

Public Function ITCReady(Message As Boolean) _
    As Boolean

' Returns True if ITC1 is ready to execute
' a new command. If the control is busy and
' the Message argument is True, displays an
' error message.

Dim msg As String

If ITC1.StillExecuting Then
    If Message Then
        msg = "The program has not finished "
        msg = msg & " executing your last request." & vbCrLf
        msg = msg & "Please wait then try again later."
        MsgBox (msg)
    End If
    ITCReady = False
Else
    ITCReady = True
End If

End Function
```

Summary

After reading this chapter, you will agree, I think, that FTP is a powerful tool. With the Internet Transfer control to help you, the power of FTP is available to any Visual Basic programmer. After you become familiar with the various FTP commands, the control makes it easy to use FTP in your Visual Basic programs.

12

Q&A

Q From the user's point of view, what are the main differences between HTTP and FTP?

A Although both protocols can be used to transfer files, only FTP provides capabilities for file management with commands for deleting and renaming files on the remote computer and similar tasks.

Q When using the Internet Transfer control for FTP, is the retrieved data always placed in the control's buffer?

A Not always. Some retrieval operations use the buffer, and others place the data directly in a disk file.

Q What is the importance of the ITC's StillExecuting property?

A If this property is True, the control is busy executing a previous request. Trying to send a new command under these conditions will cause an error.

Workshop

Quiz

1. Can anyone log on to an FTP site?

2. What is the standard password that should be sent when you log on to an FTP site as an anonymous user?

3. Can the Internet Transfer control be used to create an FTP server?

4. Do all FTP sites have URLs that start with ftp?

Exercise

Write a text editor program that gives the user the option of opening and saving his files from an FTP site.

DAY 13

Crawling the Web: Creating a Web Search Engine

The World Wide Web is a huge collection of information on every imaginable topic. The information that you need is often available on the Web, but how do you find it? Most people rely on the commercial search engines, and they can be very useful. By creating your own search engine, however, you'll have the power to customize your searches to locate information more efficiently. Today you will learn

- What Web robots are and how they work
- Robot exclusion standards
- Web search algorithms
- Programming your own search engine

What Is a Web Robot?

Computers are supposed to make our lives easier, and the same is true of robots—at least, in science fiction stories. That's the idea with a Web robot: It performs a task so that you don't have to do it yourself. With reference to the World Wide Web, the term *robot* specifically means a program that traverses Web space and retrieves information.

> **ROBOTS, SPIDERS, AND CRAWLERS**
>
> The terms *robot*, *spider*, and *crawler* have much the same meaning for a Web programmer.

What do I mean by *Web space*? It simply refers to the sum total of all Web pages and the links between them. Perhaps this is where the term *spider* came from. If you diagram Web space, it looks like an extremely complex spider's web. Figure 13.1 is a vastly over-simplified idea of what Web space looks like.

FIGURE 13.1

Web space consists of all Web pages and the links between them.

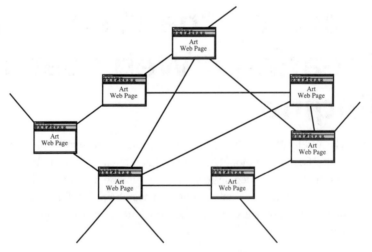

Given the way the Web is structured, some clever person soon came up with the idea that a program could be created that would automatically "crawl" around the Web, using the links to go from place to place (that is, from page to page). At each page, the program could perform various tasks: looking for information, downloading graphics, or whatever. The important thing is not the specifics of what the crawler, or robot, does but rather the concept of crawling.

A Crawling Algorithm

To create a Web crawler, you need an algorithm. This technical-sounding term means a set of specific rules to follow to achieve a desired end. A recipe for baking bread is one example of an algorithm. When you have an algorithm for crawling the Web, you can start writing the code to carry it out.

A Web robot needs a starting place. This can be a single Web site or a group of many sites; it doesn't matter. A robot also needs a termination rule: Under what conditions does it consider itself to be finished? Given a starting place and a termination rule, the algorithm can be written as follows:

1. Put the starting URLs in the URL list.
2. Go to the page specified by the first, or next, URL in the list.
3. Extract all the links from the current page and add them to the list, discarding any duplicates.
4. Perform the search or other task on the current page.
5. Is the termination rule met? If not, go to step 2. If yes, go to step 6.
6. Terminate the process.

Sometimes an algorithm such as this is more easily understood when it is diagrammed. Figure 13.2 shows a diagram, often called a *flow chart*, for this algorithm.

FIGURE 13.2

A flow chart of the Web-crawling algorithm.

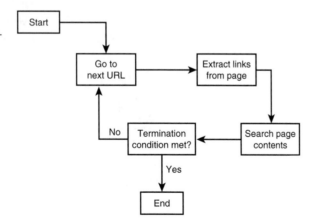

13

Searching Strategies

The way a robot traverses links can be done in two general ways, referred to as *breadth-first* and *depth-first*. A depth-first search follows a chain of links as far as possible and then backs up and follows another chain, and so on, until it is finished. In contrast, a breadth-first search follows each chain only one step down, searching all pages at that level. It then follows each chain down another step and searches that level. Figures 13.3. and 13.4 illustrate the difference in search order that would result from the two methods.

FIGURE 13.3

The order of page naviga-
tion in a depth-first
search.

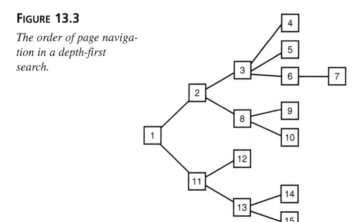

FIGURE 13.4

The order of page naviga-
tion in a breadth-first
search.

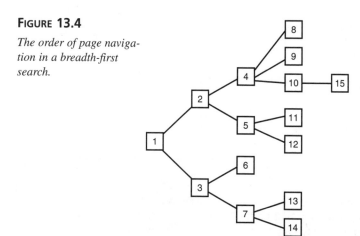

Are there any reasons to prefer one method over the other? Not that I know of.

Other Design Considerations

This section briefly discusses some other factors that you should consider when programming a search robot.

Robot Exclusion

People working in the general area of Web robots realized that there might be reasons for
certain Web sites to exclude some or all robots. Sometimes the load imposed on the site
was simply too much, or the robot would access inappropriate information such as temporary files or user input forms. The result is a Robot Exclusion Standard, which defined
ways for Web site administrators to exclude some or all robots from their site and for
robots' authors to determine which sites had a Keep Out sign hanging at the entrance.

The current policy involves creating a file named robots.txt and placing it in the root
directory of the Web site. The file contains one or more sections identifying specific
robots and listing the parts of the site they should stay away from. Here is a simple
robots.txt file:

```
User-agent: *
Disallow: /tmp/
```

This specifies that all robots (as indicated by the wildcard character *) should not examine files in the /tmp directory. Here is a more complex example that requests the
InfoSeek robot to stay out of the /bin and /temp directories:

13

```
User-agent: InfoSeek Robot
Disallow: /bin
Disallow: /temp
```

To specify that all robots should stay away from your entire site, you would write the following:

```
User-agent: *
Disallow: /
```

IT'S ALL VOLUNTARY

The Robot Exclusion Standard is voluntary. There is no way you can force a robot to stay away from parts of your site. The robots.txt file is a request and will have an effect only on robots that are programmed to look for the file, read it, and respect the wishes encoded in the file. You can find more information about this standard at `http://info.webcrawler.com/mak/projects/robots/norobots.html`.

As a programmer, it's generally in your interest to program your robots to read and respect the robots.txt file. If the Web administrator excludes part of a site from robots, it is usually for a good reason. Your search will take less time and return more accurate results if it does not include these areas. That being said, I will not include this feature in the lesson's demonstration search robot because space limitation makes it necessary to keep the program basic.

Basic Program Design

As always, it's strongly advised to start by sketching the basic design of the program. What will it do, and how will it be accomplished? The following tasks compose the basic outline:

Task 1: Define a New Search—A search is defined by its starting URLs and the keywords to look for. The program needs a form in which the user can enter this information. When the information is entered, it will be saved as a search definition.

Task 2: Save Search Information—Search information consists of the starting URLs and the keywords. Given Visual Basic's outstanding database capabilities, it makes sense to use a database file to store the information. As you will see, this same file can be used to store information about the search results: the URLs of the pages that were searched and their relevance scores.

Task 3: Open an Existing Search—This is an easy one. Given that one or more saved searches are present on disk, you can open one to continue working with it.

Task 4: Perform the Search—This is the "biggie," the heart of the program. I'll cover it in detail in the next section.

Task 5: Displaying the Results—Although various fancy report formats could be devised, stick to something simple: displaying all relevant URLs in a List Box.

THE IMPORTANCE OF RELEVANCE

Any search engine should not only locate pages that contain certain keywords, but also assign relevance scores. The way these scores are assigned will depend on the precise needs of the search, but without some way of distinguishing highly relevant sites from barely relevant ones, your search results will be much less useful.

The Search Algorithm

The search algorithm that this program uses is conceptually simple, but as you will see, many details need to be worked out in the code.

1. Make the first URL in the database current. When the search starts, this will be one of the starting URLs that the user entered.
2. See whether the current URL has already been searched. If it has, go to step 3. If not, go to step 4.
3. Make the next URL in the database current and go to step 2.
4. Retrieve the current URL's HTML text.
5. Search the HTML text for the keyword(s) and assign a relevance score to the URL.
6. Mark the current URL's entry in the database as having been searched.
7. Extract all link URLs from the page's HTML text. Add them to the URL database.
8. Are any of the termination conditions met? If so, go to step 10. If not, go to step 9.
9. Make the first URL in the database current and go to step 2.
10. Terminate the search and display the results.

The termination condition that the program uses is a simple one; it searches until a specified number of links have been searched or until all URLs in the links database have been searched. The maximum number of links to search is determined by a constant.

13

USING BRUTE FORCE

If you think about the search algorithm presented here, it relies on brute force to ensure that all URLs in the database are searched. For each new URL, it always returns to the beginning of the database and looks through the records, one at a time, until it finds a URL that has not already been searched. This is admittedly wasteful of processing time, and a more elegant solution could be worked out without too much trouble. The brute force method works perfectly well, however, and given the speed of today's computers, the time taken is insignificant.

Creating the Database Template

You have decided to use Visual Basic's database tools to maintain the program data. By keeping links information in a database, it will be simple to locate duplicate links, assign relevance values, and so on. You can also use a database table in which to keep search keywords.

I used Visual Basic's latest database technology, called ADO for ActiveX Data Objects. If you are not familiar with ADO, you owe it to yourself to learn them, because they are a significant improvement over Visual Basic's older database technologies, such as DAO. This is not a database programming book, so I cannot go into any details about how ADO works. You can just follow the code without worrying about the details.

DATABASE STRUCTURE

As a Visual Basic programmer, you are probably familiar with the fundamentals of database programming. Just in case, here's a brief refresher. A *database* consists of one or more tables (you will be using two tables). A *table* is made up of records, with each record holding a single entry. Each *record* is made up of a number of fields, with each field holding a specific item of data. In an address list database, for example, each person's address would constitute a record, and each record would contain fields such as Last Name, First Name, and Zip Code. A database also contains one or more indexes, which are used for sorting and searching the data based on information in specific fields.

The reason I am calling the database a *template* is as follows: The search robot program will let the user define and save multiple searches, and each separate search will require its own database to store the results in. The strategy is to define a template database to hold all the required information and then make a copy of the template for each saved search.

The database for the search robot will have two tables, one for URLs and one for keywords. The next task is to design these tables.

Designing the URLs Table

The first table will be organized around URLs as the basic unit of information; in other words, there will be one record in the database table for each URL. The following information will be kept in each record:

URL—The full URL of a particular Web page.

Starting—A Boolean (True/False) value indicating whether this URL is one of the base URLs for the search (value = True) or is a URL that was found during the search (value = False).

Relevance—An Integer value indicating how relevant the page is to the search. Higher values mean greater relevance.

Searched—A Date value indicating when the page was searched. A value of Null indicates that the page has not yet been searched. Although your program will not use this feature, saving the search date opens the possibility of rerunning a search in the future and searching a page again only if it has been at least a certain time since it was previously searched.

1. Start Visual Basic.

2. Select Visual Data Manager from the Add-Ins menu to start the Visual Data Manager (VisData). It will display a blank screen because no database is open at this time.

3. Select File, New, Microsoft Access, Version 7.0 MDB to create a new database in the Access version 7 format. In the Open dialog box that is displayed, navigate to your project directory and specify the name TEMPLATE for the database file. Then click Save.

4. The VisData screen will now look like Figure 13.5. You have a database file, but no tables are defined in it. That's the next task.

5. In the Database Window, right-click Properties and then select New Table from the pop-up menu. The Table Structure dialog box is displayed (see Figure 13.6).

6. Enter Links in the Table Name box.

13

FIGURE **13.5**

The Visual Data Manager after creating the TEMPLATE database file.

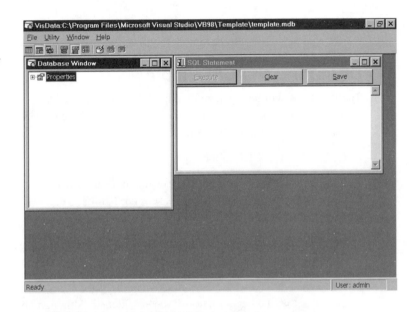

FIGURE **13.6**

Creating a new table.

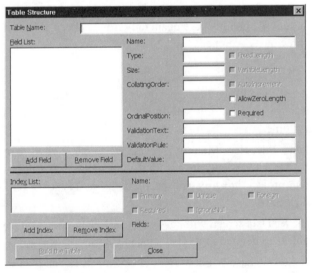

7. Click the Add Field button to add each new field (described next). The Add Field dialog box will be displayed, as shown in Figure 13.7.

8. In the Add Field dialog box, enter the name, type, and (for Text fields) size of the field; also, set other field options as needed. Then click OK to store the field and clear the dialog for another entry.

FIGURE 13.7

The Add Field dialog box.

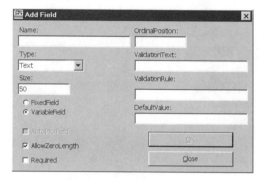

9. Repeat steps 5 and 6 for each field in the table. When done, click Close to return to the Table Structure dialog box.

Following are the definitions of the four fields that you should add to the table, using the techniques just presented:

Name	Type	Size	Other
URL	Text	120	Required = True, AllowZeroLength = False
Starting	Boolean	*n/a*	*n/a*
Relevance	Integer	*n/a*	*n/a*
Searched	Date/Time	*n/a*	*n/a*

Leave the Table Structure dialog box open because you will need it for the next step: defining indexes for the database table.

Creating Table Indexes

Every database table requires at least one index. An index provides a logical sorting of the table, based on the data in one or more of the table's fields. If you create an index based on a field, it is much easier and faster to display the table data sorted on that field and also much faster to perform searches for data in that field.

You will need two indexes for the search robot's database table: one based on the URL field and one based on the Relevance field. Here's how to define an index.

1. In the Table Structure dialog box, click the Add Index button. Visual Basic displays the Add Index to Links dialog box (see Figure 13.8).

2. Enter the index name in the Name box.

13

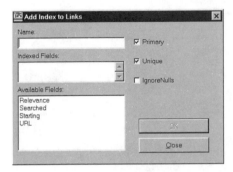

FIGURE 13.8

*Adding an index to the
Links database table.*

3. In the Available Fields box, click the field name that you want the index based on.

4. Select options as needed.

5. Click OK to store the index and clear the dialog box for entry of another index.

6. When all indexes are defined, click Close to return to the Table Structure dialog box.

Now, use the preceding steps to add the following index to the Links table:

```
Name: idxURL
Indexed Field: URL
Options: Primary = True, Unique = True, Ignore Nulls = False
```

When you are finished and have returned to the Table Structure dialog box, it will look like Figure 13.9. Click the Build Table button to create the table.

FIGURE 13.9

*The Table Structure
dialog box after de-
fining the Links table.*

Designing the Keywords Table

Now that the first database table is defined, you can turn to the second table—the one for the keywords. This table will be simpler, requiring only two fields: one for the keyword itself and another for a numerical value that specifies the keyword's importance. Using the preceding techniques, create a second table in the TEMPLATE database, assigning the name Keywords to the table. Add the following two fields to the table:

Name	Type	Size	Other
Keyword	Text	50	Required = True, AllowZeroLength = False
Importance	Integer		DefaultValue: 10, Required = True

Next, add one index to the Keywords table as follows:

Name	Indexed Field	Options
idxKeyword	Keyword	Primary = True, Unique = True, Ignore Nulls = False

Build the table as before. Then select File, Exit to close VisData and return to Visual Basic. If you look in your project directory, you'll find a file named TEMPLATE.MDB. This is the database file that is all set up to handle the data needs of the search robot.

Some Required Code

The processing that the search robot will perform requires some special types of text processing. Look at the code for these procedures before turning to the other parts of the project. Specifically, the following are needed:

- A procedure to extract all the link URLs from an HTML page
- A procedure to remove all HTML tags from a Web page and return only the content text
- A procedure to search a block of text for a keyword and return the number of times the keyword was found

Extracting URLs

After you have retrieved the text of a Web page, you need to extract all the URLs it contains so that they can be added to the list of URLs to search. With Visual Basic's powerful string-processing capabilities, this will be an easy task, but one that needs to be approached carefully. If the program cannot properly extract URLs, it will not work in the way intended.

13

What do you know about URL tags in HTML? They all have the following basic form:

```
<a href="xxxx">
```

"xxxx" is the URL. There can be other parts to the tag, but the preceding is the bare minimum. Therefore, the first part of the strategy for extracting URLs is to look for the string <a href=, being careful that you locate both uppercase and lowercase text.

After you have located the start of a URL tag (the <a href= part), you know that the URL itself will be found between the next two double-quote characters—or will it? The HTML specification permits both the double-quote and single-quote characters to be used to enclose the URL part of the tag. Therefore, both the following two tags are permitted and are equivalent:

```
<a href="xxxx">
<a href='xxxx'>
```

Although double-quote characters are almost universally used, the search program needs to take all possibilities into account. Therefore, the algorithm to extract URLs must consider both double-quote and single-quote characters.

Is this all you need to worry about? I am afraid not. More than one kind of URL can be in an <a href=> tag. Most common, of course, are the http:// URLs that lead to other Web pages. They are not the only kind permitted, however. For example, a mailto: link is used to send email to a specific address, and an ftp:// link is used to open an FTP file. Here are two examples:

```
<a href="ftp://ftp.microsoft.com">
<a href="mailto:billg@microsoft.com">
```

The URL extraction algorithm must, therefore, identify non-http:// URLs and ignore them.

OTHER TYPES OF LINKS

The complete list of possible links in an <a href=> tag would include some other possibilities, although they are rarely encountered. You will ignore them in the search robot program.

Now you are ready to write the code for the URL extraction procedure. Well, almost. You must consider one more possibility. Some URLs are complete, providing the full URL of the specified HTML file. For example:

```
<a href="http://www.pgacon.com/books.htm">
```

Other URLs are relative and refer to a file on the current site. They include only the file-name and perhaps a path, but that's all. Here's an example:

```
<a href="fishing.htm">
```

This link means "open the file fishing.htm at the current location." Another example is the following:

```
<a href="hobbies/fishing.htm">
```

which means "open the file fishing.htm in the directory 'hobbies' at the current location."

If the URL extraction procedure comes across relative URLs such as this, what should be done? The program needs complete URLs in order to function, so you need to convert these relative URLs into compete URLs. This can be done by keeping track of the full URL of the page that is currently being searched. Therefore, if the program is extracting the URLs from the page `http://www.somewhere.com/` and it locates the relative URL `fishing.htm`, the corresponding full URL is `http://www.somewhere.com/fishing.htm`.

One more possibility must be considered. Some links include submission information that is not part of the link itself but rather is submitted to the server when the link is clicked. For example, here is such a URL:

```
http://search.yahoo.com/bin/search?p=greenland
```

The part of the link before the question mark is the actual URL, and the part after the question mark is the submit information. Generally, a search engine will not want to use the submission information, so the link must be stripped of the question mark and everything following it. The same is true of the # character, which identifies a specific location in a page.

Listing 13.1 presents the procedure `GetLinks`, which accepts a block of HTML text and a base URL as arguments and returns a string containing all the `http://` links from the text. The return value is a string containing all the URLs, separated by the ¦ character. You'll see later how the program extracts the individual URLs from this string.

13

LISTING 13.1 THE `GetLinks` FUNCTION

```
Public Function GetLinks(s As String, baseURL As String) As String

' Passed some html text in s, locates all the
' hyperlinks and returns the URLs in a string
' separated by the ¦ character. Returns only
' http links and ignores mailto: and ftp://.
```

continues

Listing 13.1   CONTINUED

```
' baseURL is the base location of the html document
' that is passed in s. If a link is found that is a
' local link, this is added so the return value is
' a fully qualified URL.

Dim pos As Long, pos1 As Long, pos2 As Long
Dim buf As String, temp As String
Dim sq As String, dq As String
Dim qc As String, start As Long

buf = ""

' Make sure a nonempty string has been passed.
If s = Null Or Len(s) = 0 Then
    GetLinks = buf
    Exit Function
End If

' Make sure there is at least one link.
start = InStr(1, s, "<a href=", vbTextCompare)
If start = 0 Then
    GetLinks = buf
    Exit Function
End If

' Define the single and double quote characters.
dq = Chr$(34)
sq = Chr$(39)

Do
    ' Get the first double or single quote character.
    ' That marks the start of the URL.
    pos = InStr(start, s, dq, vbTextCompare)
    pos2 = InStr(start, s, sq, vbTextCompare)
    If pos = 0 And pos2 = 0 Then Exit Do
    ' If both a single and a double quote were
    ' found, the first one marks the start
    ' of the URL.
    If pos > 0 And pos2 > 0 Then      ' Both were found
        If pos < pos2 Then ' It is the double quote
            qc = dq
        Else     ' It is the single quote
            qc = sq
            pos = pos2
        End If
    ElseIf pos = 0 Then ' Only the single quote was found.
        qc = sq
        pos = pos2
```

```
    ElseIf pos2 = 0 Then ' Only a double quote was found.
        qc = dq
    End If
    ' Get the next quote character. That
    ' marks the end of the URL.
    pos1 = InStr(pos + 1, s, qc, vbTextCompare)
    If pos1 = 0 Then Exit Do
    temp = Mid$(s, pos + 1, pos1 - pos - 1)
    ' Don't accept mailto and ftp links.
    If LCase(Left(temp, 7)) = "mailto:" Or
➥LCase(Left(temp, 3)) = "ftp" Then
        GoTo DoNotAdd
    End If
    ' See whether it is a full URL. If not,
    ' add the base URL.
    If LCase(Left(temp, 7)) <> "http://" Then
        temp = baseURL & temp
    End If
    ' Strip off anything following a # or ?
    ' character in the link.
    pos = InStr(1, temp, "#")
    If pos > 0 Then
        temp = Left(temp, pos - 1)
    End If
    pos = InStr(1, temp, "?")
    If pos > 0 Then
        temp = Left(temp, pos - 1)
    End If
    buf = buf & temp & "¦"
DoNotAdd:
    ' Locate the next link.
    pos = InStr(pos1, s, "<a href=", vbTextCompare)
    start = pos
    ' If there are no more links, quit.
    If pos = 0 Then Exit Do
    DoEvents
Loop While True

' Strip off the trailing ¦.
GetLinks = Left(buf, Len(buf) - 1)

End Function
```

13

Stripping Out HTML Tags

When searching through a page's text for keyword matches, you should ignore text that is part of HTML tags. Clearly, text inside tags is not relevant to the search. For this purpose, I wrote a function named StripTags, which is passed the complete text of an HTML page and returns the text minus the HTML tags.

How can you remove tags? You know that all HTML tags are enclosed in angle brackets `<like this>`. If, therefore, you remove all `<` `>` pairs and whatever text is between them, you will accomplish your goal. The process can be explained in pseudocode as follows:

1. Look for the first `<` in the text; this marks the start of the first HTML tag. If it is not found, there are no tags, and you can copy the entire text to a buffer and go to step 6. Otherwise, continue with step 2.
2. Add all text to the left of the first `<` to a separate buffer.
3. Find the first `>` in the text. This marks the end of the first tag.
4. Delete all text up to and including the first `>`.
5. Go to step 1.
6. Return the contents of the buffer.

Listing 13.2 shows the procedure `StripTags`, which takes HTML text as its argument and returns the same text with all tags removed.

LISTING 13.2   THE `StripTags` FUNCTION

```
Public Function StripTags(ByVal HtmlDoc As String) As String

' Passed the text of an HTML document, returns the text
' with all HTML tags removed. Specifically, removes
' all < > pairs and the text between them.

Dim buf As String, pos As Long

' Check for no tags situation.
pos = InStr(HtmlDoc, "<")
If pos = 0 Then
    StripTags = HtmlDoc
    Exit Function
End If

Do
    ' Add text to left of first tag to buffer.
    buf = buf & Left$(HtmlDoc, pos - 1)
    ' Find end of tag.
    pos = InStr(HtmlDoc, ">")
    ' Remove everything up to the
    ' end of tag from the text.
    If pos = 0 Then Exit Do
    HtmlDoc = Mid$(HtmlDoc, pos + 1)
    ' Find the start of the next tag.
    pos = InStr(HtmlDoc, "<")
    If pos = 0 Then Exit Do
```

```
Loop While True

StripTags = buf

End Function
```

Searching for Keywords

Searching for a keyword is a relatively easy task, given the power of Visual Basic's string-handling functions. You can see how I did it in Listing 13.3, which presents the code for the function SearchForKW. The algorithm is simple: Use the Instr function to look for the first occurrence of the keyword. Then repeat until either a maximum of 10 instances have been found or the end of the text is reached.

MAXIMUM RELEVANCE

Why did I write the SearchForKW function to stop after finding 10 instances of the keyword? It seems logical that when 10 instances of a keyword are found on a Web page, you know the page is highly relevant to the search and that finding more will not make things any better. By stopping at 10, you might save some processing time.

LISTING 13.3 THE SearchForKW FUNCTION RETURNS THE NUMBER OF TIMES A KEYWORD IS FOUND IN A BLOCK OF TEXT

```
Public Function SearchForKW(str As String, kw As String) As Long

' Returns the number of times that the string kw
' is found in the string str, case-insensitive.
' Maximum count is 10 because higher hit rates will
' probably not mean higher relevance.

Dim buf As String, pos As Long, count As Integer

' Make a local copy minus HTML tags.
buf = StripTags(str)

pos = InStr(1, buf, kw, vbTextCompare)
If pos = 0 Then
    SearchForKW = 0
    Exit Function
End If

count = 0
```

13

continues

LISTING 13.3 CONTINUED

```
Do
    count = count + 1
    ' Strip off everything up to and
    ' including the just-found keyword.
    buf = Right(buf, Len(buf) - pos - Len(kw))
    pos = InStr(1, buf, kw, vbTextCompare)
Loop Until count = 10 Or pos = 0

SearchForKW = count

End Function
```

The Search Robot's Forms

The search robot program has four forms:

1. The main form with Command Buttons for selecting actions

2. A New Search form for defining a new search

3. A keyword form for entering a keyword and its relevance into a new search

4. A report form for displaying the search results

To complete this project, you must use the References dialog box (Select Project, References) to add both the Microsoft ActiveX Data Objects 2.0 Library and the Microsoft Scripting Runtime to the project.

The New Search Form

The New Search form provides the user with a place to specify the name of the search and to enter one or more starting URLs and one or more keywords with an *importance* value. This importance value is used by the program in determining the relevance of a Web page. The program is written to use importance values from 1 to 10, with 10 being the highest importance and 5 being the default importance for a keyword.

Figure 13.10 shows the New Search form in the Visual Basic design window. It contains a Text Box, two List Boxes, and several Command Buttons and labels. The form's objects and properties are presented in Listing 13.4. I have given only the important properties in this listing; you can determine the placement and size of controls from the figure or create a form layout yourself.

FIGURE 13.10

Designing the New Search form.

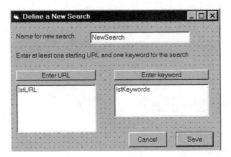

LISTING 13.4 OBJECTS AND PROPERTIES IN `frmNewSearch`

```
Begin VB.Form frmNewSearch
   Caption            =    "Define a New Search"
   Begin VB.ListBox lstKeywords
   End
   Begin VB.ListBox lstURL
   End
   Begin VB.CommandButton cmdEnterKeyword
      Caption         =    "Enter keyword"
   End
   Begin VB.CommandButton cmdEnterURL
      Caption         =    "Enter URL"
   End
   Begin VB.CommandButton Command1
      Caption         =    "Save"
      Default         =    -1   'True
      Index           =    1
   End
   Begin VB.CommandButton Command1
      Cancel          =    -1   'True
      Caption         =    "Cancel"
      Index           =    0
   End
   Begin VB.TextBox txtSearchName
      Text            =    "NewSearch"
   End
   Begin VB.Label Label2
      Caption         =    "Enter at least one starting URL
                           and one keyword for the search"
   End
   Begin VB.Label Label1
      Caption         =    "Name for new search:"
   End
End
```

13

The code in the New Search form is presented in Listing 13.5. The main tasks this code performs are accepting and verifying the user input, creating a copy of the database template file, and storing the search information (starting URLs and keywords) in the database.

LISTING 13.5   THE CODE BEHIND THE NEW SEARCH FORM

```
Option Explicit

Private Sub cmdEnterKeyword_Click()

frmKeyword.Show 1

End Sub

Private Sub cmdEnterURL_Click()

Dim s As String

s = InputBox("Enter URL", "Starting URL")
If s = "" Then Exit Sub

' Make sure the URL includes the protocol.
If LCase$(Left(s, 7)) <> "http://" Then
    s = "http://" & s
End If

lstURL.AddItem s

End Sub

Private Sub Command1_Click(Index As Integer)

Select Case Index
    Case 0 ' Cancel
        Hide
    Case 1 ' Save
        ' Be sure required info has been entered.
        If txtSearchName.Text = "" Then
            MsgBox ("You must enter a search name!")
            Exit Sub
        End If
        If lstURL.ListCount = 0 Or lstKeywords.ListCount = 0 Then
            MsgBox ("You must enter at least one URL and one keyword")
            Exit Sub
        End If
        Call SaveSearchDef
End Select
```

```
End Sub

Public Sub SaveSearchDef()

' Creates a new search based on information entered
' in the NewSearch form.

Dim NewFileName As String, i as integer
Dim TemplateFileName As String
Dim fs As New Scripting.FileSystemObject
Dim s As String, reply As String, f
Dim strConnect As String, pos As Integer

' See whether a search of this name
' already exists. If so, give the user
' the option to overwrite it.

On Error GoTo ADOError

NewFileName = App.Path & "\" & _
    frmNewSearch.txtSearchName.Text & ".mdb"

If fs.FileExists(NewFileName) Then
    s = "A search named " & txtSearchName.Text
    s = s & " already exists. Overwrite it?"
    reply = MsgBox(s, vbYesNo, "Overwite Search?")
    If reply = vbNo Then
        txtSearchName.SetFocus
        Exit Sub
    End If
End If

' Make sure the template database file exists.
TemplateFileName = App.Path & "\" & "template.mdb"

If Not fs.FileExists(TemplateFileName) Then
    s = "The search database template file 'TEMPLATE.MBD' " & vbCrLf
    s = s & " cannot be found. This file must be present " & vbCrLf
    s = s & "in the program folder."
    MsgBox (s)
    Exit Sub
End If

' Copy the template to the new search name.
Set f = fs.GetFile(TemplateFileName)
f.Copy (NewFileName)

' Now put the information in the database.

strConnect = "Provider=Microsoft.Jet.OLEDB.3.51;"
```

13

continues

LISTING 13.5   CONTINUED

```
strConnect = strConnect & "Persist Security Info=False;"
strConnect = strConnect & "Data Source = " & NewFileName

Set cnLinks = New ADODB.Connection
Set rsURL = New ADODB.Recordset
Set rsKeywords = New ADODB.Recordset

cnLinks.ConnectionString = strConnect
cnLinks.ConnectionTimeout = 10
cnLinks.CursorLocation = adUseNone
cnLinks.Open

' Put the starting URLs in the database.

rsURL.Open "Select * from Links", cnLinks, _
    adOpenDynamic, adLockOptimistic, adCmdText

For i = 0 To lstURL.ListCount - 1
    rsURL.AddNew
    rsURL!URL = lstURL.List(i)
    rsURL!Starting = True
    rsURL!relevance = 0
    rsURL!Searched = DateValue(BASEDATE)
    rsURL.Update
Next i

' Put the keywords in the database.

rsKeywords.Open "Select * from Keywords", cnLinks, _
    adOpenDynamic, adLockOptimistic, adCmdText

For i = 0 To lstKeywords.ListCount - 1
    rsKeywords.AddNew
    pos = InStr(lstKeywords.List(i), ":")
    rsKeywords!keyword = Left(lstKeywords.List(i), pos - 1)
    rsKeywords!Importance = Right(lstKeywords.List(i), _
        Len(lstKeywords.List(i)) - pos)
    rsKeywords.Update
Next i

' Destroy the database objects.
Set cnLinks = Nothing
Set rsKeywords = Nothing
Set rsURL = Nothing

gDataFileName = NewFileName
```

```
Hide

Exit Sub

ADOError:

MsgBox ("Save search: " & Err.Description)

End Sub
```

The Keyword Form

The Keyword form is displayed by the New Search form to permit the user to enter a keyword and its relative importance. It is a simple form, as shown in Figure 13.11. Its objects and properties are represented in Listing 13.6, and its code in Listing 13.7. When the user enters a keyword and property, it combines the two items, separated by a color, and puts them in the Keywords List Box on the New Search form.

FIGURE 13.11

The Keyword form.

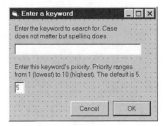

LISTING 13.6 OBJECTS AND PROPERTIES IN frmKeyword

```
Begin VB.Form frmKeyword
    Caption            =    "Enter a keyword"
    Begin VB.CommandButton Command1

        Cancel         =    -1   'True
        Caption        =    "Cancel"
        Index          =    1
    End
    Begin VB.CommandButton Command1
        Caption        =    "OK"
        Default        =    -1   'True
        Index          =    0
    End
    Begin VB.TextBox txtPriority
        Text           =    "5"
    End
```

continues

LISTING **13.6**   CONTINUED

```
Begin VB.TextBox txtKeyword
End
Begin VB.Label Label2
   Caption         =    "Enter this keyword's priority. Priority
                         ranges from 1 (lowest) to 10 (highest).
                         The default is 5."
End
Begin VB.Label Label1
   Caption         =    "Enter the keyword to search for. Case does
                         not matter, but spelling does."
End
End
```

LISTING **13.7**   THE CODE IN frmKeyword

```
Option Explicit

Private Sub Command1_Click(Index As Integer)

Dim s As String

Select Case Index
    Case 0 ' OK
        ' Make sure a keyword was entered.
        If Len(txtKeyword.Text) = 0 Then
            MsgBox ("You must enter a keyword")
            Exit Sub
        End If
        ' Is a valid priority was not entered,
        ' use the default value of 5.
        If Val(txtPriority.Text) < 1 Or _
           Val(txtPriority.Text) > 10 Then
                txtPriority.Text = "5"
        End If
        s = txtKeyword.Text & ":" & txtPriority.Text
        frmNewSearch.lstKeywords.AddItem s
        Hide
    Case 1 ' Cancel
        Hide
End Select

End Sub

Private Sub Form_Activate()
```

```
txtKeyword.Text = ""
txtPriority.Text = "5"
txtKeyword.SetFocus

End Sub
```

The Report Form

Because I decided that this search robot would be limited to a very basic report format, the report form is correspondingly simple. It consists of a form containing only one control, a List Box. When the form is loaded, code in the form's Load event procedure opens the Links database and retrieves all records for which the relevance score is greater than 0. The records are sorted by relevance and then displayed in the List Box—it's that simple! The form also contains code to make the List Box the same size as the form. Listing 13.8 presents the code in the Report form.

```
Begin VB.Form frmReport
    Caption         =   "Report"
    Begin VB.ListBox lstReport
        Height      =   1776
        Left        =   2160
        TabIndex    =   0
        Top         =   1800
        Width       =   1692
    End
End
```

LISTING 13.8 CODE FOR THE REPORT FORM

```
Option Explicit

Private Sub Form_Load()

Dim strConnect As String, buf As String
Dim SQLString As String

' Fill the form with the List Box
lstReport.Move 0, 0, ScaleWidth, ScaleHeight

' Create the database objects.
strConnect = "Provider=Microsoft.Jet.OLEDB.3.51;"
strConnect = strConnect & "Persist Security Info=False;"
strConnect = strConnect & "Data Source = " & gDataFileName

Set cnLinks = New ADODB.Connection
Set rsURL = New ADODB.Recordset
```

13

continues

LISTING 13.8 CONTINUED

```
cnLinks.ConnectionString = strConnect
cnLinks.ConnectionTimeout = 10
cnLinks.CursorLocation = adUseNone
cnLinks.Open

SQLString = "Select * from links where Relevance > 0 "
SQLString = SQLString & "order by relevance"

' Open the URLs list in the database.
rsURL.Open SQLString, cnLinks, _
    adOpenDynamic, adLockOptimistic, adCmdText

Do
    buf = rsURL!URL & " (" & rsURL!relevance & ")"
    lstReport.AddItem buf
    rsURL.MoveNext
Loop While Not rsURL.EOF

End Sub

Private Sub Form_Resize()

lstReport.Move 0, 0, ScaleWidth, ScaleHeight

End Sub
```

The Main Form

The program's main form is where most of the action takes place. Visually, it is a simple form containing a control array of five Command Buttons, as well as one Internet Transfer control and one Common Dialog control. You can see what the form looks like in Figure 13.12, and Listing 13.9 presents its objects and properties.

FIGURE 13.12

The search robot's main form.

LISTING 13.9 OBJECTS AND PROPERTIES IN THE SEARCH ROBOT'S MAIN FORM

```
Begin VB.Form frmMain
    Caption          =   "Form1"
    Begin VB.CommandButton Command1
        Caption      =   "&Cancel Search"
        Index        =   4
```

```
      End
      Begin VB.CommandButton Command1
         Caption         =   "&Quit"
         Index           =   3
      End
      Begin VB.CommandButton Command1
         Caption         =   "&Run Search"
         Index           =   2
      End
      Begin VB.CommandButton Command1
         Caption         =   "&Open Search"
         Index           =   1
      End
      Begin VB.CommandButton Command1
         Caption         =   "&New Search"
         Index           =   0
      End
      Begin MSComDlg.CommonDialog CD1
      End
      Begin InetCtlsObjects.Inet Inet1
      End
   End
End
```

The code in the main form is extensive. You have already seen much of it earlier in the lesson when you developed the procedures for carrying out specific tasks. Listing 13.10 shows the remaining code. I will not take the time to explain this code in detail, because it is well commented and easy to understand.

Tip

Always use the DoEvents statement in a program, such as this, that does a lot of processing in loops. Otherwise, the rest of the system might be slowed down unacceptably, and the program itself will not be able to respond to user input such as clicking the Cancel button.

LISTING 13.10   THE REMAINDER OF THE SEARCH ROBOT'S CODE

```
Option Explicit

Dim gCancel As Boolean

' Threshold for relevance; if a page's relevance
' is below this, its links are not added to the search.
' A setting of 0 results in all of a page's links being added.
Const RELEVANCE_THRESHOLD = 0
```

continues

13

LISTING 13.10   CONTINUED

```
Private Sub Command1_Click(Index As Integer)

Dim reply As Integer

Select Case Index
    Case 0 ' New search
        Call NewSearch
    Case 1 ' Open search
        Call OpenSearch
    Case 2 ' Run search
        Call RunSearch
        reply = MsgBox("Done - display report?", vbYesNo)
        If reply = vbYes Then Call frmReport.Show
    Case 3 ' Quit
        End
    Case 4 ' Cancel search.
        gCancel = True
End Select

End Sub

Public Sub OpenSearch()

' Opens an existing search database.

With CD1
    .Filter = "Search databases ¦ *.mdb"
    .InitDir = App.Path
    .ShowOpen
    gDataFileName = .FileName
End With

If gDataFileName <> "" Then
    Caption = gDataFileName
    Command1(2).Enabled = True
End If

End Sub


Private Sub Form_Load()

gDataFileName = ""
Command1(0).Enabled = True
Command1(1).Enabled = True
Command1(2).Enabled = False
Command1(3).Enabled = True
Command1(4).Enabled = False
gCancel = False
```

```
Caption = "No search loaded"

End Sub

Public Sub NewSearch()

' Create a new search.

gDataFileName = ""
frmNewSearch.Show 1
If gDataFileName <> "" Then ' Successful
    Caption = gDataFileName
    Command1(2).Enabled = True
End If

End Sub

Public Sub RunSearch()

' Runs a search based on the currently loaded search data.
' Terminates when MAXLINKS links have been examined or no
' more links are available.

Dim strConnect As String, buf As String
Dim count As Long, relevance As Integer
Dim oldCaption As String

' For keywords and their importance values.
Dim kw() As String
Dim impr() As Integer
' Number of keywords
Dim numKW As Integer

On Error Resume Next

' Initialize.
numKW = 0
oldCaption = frmMain.Caption

' Enable Cancel button.
Command1(4).Enabled = True
' Disable other buttons.
Command1(0).Enabled = False
Command1(1).Enabled = False
Command1(2).Enabled = False
Command1(3).Enabled = False

' Create the database objects.
strConnect = "Provider=Microsoft.Jet.OLEDB.3.51;"
```

continues

13

LISTING 13.10 CONTINUED

```
strConnect = strConnect & "Persist Security Info=False;"
strConnect = strConnect & "Data Source = " & gDataFileName

Set cnLinks = New ADODB.Connection
Set rsURL = New ADODB.Recordset
Set rsKeywords = New ADODB.Recordset

cnLinks.ConnectionString = strConnect
cnLinks.ConnectionTimeout = 10
cnLinks.CursorLocation = adUseNone
cnLinks.Open

' Get the keywords from the database and put them
' in an array. Put Importance values in their own array.

rsKeywords.Open "Select * from Keywords", cnLinks, _
    adOpenDynamic, adLockOptimistic, adCmdText

rsKeywords.MoveFirst
Do
    numKW = numKW + 1
    ReDim Preserve kw(numKW)
    ReDim Preserve impr(numKW)
    kw(numKW) = rsKeywords!keyword
    impr(numKW) = rsKeywords!Importance
    rsKeywords.MoveNext
Loop Until rsKeywords.EOF = True

' Destroy the keywords recordset because we are done with it.
Set rsKeywords = Nothing

' Open the URLs list in the database.

rsURL.Open "Select * from Links", cnLinks, _
    adOpenDynamic, adLockOptimistic, adCmdText

rsURL.MoveFirst

Do
    'Debug.Print "Trying " & rsURL!URL & ", " & rsURL!Searched
    If rsURL!Searched = DateValue(BASEDATE) Then
        'Debug.Print "Searching " & rsURL!URL
        rsURL!Searched = Now
        Call SearchURL(rsURL!URL, kw(), impr())
        count = count + 1
        frmMain.Caption = count
        rsURL.MoveFirst
    Else
        rsURL.MoveNext
```

```
        End If
        DoEvents
Loop Until count > MAXLINKS Or rsURL.EOF Or gCancel = True

' Clean up
gCancel = False
Command1(4).Enabled = False
Command1(0).Enabled = True
Command1(1).Enabled = True
Command1(2).Enabled = True
Command1(3).Enabled = True
frmMain.Caption = oldCaption

' Destroy the database objects.
Set cnLinks = Nothing
Set rsURL = Nothing

End Sub


Public Sub SearchURL(URL As String, _
    kw() As String, impr() As Integer)

' URL is the full URL to search.
' kw() is a string array of the keywords to look for.
' impr() is an integer array of the relative importance
' of each keyword in kw().

Dim buf As String, i As Integer
Dim rel As Long

On Error Resume Next

  ' Set the timeout value in seconds.
Inet1.RequestTimeout = 30

' Open the URL.
buf = Inet1.OpenURL(URL, icString)
DoEvents

' Catch time out and server not found errors.
If Err = 35761 Then
    Err.Clear
    Exit Sub
ElseIf buf = "" Then
    Exit Sub
End If

' Search for the various keywords,
' one at a time.
```

continues

13

LISTING 13.10 CONTINUED

```
rel = 0
For i = 1 To UBound(kw)
    rel = rel + (impr(i) / 5) * SearchForKW(buf, kw(i))
Next i

rel = rel \ UBound(kw)
rsURL!relevance = rel
Debug.Print rsURL!URL & ": " & rsURL!relevance

If rel >= RELEVANCE_THRESHOLD Then
    Call AddLinksToSearch(buf, MakeBaseURL(URL))
End If

End Sub

Public Sub AddLinksToSearch(s As String, baseURL As String) _

' Extracts the http:// links from s and
' adds them to the search database. s is the
' text contents of an HTML file.

' Returns True if any links were added to the
' database, False if not.

Dim links As String, newURL As String
Dim pos As Long

' Necessary so that "duplicate data"
' errors will not stop execution.
On Error Resume Next

links = GetLinks(s, baseURL)
' No links to add.
If Len(links) < 9 Then
    Exit Sub
End If

pos = 1
Do
    pos = InStr(1, links, "¦")
    If pos = 0 Then Exit Do
    newURL = Left(links, pos - 1)
    links = Right(links, Len(links) - pos)
    rsURL.AddNew
    rsURL!URL = newURL
    rsURL!relevance = 0
    rsURL!Starting = False
```

```
        rsURL!Searched = DateValue(BASEDATE)
        rsURL.Update
        ' Uncomment the following debug.print statements
        ' to see a list of accepted and duplicate URLs
        ' in the Immediate window while executing in VB.
        If Err.Number = &H80040E21 Then
            'Debug.Print newURL & " rejected as duplicate"
        Else
            'Debug.Print newURL & " added"
        End If
        DoEvents
Loop While True

End Sub


Public Function MakeBaseURL(URL As String) As String

' Passed a complete URL, returns the base part - the
' URL minus any filenames and with a trailing "/".

' For example:

' http://www.xx.com/index.htm --> http://www.xx.com/
' http://www.xx.com/sub/data.htm --> http://www.xx.com/sub/
' http://www.xx.com --> http://www.xx.com/

Dim s As String, pos As Integer

' Look for the last / in the URL.
pos = InStrRev(URL, "/")

' If it is less than 8, it is part of the http://
' protocol specifier. Therefore, we can just tack
' a / at the end and return it.

If pos < 8 Then
    MakeBaseURL = URL & "/"
    Exit Function

' Otherwise, strip off everything after
' the last /, thus removing the filename.
Else
    MakeBaseURL = Left(URL, pos)
End If

End Function
```

13

The Code Module

In addition to its four forms, the search robot project requires one code module to hold global variables and constants. Listing 13.11 shows this code.

LISTING 13.11   THE SEARCH ROBOT PROJECT'S CODE MODULE

```
Option Explicit

' The search database filename.
Global gDataFileName As String

' Maximum number of links to search.
Global Const MAXLINKS = 1000

' Date for uSnsearched links.
Global Const BASEDATE = "1/1/1900"

' For the database access.
Global cnLinks As ADODB.Connection
Global rsURL As ADODB.Recordset
Global rsKeywords As ADODB.Recordset
```

Running the Search Program

When you run the program for the first time, you must define a search. You need at least one starting URL, which should have some relevance to the subject you will be searching for. Also, you must enter at least one keyword. After a search has been defined, click the Run Search button to get things started. You can minimize the program and let it work while you do other tasks. The code presented here limits the search to 1,000 links. You might want to change that to a smaller value for your first few trial searches and to a larger value for doing real searches.

When the search is complete (or cancelled by the user), you have the option of displaying the results. Figure 13.13 shows a sample report. The relevant URLs are listed, along with their corresponding relevance scores. This is a basic display, and you might want to add the capabilities to save the list to disk, navigate to specific links, and the like.

RUN AT NIGHT

If you want to perform a serious search, I suggest that you run it at night. The Web is much less busy during the wee hours, and the search will run faster. Start your search running before you go to bed, and the results will be waiting for you in the morning.

FIGURE 13.13

The report displayed by the search robot program.

Much could be added to this program. If you find it useful and want a more sophisticated search tool, you can modify it as needed.

Summary

This lesson shows you how to utilize your Visual Basic Internet programming knowledge to create a useful, working program. I hope that it has demonstrated the big difference between textbook knowledge of Visual Basic properties, methods, and so on, and the development of a real-world program.

Searching the Web can be a very powerful tool. Although several commercial search engines are available on the Web, you might want to customize the process so that you obtain the information you need and not the information someone else thinks you need. By understanding the principles of Web crawling, you can create your own specialized search tool. Suggestions for improving the program are in the Exercise section at the end of the lesson.

Q&A

Q What is the most important characteristic of the Web that permits the operation of Web crawlers, or spiders?

A It is that Web pages are linked by hyperlinks, which permit a spider to move from page to page.

Q What is a robot exclusion file?

A It is a text file named robots.txt and located in the root directory of a Web site. It contains information in a standard format, specifying which robots should be excluded from certain parts of the Web site.

13

Q What is the advantage of using relevance scores when searching Web pages?

A In many cases, a Web search will return a large number of pages. Without some way to identify the pages most likely to interest you, the search results will not be as useful as they could be.

Workshop

Quiz

1. What is a termination rule? Why is it important?
2. Are the instructions in a robot exclusion file mandatory?
3. How can you identify the start of a hyperlink tag in an HTML document?

Exercise

The search robot program could be improved in several ways. Here are some suggestions for you to program on your own:

- Read and follow the exclusion rules in the robot exclusion files.
- Use whole-word-only matches for keyword searches. In other words, the keyword water would be a match to only *water* and not to *waterfall* or *underwater*.
- If a page's relevance score is more than a certain value, save the page to disk for later offline viewing.

DAY **14**

Email in Visual Basic

Perhaps the most popular use of the Internet is the sending and receiving of electronic mail (email). Although standalone email programs are available to anyone, it can be more convenient for some applications to have the email capability built directly in to a Visual Basic program. Visual Basic provides you with two controls that make this an easy task. Today you will learn

- What the MAPI controls are
- How to set up your email to use the MAPI controls
- Using the MAPI controls to receive messages and attachments
- Using the MAPI controls to send messages and attachments

Introducing the MAPI Controls

Visual Basic excels in hiding complex programming tasks inside easy-to-use controls, and email is no exception. Visual Basic comes with two mail-related controls, collectively named *Microsoft MAPI Controls*. Using these controls, you can read email messages, send email, use an address book, send and receive message attachments, and perform all the other related tasks that you do with your regular email program.

Although these controls could be used to create a full-fledged email program, they are more useful for adding email capabilities to other Visual Basic applications.

WHAT IS MAPI?

MAPI stands for *Messaging Application Program Interface*. The Visual Basic MAPI controls use this interface to connect your program to the underlying messaging services. In other words, to use these controls, you must have a MAPI-compliant messaging system installed, such as Microsoft Exchange.

There are two MAPI controls: `MAPISession` and `MAPIMessages`. You use the `MAPISession` control to establish an email session and then use the `MAPIMessages` control to work with individual messages in that session. Because these controls require that an underlying email system be set up, let's look at this task first and then return to the controls.

NO INTERFACE, NO EVENTS

Both the MAPI controls are invisible at runtime, having no visual interface. Neither control has any events, either.

Setting Up Your Email

Because the MAPI controls use the email system already installed on your computer, it's necessary to ensure that the email system is set up properly. Many of the settings required for a successful email session are specified in the email system itself, and are not properties of the MAPI controls, as you might expect. Your username and password are the two most important examples.

If you are regularly using email on your computer, the MAPI-compliant components are probably already installed. To check your email setup in Windows 98, open the Control Panel and double-click the Mail icon. A dialog box titled Internet Accounts will open. If one or more accounts are listed here, you are already set up. Otherwise, click the Add button to set up an account, as follows.

1. After you click Add, the Internet Connection Wizard starts and displays its first dialog box, shown in Figure 14.1. Enter your name as you want it to appear in the From field of messages you send. Then click the Next button.

FIGURE 14.1

Starting to define an email profile.

2. In the next dialog box (not shown), enter your own email address, the address people use to send you messages. Then click Next.

3. In the next dialog box, you enter the URLs of your mail servers. You also specify the type of your incoming mail server. Figure 14.2 shows this dialog box. If you do not know this information, you will have to ask your network administrator. Note that the URL may be the same for both the incoming and outgoing server. Click Next when you have entered the required information.

FIGURE 14.2

Specifying your incoming and outgoing mail servers.

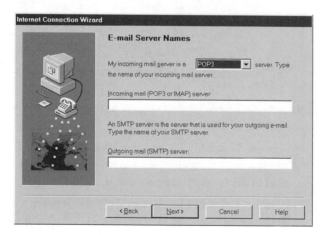

14

POP3, IMAP, AND SMTP

These three acronyms stand for different email protocols. POP3 (Post Office Protocol, version 3) and IMAP (Internet Message Access Protocol) are protocols for receiving mail, whereas SMTP (Simple Mail Transport Protocol) is a protocol for sending mail.

4. In the next Internet Connection Wizard dialog box, shown in Figure 14.3, enter your username and password for your email account. If you select the Always Prompt for Password option, you will be required to enter your password each time you log on—a useful security feature if your computer is not in a secure area. Otherwise, the system will remember your password, and logging on will be automatic. When done, click Next.

FIGURE 14.3

Entering your email account log on and password information.

5. In the next dialog box (not shown), you specify how you will connect to the Internet. Your three choices are

- Connect Using My Phone Line. Windows will use Dial Up Networking to connect to your Internet service provider (ISP). Use this option if you connect to the Internet using a modem.

- Connect Using My Local Area Network. Windows will use your existing LAN connection to access the Internet. Use this option if you have a LAN connection to the Internet.

- I Will Establish My Internet Connection Manually. Select this option for special situations in which one of the other two options is not appropriate.

USING DIAL UP NETWORKING

You must set up Windows Dial Up Networking before you can use it. The information required includes your ISP logon and password (which are not necessarily the same as your email logon and password) and the phone number to dial. See the Windows Help system for further information.

6. If you selected the LAN connection option in step 6, you are done. Click Finish, and this part of setting up your Internet connection is complete. If you selected the phone line option, the next dialog box (not shown) asks you for the phone number of your ISP. Enter the number and then click Next.

7. In the next dialog box (not shown), enter your dial up username and password and then click Next.

8. The next dialog box asks whether you want to change Advanced Settings. In almost all cases, you will not need to do so. Click Next to continue.

9. The next dialog box asks you to assign a name to this dial-up connection. You can accept the suggested default name or enter a descriptive name of your own choosing. At this point, you are done. Click Finish, and Windows will display the Internet Accounts dialog box with a list of the defined accounts. Figure 14.4 shows this dialog box with two accounts set up.

FIGURE 14.4

Your Internet mail accounts are listed in the Internet Accounts dialog box.

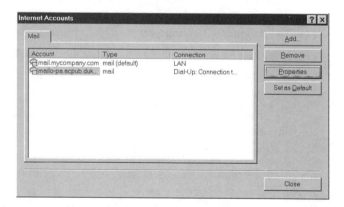

MULTIPLE MAIL ACCOUNTS

If you have set up more than one mail account, one of them will be designated as the default account. It is identified by the designation (default) in the Internet Accounts dialog box. To change the default account, click the account you want to make the default in the Internet Accounts dialog box. Then click the Set as Default button.

14

After you have an Internet mail account set up, you are ready to use the MAPI controls to work with email.

Starting a MAPI Session

To start a MAPI session, use the MAPISession control's SignOn method. First, however, you need to set some of the control's properties. The most important ones can be set in the control's property page, shown in Figure 14.5.

FIGURE 14.5

The MAPISession *control's Property Pages.*

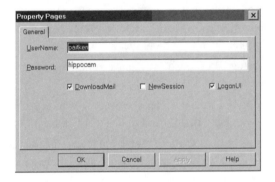

The properties are explained here:

- Username and Password—These properties are required to provide logon information to the underlying mail system. They can be set at design time, but more commonly the program will prompt the user and set them at runtime.
- DownloadMail—Select this option if you want any available messages downloaded.
- NewSession—If selected, the MAPISession control will create a new mail session even if one already exists.
- LogOnUI—If selected, the underlying mail system's logon dialog box will be displayed for the user to enter logon information. If the underlying mail system does not provide such a dialog box, this property is ignored.

What happens to downloaded messages? They will be placed in the usual location, typically the Inbox, where they can be viewed. If you want to retrieve the messages for use in your Visual Basic program, you must use the MAPIMessages control, as described later.

When the MAPISession control successfully executes the SignOn method, its SessionID property will contain a unique handle identifying the session. You need this handle when using the MAPIMessages control to work with individual mail messages.

If an error occurs during the logon, the MAPISession control generates an error. These errors are handled in the same way as other Visual Basic errors, so I will not go into any detail here. Specifics on the possible errors generated by the MAPISession control, as well as by the MAPIMessages control, are presented at the end of the chapter.

After the mail session is complete, call the MAPISession control's SignOff method to terminate the mail session.

Using the MAPIMessages Control

Two steps are required before you can use the MAPIMessages control for anything. First, you must create a valid MAPI session with the MAPISession control, as previously described. Second, you must associate the MAPIMessages control with the session. This is done by assigning the SessionID property from the MAPISession control:

```
MAPIMessages1.SessionID = MAPISession1.SessionID
```

After the control is attached to an email session, it is ready to use.

Getting Mail

To retrieve messages from the Inbox, use the Fetch method:

```
MAPIMessages1.Fetch
```

This method creates a *message set* that contains all the messages that were retrieved. Sometimes the message set is referred to as the *read buffer*. You have some control over the fetch process by setting the value of these control properties:

- FetchMsgType—Specifies the types of messages retrieved. The default setting of this property is a blank string, which causes all message types to be retrieved. The types of messages available depends on your mail system, and you need to refer to its documentation for details.

- FetchSorted—Set this property to True to retrieve messages in the same order they were received. Set it to False (the default) to retrieve messages in the order specified by the user's Inbox.

- FetchUnreadOnly—The default setting of True fetches only unread messages. Set this property to False to retrieve all messages.

A message set is indexed, and the number of messages in the set is obtained from the control's MsgCount property. To make one message in the set current, set the control's MsgIndex property to the message's index. Here is some code that loops through all the messages that were retrieved:

14

```
MAPIMessages1.Fetch
For i = 0 to MAPIMessages1.MsgCount - 1
MAPIMessages1.MsgIndex = i
' Do something with each message here.
Next I
```

Note that the available messages have indexes ranging from 0 to `MsgCount` - 1. When the `MsgIndex` property of the control points at a specific message in the message set, you use other properties of the control to obtain information and data from the message. Table 14.1 explains these properties.

ATTACHMENTS

An email message can have one or more attachments associated with it. An attachment can be any disk file or an OLE object. The `AttachmentCount` property specifies the number of attachments included with the current message, and the `AttachmentIndex` property specifies the index of the current attachment. `AttachmentIndex` ranges from 0 to `AttachmentCount` - 1.

TABLE 14.1 PROPERTIES OF THE `MAPIMessages` CONTROL

MAPIMessages *Control Property*	*Information About Current Indexed Message*
AttachmentCount	Number of attachments.
AttachmentIndex	Index of the current attachment.
AttachmentName	Name of currently indexed attachment.
AttachmentPathName	Full path of the current attachment.
AttachmentPosition	Position of the current attachment in the message body.
AttachmentType OLE object.	0 = data file, 1 = embedded OLE object, and 2 = static
MsgDateReceived	Date message was received.
MsgID	String identifier for message.
MsgNoteText	Text of message.
MsgOrigAddress	Address of message originator.
MsgOrigDisplayName	Name of message originator.
MsgRead	True if the message has been read, otherwise False.
MsgReceiptRequested	True if the message requests a return receipt.
MsgSubject	Subject of message.

With these properties, you have a great flexibility in dealing with messages. You could, for example, look through all received messages and display only those from a certain person, or you could look for messages that have a certain keyword in the subject and copy them all to a Text Box for the user to read. Listing 14.1 shows the code to perform this task.

LISTING 14.1 DISPLAYING MESSAGES RELATED TO A SPECIFIC SUBJECT

```
MAPISession1.SignOn
MAPIMessages1.SessionID = MAPISession1.SessionID

For i = 0 To MAPIMessages1.MsgCount - 1
    MAPIMessages1.MsgIndex = i
    If InStr(1, MAPIMessages1.MsgSubject, Keyword) > 0 Then
        buf = buf & "From: " & MAPIMessages1.MsgOrigDisplayName & vbCrLf
        buf = buf & "Subject: " & MAPIMessages1.MsgSubject & vbCrLf
        buf = buf & MAPIMessages1.MsgNoteText & vbCrLf & vbCrLf
    End If
    Text1.Text = buf
Next i

MAPISession1.SignOff
```

A Demonstration

To see how easily the MAPI controls enable you to retrieve mail, try this simple demonstration program. Create a standard Visual Basic EXE project and place a Text Box and two Command Buttons on it. Set their properties as follows:

Control	Property	Value
Text Box	MultiLine	True
	ScrollBars	Vertical
Command Button 1	Name	cmdQuit
Command Button 2	Name	cmdGetMail

Also, place one MAPIMessages control and one MAPISession control, leaving all their properties at the default values. Add the code shown in Listing 14.2 to the form.

14

LISTING 14.2 CODE IN THE MAPI DEMONSTRATION PROGRAM

```
Option Explicit

Private Sub cmdGetMail_Click()

Dim i As Integer, buf As String

MAPISession1.SignOn
MAPIMessages1.FetchUnreadOnly = False
MAPIMessages1.SessionID = MAPISession1.SessionID
MAPIMessages1.Fetch
For i = 0 To MAPIMessages1.MsgCount - 1
    MAPIMessages1.MsgIndex = i
    buf = buf & "From: " & _
        MAPIMessages1.MsgOrigDisplayName & vbCrLf
    buf = buf & "Subject: " & _
        MAPIMessages1.MsgSubject & vbCrLf & vbCrLf
    buf = buf & MAPIMessages1.MsgNoteText & _
        vbCrLf & vbCrLf
Next i

Text1.Text = buf
MAPISession1.SignOff

End Sub

Private Sub cmdQuit_Click()

End

End Sub
```

When you run the program, click the Get Mail button to load the Text Box with all the messages (both read and unread) that are in your Inbox. The program is shown in Figure 14.6.

FIGURE 14.6

Getting messages with the MAPI controls.

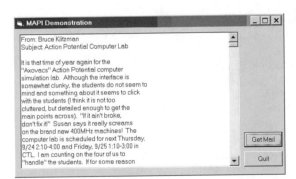

Receiving Attachments

To see whether a received message has any attachments, check the value of the MAPIMessages control's AttachmentCount property. If this property is non-zero, you access individual attachments by setting the AttachmentIndex property to a value between 0 (the first attachment) and AttachmentCount - 1 (the last attachment). After you have selected an attachment, you determine its type by the AttachmentType property, as explained in Table 14.1. Then, the AttachmentPathName will contain the full path and filename of the attachment, which will be automatically saved in your temporary directory.

Take a look at an example. Suppose that someone sends you a message with the attached file data.txt. When the message is retrieved by the MAPIMessages control, the attached file is automatically saved to your temporary directory (usually this is c:\windows\temp). When you access the message, using the MAPIMessages control, and set the MsgIndex property to point to this message and the AttachmentIndex property to point to this attachment, the AttachmentPathName property will contain the string c:\windows\temp\data.txt. Your Visual Basic program can use this path to copy the file, open it, or whatever action is appropriate.

Sending Mail

You use the MAPIMessages control's Send method to send email. This method has the following syntax:

```
MAPIMessages1.Send [ShowDialog]
```

The optional *ShowDialog* argument is a boolean value which, if True, causes the Send method to display a dialog box in which the user can enter the message information (recipients, text, and so on). If you use the default value of False, no dialog box is displayed, and the message is created by setting property values.

Before you can send a message with the MAPIMessages control, you must do two things: Set the control's MsgIndex property to -1 and call its Compose method. The first action makes the control's Send buffer current (as opposed to one of the retrieved messages), and the Compose method clears the buffer in preparation for composing a new message. The following code would let the user send a message, using the mail system's dialog box for composing the message:

```
MAPISession1.SignOn
MAPIMessages1.SessionID = MAPISession1.SessionID
MAPIMessages1.MsgIndex = -1
MAPIMessages1.Compose
```

14

```
MAPIMessages1.Send True
MAPISession1.SignOff
```

When the code is executed, the user's regular mail composition dialog box will be displayed. After the user composes the message and clicks Send, control will return to the Visual Basic program.

What if you don't want to use the mail system's compose dialog box? Then you can create your own and call the Send method with a False argument. To demonstrate this, create a project and place three Text Box controls on the form as follows:

Control	Property	Value
Text Box 1	Name	txtTo
Text Box 2	Name	txtSubject
Text Box 3	MultiLine	True
	Name	txtMessage

You should also add labels to identify the Text Boxes. Add the MAPISession and MAPIMessages controls, too, of course. Then, add a Command Button and place the code from Listing 14.3 in its Click event procedure.

LISTING 14.3 SENDING A MESSAGE WITHOUT USING THE COMPOSE DIALOG BOX

```
Command1.Click()

    MAPISession1.SignOn
    MAPIMessages1.SessionID = MAPISession1.SessionID
    MAPIMessages1.MsgIndex = -1
    MAPIMessages1.Compose
    MAPIMessages1.RecipAddress = txtTo.text
    MAPIMessages1.MsgSubject = txtSubject.Text
    MAPIMessages1.MsgNoteText = txtMessage.Text
    MAPIMessages1.Send False
    MAPISession1.SignOff

End Sub
```

The user can fill in the recipient's address, message subject, and message text and then click the command button; the message will be sent. In a real program, you would want to add some verification code—making sure, for example, that a recipient has been entered, before sending—but this demonstration gives you an idea of how easy it is to send messages with the MAPI controls.

Sending a Message to Multiple Recipients

An outgoing message can have multiple recipients, and you access them by using the RecipIndex property. When you create a new message, this value is set to 0, indicating the first recipient in the list. Therefore, the following code puts the indicated email address at the first position in the list of recipients:

```
MAPISession1.SignOn
MAPIMessages1.SessionID = MAPISession1.SessionID
MAPIMessages1.MsgIndex = -1
MAPIMessages1.Compose
MAPIMessages1.RecipAddress = "billg@microsoft.com
```

The following code shows how to add additional recipients to the message:

```
MAPIMessages1.RecipIndex = 1
MAPIMessages1.RecipAddress = "moe@harvard.edu
MAPIMessages1.RecipIndex = 2
MAPIMessages1.RecipAddress = "larry@harvard.edu
MAPIMessages1.RecipIndex = 3
MAPIMessages1.RecipAddress = "curly@harvard.edu
```

A message recipient can be one of three types: primary recipient, copy recipient, or blind copy recipient. To change the type of the currently indexed recipient, set the MAPIMessages control's RecipType property to one of the values shown in Table 14.2.

TABLE 14.2   VALUES FOR THE RecipType PROPERTY

Constant	Value	Recipient Type
mapToList	1	Primary recipient. This is the default value.
mapCcList	2	Copy recipient.
mapBccList	3	Blind copy recipient.

> **MESSAGE ORIGINATOR**
>
> There is a fourth value that the RecipType can have, mapOrigList (value = 0), specifying the message originator. This value is applicable only to messages you have received and cannot be set for messages you are composing.

The following code, modified from the preceding example, would make billg@microsoft.com the primary recipient of the message, and the other three recipients would be copy recipients:

14

```
MAPISession1.SignOn
MAPIMessages1.SessionID = MAPISession1.SessionID
MAPIMessages1.MsgIndex = -1
MAPIMessages1.Compose
MAPIMessages1.RecipAddress = "billg@microsoft.com
MAPIMessages1.RecipIndex = 1
MAPIMessages1.RecipType = mapCcList
MAPIMessages1.RecipAddress = "moe@harvard.edu
MAPIMessages1.RecipIndex = 2
MAPIMessages1.RecipType = mapCcList
MAPIMessages1.RecipAddress = "larry@harvard.edu
MAPIMessages1.RecipIndex = 3
MAPIMessages1.RecipType = mapCcList
MAPIMessages1.RecipAddress = "curly@harvard.edu
```

Sending Attachments

To send an attachment with a mail message, you use the same attachment-related properties that you learned about earlier in the chapter, as relate to receiving attachments.
Specifically:

1. Set `AttachmentIndex` to the 0-based index of the attachment you are sending.

2. Set `AttachmentPathName` to the full path and filename of the file to send.

3. Set `AttachmentName` to the name that the attachment will have on the recipient's
   computer.

Here is some sample code that sends a message with two attachments:

```
MAPISession1.SignOn
MAPIMessages1.SessionID = MAPISession1.SessionID
MAPIMessages1.MsgIndex = -1
MAPIMessages1.Compose
MAPIMessages1.RecipAddress = "joe@somewhere.com"
MAPIMessages1.MsgSubject = "Attachment"
MAPIMessages1.MsgNoteText = "Here are the files you needed"
MAPIMessages1.AttachmentPathName = "c:\marchdata\sales.txt"
MAPIMessages1.AttachmentName = "marchsales.txt"
MAPIMessages1.AttachmentIndex = 1
MAPIMessages1.AttachmentPathName = "c:\aprildata\sales.txt"
MAPIMessages1.AttachmentName = "aprilsales.txt"
MAPIMessages1.Send False
MAPISession1.SignOff
```

Note that two files with the same name were sent, but they will arrive at the recipient's
computer with different names because of the setting of the `AttachmentName` property.

MAPI Control Errors

The MAPI controls have a set of errors associated with them, and Visual Basic has defined constants for these errors to make the error trapping easier. Any program that uses the MAPI controls should trap errors and display messages to the user when necessary. Table 14.3 presents the MAPI error constants and their descriptions.

TABLE 14.3 CONSTANTS AND VALUES OF MAPI CONTROL ERRORS

Constant	Value	Description
mapSuccessSuccess	32000	Action completed successfully.
mapUserAbort	32001	The current action could not complete because the user canceled the process.
mapFailure	32002	An unspecified error occurred during the current action.
mapLoginFail	32003	Logon has failed. There was no default logon, and the user did not log on correctly.
mapDiskFull	32004	The disk is full.
mapInsufficientMem	32005	Insufficient memory.
mapAccessDenied	32006	Access denied.
mapGeneralFailure	32007	General Failure (unspecified error).
MapTooManySessions	32008	The user has too many sessions open at once.
mapTooManyFiles	32009	The message contains too many file attachments. The message was not sent or read.
mapTooManyRecipients	32010	The message has too many recipients. The message was not sent or read.
mapAttachmentNotFound	32011	The specified attachment could not be found; the message was not sent.
mapAttachmentOpenFailure	32012	The attachment couldn't be opened. The message was not sent.
mapAttachmentWriteFailure	32013	An attachment could not be written to a temporary file.
mapUnknownRecipient	32014	The recipient doesn't appear in the address list. The message was not sent.

continues

14

TABLE 14.3 CONTINUED

Constant	Value	Description
mapBadRecipType	32015	The type of recipient was incorrect. Valid recipient types are 1 (primary recipient), 2 (copy recipient), and 3 (blind copy recipient).
mapNoMessages	32016	Unable to locate the next message.
mapInvalidMessage	32017	An invalid message ID was used. The current action could not be completed.
mapTextTooLarge	32018	The message text was too large to send. Text is limited to 32KB.
mapInvalidSession	32019	An invalid session ID was used.
mapTypeNotSupported	32020	Type not supported.
mapAmbiguousRecipient	32021	One or more recipient addresses are ambiguous.
mapMessageInUse	32022	Message in use.
mapNetworkFailure	32023	Network failure.
mapInvalidEditFields	32024	The value of the AddressEditFieldCount property is invalid. It must be in the range of 0–4.
mapInvalidRecips	32025	One or more recipient addresses are invalid.
mapNotSupported	32026	The requested action is not supported by the underlying mail system.
mapSessionExist	32050	Logon failure. The MAPI messages control is already using a valid session ID.
mapInvalidBuffer	32051	Property is read-only when not using Compose Buffer. Set MsgIndex = -1.
mapInvalidReadBufferAction	32052	Action valid only for Compose Buffer. Set MsgIndex = -1.
mapNoSession	32053	The MAPI messages control does not have a valid session handle from the MAPI session control.
mapInvalidRecipient	32054	You cannot see message originator information while in the Compose Buffer (MsgIndex set to -1).

Constant	Value	Description
MapInvalidComposeBufferAction	32055	The attempted action is not valid in the Compose Buffer (MsgIndex set to -1).
mapControlFailure	32056	Cannot perform action, no messages in list.
mapNoRecipients	32057	Cannot perform action, no recipients.
mapNoAttachment	32058	Cannot perform action, no attachments.

Summary

With the MAPISession and MAPIMessages controls, adding sophisticated email capability to your Visual Basic programs is almost as easy as falling off a log. These two controls work in cooperation with your existing MAPI-compliant email system, which performs most of the work. Given the popularity and importance of email in today's business world, the ability to incorporate the sending and receiving of messages and attachments in your Visual Basic applications is very important.

Q&A

Q Suppose you have written a Visual Basic application that uses the MAPI controls to send and receive email. Can anyone use it?

A No, users must have a MAPI-compliant email system installed on their computer for the MAPI controls to work.

Q What is the difference between the MAPISession control and the MAPIMessages control?

A The MAPISession control is used only to open a MAPI session and to close it. The MAPIMessages control is used for all message-related tasks, such as retrieving and sending mail.

Q Suppose that you have executed the Fetch method, and one of the downloaded messages has a file attachment. How do you save that attachment to disk?

A This is a trick question. You need not do anything because the attached file is automatically saved in your temporary directory when the message is fetched.

14

Workshop

Quiz

1. What MAPIMessages control event is fired when a mail message is received?
2. What is the first thing that a Visual Basic program must do before accessing email with the MAPI controls?
3. How do you determine whether the MAPIMessages control downloads all messages or only unread messages?
4. After executing the Fetch method, how can you determine how many messages were downloaded?
5. When examining a specific message that has been received, how can you tell whether it has any attachments with it?

Exercise

Write a Visual Basic application that runs minimized and notifies the user whenever a message with a specified subject is received.

WEEK 2

In Review

Congratulations! You have completed the second week of your lessons and are well on your way to becoming a skilled Visual Basic Web developer. The first week concentrated mainly on the ActiveX technology. This week, you finished that topic and moved on to dynamic HTML and the Internet-related controls. You understand how both ActiveX and DHTML can be used to provide dynamic content on your Web site, each method having its own strengths and weaknesses. You also saw how to use your knowledge to create real-world, useful applications: a link validity checker and a search robot. Finally, you learned how to integrate email in your Visual Basic applications.

Where You Have Been

This week's first lesson finished up the ActiveX topic that was started last week, showing you how existing Visual Basic applications can be migrated to the ActiveX document format. The next two days taught you about DHTML, a flexible technology that combines HTML, the language of the Web, with Visual Basic programming to create dynamic and powerful Web applications. You also saw how to use the Internet transfer control to send and receive data over the Internet, a capability that offers many possibilities in creating Web-aware applications. You also learned how easy it is to include email capabilities in your Visual Basic applications, with the email controls. As always, Visual Basic lives up to its reputation for making complex programming tasks easy.

8

9

10

11

12

13

14

WEEK 3

15

16

17

18

19

20

21

At a Glance

After completing your first two weeks of lessons, you have already learned a lot about using Visual Basic for Web programming, but Visual Basic has quite a few more goodies that you need to know about. In this last week, the first two lessons explain the WebBrowser control, which lets you drop a fully functional Web browser into your applications. Then you will spend a few lessons learning about VBScript, Active Server Pages, and database connectivity. You'll wrap things up with a lesson on common gateway interface programming, one of most important and widely supported standards for Web development.

Where You Are Going

The WebBrowser control provides almost all the capabilities of a standalone browser in a control you can drop into your Visual Basic applications. Most important, it can be customized, enabling you to do things such as restrict browsing to approved sites. After the first two lessons, you start learning about Active Server Pages (ASP), which permits Web pages to be generated on-the-fly, and VBScript, a simplified version of the Basic language that you can use to write scripts, or small programs, to execute on the Web server or in the Web browser. Then you will see how you can combine ASP and Visual Basic's ActiveX Data objects to provide complete database connectivity in your Web projects. Finally, in the book's last lesson, you will learn how to create common gateway interface programs with Visual Basic.

DAY **15**

Understanding the WebBrowser Control

One of the most sophisticated controls supplied with Visual Basic is the WebBrowser control, which lets you drop a nearly complete Web browser into your projects. Despite this sophistication, it is quite easy to use. Understanding this control's properties, methods, and events will enable you to create browser applications customized to your precise needs. Today you will learn

- The relationship between the WebBrowser control and the Internet Explorer browser
- How to create a basic but functional Web browser
- Details of the WebBrowser control's most important properties, methods, and events

Some Background

To understand the origins of the WebBrowser control, you need a little background information. When Microsoft decided it needed to seriously compete in the browser wars, it developed the Internet Explorer browser. The programmers at Microsoft followed their own advice and used a component-oriented approach in creating the browser. When you use the Internet Explorer browser, therefore, you are actually using this integrated set of components that work together to provide the needed functionality. Let's take a look at the details.

The Internet Explorer application itself—IEXPLORE.EXE—is a surprisingly small application whose primary function is to host and coordinate the various components that make up the browser application. It is the components that perform the actual work of downloading, navigation, HTML parsing, and so on.

The primary component directly hosted by IEXPLORE.EXE is SHDOCVW.DLL, the WebBrowser control. SHDOCVW.DLL provides functionality for navigation, in-place hyperlinking, favorites and history management, and similar tasks. SHDOCVW.DLL in turn hosts the MSHTML.DLL component, which has the main task of parsing and rendering the HTML document. Figure 15.1 shows the overall arrangement.

FIGURE 15.1

The Internet Explorer component model.

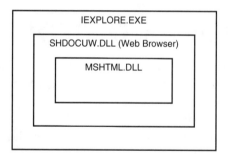

> **WHAT ARE PARSING AND RENDERING**
>
> *Parsing* is the process of going through a data stream and separating it into meaningful parts. The main part of parsing an HTML document is separating the HTML tags from the document content. *Rendering* is the process of interpreting the HTML tags and displaying the document contents onscreen as specified by the formatting tags.

As a result of the way that Microsoft created the Internet Explorer browser, its components are available for other programmers to use. Of most interest is the WebBrowser

15

control. By dropping this control into a Visual Basic project, you have instant access to most of the functionality of a full-blown Web browser.

Don't expect the WebBrowser control to provide all the functionality of the full Internet Explorer browser. Certain features of the browser, such as the menus and toolbar, are provided by the IEXPLORE container and are not part of the WebBrowser control itself. Your Visual Basic program must provide whatever menus and other user interface elements you need.

See How Easy It Is

If you still don't believe me, try this simple project. It will convince you how easy it is to use the WebBrowser control.

1. Start a new Visual Basic Standard EXE project.
2. Use the Components dialog box (press Ctrl+T) to add the Microsoft Internet Controls to the Toolbox.
3. Add a WebBrowser control to the project's form (this control is represented by a globe icon in the Toolbox). Size the control so that it fills most of the form. Leave all its properties at their default values.
4. Add a Text Box and a Command Button to the form. Change the Command Button's Caption property to Go. Do not change any other properties.
5. Put the following line of code in the Command Button's Click event procedure:

```
WebBrowser1.Navigate Text1.Text
```

That's it. You have just programmed a Web browser. Run the program, enter a URL in the text box, and click the Go button. The program will navigate to the site and display it. All the hyperlinks will work, animated elements will move, and scripts will execute—just as in Internet Explorer. You can see my Visual Basic page displayed in the "quick and easy" browser in Figure 15.2.

Just because it is so easy to use the WebBrowser control does not mean that greater flexibility is not available. The control has properties, methods, and events that provide the programmer with the tools needed to create custom browser applications.

The following sections explain these properties, methods, and events of the WebBrowser control. I cover only those aspects of the control that are needed for most development tasks. Then, in tomorrow's lesson, I will show you how to use this control to create a customized Web browser application.

FIGURE 15.2

Displaying a Web page in the "quick and easy" browser.

WebBrowser Control Properties

The WebBrowser control has the standard Visual Basic properties, Height, Width, Top, and Left, that specify its size and location within its container. The WebBrowser control has a Visible property as well. The following are several other properties that you need to know about if you are going to use the control in your projects.

Busy—Returns True if the control is engaged in a navigation or download operation and False otherwise. If Busy is True, you can use the Stop method to terminate the current action.

Container—Returns a reference to the control's container object.

Document—Returns a reference to the automation object of the current HTML document (if there is any). You can use the properties and methods of this Document object to access the contents of the HTML page. See the Visual Basic documentation for details of the Document object.

LocationName—Returns a string that contains the name of the resource currently loaded in the WebBrowser control. If the resource is an HTML page on the World Wide Web, the name is the title of that page. If the resource is a folder or file on the network or local computer, the name is the full path of the folder or file.

LocationURL—Returns a string that contains the URL of the resource currently loaded in the WebBrowser control. If the resource is a folder or file on the network or local computer, the name is the full path of the folder or file.

Offline—Specifies whether the WebBrowser control is operating in offline mode. If False (the default), the control attempts to read the source document. If True, the control uses the local cached copy of the document.

Parent—Returns a reference to the Visual Basic form on which the WebBrowser control located.

ReadyState—Returns the WebBrowser control's ready state. Table 15.1 shows the possible values.

TABLE 15.1 POSSIBLE RETURN VALUES OF THE ReadyState PROPERTY

READYSTATE_UNINITIALIZED	The object is uninitialized.
READYSTATE_LOADING	The object is loading its properties.
READYSTATE_LOADED	The object has been initialized.
READYSTATE_INTERACTIVE	The object is interactive, but not all of its data is available.
READYSTATE_COMPLETE	The object has received all its data.

RegisterAsBrowser—True or False, specifying whether the WebBrowser control is registered as a top-level browser for target name resolution.

RegisterAsDropTarget—True or False, specifying whether the WebBrowser control is registered as a drop target for navigation.

Silent—Specifies whether the WebBrowser control can display any dialog boxes. The default setting, False, means that no dialog boxes can be displayed.

TopLevelContainer—Returns True if the object is a top-level container and False otherwise.

WebBrowser Control Methods

The methods of the WebBrowser control are related mostly to navigation. You will see that most of these methods correspond to commands available in the Internet Explorer Web browser.

GoBack—Navigates to the previous location in the history list.

GoForward—Navigates to the next item in the history list.

> **THE HISTORY LIST**
>
> The WebBrowser control automatically maintains an ordered list of all locations that have been visited during the current session. The GoBack and GoForward methods can be used to move from item to item in this list. If you are currently at the last item in the history list, the GoForward method should not be used. Likewise, the GoBack method is inappropriate if you are at the first item in the list. You can use the CommandStateChange event (described later in the chapter) to determine whether the history list contains a "next" or a "previous" item.

GoHome—Navigates to your home page. You specify your home page under Internet in the Windows control panel (see the sidebar for details).

> **SPECIFYING A HOME PAGE**
>
> To specify your default home page on the Web, open the Windows control panel and double-click the Internet icon. In the Internet Properties dialog box, select the General tab and enter the desired home page URL.

Navigate—Navigates to a URL or local file. The syntax of this method is

```
Navigate URL [Flags,] [TargetFrameName,] [PostData,] [Headers]
```

- The PostData and Headers arguments are for advanced uses beyond the scope of this book, so I will not cover them further. I mention them only so that you will know they exist and can investigate further on your own if you like.

- URL is the only required argument. It specifies the URL or full pathname of the resource to open.

- Flags is an optional argument that determines details of how the new resource is opened. It can be a combination of the values shown in Table 15.2. If no Flags argument is used, the new resource is opened in the current window, added to the history list, loaded from the disk cache if it is available, and written to the disk cache if downloaded.

TABLE 15.2 VALUES FOR THE Navigate METHOD'S Flags ARGUMENT

Constant	Value	Effect
navOpenInNewWindow	1	Opens the resource in a new window.
navNoHistory	2	Do not add the current page to the history list. The new page replaces the current page in the list.
navNoReadFromCache	4	Do not read the new page from the disk cache.
navNoWriteToCache	8	Do not write the new page to the disk cache.

TargetFrameName specifies the target frame for the new URL. It is relevant only if the new resource has defined frames. Table 15.3 lists the possible values.

TABLE 15.3 VALUES FOR THE Navigate METHOD'S OPTIONAL TargetFrameName ARGUMENT

Argument	Loads the Resource into...
_blank	A new unnamed window.
_parent	The immediate parent of the current document.
_self	The current frame.
_top	The full body of the current window.
name	The frame identified by *name*. If *name* does not exist, a new window is opened.

Quit—Closes the WebBrowser control.

Refresh—Reloads the page currently displayed in the WebBrowser control. Forces a load over the network, ensuring that the latest data is displayed (in other words, will not load from the cache).

Stop—Cancels any ongoing navigation or download operations and stops any dynamic page elements, such as background sounds and animations. This has an effect only when the Busy property is True.

WebBrowser Control Events

The events detected by the WebBrowser control are related to navigating and other state changes. Your program can use these events to keep track of the control's status.

CommandStateChange

This event is used mainly to enable and disable a browser's Forward and Back buttons. As mentioned earlier in the chapter, the WebBrowser control's GoBack and GoForward methods are appropriate only if the history list contains a URL to go back or forward to. You can place code in the CommandStateChange event procedure to perform this task. The event procedure has the following syntax:

```
Private Sub object_CommandStateChange (ByVal Command As Long,
    ByVal Enable As Boolean)
```

The Command argument identifies the command whose enabled state has changed. The two relevant values are CSC_NAVIGATEFORWARD (value = 1) and CSC_NAVIGATEBACK (value = 3), which identify the GoForward and GoBack commands, respectively. The Enable argument is True if the command identified by Command is now enabled, and False if not.

The following code shows how this is done. Assume that your browser application has two Command Buttons for the Forward and Back commands. Then this code, in the CommandStateChange event procedure, will enable and disable the Forward and Back buttons appropriately, depending on the state of the history list:

```
Private Sub brwWebBrowser_CommandStateChange (ByVal Command _
    As Long, ByVal Enable As Boolean)

If Command = CSC_NAVIGATEBACK Then
    cmdForward.Enabled = Enable
End If

If Command = CSC_NAVIGATEFORWARD Then
    cmdBack.Enabled = Enable
End If

End Sub
```

DocumentComplete

The DocumentComplete event fires when the document being navigated to reaches the READYSTATE_COMPLETE state (as described earlier for the ReadyState property). The event procedure syntax is as follows:

```
Private Sub object_DocumentComplete(ByVal pDisp As Object, URL As Variant)
```

The pDisp argument returns a reference to the WebBrowser control that received the event. The URL argument is the URL or filename that was navigated to.

Why does this event receive a reference to the WebBrowser control that fired it? For a document without frames, this argument is not needed. In a multiple frame document, however, each frame is represented by a WebBrowser object. This is in addition to the top-level WebBrowser object that contains the entire document. As each individual frame loads, it will fire the DocumentComplete event. After all frames are loaded, this event will fire one last time. The top-level object can identify this event by using the value of the *pDisp* argument.

Suppose the top-level WebBrowser control is named WB1. The following code will identify when the final DocumentComplete event has occurred:

```
Private Sub WB1_DocumentComplete(ByVal pDisp As Object, _
    URL As Variant)
    If (pDisp Is WB1.Object) Then
        ' All frames loaded.
    End If

End Sub
```

THE URL ARGUMENT

The URL argument passed to the DocumentComplete event procedure may be different from the URL that the WebBrowser control was told to navigate to. The URL argument is fully qualified, so if the WebBrowser control was told to navigate to www.pgacom.con, this argument will contain http://www.pgacon.com/. Also, if the server directed the browser to another URL, this URL will be passed to the event procedure and not the original URL.

DownloadBegin

The DownloadBegin event fires when a navigation operation is beginning. This event procedure takes no arguments. The browser can use this event to commence the display of any "busy" message or other indication that a download is in progress.

DownloadComplete

The DownloadComplete event fires when a navigation operation finishes, is cancelled by the user, or fails because of an error. Use this event to terminate the display of a "busy" indicator. There is always a DownloadComplete event for each DownloadBegin event.

ProgressChange

The ProgressChange event occurs when the progress of a download operation is updated. It has the following syntax:

```
Private Sub object_ProgressChange(ByVal Progress As Long, _
    ByVal ProgressMax As Long)
```

The *Progress* argument specifies the amount of progress (in bytes downloaded) and has a value of -1 when the operation is complete. The *ProgressMax* argument indicates the total number of bytes to download. Use this event procedure to display a progress indicator to the user during downloads. Any time that this event fires and `Progress` is not -1, the formula

```
(Progress/ProgressMax) * 100
```

can be used to calculate the percent of the download that is complete. You need to include code to check for cases in which `ProgressMax` is 0, to avoid a Divide by Zero error. For example:

```
If ProgressMax <> 0 Then
    txtProgress.Text = (Progress / ProgressMax) * 100
End If
```

INACCURATE BYTE COUNTS

In my experience, the values passed to the `ProgressChange` event procedure do not always give accurate byte counts, although the percentage values calculated by Progress/ProgressMax seem to be accurate. For this reason, I have used this event procedure to display "percent done" indicators but not to display "bytes remaining" values.

Summary

The capability to browse the Web is an important part of many Visual Basic applications. Although the standard Microsoft Internet Explorer is a fine browser, it is designed for general use and might not be suitable for a business setting in which unrestricted Web access is inappropriate. By utilizing the WebBrowser control, you can create a customized browser that is designed specifically for the tasks your end users need to accomplish.

This lesson explains the basic operation of the WebBrowser control and teaches you its important properties, methods, and events. With this background information, you are ready to tackle tomorrow's lesson, creating a custom browser.

15

Q&A

Q When you place a WebBrowser control in your Visual Basic project, is the end result identical to the standalone Internet Explorer browser?

A No. The WebBrowser control provides some of the functionality of the standalone browser—loading and displaying HTML documents, hyperlinking, and so on. Other aspects of the browser, such as its menus and toolbar, are not part of the WebBrowser control.

Q When an HTML document is loaded into the WebBrowser control, how do you access details of the document contents?

A By means of the Document object, referenced by the WebBrowser control's Document property.

Workshop

Quiz

1. Which of the WebBrowser control's events can you use to enable and disable the application's Forward and Back buttons?

2. How do you know that the WebBrowser control has loaded all its data?

3. Can you use the `DownloadComplete` event to tell that the WebBrowser control has completed loading an HTML page?

4. How would you navigate to a new URL without adding the current URL to the history list?

Creating a Customized Web Browser

The WebBrowser control provides a lot of functionality in an easy-to-use package. In this lesson, you will see how to use this control to create a custom Web browser that restricts users to a list of approved URLs. Today you will learn

- Why you might need to create a custom browser
- How to use the Visual Basic Application Wizard to create a basic browser
- How to limit the browser to those URLs on an approved URL list

Why a Custom Browser?

Perhaps you are wondering why you would need to program a custom Web browser. Isn't the Internet Explorer browser, available free from Microsoft, good enough? Certainly, Internet Explorer is a terrific browser, and for general browsing, I think it is hard to beat. But that's where the problem lies—it *is* a general-purpose browser and does not impose any guidelines or limitations on what the user does.

Suppose, for example, that you have created a set of ActiveX documents or dynamic HTML pages for an important company function. The various users will need a browser to access these pages, and the standalone version of Internet Explorer will work just fine. Unfortunately, it will also work just fine for visiting the Hawaii Tourism Bureau pages, doing a little online shopping, or checking stock quotes. Unless you have an awful lot of trust in your employees, you might want to equip them with a browser that lets them perform their work but limits the playing until after hours.

This is only one of many potential advantages to writing a custom browser designed specifically for a particular task. Even if you trust your employees 100%, you can simplify and streamline many business procedures by writing a custom browser.

Getting Started

The easiest way to begin building a customized Web browser is to let Visual Basic do the work for you. That's right, the Visual Basic Application Wizard will create a basic browser for you, complete with a nice-looking toolbar. You can then add custom features as needed. Here's how:

1. Select New from the File menu to display the New Project dialog box.

2. Click the VB Application Wizard icon; then click Open.

3. Continue through the wizard screens, accepting the default settings, until you come to the Application Wizard - Internet Connectivity dialog box, which is shown in Figure 16.1.

FIGURE **16.1**

The Application Wizard - Internet Connectivity dialog box.

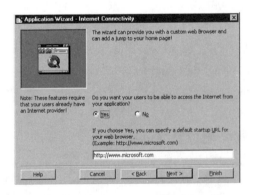

4. Select the Yes option. If you want your browser to have a default home page, enter the page URL in the text box at the bottom of the dialog box. Otherwise, erase the contents of this text box and leave it blank.

5. Click Finish. Visual Basic will create the application as you defined it in the wizard.

If you examine the modules created by the wizard, you will see a form named frmBrowser. This is the browser part of the application, and it is the only part you need. You can delete the other modules from the disk, if desired. Then, to create the custom browser project, follow these steps:

1. Create a new Standard EXE project.

2. Select Project, Add Form to display the Add Form dialog box. Click the Existing tab (see Figure 16.2). Navigate to the location where you saved the browser form (frmBrowser.frm) from the project that the wizard created. Select that form and click Open.

16

FIGURE 16.2

Adding the existing browser form to your project.

3. In the Project window, select the project's original form, Form1.

4. Select Project, Remove Form 1. Now the project will contain only the browser form.

5. Select Project, Project1 Properties to display the Project Properties dialog box. On the General tab, pull down the Startup Object list and select frmBrowser; then click OK.

6. Make sure that the MDIChild property of frmBrowser is set to False.

Don't forget to save the project under a name of your choosing. The browser is ready, and you can run it to see how it works. When it starts, it displays a blank screen, shown in Figure 16.3. If you enter a URL in the Combo Box and press Enter, you will navigate to that URL. Try it!

Figure 16.3

Running the basic browser.

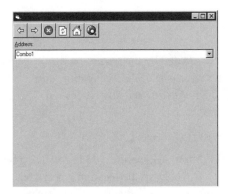

Under the Hood

It's worthwhile to look at the objects and code in the browser that the wizard created to see what features it already has, which features you might want to change, and which ones you will need to add. The form contains the following controls:

- A WebBrowser control
- A Combo Box for entering and keeping track of URLs
- A Picture Box that serves as a container for the Combo Box
- A Toolbar with six buttons
- An Image List that holds the images for the toolbar buttons
- A Timer control used to display status messages to the user

Listing 16.1 presents the code in the form. Following is a brief description of each procedure and what tasks its code accomplishes. It's a good idea for you to examine the code and be sure that you understand how it works.

Form_Load procedure—Code in this procedure positions the Combo Box at the proper location. Then, if the global variable StartingAddress contains a URL, it navigates to that URL. If you want the browser to automatically open a URL when it starts, add a line of code to this procedure, setting the variable StartingAddress to the desired URL.

Form_Resize procedure—This code sets the width of the address Combo Box to extend across the form and then resizes the WebBrowser control to fill the remainder of the form.

DownloadComplete—Code in this event procedure sets the form's caption to the URL just downloaded.

NavigateComplete2—This event fires when a successful navigation completes. Code here removes the current URL from the Combo Box if it is present and then adds it at the top of the list.

cboAddress_Click—If the address box is clicked, code in this procedure instructs the WebBrowser control to navigate to the selected URL.

cboAddress_KeyPress—If the user presses Enter on the Combo Box, this code simulates a click on the control, so the cboAddress_Click event procedure will be executed.

timTimer_Timer—The timer is used to display a Working... message in the form's title bar while the WebBrowser control is busy with a transfer.

tbToolBar_ButtonClick—This event procedure responds to clicks of toolbar buttons. The code sends the appropriate command to the WebBrowser control.

Note also the two module-level global variables. The variable StartingAddress is a remnant from the original wizard-generated program and was used to pass a starting URL to the browser form. The Boolean variable mbDontNavigateNow is used to prevent the browser from navigating to a new URL in the brief period when the address Combo Box is being updated.

LISTING 16.1 CODE IN THE WIZARD-CREATED BROWSER FORM

```
Public StartingAddress As String
Dim mbDontNavigateNow As Boolean

Private Sub Form_Load()

    On Error Resume Next
    Me.Show
    tbToolBar.Refresh
    Form_Resize

    cboAddress.Move 50, lblAddress.Top + lblAddress.Height + 15

    If Len(StartingAddress) > 0 Then
        cboAddress.Text = StartingAddress
        cboAddress.AddItem cboAddress.Text
        'try to navigate to the starting address
        timTimer.Enabled = True
        brwWebBrowser.Navigate StartingAddress
    End If

End Sub
```

continues

LISTING 16.1 CONTINUED

```
Private Sub brwWebBrowser_DownloadComplete()

    On Error Resume Next
    Me.Caption = brwWebBrowser.LocationName

End Sub

Private Sub brwWebBrowser_NavigateComplete2 _
    (ByVal pDisp As Object, URL As Variant)

    On Error Resume Next

    Dim i As Integer
    Dim bFound As Boolean

    Me.Caption = brwWebBrowser.LocationName
    For i = 0 To cboAddress.ListCount - 1
        If cboAddress.List(i) = brwWebBrowser.LocationURL Then
            bFound = True
            Exit For
        End If
    Next i
    mbDontNavigateNow = True
    If bFound Then
        cboAddress.RemoveItem i
    End If
    cboAddress.AddItem brwWebBrowser.LocationURL, 0
    cboAddress.ListIndex = 0
    mbDontNavigateNow = False

End Sub

Private Sub cboAddress_Click()

    If mbDontNavigateNow Then Exit Sub
    timTimer.Enabled = True
    brwWebBrowser.Navigate cboAddress.Text

End Sub

Private Sub cboAddress_KeyPress(KeyAscii As Integer)
    On Error Resume Next
    If KeyAscii = vbKeyReturn Then
        cboAddress_Click
    End If
End Sub

Private Sub Form_Resize()
```

```
    On Error Resume Next

    cboAddress.Width = Me.ScaleWidth - 100
    brwWebBrowser.Width = Me.ScaleWidth - 100
    brwWebBrowser.Height = Me.ScaleHeight - _
        (picAddress.Top + picAddress.Height) - 100

End Sub

Private Sub timTimer_Timer()

    If brwWebBrowser.Busy = False Then
        timTimer.Enabled = False
        Me.Caption = brwWebBrowser.LocationName
    Else
        Me.Caption = "Working..."
    End If

End Sub

Private Sub tbToolBar_ButtonClick(ByVal Button As Button)

    On Error Resume Next

    timTimer.Enabled = True

    Select Case Button.Key
        Case "Back"
            brwWebBrowser.GoBack
        Case "Forward"
            brwWebBrowser.GoForward
        Case "Refresh"
            brwWebBrowser.Refresh
        Case "Home"
            brwWebBrowser.GoHome
        Case "Search"
            brwWebBrowser.GoSearch
        Case "Stop"
            timTimer.Enabled = False
            brwWebBrowser.Stop
            Me.Caption = brwWebBrowser.LocationName
    End Select

End Sub
```

Some Preliminary Modifications

The browser form created by the wizard is a good start, but it is pretty basic. Let's make some changes to improve it.

Enabling and Disabling Toolbar Buttons

A well-designed application will not make it appear as though actions can be carried out when, in fact, they cannot. For a browser, one example is that the Forward and Back commands should not be available unless URLs are available in the history list to go forward or back to. Likewise, the Refresh command is not relevant until a resource has been loaded. The first modifications to the custom browser, therefore, will be to enable and disable the toolbar buttons appropriately, depending on the state of the browser. Here are the steps required:

1. Add the following code to the `Form_Load` event procedure to disable the Forward, Back, Stop, and Refresh buttons when the browser is first loaded.

   ```
   tbToolBar.Buttons("Back").Enabled = False
   tbToolBar.Buttons("Forward").Enabled = False
   tbToolBar.Buttons("Stop").Enabled = False
   tbToolBar.Buttons("Refresh").Enabled = False
   ```

2. Add this line of code to the `brwWebBrowser_NavigateComplete2` event procedure, to enable the Refresh button as soon as the browser has loaded a resource.

   ```
   tbToolBar.Buttons("Refresh").Enabled = True
   ```

3. Create an event procedure for the WebBrowser control's `CommandStateChange` event and the code shown here. This code enables or disables the Forward and Back buttons, depending on the state of the history list. See Day 15, "Understanding the WebBrowser Control," for details on how this event procedure works.

   ```
   Private Sub brwWebBrowser_CommandStateChange _
       (ByVal Command As Long, ByVal Enable As Boolean)

   If Command = CSC_NAVIGATEBACK Then
       tbToolBar.Buttons("Back").Enabled = Enable
   End If

   If Command = CSC_NAVIGATEFORWARD Then
       tbToolBar.Buttons("Forward").Enabled = Enable
   End If

   End Sub
   ```

4. Edit the `timTimer_Timer` event procedure so that the Stop button will be enabled during downloads (when the WebBrowser control's `Busy` property is `True`) and disabled at other times. Listing 16.2 shows the code for the entire procedure; the two lines that refer to the toolbar control are new.

LISTING 16.2   THE `timTimer_Timer` EVENT PROCEDURE

```
Private Sub timTimer_Timer()

    If brwWebBrowser.Busy = False Then
        timTimer.Enabled = False
        Me.Caption = brwWebBrowser.LocationName
        tbToolBar.Buttons("Stop").Enabled = False
    Else
        Me.Caption = "Working..."
        tbToolBar.Buttons("Stop").Enabled = True
    End If

End Sub
```

After adding this code, run the browser, and you will see that the toolbar buttons are enabled and disabled appropriately according to the state of the program.

FINDING TEXT

The ability to search for text in the currently loaded document is a useful feature. I thought it would take a bit of programming, but to my delight, I found the capability already built in to the WebBrowser control. All the user needs to do is click anywhere in the document and then press Ctrl+F to open a Find dialog box.

Adding Menu Commands

I don't know about you, but I like to use menus for most program functions. Therefore, I decided to give the custom browser a menu, albeit a simple one. At this stage, the menu will contain only commands for opening a new URL, quitting the program, and displaying an About dialog box.

Open the Visual Basic menu editor and create two top-level menus as follows:

First Level	Second Level	Caption	Shortcut
mnuFile		&File	
	mnuFileOpen	&Open	Ctrl+O
	mnuFileExit	E&xit	
mnuHelp		&Help	
	mnuHelpAbout	&About	

To create the About dialog box, select Project, Add Form to display the Add Form dialog box. I suggest you select the About Dialog icon to used the About dialog box template provided with Visual Basic (shown in Figure 16.4). Of course, you need to edit this form to reflect information about your program.

FIGURE 16.4

Visual Basic's default About dialog box template.

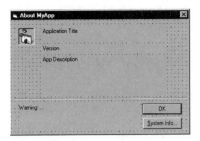

Listing 16.3 shows the code to handle the menu commands. This code is quite simple, and I am sure you do not need any explanation.

LISTING 16.3 CODE FOR THE MENU COMMANDS

```
Private Sub mnuFileExit_Click()

    Dim reply

    reply = MsgBox("Exit - are you sure?", vbYesNo)
    If reply = vbYes Then End

    End Sub

Private Sub mnuFileOpen_Click()

    Dim newURL As String

    newURL = InputBox("Enter URL or file name:", "Open")

    If newURL <> "" Then
            brwWebBrowser.Navigate2 (newURL)
        End If

End Sub

Private Sub mnuHelpAbout_Click()

    frmAbout.Show 1

End Sub
```

> **THE ABOUT DIALOG BOX**
>
> When you add one of Visual Basic's default About dialog boxes to a project, you get a lot more than a form with some labels you can edit. The form includes code to display detailed system information, including some information obtained from the Windows Registry. It can be a real timesaver if you want this sort of functionality in your application's About box.

So far, you have a perfectly serviceable browser, but it offers no advantages over the standalone Internet Explorer browser and, in fact, is not nearly as flexible. The remainder of the chapter is devoted to adding special customization features that the standalone Internet Explorer browser cannot offer.

Restricting Access

The most important feature for a custom browser is some way to restrict access. In other words, the user should not be able to navigate to any Web sites other than those specified in an approved list. How do you accomplish this?

> **FORBIDDING SITES**
>
> Another way to limit access is the other side of the coin from permitting only a selected list of sites to forbid specific sites and permit all others. Although logically feasible, this approach must deal with the constant and rapid expansion of the Web. Will you really be able to keep the "forbidden sites" list up to date?

One approach would be to simply program the approved URLs into the application. However, there is an immediately obvious weakness to this method—what if the list changes? You'll have to reprogram and redistribute the entire application. Not a good idea!

Another method would be to publish the list of approved sites in a file that is then distributed to the users, perhaps by email. Aside from the trouble of distributing the file, there is always the possibility that a clever user will figure out how to edit the file and add unauthorized sites to the approved list.

Perhaps the best approach, and the one you will follow here, is to maintain a single approved list file on a server and have the program retrieve the list each time it starts. There is no chance of unauthorized tampering with the file, and changes to the list can be easily made.

Approved File List Format and Retrieval

The format for the approved sites list can be anything you like, as long as it works. I have taken the simplest approach, using a simple text file containing one URL per line.

Retrieving the file will be an easy task with the help of the Internet Transfer control (ITC). You learned how to use the ITC for http:// transfers on Day 11, "The Internet Transfer Control." Please refer back to that lesson if you want to brush up on the details.

After the program has retrieved the approved URL list, then what? It would be a simple matter to compare the URLs entered by the user with the list and accept them only if they are found on the list. However, this would require the user to remember URLs. A better idea would be to make the list of approved URLs available to users so that they can select the desired URL. You do this by adding a menu and placing the approved URLs on it.

ADDING MENUS AT RUNTIME

Adding menu commands to an application at runtime can be a very useful technique. You must create at least one menu item of the same name at design time and make it an element of a control array by assigning it an Index property of 0. Then, at runtime use the Load statement to add as many more items as you want. Suppose you added a menu item with the name mnuDummy and the Index of 0. At runtime the following code would add two more items to the menu:

```
Load mnuDummy(1)
Load mnuDummy(2)
MnuDummy(1).Caption = "This"
MnuDummy(2).Caption = "That"
```

With the Unload statement, you can also remove menu items that are part of a control array.

To prepare the browser for adding URLs to a menu, open the menu editor and add a new top-level menu item with the name mnuGoto and the caption &Go To. Then add a sub-item under it with the name mnuGotoURL, the Caption of (unavailable), and the Index property of 0. When you are finished, the Menu Editor will look like Figure 16.5.

To download the approved URL file, the project needs one Internet Transfer control. Add this control to the form and leave all its properties at their default values.

FIGURE **16.5**

After adding the Go To menu for placing the approved URLs.

The task of downloading the approved URL file and adding its contents to the menu is performed by the LoadApprovedList function. The code is shown in Listing 16.4. Note that the URL of the approved URL file is specified by the constant URL_LIST that must be declared and initialized at the module level. You must add this constant at the module level of your code, being sure to replace the xxxx with the proper URL:

```
Const URL_LIST = http://xxxx/allowed.txt
```

Then the code downloads the file, extracts each URL (there is one URL per line), and adds it to the menu. The function returns True on success and False if an error condition prevents the file from being downloaded.

LISTING **16.4** THE LoadApprovedList FUNCTION

```
Public Function LoadApprovedList() As Boolean

On Error GoTo InetError

Dim s As String, temp As String
Dim pos As Integer, pos1 As Integer
Dim i As Integer

s = Inet1.OpenURL(URL_LIST)

pos = 1
i = 0
pos1 = InStr(pos, s, vbCrLf)
Do While pos1 > 0
    temp = Mid(s, pos, pos1 - pos)
    If i > 0 Then Load mnuGotoURL(i)
    mnuGotoURL(i).Caption = temp
    i = i + 1
```

continues

LISTING 16.4   CONTINUED

```
        pos = pos1 + 2
        pos1 = InStr(pos, s, vbCrLf)
        DoEvents
Loop

LoadApprovedList = True
Exit Function

InetError:
    LoadApprovedList = False

End Function
```

The `LoadApprovedList` function is called from the `Form_Load` event procedure. At the beginning, add the following code to that procedure. Don't forget to declare a string variable s to hold the error message.

```
If Not LoadApprovedList Then
    s = "Cannot download URL list." & vbCrLf
    s = s & "Please try again later."
    MsgBox (s)
    End
End If
```

So far so good. Figure 16.6 shows the custom browser in operation, displaying the menu with the URLs downloaded from the approved list. The user can select the desired destination by opening the menu and selecting.

FIGURE 16.6

The approved URLs are displayed as menu commands.

You have one more problem to solve, as you are probably aware. Although the approved list works fine as menu commands, there is no restriction on URLs that the user enters in the Address box or enters using the File, Open command. To prevent users from circumventing the approved list in these ways, you can save the list of approved URLs in a global string and then check any user-specified URL against the list. If the URL is found, fine; otherwise, the program will display a message to the effect that the URL is not approved.

1. Add the following declaration to the frmBrowser module, at the module level. This creates a global string variable to hold the approved URL list.

   ```
   Dim OkURLs As String
   ```

2. Modify the code in the LoadApprovedList function so that the downloaded list is placed in this global variable rather than in the local variable s. Then, assign the value to s for local processing:

   ```
   OkURLs = Inet1.OpenURL(URL_LIST)
   s = OkURLs
   ```

3. Add a function named UrlIsOK with the code shown in Listing 16.5.

LISTING 16.5 THE FUNCTION UrlIsOk CHECKS URLs AGAINST THE APPROVED LIST

```
Public Function UrlIsOk(URL As String) As Boolean

Dim s As String

If InStr(1, OkURLs, URL) = 0 Then
    s = "Sorry but " & URL & " is not an approved location."
    MsgBox (s)
    UrlIsOk = False
Else
    UrlIsOk = True
End If

End Function
```

4. Modify the cboAddress_Click and mnuFileOpen_Click event procedures, as shown in Listing 16.6, so that the new URL is checked against the list and opened only if found.

LISTING 16.6 CHECKING NEW URLs AGAINST THE APPROVED LIST BEFORE OPENING THEM

```
Private Sub cboAddress_Click()

    If mbDontNavigateNow Then Exit Sub
    If UrlIsOk(cboAddress.Text) Then
        timTimer.Enabled = True
```

continues

LISTING 16.6   CONTINUED

```
        brwWebBrowser.Navigate cboAddress.Text
    End If

End Sub

Private Sub mnuFileOpen_Click()

Dim newURL As String

newURL = InputBox("Enter URL or file name:", "Open")

If newURL <> "" And UrlIsOk(newURL) Then
    brwWebBrowser.Navigate2 (newURL)
End If

End Sub
```

The final bit of code needed is the click event procedure for the mnuGoToURL menu command. This command lets the user navigate to one of the URLs on the loaded approved list. It is shown in Listing 16.7.

LISTING 16.7   THE Click EVENT PROCEDURE FOR THE mnuGoToURL COMMAND

```
Private Sub mnuGotoURL_Click(Index As Integer)
    brwWebBrowser.Navigate2 (mnuGotoURL(Index).Caption)
End Sub
```

With the addition of this code, the browser is finished—at least, as far as you are going to take it! Run it, and you'll see that the browser will not navigate to any URL that is not on the approved list, regardless of how the user specifies the URL.

Listing 16.8 presents the browser form's full code. You have seen much of this code in bits and pieces throughout the chapter, but seeing it all together might help you to understand how the different parts of the program work together.

LISTING 16.8   THE COMPLETE CODE FOR THE CUSTOM BROWSER FORM

```
Public StartingAddress As String
Dim mbDontNavigateNow As Boolean
Const URL_LIST = "http://www.pgacon.com/ipbook/allowed.txt"
Dim OkURLs As String

Private Sub brwWebBrowser_CommandStateChange _
    (ByVal Command As Long, ByVal Enable As Boolean)
```

```
If Command = CSC_NAVIGATEBACK Then
    tbToolBar.Buttons("Back").Enabled = Enable
End If

If Command = CSC_NAVIGATEFORWARD Then
    tbToolBar.Buttons("Forward").Enabled = Enable
End If

End Sub

Private Sub Form_Load()

    Dim s As String

    On Error Resume Next
    Me.Show
    tbToolBar.Refresh
    Form_Resize
    StartingAddress = ""

    If Not LoadApprovedList Then
        s = "Cannot download URL list." & vbCrLf
        s = s & "Please try again later."
        MsgBox (s)
        End
    End If

    cboAddress.Move 50, lblAddress.Top + lblAddress.Height + 15

    tbToolBar.Buttons("Back").Enabled = False
    tbToolBar.Buttons("Forward").Enabled = False
    tbToolBar.Buttons("Refresh").Enabled = False
    tbToolBar.Buttons("Stop").Enabled = False

    If Len(StartingAddress) > 0 Then
        cboAddress.Text = StartingAddress
        cboAddress.AddItem cboAddress.Text
        'Try to navigate to the starting address
        timTimer.Enabled = True
        brwWebBrowser.Navigate StartingAddress
    End If

End Sub

Private Sub brwWebBrowser_DownloadComplete()
    On Error Resume Next
    Me.Caption = brwWebBrowser.LocationName
End Sub
```

16

continues

LISTING 16.8   CONTINUED

```
Private Sub brwWebBrowser_NavigateComplete2 _
    (ByVal pDisp As Object, URL As Variant)

    Dim i As Integer
    Dim bFound As Boolean

    On Error Resume Next

    Me.Caption = brwWebBrowser.LocationName
    For i = 0 To cboAddress.ListCount - 1
        If cboAddress.List(i) = brwWebBrowser.LocationURL Then
            bFound = True
            Exit For
        End If
    Next i
    mbDontNavigateNow = True
    If bFound Then
        cboAddress.RemoveItem i
    End If
    cboAddress.AddItem brwWebBrowser.LocationURL, 0
    cboAddress.ListIndex = 0
    mbDontNavigateNow = False
    tbToolBar.Buttons("Refresh").Enabled = True

End Sub

Private Sub cboAddress_Click()

    If mbDontNavigateNow Then Exit Sub
    If UrlIsOk(cboAddress.Text) Then
        timTimer.Enabled = True
        brwWebBrowser.Navigate cboAddress.Text
    End If

End Sub

Private Sub cboAddress_KeyPress(KeyAscii As Integer)

    On Error Resume Next

    If KeyAscii = vbKeyReturn Then
        cboAddress_Click
    End If

End Sub

Private Sub Form_Resize()
    On Error Resume Next
    cboAddress.Width = Me.ScaleWidth - 100
```

```
    brwWebBrowser.Width = Me.ScaleWidth - 100
    brwWebBrowser.Height = Me.ScaleHeight - _
        (picAddress.Top + picAddress.Height) - 100
End Sub

Private Sub mnuFileExit_Click()

    Dim reply

    reply = MsgBox("Exit - are you sure?", vbYesNo)
    If reply = vbYes Then End

End Sub

Private Sub mnuFileOpen_Click()

    Dim newURL As String

    newURL = InputBox("Enter URL or file name:", "Open")

    If newURL <> "" And UrlIsOk(newURL) Then
        brwWebBrowser.Navigate2 (newURL)
    End If

End Sub

Private Sub mnuGotoURL_Click(Index As Integer)

    brwWebBrowser.Navigate2 (mnuGotoURL(Index).Caption)

End Sub

Private Sub mnuHelpAbout_Click()

    frmAbout.Show 1

End Sub

Private Sub timTimer_Timer()

    If brwWebBrowser.Busy = False Then
        timTimer.Enabled = False
        Me.Caption = brwWebBrowser.LocationName
        tbToolBar.Buttons("Stop").Enabled = False
    Else
        Me.Caption = "Working..."
        tbToolBar.Buttons("Stop").Enabled = True
    End If
```

continues

LISTING 16.8   CONTINUED

```
End Sub

Private Sub tbToolBar_ButtonClick(ByVal Button As Button)

    On Error Resume Next

    timTimer.Enabled = True

    Select Case Button.Key
        Case "Back"
            brwWebBrowser.GoBack
        Case "Forward"
            brwWebBrowser.GoForward
        Case "Refresh"
            brwWebBrowser.Refresh
        Case "Home"
            brwWebBrowser.GoHome
        Case "Search"
            brwWebBrowser.GoSearch
        Case "Stop"
            timTimer.Enabled = False
            brwWebBrowser.Stop
            Me.Caption = brwWebBrowser.LocationName
    End Select

End Sub


Public Function LoadApprovedList() As Boolean

    'On Error GoTo InetError

    Dim s As String, temp As String
    Dim pos As Integer, pos1 As Integer
    Dim i As Integer

    OkURLs = Inet1.OpenURL(URL_LIST)
    s = OkURLs

    pos = 1
    i = 0
    pos1 = InStr(pos, s, vbCrLf)
    Do While pos1 > 0
        temp = Mid(s, pos, pos1 - pos)
        If i > 0 Then Load mnuGotoURL(i)
        mnuGotoURL(i).Caption = temp
        i = i + 1
        pos = pos1 + 2
        pos1 = InStr(pos, s, vbCrLf)
```

```
        DoEvents
    Loop

    LoadApprovedList = True
    Exit Function

InetError:
        LoadApprovedList = False

End Function

Public Function UrlIsOk(URL As String) As Boolean

    Dim s As String

    If InStr(1, OkURLs, URL) = 0 Then
        s = "Sorry but " & URL & " is not an approved location."
        MsgBox (s)
        UrlIsOk = False
    Else
        UrlIsOk = True
    End If

End Function
```

Possible Improvements

Although this customized browser does a good job of keeping your users from visiting unauthorized sites, I can think of several improvements. For one, the approved file list could contain meaningful titles of the various URLs, as well as the URLs themselves. These titles could be displayed on the Go To menu, which would make it easier for the user to locate the needed location.

There is also the potential problem that an approved URL itself might have links out to the Web, permitting users to "escape" from the restricted list. You can use the BeforeNavigate2 event procedure to check the URL against the approved list, and cancel the operation if needed.

Summary

The WebBrowser control provides most of the functionality of a standalone browser in a package that you can easily reuse in your Visual Basic programs. You can use the Visual Basic Application Wizard to create basic browser application, and then you can customize it to meet your specific needs. By designing the browser so that only approved

URLs can be visited, you can provide your customers with a tool that enables them to perform the needed Web-based tasks without the temptation of wasting time surfing the Web.

Q&A

Q What is the easiest way to create a browser in a Visual Basic project?

A By running the Visual Basic Application Wizard and specifying Yes when the wizard asks whether you want Internet connectivity. The project created by the wizard will have a form that uses the WebBrowser control to provide basic browsing capabilities.

Q In an application that uses the WebBrowser control, what is the easiest way to program the capability to search the loaded document?

A You do not have to program this capability at all. The control has its own Find dialog box that is displayed when the user presses Ctrl+F.

Q What is the main advantage of using Visual Basic's template for an About dialog box rather than creating one from scratch?

A The About dialog box template includes code to display detailed system information, something that your users might find useful.

Workshop

Quiz

1. How do you display the WebBrowser control's toolbar?
2. Ideally, when should a browser's Stop button be enabled?
3. The user clicks on a hyperlink in the displayed page. Is it possible to prevent the browser from navigating to that URL?

Exercise

Near the end of this lesson, the section titled "Possible Improvements" suggests some additions that could be made to the custom browser developed in the chapter. Adding either, or better yet both, of the suggested improvements would be a great way to hone your Visual Basic programming skills.

DAY 17

Client-Side Scripting with VBScript

Web scripting languages enable you to embed programming statements directly in a Web page. When the page is loaded into a browser, the code is executed. VBScript is Microsoft's Web scripting language, and as the name suggests, it is closely based on Visual Basic. The use of VBScript enables you to do things in your Web pages that would be otherwise difficult or impossible. Today you will learn

- The origins of VBScript
- How scripting languages work
- The advantages of client-side scripting
- Details of VBScript variables, syntax, and procedures
- How to respond to user actions in VBScript
- Using VBScript for data validation

Hello, VBScript

The *VB* in *VBScript* stands for *Visual Basic*, of course, but that doesn't explain what VBScript is. Where did VBScript come from, and what is it used for? You need to go back a few years to answer these questions.

As the popularity of the World Wide Web began to increase dramatically, Web developers saw the need for a Web page specification that would provide them with more flexibility and power. A Web page should not be limited to being static, but should offer the capability to perform actions that would assist in the display and processing of data. As a result, the first Web scripting language was born. It was called *JavaScript* and was the brainchild of Netscape Communications, the same company that publishes the Netscape Navigator browser. JavaScript soon became very popular with Web page developers.

VBScript Versus JavaScript

Both VBScript and JavaScript are powerful and flexible scripting languages. Little if anything can be done with one that cannot also be done with the other. The syntax and structure of JavaScript and Java are loosely based on C and C++.

Microsoft immediately decided to jump on the bandwagon and create its own Web scripting language. The result was VBScript, a language based on standard Visual Basic syntax but specially adapted for Web scripting needs. You'll be happy to know that as a Visual Basic programmer, you already know most details of VBScript, so you should be up and running in a short time.

In the remainder of this lesson, I will cover the fundamentals of VBScript, taking the approach that readers already have a good grounding in Visual Basic. Complete coverage of VBScript would consist mainly of repeating things that a Visual Basic programmer already knows, because there is so much similarity between the two.

Client-Side and Server-Side Execution

One of the main advantages of a scripting language is that it is processed on the user's computer, referred to as *client-side execution*. Previously, all requests for data processing had to be sent to the server. Even extremely simple tasks, such as verifying data input by the user, required the round trip of sending the data to the server and then sending the response back to the client. This arrangement not only increased the processing load on the server, but it also increased traffic over the network and often introduced an annoying delay for the user.

VBScript (or any scripting language) permits certain types of data processing to be performed locally, on the user's machine. There is no need to send a request to the server and wait for the reply; server load and network traffic are both reduced. Figure 17.1 illustrates these two situations.

FIGURE 17.1

A scripting language permits some data processing requests to be processed locally rather than sent to the server.

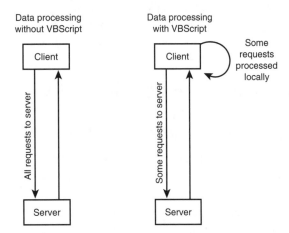

17

SERVER-SIDE SCRIPTING

VBScript can also be used for server-side scripting, a topic that I will cover on Day 18, "Creating Dynamic Content with Active Server Pages."

How Scripts Work

A scripting language is used inside an HTML document. Statements and other language elements are separated from the rest of the document by special tags. When the page is loaded into a browser that supports the scripting language, the script is parsed from the document and executed. Browsers that do not support the scripting language simply ignore the script.

Script is set off from the rest of the HTML document by <SCRIPT>...</SCRIPT> tags. In almost all cases, the first <SCRIPT> tag also identifies the language in use:

```
<SCRIPT LANGUAGE=VBSCRIPT>
...
</SCRIPT>
```

It is standard practice to enclose script code inside the HTML comment tags <!-- and -->, which prevents the code from being displayed as plain text by browsers that do not support the scripting language:

```
<script language = VBScript>
<!--
VBScript code goes here
-->
</script>
```

In this book, I will often omit the HTML comment tags because it's safe to assume that readers are using a VBScript-enabled browser. You should always include them in your own VBScript scripts unless you can be sure than no one who visits the page will be using an incompatible browser.

Differences Between VBScript and Visual Basic

Although VBScript is very similar to Visual Basic—or more precisely, to the Basic language used by Visual Basic—there are many significant differences.

- VBScript has nothing to do with the Visual Basic development environment. It is simply a language specification and does not support forms, controls, dialog boxes, and so on.

- VBScript does not support any file operations. This makes perfect sense because you would not want to download a Web page that has the potential to delete or otherwise harm your disk files.

- VBScript has no graphics capabilities whatsoever.

- Visual Basic has an assortment of data types, but VBScript has only one. All variables in VBScript are the same type, which is essentially equivalent to Visual Basic's Variant type.

So far, it seems that VBScript is only a subset of the full Basic language, and this, in fact, is a perfectly accurate assessment. However, you should not look on this as a limitation. VBScript was designed for a specific purpose, and it has those capabilities that are needed by a Web scripting language.

Table 17.1 summarizes other differences between VBScript and Visual Basic, which are also mentioned as needed throughout the remainder of the chapter.

TABLE 17.1 VISUAL BASIC FEATURES NOT SUPPORTED IN VBSCRIPT

Category	Feature or Keyword Not Supported
Arrays	Option Base. Arrays with lower bound other than 0
Collection	Add, Count, Item, Remove. Access to collections using the ! character
Conditional compilation	#Const, #If...Then...#Else

Category	Feature or Keyword Not Supported
Control flow	DoEvents, GoSub...Return, GoTo, On...GoSub, On...GoTo line numbers, line labels With...End With
Conversion	CVar, CVDateStr, Val
Date/Time	Date statement, Time statement, Timer
DDE	LinkExecute, LinkPoke, LinkRequest, LinkSend
Declaration	Declare New Optional ParamArray, Property Get, Property Let, Property Set Static
Error handling	Err, Error, On Error...Resume, On Error.GoTo...Resume, Resume Next
Financial	All financial functions
Object manipulation	TypeOf
Objects	Clipboard collection
Operators	Like
Options	Deftype, Option Base, Option Compare, Option Private Module
Select case	Expressions containing the Is keyword, any comparison operators, or a range of values using the To keyword
Strings	LSet, RSet, Mid statement, StrConv

17

Variables and Arrays in VBScript

As I mentioned earlier, VBScript has only a single data type, Variant. You should know from your experience with Visual Basic that the Variant data type is a catch-all and can be used to hold nearly any type of data, including numbers, strings, and object references.

You declare variables with the Dim statement. For example:

```
Dim X, Y, Z
```

As in Visual Basic, variables do not have to be declared unless the Option Explicit statement is included in the code. You should place this statement at the beginning of the VBScript code, as shown here:

```
<SCRIPT LANGUAGE=VBSCRIPT>
Option Explicit
Dim X, Y, Z
... more code
</SCRIPT>
```

If you omit `Option Explicit`, you can simply use variables in code without declaring them. I strongly recommend that you always include `Option Explicit`, for the same reason that you should use it in all regular Visual Basic programs: to prevent errors caused by misspelled variable names.

COMMENTS IN VBSCRIPT

You create comments in VBScript by using the apostrophe or the Rem keyword, the same as in regular Basic.

```
' This is a comment.
X = 20 ' This is a comment.
Y = 0 : Rem This is a comment, too.
Rem And so is this.
```

Note that if you use Rem anywhere other than the beginning of a line, there must be a colon between it and the preceding code.

Arrays

You declare arrays in VBScript by using the `Dim` statement and the same syntax as used in Basic. Here are some examples:

```
Dim MyArray(10)
Dim AnotherArray(5, 5)
```

The lower bound of VBScript arrays is always 0. The first `Dim` statement above, therefore, creates an array with 11 elements indexed 0–10.

NO USER-DEFINED TYPES

VBScript does not permit the definition of user-defined types, or structures, with the Type ... End Type statement.

When you specify an array's dimensions in the `Dim` statement, it is a *static* array with fixed size. You can create a *dynamic* array by using empty parentheses in the `Dim` statement:

```
Dim MyArray()
```

Then, you can set the size of the array with the `ReDim` statement and change it as needed during script execution:

```
ReDim MyArray(10)
' MyArray has 11 elements
Redim MyArray(45)
' MyArray has 46 elements
```

Use the `Preserve` keyword to retain existing data in the array when redimensioning it:

```
Redim Preserve MyArray(45)
```

For multidimensional arrays, you can use `Preserve` only when changing the size of the last dimension.

```
Dim MyArray(10, 10)
' The following is OK.
ReDim Preserve MyArray(10, 20)
' The following is illegal.
ReDim Preserve MyArray(20, 10)
```

The `Erase` statement reinitializes static arrays and frees the memory used by dynamic arrays. When you erase a static array, no memory is freed, but all array elements are set to 0 or a blank string. Erasing a dynamic array frees its memory, and you must use `ReDim` to set the array dimensions before using it again.:

You can use the `UBound` function to determine the upper bound of an array index. The syntax for `UBound` is the same as in regular Basic. VBScript supports the `LBound` function as well, but because all arrays start at element 0, it is never really needed.:

Constants in VBScript

You can define constants in a VBScript program by using the `Const` keyword, just as you do in regular Basic.

Operators and Control Expressions

This is a short section because with few exceptions, the operators and control expressions supported by VBScript are identical to those in standard Basic. You have the full array of mathematical, logical, and comparison operators at your disposal in VBScript. The symbols and syntax are exactly the same as you use in standard Basic.

You also have most of the same control expressions in VBScript. This includes the following:

```
For...Next
For Each...Next
If...Then...Else
Do...Loop
While...Wend
```

The following are not supported:

```
Goto
With...End With
```

Procedures in VBScript

A VBScript procedure is an independent block of code that has been assigned a name. The code in the procedure can then be executed by referring to its name. In most ways, procedures in VBScript work the same as procedures in regular Basic. You have function procedures, which return a value to the code that called it, and sub procedures, which do not return a value. The syntax is identical to regular Basic, with the main differences related to VBScript not having different data types, only the one Variant type.

There are some other restrictions. VBScript does not permit optional procedure arguments or parameter arrays, nor does it support Static local variables in procedures.

When a script executes, you cannot call a procedure until its definition has been processed. This means that procedure definitions must be placed before any script code that calls them. The ideal place for this is in the HTML file header between the <HEAD> and </HEAD> tags. There is no rule against defining procedures in the body of the HTML file, as long as the definition precedes any call to the procedure. However, I think it's advisable to keep all procedure definitions together in the header.

Take a look at a simple example. I have created a VBScript function named MakeBold that takes some text as its argument and returns the text enclosed in HTML bold tags. It is a simple function, as shown in Listing 17.1.

LISTING 17.1   A VBSCRIPT FUNCTION TO ENCLOSE TEXT IN BOLD TAGS

```
function MakeBold(msg)
' Returns msg enclosed in HTML bold tags.
Dim s
s = "<B>" & msg & "</B>"
MakeBold = s
end function
```

The HTML page shown in Listing 17.2 includes this function and shows how to call it from VBScript located elsewhere on the page.

LISTING 17.2   USING THE MakeBold FUNCTION IN AN HTML PAGE

```
<html>
<head>
<script language = vbscript>
function MakeBold(msg)
' Returns msg enclosed in HTML bold tags.
Dim s
s = "<B>" & msg & "</B>"
MakeBold = s
end function
</script>
</head>
<body>
<script language = vbscript>
document.write("This line is in regular text<P>")
document.write(MakeBold("This line is in bold text<P>"))
</script>
</body>
</html>
```

17

When you load this HTML page into Internet Explorer, it displays two lines of text, as shown in Figure 17.2. As you can see, the second line is displayed in boldface.

FIGURE 17.2

The output of the demonstration VBScript script.

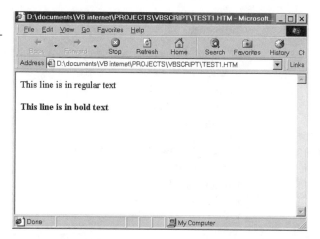

THE Document OBJECT

In a VBScript program, and in fact in any HTML page, you have access to the Document object, which provides properties and methods for working with the contents of the page. The Document object is defined by the <body>...</body> tags in the HTML text. I will present more information about this object later in the chapter.

Responding to User Actions

When you use VBScript to go beyond simple, static Web pages, you will almost always want your page to respond to user input. Sure, plain HTML can provide some response to user actions, such as a Submit button, but that's not enough. What you need is some way to execute VBScript code in response to what the user does.

Events are detected by objects. At the most fundamental level are the standard HTML objects. A `Button` object can detect when it has been clicked, a `Text` object can detect when its contents have changed, and so on. The events that can be detected and the HTML objects that can respond to them are listed here:

Event	Occurs	Detected by
OnBlur	When an object loses the focus	Text, TextArea, and Select objects
OnChange	When an object loses the focus after its contents have been modified	Text, TextArea, and Select objects
OnClick	When the user clicks the object with the the mouse	Button, Checkbox, Radio, Link, Reset, and Submit objects
OnFocus	When an object receives input focus by tabbing with the keyboard or clicking with the mouse	Text, TextArea, and Select objects
OnLoad	When the browser finishes loading a window or all frames within a \<FRAMESET> tag	Window object*
OnMouseOver	Once each time the mouse pointer moves over an object from outside that object	Link object

Event	Occurs	Detected by
OnSelect	When a user selects some text	Text and TextArea objects
OnSubmit	When the user submits a form	Form object
OnUnload	When the user exits a document	Window object*

Technically, these events are detected by the Window object, but your program accesses them via the Document object.

A VBScript program can also respond to events detected by other objects on the page, such as ActiveX controls. The events that can be detected by ActiveX controls and other objects depend on the way the objects are programmed and which events are raised to be detected by the container. Given that an object detects an event, responding to it in VBScript requires the same techniques.

As in Visual Basic, events are responded to by creating event procedures. The name of the event procedure consists of the object name followed by an underscore and the event name. The connection between the event and the procedure is defined by the procedure name.

Suppose your page contains a Button object defined as follows:

```
<input type="button" name="OKButton" value'"OK">
```

Here is the OnClick event procedure for this button:

```
Sub OKButton_OnClick()
...
End Sub
```

The only requirement for writing event procedures is that the object have an assigned Name or ID attribute. For HTML objects, the Name attribute is used, as in the preceding example. For other objects, such as ActiveX controls, that are defined by <OBJECT> tags, you use the ID attribute. For example:

```
<OBJECT classid="clsid:whatever" id="MyControl"></OBJECT>
```

Then the event procedure would be as follows:

```
Sub MyControl_OnClick()
...
End Sub
```

17

ANOTHER WAY TO DETECT EVENTS

VBScript offers another way to connect an event to an object: by including the event code as part of the tag that defines the object. To define a Button object with an OnClick event procedure, you could write the following:

```
<INPUT TYPE="button" VALUE="Click Me" OnClick="XYZ()">
```

XYZ() is the function to be executed when the object is clicked.

Listing 17.3 is a simple demonstration of how to respond to events in VBScript. This HTML page displays a Button element and a Text element. If the user clicks the Button, moves the focus away from the Text element (with or without having changed the text), a message is displayed. Figure 17.3 shows the program operating.

LISTING 17.3 RESPONDING TO USER EVENTS IN VBSCRIPT

```
<HTML>
<HEAD>
<script language="vbscript">

sub text1_onblur()
msgbox("Text1 has lost the focus.")
end sub

sub text1_onchange()
msgbox("Text1 has been changed.")
end sub

sub button1_onclick()
msgbox("Button1 has been clicked.")
end sub

</script>
</HEAD>
<BODY>
<INPUT TYPE="button" NAME="button1" VALUE="Click Here">
<INPUT TYPE="text" NAME="text1" VALUE="Change this text">
</BODY>
</HTML>
```

FIGURE 17.3

*Responding to user
events in VBScript.*

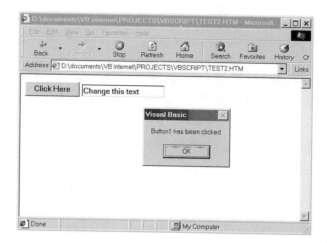

The **Document** Object

In any HTML page, the top-level object is the Document object. This is true regardless of
whether the page uses VBScript. A page's Document object is defined by the
<BODY>...</BODY> tags in the file and whatever is between them. All other page-related
objects are subsumed within the Document object.

The Document contains information about the document and provides methods for displaying HTML. Within the HTML text, the Document object is defined using standard
HTML syntax for the <BODY> tags:

```
<BODY
    BACKGROUND="backgroundImage"
    BGCOLOR="backgroundColor"
    TEXT="foregroundColor"
    LINK="unfollowedLinkColor"
    ALINK="activatedLinkColor"
    VLINK="followedLinkColor"
    onLoad="loadHandler"
    onUnload="unloadHandler">
...
Document contents go here
...
</BODY>
```

All the attribute tags are optional; you can define the Document simply with
<BODY>...</BODY> tags, and the various Document properties will have default values. If
you do use the attribute tags, here's what they mean:

17

backgroundImage is a filename or URL specifying an image file to use as the document's background.

The various *Color* arguments specify the color to be used to display the associated element in the document. They can be expressed as a hexadecimal RGB triplet (in the format rrggbb or #rrggbb) or as one of the standard HTML color constants.

loadHandler and *unloadHandler* are VBScript code to execute when the document is loaded and unloaded.

The Document object has a number of properties (see Table 17.2) that can be very useful to you in your VBScript programs. This object also has several methods, which are explained in Table 17.3.

TABLE 17.2 PROPERTIES OF THE Document OBJECT

Property	Description
AlinkColor	Displays color for activated links (ALINK attribute)
Anchors	An array containing all the anchors in the document
BgColor	Document background color (BGCOLOR attribute)
Cookie	Specifies a cookie
FgColor	Text display color (TEXT attribute)
Forms	An array reflecting all the forms in a document
LastModified	The date the document was last modified
LinkColor	Displays color for nonactivated links (LINK attribute)
Links	An array reflecting all the links in the document
Location	The complete URL of the document
Referrer	The URL of the calling document
Title	The contents of the <TITLE> tag
VlinkColor	Displays color for followed links (VLINK attribute)

TABLE 17.3 Document OBJECT METHODS

Method	Effect
clear	Erases the contents of the document window
Close	Closes the document output stream, forcing display of all elements
Open	Opens a stream to collect the output of write or writeln methods
write	Writes text to the document
writeln	The same as write(), but adds a newline character at the end of the output

VBScript Functions

VBScript provides a rich set of built-in functions, just like Visual Basic. Many are used for data type checking and some for other purposes.

Data Type Checking

Because VBScript has only a single data type, Variant, there is no way to know what type of data a variable holds, based on the type of the variable. To solve this problem, the VBScript specification includes a set of functions that are passed a variable and return a value indicating the type of data stored there. Most of these functions are of the following form:

IsXXXX(VarName)

XXXX represents a possible data subtype, and VarName is the name of the variable you are interested in. The functions return True if the variable contains data of the specified type and False otherwise. Table 17.4 describes the functions.

17

TABLE 17.4   DATA TYPE DETERMINATION FUNCTIONS

Function	Returns True If...
IsArray(x)	x is an array.
IsDate(x)	x is a date.
IsEmpty(x)	x contains Empty.
IsNull(x)	x contains Null.
IsNumeric(x)	x contains a numeric value.
IsObject(x)	x contains an object reference.

SPECIAL DATA VALUES IN VBSCRIPT

In addition to the usual predefined constants True and False, VBScript has three other constants for special data values.

Empty indicates an uninitialized variable.

Null indicates an invalid value.

Nothing is used to dissociate an object variable from the object it refers to, as in Set MyObj = Nothing.

It's important to note that Empty and Null are not the same. For instance, a variable that holds a phone number would be set to Empty if the phone number has not been entered yet and to Null if an invalid phone number was entered.

There is one more data classification function: VarType. Passed a variable name, this function returns a value identifying the type of data the variable contains. For example:

```
X = VarType(Y)
```

Table 17.5 gives the possible values returned by this function.

TABLE 17.5 RETURN VALUES OF THE VarType FUNCTION

Constant	Value	Description
VbEmpty	0	Empty
VbNull	1	Null
VbInteger	2	Integer
VbLong	3	Long integer
VbSingle	4	Single-precision floating-point number
VbDouble	5	Double-precision floating-point number
VbCurrency	6	Currency
VbDate	7	Date
VbString	8	String
VbObject	9	Automation object
VbError	10	Error
VbBoolean	11	Boolean
VbVariant	12	Variant (used only with arrays of Variants)
VbDataObject	13	Data-access object
VbByte	17	Byte
VbArray	8192	Array

Other VBScript Functions

VBScript provides a rich set of built-in functions for mathematics, string manipulation, Date and Time handling, data conversion, and so on. For the most part, these functions are the same ones you use in Visual Basic. I do not cover these functions in this book because you probably already know how to use them; if not, you can turn to your Visual Basic documentation for information.

Data Validation with VBScript

Perhaps the most common task that Web developers use VBScript for is data validation. When the user enters data on a Web page form, you can use VBScript to validate that the data meets certain criteria before submitting it to the server. Performing validation on the client side speeds up things and removes processing load from the server. Furthermore, VBScript is an excellent language for data verification tasks because of its many built-in string manipulation and data classification functions.

In this section, I will show you how to perform certain basic data verification functions in VBScript. You can extend these principles to other more involved verification tasks. You can also drop the functions that I develop right into your VBScript projects.

Text Length

Checking the length of entered text is one of the most fundamental verification tasks. This includes preventing blank input fields. VBScript's len() function makes text length validations a trivial task. Listing 17.4 presents a function that checks whether the length of a text string is between two specified values. To verify a non-zero length, call the function with the min argument set to 1 and the max argument set to some huge value.

LISTING 17.4 THE LengthOfText FUNCTION CHECKS THE LENGTH OF TEXT

```
function LengthOfText(s, max, min)

' Returns True if the length of the text in s
' is between max and min.
' Otherwise, returns False.

if (len(s) <= max And len(s) >= min) then
    LengthOfText = True
else
    LengthOfText = False
end if

end function
```

Zip Codes

If your application deals with addresses, it will also have to deal with zip codes. If an address has an invalid zip code, delivery of mail might not be reliable. Although you cannot verify that a zip code entered by the user is correct, you can make sure it is in the proper format: either 5 digits alone or 5 digits followed by a dash and four more digits for ZIP + 4.

The function IsZipCode in Listing 17.5 validates zip codes. Pass it the text containing the zip code, and the function returns True only if the text is in a valid 5-digit or 9-digit format. These are what it checks:

- The zip code must be either 5 or 10 characters long.
- If 5 characters long, it must evaluate to a number as tested with VBScript's built-in isNumeric() function.
- If 10 characters long, the first 5 characters must evaluate to a number, the sixth character must be a hyphen, and the last 4 characters evaluate to a number.

LISTING 17.5 THE FUNCTION IsZipCode VALIDATES PROPER FORMAT FOR BOTH 5-DIGIT AND 9-DIGIT ZIP CODES

```
function IsZipCode(zip)

' Returns True if zip is a 5- or 9-
' digit ZIP code.
' Otherwise, returns False.

Dim l
IsZipCode = False

l = len(zip)
if (l <> 5) And (l <> 10) then exit function

' First 5 digits must be numbers.
if (Not isNumeric(left(1, 5))) then exit function

'If it's a 5 digit ZIP, we're done.
if (l = 5) then
    IsZipCode = True
    exit function
end if

'Sixth character must be "-".
if (instr(zip,"-") <> 6) then exit function

'The last 4 characters must be digits.
if (Not isNumeric(right(zip, 4))) then exit function

'Zip validates OK
IsZipCode = true

end function
```

Phone Numbers

Validation of telephone numbers is another common data validation task. The function IsPhoneNumber, presented in Listing 17.6, verifies that the phone number entered by the user is in the correct format, including area code. Specifically, the function checks the following items:

- The overall length should be 12 characters.
- The first 3 characters should be numeric and evaluate to a value greater than 100 because no area codes begin with 0.
- The fourth character should be a hyphen.
- The fifth through seventh characters should evaluate to a number greater than 100 because no exchanges begin with 0.
- The eighth character should be a hyphen.
- Finally, the ninth through twelfth characters should evaluate to a number.

LISTING 17.6 CHECKING FOR PROPER PHONE NUMBER FORMAT

```
function IsPhonenumber(pn)

' Returns True if pn is in valid phone number
' format (xxx-xxx-xxxx).
' Otherwise, returns False.

IsPhonenumber = False

if (len(pn) <> 12) then exit function
if (left(pn, 3) < 100) then exit function
if (mid(pn, 4, 1) <> "-") then exit function
if (mid(pn, 5, 3) < 100) then exit function
if (mid(pn, 8, 1) <> "-") then exit function
if (Not isNumeric(right(pn, 4))) then exit function

isPhonenumber = True

end function
```

A VBScript Demonstration

VBScript is a surprisingly flexible language. Although it does not offer anywhere near the power of the full Visual Basic version of Basic, you can still do sophisticated things with it. To demonstrate, I have created an onscreen calculator in VBScript. This is a basic calculator, providing only the four fundamental mathematical operations, but it is a terrific demonstration of what can be done with VBScript.

Figure 17.4 shows what the calculator looks like, and its code is presented in Listing 17.7. I will not explain the code workings because you will learn more by looking through it and figuring it out for yourself. I will mention that the calculator buttons are arranged by putting them in the cells of an HTML table. That's what all the strange tags are for, such as the <TD> and <TR> tags: defining the table structure.

FIGURE 17.4

The VBScript calculator in operation.

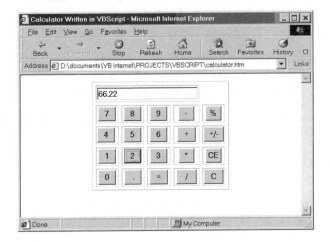

LISTING 17.7 THE VBSCRIPT CALCULATOR CODE

```
<HTML>
<HEAD>
<TITLE>Calculator Written in VBScript</TITLE>
<SCRIPT LANGUAGE="VBScript">
<!--
Option Explicit

Dim X
Dim EnteringNew
Dim Operation

sub KeyPressed(Byval Number)

If EnteringNew Then
    Document.formcalc.output.value = Number
        EnteringNew = False
    Else
        If Document.formcalc.output.value = "0" Then
            Document.formcalc.output.value = CStr(Number)
```

```vbscript
            Else
                Document.formcalc.output.value = _
                    Document.formcalc.output.value & CStr(Number)
            End If
    End If

end sub

sub Decimal_onClick()
    Dim CurrentVal
    CurrentVal = Document.formcalc.output.value
    If EnteringNew Then
        CurrentVal = "0."
        EnteringNew = False
    Else
        If instr(CurrentVal, ".") = 0 Then
            CurrentVal = CurrentVal & "."
        End If
    End If
    Document.formcalc.output.value = CurrentVal
end sub

sub calculate(ByVal Op)
    Dim cd        ' Current display
    cd = Document.formcalc.output.value
    If Not EnteringNew Or Op = "=" Then
        Select Case Operation
            Case "+"
                X = CDbl(X) + CDbl(cd)
            Case "-"
                X = CDbl(X) - CDbl(cd)
            Case "/"
                X = CDbl(X) / CDbl(cd)
            Case "*"
                X = CDbl(X) * CDbl(cd)
            Case Else
                X = cd
        End Select
        Document.formcalc.output.value = X
        EnteringNew = True
        Operation = Op
    End If
end sub

sub ClearEntry_onClick()
    Document.formcalc.output.value = "0.0"
    EnteringNew = True
end sub
```

17

continues

LISTING 17.7   CONTINUED

```
sub ClearAll_onClick()
    X = 0
    ClearEntry_onClick
end sub

sub ChangeSign_onClick()
    Document.formcalc.output.value = -1 * _
        CDbl(Document.formcalc.output.value)
end sub

sub Percent_onClick()
    Document.formcalc.output.value = _
        (CDbl(Document.formcalc.output.value) / 100)
end sub

-->
</SCRIPT>
</HEAD>

<BODY>
<SCRIPT LANGUAGE="VBScript">
EnteringNew = True
</Script>
<CENTER>
<FORM Name="formcalc">
<TABLE BORDER=1 WIDTH=60 HEIGHT=60 CELLPADDING=2 CELLSPACING=7>
<TR>
<TD COLSPAN=4 ALIGN=MIDDLE>
<INPUT NAME="output" TYPE="Text" SIZE=25 VALUE="0.0" WIDTH=100%>
</TD>
</TR>
<TR>
<TD ALIGN=MIDDLE>
<INPUT TYPE="Button" VALUE="  7  " OnClick="KeyPressed(7)">
</TD>
<TD ALIGN=MIDDLE>
<INPUT TYPE="Button" VALUE="  8  " OnClick="KeyPressed(8)">
</TD>
<TD ALIGN=MIDDLE>
<INPUT TYPE="Button" VALUE="  9  " OnClick="KeyPressed(9)">
</TD>
<TD ALIGN=MIDDLE>
<INPUT NAME="Minus" TYPE="Button" VALUE="  -  " OnClick='calculate("-")'>
</TD>
<TD ALIGN=MIDDLE>
<INPUT NAME="Percent" TYPE="Button" VALUE=" % " >
</TD>
</TR>
<TR>
```

```
<TD>
<INPUT NAME="Four" TYPE="Button" VALUE="  4   " OnClick="KeyPressed(4)">
</TD>
<TD ALIGN=MIDDLE>
<INPUT NAME="Five" TYPE="Button" VALUE="  5   " OnClick="KeyPressed(5)">
</TD>
<TD ALIGN=MIDDLE>
<INPUT NAME="Six" TYPE="Button" VALUE="  6   " OnClick="KeyPressed(6)">
</TD>
<TD ALIGN=MIDDLE>
<INPUT NAME="Plus" TYPE="Button" VALUE="  +   " OnClick='calculate("+")'>
</TD>
<TD ALIGN=MIDDLE>
<INPUT NAME="ChangeSign" TYPE="Button" VALUE=" +/- " >
</TD>
</TR>
<TR>
<TD ALIGN=MIDDLE>
<INPUT NAME="One" TYPE="Button" VALUE="  1  " OnClick="KeyPressed(1)">
</TD>
<TD ALIGN=MIDDLE>
<INPUT NAME="Two" TYPE="Button" VALUE="  2  " OnClick="KeyPressed(2)">
</TD>
<TD ALIGN=MIDDLE>
<INPUT NAME="Three" TYPE="Button" VALUE="  3   " OnClick="KeyPressed(3)">
</TD>
<TD ALIGN=MIDDLE>
<INPUT NAME="Multiply" TYPE="Button" VALUE="  *   "
OnClick='calculate("*")'>
</TD>
<TD ALIGN=MIDDLE>
<INPUT NAME="ClearEntry" TYPE="Button" VALUE="CE" >
</TD>
</TR>
<TR>
<TD ALIGN=MIDDLE>
<INPUT NAME="Zero" TYPE="Button" VALUE="  0   " OnClick="KeyPressed(0)">
</TD>
<TD ALIGN=MIDDLE>
<INPUT NAME="Decimal" TYPE="Button" VALUE="   .  " >
</TD>
<TD ALIGN=MIDDLE>
<INPUT NAME="Equals" TYPE="Button" VALUE="  =   " OnClick='calculate("=")'>
</TD>
<TD ALIGN=MIDDLE>
<INPUT NAME="Divide" TYPE="Button" VALUE="   /    "
OnClick='calculate("/")'>
</TD>
<TD ALIGN=MIDDLE>
```

continues

LISTING 17.7 CONTINUED

```
<INPUT NAME="ClearAll" TYPE="Button" VALUE="  C  " >
</TD>
</TR>
</TABLE>
</CENTER>
</FORM>
</BODY>
</HTML>
```

Summary

By embedding VBScript code directly in a Web page, you obtain a lot of power and flexibility. The code is executed locally, on the client machine, which provides the significant advantages of improved response speed and lessened server workload. VBScript lacks those language features, such as file manipulation, that have the potential to cause harm on the client computer. Even without these features, it is a robust and flexible language. Its primary use is data validation, but it can be used for many other important Web programming tasks.

Q&A

Q How can users be sure that VBScript code in a Web page will not contain viruses or harm their system in other ways?

A The VBScript language is limited to performing tasks that do not have the potential for causing harm. File system access and memory manipulation, for example, are not supported.

Q Not all Web browsers support VBScript. How can you design a Web page that uses VBScript but also can be viewed in other browsers?

A Script code should always be enclosed in HTML comment tags <!--...-->. This will prevent the code from displaying as regular text in a browser that does not support scripts.

Q In a VBScript Web page, where should procedure definitions be placed?

A Procedure definitions must be placed before any code that calls the procedures. Although not required, it is generally a good idea to place procedure definitions in the HEAD section of the HTML document.

Workshop

Quiz

1. How do you identify VBScript code in an HTML page?

2. What graphics capabilities does VBScript have?

3. Your VBScript program needs a variable to hold a number whose value will range between -2500 and +4500. Which data type should you use?

4. Is the following array declaration legal in VBScript?

   `Dim array(5 to 15)`

5. How can VBScript code access information about the loaded document?

6. How can VBScript code write text to the HTML page?

Exercise

Use VBScript to create a Web page that presents a guessing game to the user. The program generates a random number between 1 and 100 and then accepts guesses from the user. After each guess, the program tells the user whether the guess was high, low, or correct, while keeping track of the number of guesses.

17

DAY 18

Creating Dynamic Content with Active Server Pages

In my opinion, one of the most exciting Internet technologies that Microsoft has come up with is Active Server Pages (ASP). With ASP, a script running on the server receives a request from the client and generates a customized HTML page to send back. Today's lesson is the first of three lessons devoted to this important topic. Today you will learn about

- The basics of ASP
- Scripting languages supported by ASP
- Server objects available to ASP scripts
- Receiving data from the client
- Reusing script and HTML with #include
- Server-side file access
- Using cookies

What Are Active Server Pages?

Active Server Pages is a technology that is available with Microsoft Internet Information Server (IIS) and enables you to write programs, or scripts, that execute on a Web server. It is one of the most powerful ways to generate dynamic Web content, and every Web developer needs to know about it.

IIS ONLY

One of the few limitations of ASP technology is that it runs on Microsoft Web servers only. Specifically, ASP is available only on Microsoft Internet Information Server version 3 and better and on Microsoft Peer Web services running on Windows NT. It is also available on the Microsoft Personal Web Server on Windows 95/98. This means that if your Web page is hosted on a server that runs another Web server, you can forget about using ASP. In Chapter 20, "Implementing a Web Database Application," you will find information about where to get the Personal Web Server and how to set it up.

How exactly does ASP work? An ASP Web page consists of an HTML document with script code embedded in it. ASP Web pages are saved with the .ASP extension to differentiate them from "regular" HTML pages. When a user navigates to an ASP page, here is what happens:

1. The server receives the request for the ASP page, for example, default.asp.
2. The server loads the ASP page and processes the script and HTML in the page.
3. Based on the script logic and HTML in the ASP page, a new HTML page is generated.
4. The newly generated HTML page is returned to the user and viewed in the browser.

Figure 18.1 illustrates this process.

One advantage of ASP technology is that it is largely browser independent. Because the scripts are executed on the server and only HTML is returned to the client, there are no special requirements for script support in the browser.

ASP Scripting Languages

It is important to realize that ASP is a technology and not a language. The script in an ASP Web page can be written in VBScript, JavaScript, JScript (Microsoft's version of JavaScript), Perl, or another language. As long as the Web server has an interpreter for the script language in use, that's all that matters. Because this is a Visual Basic book, I will be limiting myself to using VBScript in ASP Web pages.

FIGURE 18.1

The ASP is processed by the Web server, which generates an HTML document to return to the user.

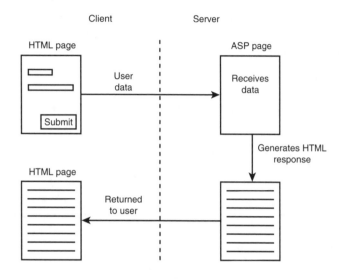

ASP AND VISUAL BASIC

ASP programming is not directly related to Visual Basic in that you do not use the Visual Basic development environment to write and test ASP applications. The scripting language you will probably use, VBScript, is definitely related to Visual Basic (as you learned in yesterday's lesson), so that is why this topic is appropriate for a Visual Basic programming book.

When you write your ASP pages in VBScript, two of VBScript's features are not available: user interface statements such as MsgBox and InputBox and the object-related functions CreateObject and GetObject. Because the script is executing on the server instead of the client, the user-interface statements are clearly not relevant. As for objects, a server-side script should use the Server object's CreateObject function in place of VBScript's function of the same name (as described later in the chapter).

18

The Structure of an ASP Web Page

An ASP Web page is a text document, like regular HTML pages. It can contain the same content and HTML tags and differs only in having script logic embedded within it. The script is special <%...%> tags to separate it from the rest of the document. The final HTML document returned to the user is a combination of the HTML originally present in the ASP page and the HTML generated by the script.

ASP uses two types of script delimiters. You have already met one type, the <%...%> pair. The second type is used specifically for output expressions; it looks like this:

```
<%= ... %>
```

These tags mean "display the value of whatever expression is inside the tags in the browser." If, for example, Total is a VBScript variable, the following will display its value in the browser:

```
<%= Total %>
```

A Simple Demonstration of an ASP Web Page

You'll develop a better feel for what ASP is and how it works by trying a simple demonstration. Using your HTML editor or any text editor, create a text file with the HTML shown in Listing 18.1 and save it as GREAT.ASP.

LISTING 18.1   A SIMPLE ASP PAGE

```
<HTML>
<HEAD>
<TITLE>ASP Test Page</TITLE>
</HEAD>
<BODY>
<% for I = 1 to 7 %>
<FONT SIZE=<%= I %>> ASP is great!<BR>
<% Next %>
</BODY>
```

Next, publish the page to your Web site, either remotely or using the local server, depending on your setup. Remember, the server must be running one of the Microsoft Web servers mentioned earlier in the chapter in order to have ASP support.

> **TRY IT OUT**
>
> If you do not have access to an ASP-compatible Web server, you can try this ASP application on my site at http://www.pgacon.com/ipbook/great.asp.

Next, open your Web browser and navigate to the ASP Web page. If everything is working as it is supposed to, you'll see a page like that shown in Figure 18.2. It displays the phrase ASP is great! in seven font sizes.

Still in your browser, examine the HTML source code for the page. In Internet Explorer, the command to do this is View, Source. You'll see that the HTML source is different from the contents of the original ASP page, as shown in Listing 18.2.

FIGURE 18.2

Testing the ASP demonstration page.

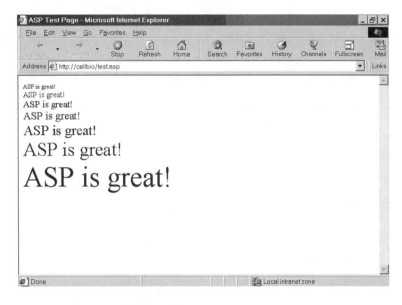

LISTING 18.2 THE HTML RETURNED BY GREAT.ASP

18

```
<HTML>
<HEAD>
<TITLE>ASP Test Page</TITLE>
</HEAD>
<BODY>
<FONT SIZE=1> ASP is great!<BR>
<FONT SIZE=2> ASP is great!<BR>
<FONT SIZE=3> ASP is great!<BR>
<FONT SIZE=4> ASP is great!<BR>
<FONT SIZE=5> ASP is great!<BR>
<FONT SIZE=6> ASP is great!<BR>
<FONT SIZE=7> ASP is great!<BR>
</BODY>
```

Let's analyze what happened. If you return to Listing 18.1, you can see that most of the original ASP file is standard HTML that ends up being copied without modification to the result page returned to the user. There are only three script lines:

```
<% for I = 1 to 7 %>
<FONT SIZE=<%= I %>> ASP is great!<BR>
<% Next %>
```

The first and third lines should look familiar to you; in fact, they are a standard Basic For...Next loop that executes seven times. The middle line is more complex. It uses the output tag <%=...%> to write the value of the variable I to the document, along with some other text. Therefore, the first time the loop executes, the following text is written to the output HTML document:

```
<FONT SIZE=1> ASP is great!<BR>
```

The second time the loop executes, this is written:

```
<FONT SIZE=2> ASP is great!<BR>
```

This continues until all seven lines have been written. The result, as you have seen, is to display the message in seven different font sizes.

The GLOBAL.ASA File

Every ASP application has a GLOBAL.ASA file that resides on the server. Strictly speaking, this file is not absolutely necessary, but without it, you can perform only relatively simple ASP tasks.

The GLOBAL.ASA file is executed by the Web server. It typically contains scripts to initialize application or session variables, connect to databases, send cookies, and perform other operations that pertain to the application as a whole. You must create the GLOBAL.ASA file for your application and upload it to the application's main directory. The code you put in the file will depend on the needs of your application; I will provide some examples later in the chapter.

Active Server Objects

A server that supports ASP will offer a number of objects that your scripts can use. These objects, through their properties and methods, provide information about the server environment, perform tasks relating to form management, and allow for data storage. You need to know about these server-side objects to program ASP Web pages efficiently.

Application

The Application object is used to share data among all the users of your ASP application. An *application* is defined as all the ASP files within the virtual directory (where GLOBAL.ASA resides) and its subfolders. Information stored in the Application object is available on all pages in the application and to all users.

DON'T OVERDO IT!

The Application object can store data, but it is intended for relatively small quantities. Your ASP scripts should not try to use the Application object for storage of large quantities of data.

To create a variable in the Application object, use the following syntax:

```
Application(varname) = value
```

varname is the variable name, and value is the data to be stored there. For example:

```
Application("MyName") = "Peter Aitken"
```

Then, retrieve the value as follows:

```
Dim MyName
MyName = Application("MyName")
```

One popular use for the Application object is to implement a hit counter. Incrementing an Application variable by 1 each time a page is loaded will keep track of your visitors. Listing 18.3 presents an example.

LISTING 18.3 SAMPLE CODE TO IMPLEMENT A HIT COUNTER

```
<HTML>
<HEAD>
<TITLE>ASP Counter Test Page</TITLE>
</HEAD>
<BODY>
<% Application("hits") = Application("hits") + 1 %>
This page has had <%= Application("hits") %> visitors. <BR>
</BODY>
</HTML>
```

18

Because all users have access to the Application object, a potential problem exists: What if two users try to access it at the same instant? For this, the Application object has Lock and Unlock methods. The Lock method puts a freeze on the object so that no other instances of the application can perform an operation on it. The Unlock method removes the lock. Proper coding of the preceding example would therefore be as follows:

```
Application.Lock
Application("hits") = Application("hits") + 1
Application.UnLock
```

To prevent other users from having to wait to access it, you should lock the Application object for as brief a time as possible.

The information stored in the Application object is persistent, which means that it is "remembered" between visits. However, it is not remembered when the application shuts down. To make information truly persistent, it must be saved to disk at the server. I'll show you show to do this in the section "File Access on the Server" later in this chapter.

The `Application` object has two events, `Application_OnStart` and `Application_OnEnd`. They are fired, as you might have guessed, when the application first starts and when it terminates. You can use these events to perform initialization actions that affect the entire application, such as setting up a database connection and storing or retrieving information from disk.

WHEN DO APPLICATIONS START AND END?

An ASP application starts the first time a user logs on to one of the application's ASP pages. It does not end, however, when the last user leaves your pages. Rather, it ends only when the Web server shuts down. After the Web service is shut down and restarted, the `Application_OnStart` event will again fire the first time someone visits one of your ASP pages.

Session

The `Session` object represents a single-user session. It is similar to the `Application` object in that it provides a place to store data, but a separate `Session` object is created for each visitor to your application. The `Session` object is available throughout all pages in the application, but only to the single user whose session it is associated with. You save and retrieve data by using the same syntax that you learned before for the `Application` object:

```
Session("VisitorName") = v_name
...
v_name = Session("VisitorName")
```

The `Session` object has `OnStart` and `OnEnd` events, and you place code for these event procedures in the GLOBAL.ASA file. One use for the `Session_OnStart` event is to provide a more accurate count of site visitors. Code placed in this event procedure will be executed only once for each visitor, unlike code in an ASP file, which can be executed multiple times for a single visitor if he or she visits that page more than once during a session. Therefore, you could have the following in GLOBAL.ASA:

```
<script RUNAT="Server" LANGUAGE = "vbscript">
Sub Session_OnStart()
Application.Lock
Application("hits") = Application("hits") + 1
Application.UnLock
End Sub
</script>
```

The `Session` object also has two properties. The `SessionID` property returns a unique type `Long` value that uniquely identifies the session on the server. The `TimeOut` property specifies, in minutes, how long the server will wait before terminating the session if there is no activity from the user. The default value is 20 minutes.

SessionID Is Only Temporarily Unique

You cannot be sure that the value returned by the SessionID property will remain unique. If the Web server is shut down and restarted, the same SessionID value can be reused. For this reason, you should not use the SessionID as the primary key in a database.

The Session object has one method, Abandon. When you call this method, the session is closed, and all its objects and data are destroyed. Calling Abandon has the same effect as if the session timed out.

Request

The Request object lets your script access data that was passed to the server from the client in an HTTP request. The object has three collections used to access client data:

- The Cookies collection retrieves the value of a cookie.
- The Form collection retrieves data sent with a client HTML POST request.
- The QueryString retrieves data sent with a client HTML GET request.

Cookies?

A *cookie* is a small bit of information stored on the client machine by the server.

I will cover the use of these three Request object collections later in the chapter.

Response

The Response object is used to send output from the server to the client. It has a number of properties and methods, but you will use the Response object most often for sending cookies. This is covered later in the chapter.

Server

The Server object represents the Web server that the ASP application is running on. Using this object, you can access information and tools provided by the Server.

The only property of this object is ScriptTimeOut, which specifies (in seconds) the length of time that a script can run before being terminated by the server. The default

18

value is 90 seconds. You cannot set a lower value than the server's default, but you might want to set a higher value if you have scripts that require a long time to process.

In addition to this one property, the `Server` object has three methods. The `HTMLEncode` method takes a string and encodes it as HTML. This means that characters with special meaning in HTML are converted to their special HTML representations. For example, the < and > characters are used to enclosed HTML tags. To display them on a Web page, you would use the codes `&lt` and `&gt` (for *less than* and *greater than*). Therefore, the method call

```
Server.HTMLEncode("HTML uses <B> for boldface")
```

would produce the following output:

```
HTML uses &ltB&gt for boldface
```

The `MapPath` method maps a specified relative or virtual path to the corresponding physical directory on the server. Because of the way files and directories are arranged and rearranged on Web servers, you sometimes need this method when all you know is the relative location. The syntax is as follows:

```
server.MapPath(path)
```

If *path* begins with a forward or backward slash, `MapPath` interprets *path* as being a full virtual path. Otherwise, `MapPath` returns a path that is relative to the location of the ASP file where the script is located.

There are two special ways to use `MapPath` that can be very useful. You can obtain the path information for the current page, relative to the application's root, by using the `ServerVariables` collection of the `Request` object:

```
Request.ServerVariables("PATH_INFO")
```

If you then pass this value to the `MapPath` method, you will obtain the full physical path to the current file:

```
server.MapPath(Request.ServerVariables("PATH_INFO"))
```

Likewise, passing a single slash to `MapPath` can be used to obtain the path to the home, or root, publishing directory.

Here's an example. Suppose your home publishing directory is c:\inetpub\wwwroot and your ASP application is located in \asp_test off the root. The file pathtest.asp contains the script and is located in the application directory \asp_test. Then, the following script:

```
<%= Request.ServerVariables("PATH_INFO")%><p>
<%= server.MapPath(Request.ServerVariables("PATH_INFO")) %><p>
<%= server.MapPath("/") %>
```

results in the following output:

```
/asp_test/pathtest.asp
C:\Inetpub\wwwroot\asp_test\pathtest.asp
C:\Inetpub\wwwroot
```

The final Server object method is CreateObject, and it is such an important topic that it deserves its own section.

Creating Objects on the Server

Some of the most interesting things you can do with ASP involve creating objects on the server. These are not the server objects, such as Application and Request, that you looked at earlier in this chapter. Rather, they are creatable components that are provided by the Web server for use in your ASP applications. You use the Server object's CreateObject method to create instances of these objects. The syntax is

```
Server.CreateObject(ObjID)
```

The argument ObjID identifies the object to create. For example, to create an instance of the AdRotator object, your script code would look like this:

```
Set MyAR = Server.CreateObject("MSWC.AdRotator")
```

What components are available? The Microsoft Web servers come with a set of components that perform a wide variety of commonly needed Web programming tasks, such as accessing databases, creating hit counters, and determining the browser being used by a client.

 Tip

Learn the fundamentals of the components available for use in your ASP applications. They can make your programming much easier.

Table 18.1 lists the available components and provides a brief description of what each does. I will go into more detail on a few of the components that I think are the most useful.

18

> **DATABASE ACCESS**
>
> One of the most powerful types of components is the ADO (ActiveX Database), related components that enable your ASP scripts to manipulate information in a database file. These are covered in detail on Day 19, "Connecting to a Database with ASP."

TABLE 18.1 ASP SERVER COMPONENTS

Component	Function
AdRotator	Automatically rotates advertisements displayed on a page according to a specified schedule.
BrowserType	Determines the capabilities, type, and version of clients' browsers
NextLink	Creates tables of contents for Web pages and links pages together like pages in a book
FileSystemObject	Provides access to file input and output
Tools	Provides utilities to add sophisticated functionality to your Web pages
MyInfo	Keeps track of personal information, such as the site administrator's name, address, and display choices
Counters	Creates, stores, increments, and retrieves counters
ContentRotator	Automates the rotation of HTML content on a Web page
PageCounter	Counts and displays the number of times a Web page has been visited
PermissionChecker	Uses password authentication protocols to determine whether a client has been granted permission to read a file

Using Server Components

Using a Server component is no different from using any other object in Visual Basic. You access the object's properties, methods, and events by using the same syntax that you already know. You must know exactly what properties and other capabilities the object provides, of course!

The default scope of a component is the page that contains the script code that created the instance of the component. This means that the component is destroyed by the server as soon as it is finished processing the page. If you want an object to have session scope, store its reference in a Session variable. For example:

```
Set Session("AR") = Server.CreateObject("MSWC.AdRotator")
```

The object will remain in existence as long as the session is still running. To destroy the component, set the reference to `Nothing`:

```
Set Session("AR") = Nothing
```

The `BrowserType` Component

The `BrowserType` component permits you to obtain information about the type and capabilities of the browser that a client is using. Its operation is based on the fact that all browsers, when they first connect to a site, send a User Agent HTTP Header that identifies the browser and its version number. This information is then used to look up the browser in the BROWSCAP.INI file maintained on the server. This file has entries for all popular browsers and some you have never heard of. Each browser entry contains information on that browser's specific capabilities, such as whether it supports frames and whether it can host ActiveX components. Here, for example, is the BROWSCAP.INI entry for the Internet Explorer version 3 browser:

```
[IE 3.0]
browser=IE
Version=3.0
majorver=3
minorver=0
frames=TRUE
tables=TRUE
cookies=TRUE
backgroundsounds=TRUE
vbscript=TRUE
javascript=TRUE
javaapplets=TRUE
ActiveXControls=TRUE
Win16=False
beta=False
AK=False
SK=False
AOL=False
Crawler=False
```

Although I do not know the meaning of each entry, it's clear that this browser supports VBScript, ActiveX controls, cookies, tables, and so on.

The information about a client's browser is made available to your script through the `BrowserType` object. Create an instance of the object and then access its properties, which correspond to the entries in the BROWSCAP.INI file.

```
Set BrType = Server.CreateObject("MSWC.BrowserType")
```

18

Now, for example, you can determine whether the browser supports frames, as follows:

```
<% if BrType.Frames = True then
' frames are supported
else
' frames not supported
end if %>
```

The BROWSCAP.INI file can also contain a set of default capabilities that will be reported if the client's browser is not among those in the file. If the specific property cannot be found, the return value is the string UNKNOWN.

Table 18.2 lists some of the more commonly used browser capabilities and the corresponding property names that you use with the BrowserType object.

TABLE 18.2 SOME BROWSER CAPABILITY PROPERTIES OF THE BrowserType COMPONENT

Property	Description
ActiveXControls	Specifies whether the browser supports ActiveX controls
backgroundsounds	Specifies whether the browser supports background sounds
beta	Specifies whether the browser is beta software
browser	Specifies the name of the browser
cdf	Specifies whether the browser supports the Channel Definition Format for Webcasting
cookies	Specifies whether the browser supports cookies
frames	Specifies whether the browser supports frames
Javaapplets	Specifies whether the browser supports Java applets
javascript	Specifies whether the browser supports JScript
platform	Specifies the platform that the browser runs on
tables	Specifies whether the browser supports tables
vbscript	Specifies whether the browser supports VBScript
version	Specifies the version number of the browser

The Tools Component

The Tools object provides several utility functions. Create an instance as follows:

```
Set Tools = Server.CreateObject("MSWC.Tools")
```

The component has the following methods:

- FileExists checks whether a file exists on your site. Pass the relative URL of the file, and the method returns True if the file exists and False otherwise.
- Random returns a pseudo-random integer in the range of -32768–32767. This method takes no arguments.

Reusing Script with #include

The #include directive enables you to insert the contents of one file into another. It can be very useful, particularly if you reuse various page elements. You can include anything with this directive, HTML or script. For example, if you have created a set of general-purpose VBScript procedures, you can put them in a separate file and then #include that file in every page that needs to use the procedures.

By tradition, files that are meant to be included in other files and not viewed on their own, are given the .INC extension. This is not required, however; you can use any extension you like. Some people like to use the .SCR extension for files that contain script. If you had placed your VBScript procedures in the file proc1.inc, you would include it as follows:

```
<!-- #include file="proc1.scr" -->
```

Note that the directive is placed within HTML comment tags. The end result is exactly the same as if the script (or other text) were a part of the file where the #include directive was placed. If you modify the script code, all you need to do is change the one file, proc1.inc, and the changes will automatically be reflected in all the HTML or ASP files that include it.

18

> **#include file VERSUS #include virtual**
> The #include file = "name" directive specifies a path to the filename relative to the current file. If you use #include virtual = "name", the path is specified as relative to the virtual root directory.

You can nest included files. For example, file A can include file B, which in turn includes file C. You cannot have circular references, however. If file A includes file B, then file B cannot include file A.

Receiving Data from the Client

Much of what you will want to do with ASP Web pages involves obtaining some information from the client and then using server-side scripting to generate the appropriate response. The following is a typical sequence of events:

1. The user views an HTML document that has input elements for the user to enter information, such as keywords to use in a search.
2. After entering the required information, the user clicks a button or performs some other action to submit the data to the server.
3. On the server, the data is received by a script in an ASP page.
4. The ASP page generates an HTML response—in this case, the results of the query—and returns it to the user.

How does a client send data to the server? The answer lies in the Form object, which is a part of the HTML specification and has nothing to do with Visual Basic forms. An HTML form is defined within <FORM> ... </FORM> tags. Within the Form, you use HTML input elements to permit the user to enter information. The Form will also have a Submit button that the user clicks to send all the information to the server.

The submitting process is automatic and requires no programming on your part. The details of the submission are defined by attributes within the <FORM> tag. You need to know about two of these: ACTION and METHOD.

The ACTION attribute specifies the URL of the page that will process the data. ACTION is optional, and if omitted, the data will be sent to the same URL as the page containing the <Form >tag (in other words, the page contains script to process its own data).

The METHOD attribute can be set to either POST or GET; these are two different ways of sending data to the server. GET tacks the data at the end of the ACTION URL, separated by a question mark, whereas POST sends the data separately, not associated with the URL. Both methods work perfectly well, but you must use different script code on the server to retrieve data from each.

GET VERSUS POST

The main difference between GET and POST is that GET limits you to a total of 255 characters for the data being sent to the server, whereas POST has no data length limitation.

In your ASP script, you use the Request object to retrieve data sent by the client. If the data was sent using the GET method, you use the Request object's QueryString collection. The syntax is as follows:

```
var = Request.QueryString("InputName")
```

If the data was sent with POST, you use the Request object's Form collection:

```
var = Request.Form("InputName")
```

In both these examples, *InputName* is the name of the HTML input element whose data you are retrieving. Here's an example. Suppose your HTML page contains the following (this is not the entire page HTML, just the Form element):

```
<FORM ACTION="myasp.asp" method=GET>
<INPUT name="firstname">
<INPUT type=SUBMIT>
</FORM>
```

Then, your ASP file, MYASP.ASP, would use the following script to retrieve the value that the user enters in the FirstName input element:

```
UserFirstName=request.querystring("firstname")
```

If, however, the FORM tag had specified the POST method, the ASP script would look like this:

```
UserFirstName = request.form("firstname")
```

A Demonstration of Responding to Information from a Client Interaction

I wrote a simple application that demonstrates how to send data from a client, receive it in an ASP script, and return a custom response to the user. The data entry page is pure HTML, with no VBScript required to perform its task. It is called GETINFO.HTM, and Listing 18.4 shows its HTML. You can see what the page looks like in Figure 18.3.

18

FIGURE **18.3**

*The GETINFO.HTM
page for data entry.*

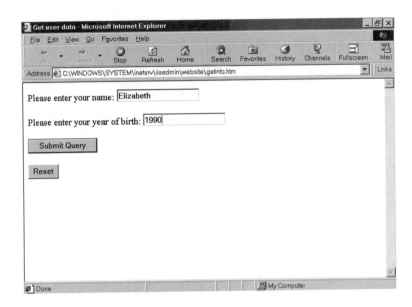

LISTING **18.4**   GETINFO.HTM ACCEPTS NAME AND BIRTH YEAR INFORMATION FROM THE USER
AND SUBMITS IT TO GETINFO.ASP

```
<html>
<head>
<title>getinfo.htm </title>
</head>
<body>
<form action="getinfo.asp" method=post>
Please enter your name: <input Name = "username" MaxLength = 25><p>
Please enter your year of birth: <input Name = "birthyear"
MaxLength = 4><p>
<INPUT TYPE=submit><p><INPUT TYPE=reset></form>
</body>
</html>
```

When the user submits data from GETINFO.HTM, it is sent by using the POST method to
GETINFO.ASP. Script code in this ASP file accepts the data sent by the user and then
generates a custom response based on the user's name and age. The code in
GETINFO.ASP is shown in Listing 18.5, and Figure 18.4 shows one of the responses it
generates.

FIGURE 18.4

Output created by GETINFO.ASP.

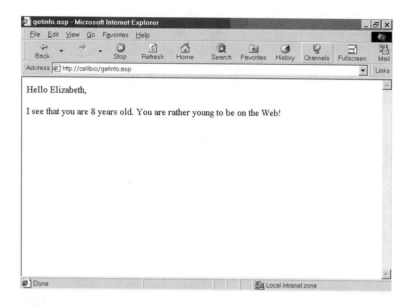

LISTING 18.5 GETINFO.ASP GENERATES A CUSTOM RESPONSE FROM INFORMATION ENTERED BY THE USER IN GETINFO.HTM

18

```
<html><head>

<TITLE>getinfo.asp</TITLE>

</head><body>

<%

name=request.form("username")
birth=request.form("birthyear")
age = 1998 - birth %>
Hello <%=name%>,<p>
<%If age < 15 then %>
I see that you are <%=age%> years old. You are rather
young to be on the Web!
<%elseif age > 60 then %>
I see you are over 60 years old. Shouldn't you be off
playing golf somewhere?
<%else%>
Nice to Meet You.
<%end if%>
</body></html>
```

File Access on the Server

The server-side scripting model of ASP permits you to create, read, and write files on the server. This capability can be useful for a variety of tasks, such as ensuring that data saved in the Application is really persistent and will be retained even if the Web server is shut down and restarted.

ISN'T THIS DANGEROUS?

You might be wondering why file access is supported by server-side scripting when it is not supported by client-side scripting. One of the reasons that VBScript is considered safe is that it cannot access files, isn't it? That's true, but relevant only for client-side scripting. On a server, you will be able to read and write files only within the directories of your Web. In no way can you cause problems with critical system files or other people's data.

File access in an ASP script is done using the same FileSystemObject (FSO) model available in Visual Basic itself. If you have used this technique in your regular Visual Basic programs, it will carry over to your scripts.

WHAT IS THE FSO MODEL?

If you have not worked much with Visual Basic version 6, you might not be familiar with the FSO model. Visual Basic still supports all the traditional file access statements, such as Open, Write, and Put. However, the new object-oriented FSO model has been added and probably will eventually replace the old model. The FSO model is based on the FileSystemObject, which is created as follows:

```
Set fs = CreateObject("Scripting.FileSystemObject")
```

After you create the object, you use its properties and methods to create, open, write, read, and otherwise manipulate files. At present, the FSO model is limited to working with text files.

The first step in reading or writing files in an ASP script is to create an instance of the FileSystemObject, as follows:

```
set fs = Server.CreateObject("Scripting.FileSystemObject")
```

After you have created a FileSystemObject object, you next create a TextStream object, which is simply a regular text file enclosed in an FSO wrapper. The FileSystemObject has two methods for creating TextStream objects:

- `CreateTextFile` creates a new file. If a file of the specified name already exists, it is overwritten.

- `OpenTextFile` opens a file for reading or writing. If the specified file already exists, new data is appended at the end of existing data.

The syntax for the `CreateTextFile` and `OpenTextFile` methods is similar.

```
Set ts = fs.CreateTextFile(filename[, overwrite[, unicode]])
Set ts = fs.OpenTextFile(filename[, iomode[, create[, format]]])
```

Filename specifies the name, including path information, of the file.

Overwrite is `True` if an existing file is to be overwritten and `False` if not. If this argument is omitted, the default is `False`. An error occurs if *overwrite* is `False` and *filename* already exists.

Unicode is `True` to create a Unicode file and `False` (the default) for an ASCII file.

IOMode is set to `ForReading` to read data from the file or to `ForAppending` to write data to the end of the file. You cannot write data to a file that was opened in `ForReading` mode.

Create is `True` or `False`, specifying whether a new file will be created if *filename* does not exist. The default is `False`.

Format is a tristate argument that specifies the format of the file. Use `TriStateTrue` to open the file as Unicode, `TriStateFalse` (the default) to open the file as ASCII, and `TristateUseDefault` to use the system default file format setting.

18

UNI-WHAT?

Computers use numbers to represent text characters, punctuation marks, and other symbols. There are two systems for assigning numbers to characters: ACSII (or ANSI) and Unicode. ASCII uses one byte per character, which permits 256 different symbols to be represented. Although this is adequate for English, it cannot support many other languages. Unicode uses 2 bytes per character, which permits more than 65,000 different symbols. Which format you use depends on the specific requirements of your project.

After creating the `TextStream` object associated with a file, you then use its methods to write and read file data. Tables 18.3 and 18.4 describe the `TextStream` object's methods and properties, respectively.

TABLE 18.3   TextStream Object Methods

Method	Description
Close	Closes the file. You should always execute this method when you are finished accessing the file.
Read(n)	Reads the next n characters from the file.
ReadAll	Reads the entire file.
ReadLine	Reads an entire line up to, but not including, the newline character from a file.
Skip(n)	Skips ahead by n characters.
SkipLine	Skips to the beginning of the next line.
Write(s)	Writes the string s to the file. No newline character is added.
WriteBlankLines(n)	Writes n blank lines to the file.
WriteLine(s)	Writes the string s to the file, followed by a newline character.

TABLE 18.4   TextStream Object Properties

Property	Description
AtEndOfLine	True if the file pointer is at the end of a line and False otherwise. Applies only to files that are open for reading; otherwise, an error occurs.
AtEndOfStream	True if the file pointer is at the end of the file and False otherwise. Applies only to files that are open for reading; otherwise, an error occurs.
Column	Returns the file pointer's column number. The first character on a line is at column 1.
Line	Returns the current line number.

Use of the FSO system to read and write files is fairly straightforward and really no different in an ASP script than it would be in a regular Visual Basic application. For example, Listing 18.6 shows the code you could put in your Session_OnStart event procedure (in GLOBAL.ASA) to save the current hit count to disk so that if the Web server is ever shut down and restarted, you will have a record.

LISTING 18.6 THE SERVER Session_OnStart PROCEDURE

```
<SCRIPT LANGUAGE="VBScript" RUNAT="server">

Sub Session_OnStart

Application.Lock
hits = Application("hits")
hits = hits + 1
Application("hits") = hits
set fs = Server.CreateObject("Scripting.FileSystemObject")
set hitfile = fs.CreateTextFile("hits.txt", True, False)
hitfile.WriteLine(hits)
hitfile.Close
Application.Unlock

End Sub

</SCRIPT>
```

Using Cookies

18

Have you ever visited a Web site that seems to remember things about you from your last visit? This can be a very convenient feature. For example, when I log on to my favorite online bookseller, they know it's me and can retrieve information about me that I have entered previously, such as my shipping address and credit card number. Then, I can place orders without again having to enter all that information each time.

This type of memory is accomplished with cookies. A *cookie* is a small bit of information that the server stores on the client machine. Whenever a client visits a site, the site can see whether any of its cookies are present on the client machine and, if they are, use the values to identify the visitor.

COOKIES ARE SAFE!

As a client, you usually have no idea that cookies are being used by the sites you visit. They are totally harmless, and other than taking up a few bytes of disk space, they have no adverse effects.

Sending Cookies

In an ASP application, you use the `Response` object for placing a cookie on the client machine and the `Request` object to read it back. The syntax for setting a cookie with `Response` is as follows:

```
Response.Cookies(cookie)[(key)] = value
```

In this example, `cookie` is the cookie name, and `value` is the data assigned to it. Therefore, to set a cookie named `fiction` to the value `Michael Crichton`, you would write

```
Response.Cookies("fiction") = "Michael Crichton"
```

You can use the optional *key* argument to create a *cookie dictionary*, which contains multiple values with different keys under the same cookie name:

```
Response.Cookies("favorite")("team") = "Panthers"
Response.Cookies("favorite")("flavor") = "Vanilla"
Response.Cookies("favorite")("car") = "Corvette"
```

Each cookie has a set of attributes that control certain aspects of its lifetime and operation. Table 18.5 describes these.

TABLE 18.5 COOKIE ATTRIBUTES

Cookie Attribute	Meaning
Expires	The date on which the cookie *expires* (can no longer be retrieved from the client machine).
Domain	If specified, the cookie can be retrieved only from this domain.
Path	If specified, the cookie can be retrieved only from this path.
Secure	Specifies whether the cookie is secure (encrypted).
HasKeys	Specifies whether the cookie is a dictionary.

The `HasKeys` cookie attribute is read-only, whereas the others are all write-only. To set a cookie attribute, use the following syntax:

```
Response.Cookies(cookie).attribute = value
```

Here, `attribute` is the attribute you are setting, from Table 18.5. For example, to specify that the cookie named `favorites` will expire on January 1, 1999, you would write the following code:

```
Response.Cookies("favorites").Expires = #January 1, 1999#
```

If you set an expiration date for a cookie dictionary, all its entries expire on that date. If you assign a single value to a cookie dictionary, all its individual key values are lost.

Retrieving Cookies

You use the `Request` object to retrieve cookie values from a client computer. The syntax to retrieve a single cookie named *cookiename* is as follows:

```
cv = Request.Cookies(cookiename)
```

If the cookie does not exist, the method returns a blank string. To retrieve a specific cookie *key* from the cookie dictionary *cookiename*, here is the syntax:

```
cv = Request.Cookies(cookiename)(key)
```

To check whether a cookie is a single or a dictionary, query the `HasKeys` property:

```
If Request.Cookies(cookiename).HasKeys Then
' It is a dictionary
Else
' it is a single cookie
End If
```

When you know that a cookie is a dictionary, you can loop through all its keys with the following code, which lists the cookies in the document:

```
<% For Each Key in Request.Cookies(cookiename) %>'
The key <%= key %> has the value
<%= Request.Cookies(cookiename)(key) %><P>
<% Next %>
```

Summary

ASP pages contain regular HTML, as well as scripts that execute on the server. The scripts can obtain information from the client and generate a customized HTML response to return for viewing in the client browser. This is a very powerful technique for creating dynamic Web pages that react to the user. The technology's one major limitation is that ASP pages run only on Web servers from Microsoft. It is, however, browser independent.

You saw today how the `Server` object provides a number of objects that your scripts can use for tasks such as database manipulation and file access. You also learned how to use cookies to store state information on the client machine. Although this has been a good introduction to ASP pages, there is much more to learn. In the next two lessons, you will look at how to use ASP for database applications and work through creating a full-fledged ASP program.

Q&A

Q **What is the primary limitation of ASP technology?**

A ASP pages can be hosted only on Web servers that are running one of Microsoft's servers, such as the Internet Information Server. If your Web site is hosted by another type of server, you cannot use this technology—at least, not at present.

Q **Do ASP scripts require a specific browser in order to work properly?**

A No. Because ASP scripts execute on the server, their proper operation is not dependent on the type of browser used by the client.

Q **What method do you use in an ASP script to retrieve data sent from a form on the client's machine?**

A It depends on the method used to send the data. If the form uses GET, the script must use the Request object's QueryString collection. On the other hand, if the form uses POST, the script must use the Request object's Form collection.

Q **How can an ASP page send HTML to the client?**

A One simple way is to have the desired HTML in the ASP page, outside any script tags. The other way involves using the special tag <%= to display the value of VBScript variables in the final HTML page.

Workshop

Quiz

1. How can an ASP application determine whether a client's browser supports frames?

2. To create an object in an ASP script, do you use VBScript's CreateObject method?

3. How can an ASP script convert regular text into HTML encoded text for viewing in the client's browser?

4. From the client's point of view, what is the main difference between the GET and POST methods?

5. What does the #include directive do?

DAY 19

Connecting to a Database with ASP

One of the things that Web developers want to do most often is to connect a Web page to a database. This can be a very powerful approach to dynamic Web pages because, properly done, it enables the user to see only the information he or she is interested in. Today you will learn

- Why Web database access is so powerful
- The basics of database design and programming
- How Web database connections work
- The use of ActiveX Data Objects (ADO) for database access
- How to create and use ADO in ASP scripts

Why Database Access?

Perhaps the hottest topic in Web programming these days is database access. Why all the fuss? I think that when you realize the potential power of combining database technology with the worldwide reach of the Internet, you will understand.

- Database technology is the most powerful and efficient means of organizing and manipulating many kinds of information.
- The Internet is the most efficient and widely used means of distributing information.

Put these two facts together, and you'll have some idea of what's going on. In fact, I bet that many of the Web sites you like to visit are using database technology, even though you might not be aware of it.

Database programming takes many forms. As a Visual Basic programmer, you might have already done some database programming. Visual Basic is perhaps the most powerful database programming tool available and is probably used more for database projects than for any other kind.

Types of Database Applications

Forget about the Internet for a moment. Database programming can be divided into the following two categories:

- *Single user databases* are located on a single computer and are designed to be used by one person at a time. If you used Visual Basic to write a database program to keep track of your video tape collection, for example, this would be a single user database.
- *Multiuser databases* are located on a network and are designed for simultaneous use by more than one person. They are sometimes called *client/server databases* or *distributed databases*. Typically, the actual data resides on a central server computer, and each user is at a remote computer connected via a local area network (LAN). Multiuser databases are significantly more difficult to program because of the need to control and coordinate input and requests from multiple users.

Any database designed to be deployed on the Web will clearly be a multiuser database. However, the general category of multiuser databases can be further divided as follows:

- *Decision support applications* permit the users to view and query the information in the database, but not to add new data or make changes.
- *Transaction processing applications* allow the users not only to view the database information, but also to add, delete, and modify data.

As you might guess, a decision support application is much easier to program than a transaction processing application. That's good news for us because in almost all cases a Web database application falls into this category, making the programmer's job easier.

How does this work? Someone has to be able to enter and modify database information. This is accomplished by having two separate applications access the same database file (where the information is stored). You, or the Web site administrator, would have a transaction processing application that lets you add, delete, and modify information in the database. This could be a custom database program created with Visual Basic or a dedicated database application such as Microsoft Access. Then there would be a second decision support application, which links the database to the Web. Figure 19.1 shows this arrangement.

FIGURE 19.1

Database deployment on the Web.

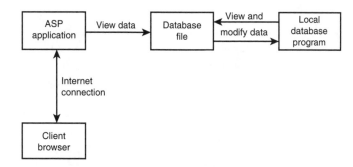

Database Programming Versus Web Programming

It's important for you to realize that database programming and Web programming are two separate topics. To implement a Web database application, you must understand both. Although the fundamentals of database programming are relatively easy to understand, more advanced database topics can be complicated. Entire books have been devoted to the topic of Visual Basic database programming, and I can do no more than scratch the surface here. This is, after all, a Web programming book! My goal is to present the basics of database programming and concentrate on the Web connection topics. If your database programming needs go beyond what I cover, you can explore the topic further on your own.

Database Basics

There's nothing mysterious about a database. If you maintain an address list, you are using a database, even though you might not know it. A *database* is simply a collection of information that is arranged in a specific manner. The most fundamental unit of

19

information in a database is a *record*. In an address list, for example, each person's entry is a record. Every record in a database contains *fields* that hold individual bits of information. In an address list, each record contains fields for the last name, first name, address, and so on. Each record in a database has the same fields, although these contain different information for each record, of course.

DATABASES AND APPLICATIONS

Remember that the term *database* refers to the information itself, whereas a *database application* is the program that permits you to access and manipulate that information. A given database can be accessed by several applications, and one application can access several databases.

The information in a database can be displayed in row and column format, with one row for each record and one column for each field. Figure 19.2 illustrates this. You will sometimes hear the terms *row* and *column* used as synonyms for *record* and *field*. The entire set of records is called a *table*. A database that contains only a single table is called a *flat-file database*.

FIGURE 19.2

A database has a row and column structure.

LASTNAME	FIRSTNAME	PHONE
SMITH	JOAN	555-1212
JONES	BILL	555-1213
CHANG	WALTER	555-1214

One record

One field

Relational Databases

Some databases contain more than one table. Multi-table databases are called *relational* databases because the tables are designed so that the data in one is related to the data in another.

Take a look at an example. Suppose you are a music buff and collect recordings of female jazz singers. You want to create a database that will enable you to keep track of your records, CDs, and tapes, so you design a database table named Recordings with the following field structure:

ItemNumber

ArtistName

Label

Title

Location

Format

A real database table would have more fields than this, of course, but this will serve for an example. Next, you want to keep track of biographical information about individual singers. That database table, called Artists, might have the following structure:

ArtistName

BirthDate

BirthPlace

Notes

> Every database table should have one field whose data is unique for every record. If the data itself does not provide unique values, as is often the case, you can simply create an ItemNumber field and assign sequential numbers to records. Many database programs do this automatically.

Note that these two database tables have one field in common: ArtistName. This is the basis of the relationships in a relational database—one or more fields in common. When you start entering data in the two tables, you will know that for every entry in the Recordings table, there will be one related entry in the Artists table. For every entry in the Artists table, there will be one or more related entries in the Recordings table.

19

Setting up a relational database creates many possibilities that are unavailable with flat-file databases. Continuing with the example, you could use the database's relation features to

- Display a list of all recordings by artists born in New York City.
- Find all artists who have made recordings with *Gershwin* in the album title.
- List all artists who have released two or more recordings on the Polygram label.

The potential of the relational database model is impressive, but not all applications require it. I will not cover relational databases any further because they are a database topic, not an Internet programming topic. Now that you know what they are, you can explore them further if you think that your application requires this technology.

Front End/Back End

Almost all database programming, whether single user or multiuser, uses the front end/back end model. In this model, two elements exist between the user and the actual data:

- The *front end* is the program that the user interacts with. It permits data entry, report generation, printing, and whatever other tasks the user needs to do. When you write a database program in Visual Basic, you are creating a front end.

- The *back end* sits between the front end and the database itself. You do not write the back end; it is provided as part of the operating system or by a database application vendor. The Microsoft Jet Database Engine is one example of a back end. The back end receives requests from the front end, carries them out, and returns the results to the front end.

The primary reason that this model was developed is that there are many database file formats. It was unrealistic to expect programmers to learn how to deal with all the various file formats. A back end provides a uniform set of commands that the user, or front end, can call. These general commands are then translated, by means of a specific database driver, into the specific commands required by the database file format in use. Whether you are programming for an Access database, a dBase database, or an Oracle database, your front-end program can simply issue the sort command, and the back end will take care of the details.

For a single-user database, the front and back ends are located on the same computer. A multiuser database locates the back end on the server, with each user running the front end on his or her local computer. The arrangement is shown schematically in Figure 19.3.

FIGURE 19.3

The relationship between a user, the front and back ends, and the database file.

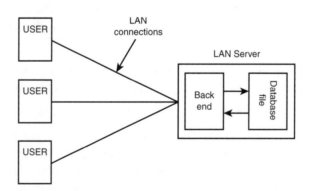

Web Database Connections

There are many ways to connect a Web page to a database, but they all have certain things in common. When you understand these common elements, you can explore the details of how it is done. As you will see, it has much in common with the way things are done for non-Web database programs, as discussed in the previous section.

For a Web-based database application, the actual database files are almost always located on the Web server. If you are publishing your database application on a server you maintain, you will simply copy the database file to an appropriate directory. If you are publishing to your Web site on a remote server, you'll upload the file just as you upload other files that are part of your Web.

The Web server will also be running a database back end that supports your database file format. In fact, it is probably the same back end that would be used for a local database program on the server computer—after all, the back end does not know or care whether the requests it's receiving are coming from a local program, over the LAN, or via the Internet.

Already, you have two of the three required parts of a database application: the database file and the back end. All that remains is the front end, and this is exactly what the term *Web database programming* refers to. The front end you create will be an ASP page that executes on the server.

In terms of *what* you do, creating a Web-based front end is no different from programming a standalone front end by using Visual Basic (or any other development tool, for that matter). In broad outline, you would do the following:

1. Collect information and commands from the user.
2. Send the appropriate requests to the back end.
3. Retrieve the results returned by the back end.
4. Display the results for the user to view.

In terms of *how* you perform these tasks, steps 1 and 4 are different for Web development:

- Information and user actions are obtained by means of an HTML document displayed on the user's browser. Information is entered into HTML input elements and sent to the server by using the GET or POST method. The front end application, executing on the server, obtains this information by using the Request object (as you learned in the previous lesson).

19

- Results are displayed to the user by generating a custom HTML page, which is returned to the client.

You can see, I think, that Web database programming is really just the combination of two programming technologies that you probably already know: ASP scripts, which you learned about in the previous lesson, and Visual Basic database programming, which you perhaps already know from your programming experience.

ActiveX Data Objects

You can connect Web pages to a database in numerous ways, but the best one by far (at least in my opinion) is ActiveX Data Objects (ADO). ADO is a relatively new database access model, partially supported in Visual Basic version 5 and fully supported only with the most recent release of Visual Basic.

OLE DB

To understand ADO, you must know a little about OLE DB. *OLE DB* is a set of COM Component Object Model interfaces that you can use to access a variety of information sources. OLE DB was designed to provide universal data access that is not limited to certain data sources but can deal with any type of data in any format. Different data sources have different data management capabilities, and the OLE DB interfaces take this into account. You do not access OLE DB directly, but indirectly by means of ActiveX Data Objects (ADO).

ADO

ActiveX Data Objects provide programmers with an application-level interface to OLE DB. You never have to think about OLE DB, which sits quietly in the background doing its job. In other words, now that you know about OLE DB, you can forget about it and simply think of ADO as an interface directly to the data source.

ADO supplants several early data access technologies, such as Remote Data Objects (RDO) and Data Access Objects (DAO). These data interfaces are still supported, and you can use them in your ASP pages to create a Web database application. ADO is, however, a much superior approach. A database program written using ADO is much simpler and easier to maintain than one created using the older database technologies. Therefore, I strongly suggest that you use ADO for all new projects. I used ADO exclusively for this book's Web database lessons.

THE ADO DATA CONTROL

In a standard Visual Basic program, you can access ADO in two ways: by creating and manipulating ADO objects in code or by placing an ADO Data Control on a form. In an ASP page, however, the ADO Data Control cannot be used.

What follows is a brief introduction to the most important features of the ADO model, enough to get you started creating Web database projects.

The ADO Object Model

The ADO object model contains only seven objects. If you have worked with any of the earlier data access models, you realize what an improvement this is! These objects are described here:

- `Connection` object—The link between the program and the database file
- `Command` object—A query or statement that is sent to the data source for processing
- `Recordset` object—A set of data records that is returned by the data source in response to a query
- `Field` object—A single column of data within a `Recordset` object
- `Error` object—Information about error conditions reported by the data source
- `Parameter` object—A single piece of information, or parameter, associated with a `Command` object
- `Property` object—A property of an ADO object

The ADO objects are related as follows:

- Each `Connection` object has a property named `Errors`, which references a collection of `Error` objects representing any errors that have occurred.
- Each `Command` object contains a property named `Parameters`, which references a collection of `Parameter` objects. There will be one `Parameter` object for each parameter required by the current command.
- Each `Recordset` object contains a property named `Fields`, which references a collection of `Field` objects, one for each column in the recordset.
- Each of these six object types has a `Properties` property, which references a collection of `Property` objects, one for each provider-specific property.

19

The ADO model is very flexible, and it's impossible to specify a sequence of steps or events to always follow. Here is a typical sequence:

1. Create a Connection object.
2. Set the Connection object's properties. For example, you must specify the name and location of the database file you want to connect to.
3. Call the Connection object's Open method to establish the link to the database file.
4. Create a Command object.
5. Set the Command object's properties to create the query or statement that you want to execute.
6. Send the command to the data source. This is done by associating the Command object with the Connection object.
7. The results of the query are returned in a RecordSet object. Use the contents of the RecordSet as needed.
8. Terminate the connection.

As you will see, you can usually take shortcuts. Only for the most sophisticated types of database operations will you need to use the full set of ADO objects. Usually, you can accomplish what you want in a much simpler way.

The Connection Object

The Connection object has a number of properties, but only one that you need to know about at this time: ConnectionString. As the name implies, this property is a string that specifies details of the connection that you want to establish. Among the specifics that the connection string can specify are the database filename, the user ID and password (for databases that require a login), and the mode (read/write/share settings). A sample ConnectionString is shown here:

```
Provider=Microsoft.Jet.OLEDB.3.51;Persist Security Info=False;

Data Source="c:\data\sales.mdb";Mode=Read¦Write¦Share Deny None
```

For most applications, all you need is the proper `ConnectionString` to link the `Connection` object to a database file. Fortunately, although the syntax of the string seems complex, there is an easy way to create one. Here's how:

1. Start Visual Basic and create a new Standard EXE project.

2. Place an ADO Data control on the form. You first select the ADO Data Control in the components list.

3. Right-click ADO Data Control and select Properties to display the property pages for the control. Be sure the General tab is selected (see Figure 19.4).

FIGURE 19.4

The ADO Data control's General property page.

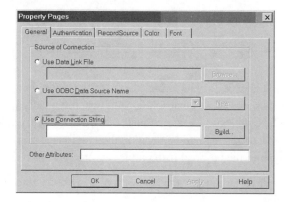

4. Select the Use Connection String option and then click the Build button. The Data Link Properties dialog will be displayed, as shown in Figure 19.5.

5. On the Provider tab, select the correct provider for the database file you will be connecting to. Hint: For Microsoft Access database files, use the Microsoft Jet 3.51 OLE DB Provider.

6. Use the Data Link Properties dialog box's other tabs to set other details of the link, such as the name of the database file.

7. When done, click OK. Visual Basic will create the connection string and display it on the property page.

8. Copy the connection string from the dialog box for use in your ASP script.

19

FIGURE **19.5**

Setting the Data Link properties.

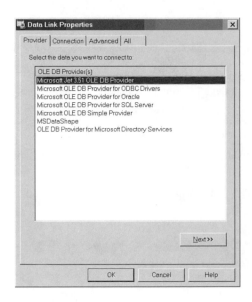

One modification is necessary to a connection string created in this manner. The path to the data source is specified as an absolute path, which typically will be incorrect after the application and the database file are published to your Web server. You must use the Server object's MapPath method (covered in the previous lesson) to map the database file's relative path to the physical path on the server.

Here's an example. Suppose that the connection string created for the ADO Data control was the following:

```
Provider=Microsoft.Jet.OLEDB.3.51;Persist Security Info=False;

Data Source="c:\data\sales.mdb";Mode=Read¦Write¦Share Deny None
```

On your Web site, you plan to place the sales.mdb database file in the same directory as the ASP file where the script will be located. Then, in your script, you would construct the connection string as follows:

```
<% CS = "Provider=Microsoft.Jet.OLEDB.3.51;"
CS = CS & "Persist Security Info=False;"
CS = CS & "Data Source=" & Server.mappath("sales.mdb") & ";"
cs = cs & "Mode=Read¦Write¦Share Deny None" %>
```

The Connection object has three methods that you need to know about. The Open method opens a connection to a data source. The syntax is

```
connection.Open ConnectionString, UserID, Password
```

All the arguments to this method are optional. You can put the connection string in the `ConnectionString` property and call `Open` without arguments, or you can pass the connection string as an argument to the method. Likewise, if the user ID and password are specified in the connection string, they can be omitted from the method call. If the `Open` method fails, an error will be raised, and the `Connection` object's `Errors` collection will contain one or more `Error` objects with information about the error.

The `Execute` command sends a command to the database and returns the results. The syntax is

```
connection.execute command
```

Command is a string specifying the command to execute. The results of the command are always returned in a read-only `RecordSet`. Here is an example, which assumes that `cnn` is a `Connection` object that has already been connected to a data source:

```
Dim rs As New ADODB.Recordset
Set rs = cnn.Execute("select * from saledata")
```

After this command is executed, the `RecordSet` `rs` will contain all records from the database table named saledata.

The `Connection` object's third method is `Close`, which closes the connection to the data source and frees any associated resources. Executing `Close` does not destroy the `Connection` object, which is accomplished by setting the reference variable to `Nothing`.

The `RecordSet` Object

All data manipulation and access with ADO is done with `RecordSet` objects. Basically, you create one or more `RecordSet` objects that contain the records and fields from a database table that you need. At one extreme, a `RecordSet` can contain all records and all fields from a table. You can also specify that a `RecordSet` be limited to specific records (for example, where `STATE` is `New York`) and specified fields.

Given the power and flexibility of the `RecordSet` object, it's not surprising that it has many properties and methods. Fortunately, you will not have to deal with most of them. Many are related to procedures for adding new data or editing existing data in a database—a topic that I am not covering because the vast majority of Web database projects do not need these capabilities. Other properties and methods are used only for advanced programming tasks, again something beyond the scope of this book. My goal, remember, is to get you up and running with your Web database projects as soon as possible.

Before diving into the details, let me explain the basic structure of a `RecordSet`. It is organized in row and column format, like a database table, with the rows corresponding to records and the columns to fields. A RecordSet has a current record position, or record pointer, that indicates which record is current. The record pointer can also be at the beginning or the end of the RecordSet, in which case it does not point at any record.

Table 19.1 lists the essential properties of the RecordSet object.

TABLE 19.1 ESSENTIAL RecordSet OBJECT PROPERTIES

Property	Description
BOF	True if the record pointer is at the beginning of the RecordSet.
EOF	True if the record pointer is at the end of the RecordSet.
MaxRecords	The maximum number of records to return to the RecordSet from a query. The default value of 0 means there is no limit.
RecordCount	Returns the number of records in the RecordSet. Returns -1 if for some reason the number of records cannot be determined.

EMPTY RecordSet?

If a RecordSet is empty, both the BOF and EOF properties will be True.

The RecordSet object also has a variety of methods. The most important ones are explained in Table 19.2. You'll see that all these methods have to do with moving around in the RecordSet.

TABLE 19.2 THE ESSENTIAL METHODS OF THE RecordSet OBJECT

Method	Description
Move NumRecs	Moves the record pointer by *NumRecs* records. Positive values move toward the end of the RecordSet, and negative values move toward the beginning. If the Move method goes past the beginning or end of the file, the pointer is set to the beginning or end of the RecordSet, respectively.
MoveFirst	Moves to the first record in the RecordSet.
MoveLast	Moves to the last record in the RecordSet.
MoveNext	Moves forward one record.
MovePrevious	Moves back one record.

Getting Data from `RecordSets`

After you have populated a `RecordSet` with the desired records, how do you obtain the data from the `RecordSet` so that you can use it in your script? Remember that the `RecordSet` object has a `Fields` collection that contains one entry for each field, or column, in the `RecordSet`. The number of fields is obtained as follows:

```
NumFields = RecordSet.fields.count
```

The fields themselves are indexed from `0` through `NumFields - 1`. You can access the data in the current record by specifying the index of its field. For example, the following script code displays the contents of the second field in the `RecordSet`'s current record:

```
<%= RecordSet.fields(1).value %>
```

You can also access members of the `Fields` collection by their names. This code displays the contents of the Name field:

```
<%= RecordSet.fields("name").value %>
```

A Simple Demonstration

To give you a feel for how simple database access on the Web can be, I put together a short ASP page that opens a database table and displays all its records in a table. This task takes surprisingly few lines of code, presented in Listing 19.1. Figure 19.6 shows the program output, displaying the contents of my stamps database.

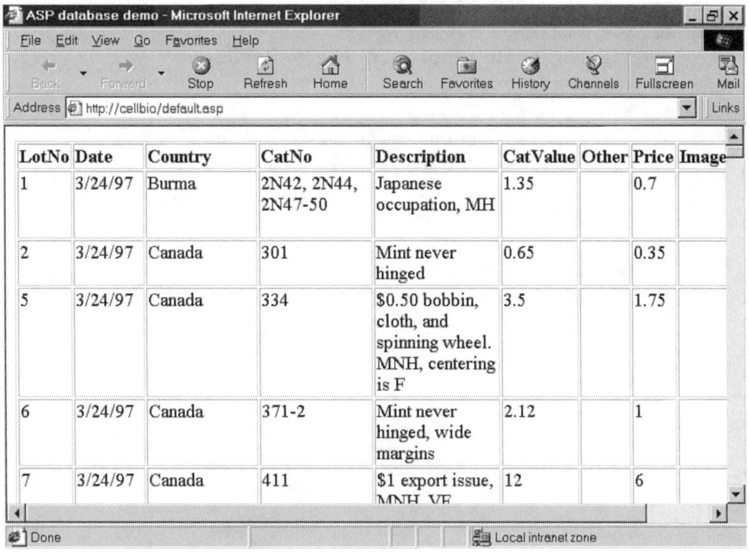

FIGURE 19.6

The output of the ASP database demonstration program.

19

LotNo	Date	Country	CatNo	Description	CatValue	Other	Price	Image
1	3/24/97	Burma	2N42, 2N44, 2N47-50	Japanese occupation, MH	1.35		0.7	
2	3/24/97	Canada	301	Mint never hinged	0.65		0.35	
5	3/24/97	Canada	334	$0.50 bobbin, cloth, and spinning wheel. MNH, centering is F	3.5		1.75	
6	3/24/97	Canada	371-2	Mint never hinged, wide margins	2.12		1	
7	3/24/97	Canada	411	$1 export issue, MNH, VF	12		6	

LISTING 19.1   DISPLAYING THE CONTENTS OF A DATABASE TABLE WITH AN ASP SCRIPT

```
<html>
<head>
<title>ASP database demo</title>
</head>
<body>
<%
' Build the connection string.
CS = "Provider=Microsoft.Jet.OLEDB.3.51;"
CS = CS & "Persist Security Info=False;"
CS = CS & "Data Source=" & Server.mappath("sales.mdb") & ";"
cs = cs & "Mode=Read¦Write¦Share Deny None"
' Create the Connection object and open it.
set adocon = Server.CreateObject("adodb.connection")
adocon.open cs
' Execute a query. This selects all fields and all
' records from the table "stamps" and sorts the
' records by the data in the LotNo field.
set rs = adocon.execute("select * from stamps order by LotNo")
' Get the number of fields in the table.
numfields=rs.fields.count
' Create a table with one column per field. %>
<table border = 1>
<tr>
<% for i = 0 to numfields -1 %>
<td><b><%= rs(i).name %></b></td>
<% next %>
</tr>
<%' Move to the first record.
rs.movefirst
' Loop for each record in the RecordSet.
do while not rs.eof %>
<tr>
<% ' Populate the row with field values.
for i = 0 to numfields - 1 %>
<td valign=top><%= rs.fields(i).value %>
 </td>
<% next %>
</tr>
<% ' Go to the next record.
rs.movenext
loop %>
</table>
</body>
</html>
```

This is a simple program, but it performs many of the actions required by all Web database applications—opening a database, selecting records, and displaying them. You can use the same code to display the contents of any database table by simply changing the connection string to point at the correct database file and changing the command to select records from the proper table.

Summary

With the tools and technologies available today, creating database-aware Web applications is not nearly as complex as it used to be. ActiveX Data Objects, available on Microsoft Web servers, enable you to access and manipulate database files in the same ways you would in a standard Visual Basic program. Active Server Pages (ASP) technology enables you to obtain information from users and return database results to them. If you put these two technologies together, you have a database-aware Web application.

In tomorrow's lesson, you will pull together what you have learned yesterday and today and create a fully functional database-aware Web application.

Q&A

Q How does the way you would access a database from an ASP script differ from how it is done in a regular Visual Basic program?

A The only significant difference is that a standard Visual Basic program can use data-aware controls, whereas an ASP script cannot. Otherwise, the procedures for creating and using ActiveX Data Objects are essentially the same.

Q Database applications are traditionally composed of a front end and a back end. With a Web database application, does the front end execute on the server or the client?

A Actually, it executes in both locations. ASP scripts that are part of the front end run on the server while the HTML is viewed, and optionally, client-side VBScript is executed on the client machine.

Q Suppose the data that will be stored in your database does not provide a field that is guaranteed to have a unique value for each record. Is this okay?

A No, it should be avoided. Databases work better if there is a primary key field whose data is different for each record. You can generate the data for this field, if necessary.

19

Workshop

Quiz

1. How would a database-aware Web application obtain input from the user?

2. Do all database applications permit the user to enter, delete, and edit data?

3. In the ADO model, which object represents the link between your program and the database file?

4. After populating a `RecordSet` object, how do you know how many fields it contains?

5. Give two ways to tell whether a `RecordSet` is empty.

DAY **20**

Implementing a Web Database Application

There's no teacher like experience, they say, and that holds for programming as well. You have learned enough about Active Server Pages and Web database connectivity to create database-aware Web applications, but seeing these principles put into practice will be a useful experience. Today you will learn

- How to use the Personal Web Server to test your ASP applications
- The basics of Structured Query Language (SQL)
- How to design the overall application
- How to create the user request form
- How to write an ASP page to respond to user requests
- How to deploy and test the application

Using the Personal Web Server

When you are working on a Web database project, or any ASP application for that matter, you should not publish it to your Web site until it is thoroughly tested and debugged. This avoids the various problems, both minor and serious, that untested software can cause for other applications and pages on the Web site. Another consideration is that the process of publishing to the Web site is usually time-consuming, necessitating the upload of one or more files across the Internet. To test an ASP application, you require a Web server of some sort. Simply opening the ASP pages in local mode as files does not execute the script; that is the job of the Web server. Fortunately, Microsoft provides its Personal Web Server as part of Windows 98.

The Personal Web Server is not normally installed, so you must do it yourself. On your Windows 98 CD-ROM, go to the /add-ons/pws folder and execute the setup.exe program. Unless you have special requirements, you can select the "typical" installation options. Once installed, the Personal Web Server will start and run in the background every time you turn on your computer. It will display as an icon in the taskbar tray, and you can open it by clicking the icon and selecting Properties. Figure 20.1 shows the Personal Web Manager, where you set the Personal Web Server's properties.

> **FRONTPAGE WON'T WORK**
>
> A version of the Personal Web Server is included with the Microsoft FrontPage Web editing package, but it does not support ASP. You need the version of the PWS that is provided on the Windows 98 CD-ROM.

Two particularly important things are shown on this page in the Publishing box. Where it says `Your home page is available at:`, you'll see the URL of your Web server directory. On my computer, as you can see in the figure, the URL is `http://cellbio`. This is not like a standard Web URL, and it does not have to be, because it is only for local use on this computer. Where it says `Your home directory`, you see the full path to your local publishing folder, which by default is c:\inetpub\wwwroot.

What this means is that when the Personal Web Server is running, HTTP requests to your home page URL will access files located in your home directory. Suppose, for example, that you have created a Web page called mypage.asp and placed the file in the folder c:\inetpub\wwwroot. If you open your Web browser and navigate to `http://oemcomputer/mypage.asp`, you will access this file. Most important, you'll be accessing the file by means of the Web server and the HTTP protocol and not simply opening it as a file. This means that server-side scripts will be executed, which is exactly what you need for testing your ASP applications.

FIGURE 20.1

Personal Web Server properties.

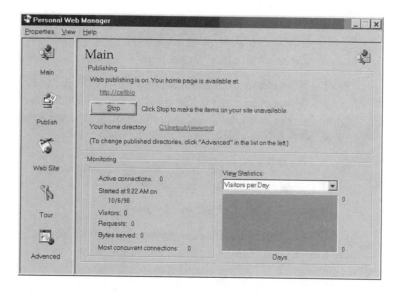

There is much more to the Personal Web Server. For example, if your computer is connected to the Internet, you can use the server to host a "real" Web page that can be accessed from anywhere on the Internet. You can explore the Personal Web Server further if you want.

SQL Basics

Structured Query Language is a widely accepted standard for manipulating databases. It is different from Basic and other programming languages in that it is nonprocedural, which means it has no statements for controlling program flow (such as Basic's If...Then...Else statement). SQL is limited to expressing what you want done, and the details of how are left to the underlying program.

> **IT IS PRONOUNCED *S-Q-L*, NOT *SEQUEL***
>
> Some people pronounce SQL *sequel*, but this is not correct. There was a data definition language called *Sequel*, and it was a precursor of today's SQL. However, they are two different things.

SQL has a variety of statements for performing actions such as adding, deleting, and modifying records. For present purposes, however, you need only to select records to

20

specify which fields and records in a database table should be copied to a `RecordSet`. For this, you use the `Select` statement. This SQL statement has the following syntax:

```
SELECT fields FROM table WHERE criteria ORDER BY sort
```

The `fields` argument specifies which fields should be included in the result set. You can use the wildcard character * to specify all fields or include a list of field names separated by commas. For example, if you want the result set to include only the First Name and Last Name fields, you could write

```
SELECT FirstName, LastName FROM ...
```

If a field name includes a space or punctuation, enclose it in brackets:

```
SELECT [First Name], [Last Name] FROM ...
```

The `table` argument specifies the database table to extract records from. In this book, I have used database files that contain only a single table, but a database file can contain multiple tables. Therefore, you have to specify the table name in an SQL query.

The `WHERE` part of the `SELECT` statement is optional; if it is omitted, the query will retrieve all records from the table. The `criteria` part of the `WHERE` clause is an expression that includes field names, comparison and logical operators, and criteria. Here are a few examples:

```
WHERE Country="Germany"
WHERE Price > 1
WHERE Country<>"Britain"
WHERE CatNo < 100
WHERE Country="Brazil" Or Country="Argentina"
```

The `ORDER BY` clause is also optional. If it is omitted, the order of the records in the result set will be determined by the database table's default index. To sort on a single field, the syntax is

```
... ORDER BY Country
```

To sort on two fields,

```
... ORDER BY Country, Price
```

The records will be sorted by `Country`; records with the same `Country` value will be sorted by price. The default sort order is ascending (A–Z, 0–9). For a descending order, include the `DESC` keyword:

```
... ORDER BY Country DESC
```

There is much more to SQL, but now you know the basics required for your Web database project.

Designing the Application

Like all programming projects, a Web database application benefits from planning ahead. This does not mean that your plans are set in stone, but forming at least a general idea of what you want to do makes later programming tasks easier.

The goal of this project is to create a database-aware Web page for selling postage stamps to collectors. Most stamp collectors, myself included, have numerous duplicate or unwanted stamps that we would like to sell to help finance the hobby. A Web page is a great place to do this. Because I keep a listing of my duplicate stamps in a Microsoft Excel database, a Web database application seems an ideal approach.

I planned the application to have two pages. The first one that visitors would see would provide some introductory information and also permit the user to specify the following:

- Which country or category of stamps to view
- How to sort the listing

The second page would be displayed in response to submission of the data from the first page. It would contain a tabular list of all the items in the selected category. The user could select items to purchase or could return to the first page to specify a new search.

Overall, this is a relatively simple Web database application. Even so, it uses most of the techniques that you would use in more complex projects and will serve well as a first Web database project.

Most Web database applications can be divided into three parts: the database itself, the user input page, and the custom data page that is generated in response to the user's request. You also must consider the global.asa file. Let's look at each of these in turn.

The Database

If you are starting from scratch, you can design your database file exactly as you want it. Based on the projected needs of the Web database application, you can design fields, assign field names, create indexes, and so on, in the most effective and efficient way. For example, data should be divided into fields, based on the needs of your application, and a field name should be relatively short but sufficiently descriptive of the data that the field contains.

In many situations, however, the database file that you want to deploy on the Web already exists. Opportunities to modify the file to suit the particular needs of your Web application might be limited. This is particularly true if the database file is used by other applications. It's unlikely you will be able to change field names or rearrange the data without causing these other applications to function improperly.

20

One thing you can do is create indexes as needed. An index greatly speeds the process of searching or sorting the records of the database, based on the data in a particular field. If your Web application will have to perform searches or sorts, you should be sure that the database of file definitions includes indexes based on the corresponding fields.

The stamp database that this project will use is a Microsoft Access database file. Table 20.1 describes its fields.

TABLE 20.1 FIELDS IN THE STAMPS DATABASE

Field Name	Data Type	Description
LotNo	Number	A sequential number unique for each record.
Date	Date/Time	The date the record was added to the database.
Country	Text	The country or category of the stamp.
CatNo	Text	The number of the stamp is a standard postage stamp catalog. The Text data is used because some catalog numbers include letter suffixes.
Description	Memo	A detailed description of the item. The Memo data type is used because the Text type is limited to 255 characters, and item descriptions might exceed this limit.
CatValue	Currency	The value of the stamp taken from a standard postage stamp catalog.
Price	Currency	The sale price of the item.
Image	Text	If an image of the stamp is available, the name of the JPG file.

The global.asa File

As you learned in the previous lesson, each ASP application has a global.asa file associated with it. This file contains script. More specifically, it contains event procedures that execute when a session or the application starts or terminates. This is the ideal place to establish a database connection. Each session requires its own Connection object, associated with the sales database. You can create the connection in the Session_OnStart() event procedure and then store the object reference as a session variable. Then all the pages in the application can reference the database connection. This is more efficient that having each individual ASP page create its own Connection object.

WATCH FOR A BUG

There have been reports that the Personal Web Server does not properly execute Session_OnStart when it should. If you have problems, this might be the cause. You should check the Microsoft Web site for updates to fix this problem.

Listing 20.1 shows the project's global.asa file. You can see that the code in the Session_Onstart() event procedure creates an ADO Connection object and stores the object reference in session sdb. At any time during the session, an ASP script can reference the Connection object by retrieving this value.

LISTING 20.1   THE GLOBAL.ASA FILE FOR THE STAMPS PROJECT

```
<script language="vbscript" runat="server">

' This is the global.asa file for the stamps database
' project. It creates a Connection object to the
' database file and stores the reference as the
' session variable "sdb".

sub session_onstart

cs = "Provider=Microsoft.Jet.OLEDB.3.51;"
cs = cs & "Persist Security Info=False;"
cs = cs & "Data Source="
cs = cs & server.mappath("Sales.mdb") & ";"
set session("sdb") = server.createobject("adodb.connection")
session("sdb").open cs

end sub

</script>
```

Do	**DON'T**
DO create database connections at the session level so that they will be available to all pages in the application.	**DON'T** create database connections at the application level. There is no need to load the server with a connection when no one is using it.

20

The User Input Page

The user input page will provide a place for the user to select which country/category to view, with a "view everything" choice included as well. There will also be an option to sort the listing by catalog number or by price and, of course, a Submit button. Figure 20.2 shows the appearance of this page.

FIGURE 20.2

The user input page.

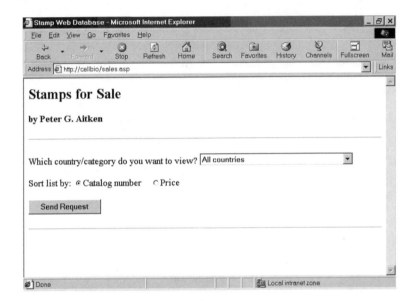

For choosing a country, a Select element is ideal. This is like a regular Visual Basic Combo Box, in which the user can pull down a list of items and select one. The HTML code for a Select element is

```
<select name = "name" size = "n">
<option value = "value1">text1</option>
<option selected value = "value2">text2</option>
...
</select>
```

The Select element's Name is specified by *name* and its size (height in lines) by *n*. The element's width is automatically set to fit its widest entry.

Each item in the Select element is specified by an <option>...</option> tag. Each Option tag has a Value attribute, which is the value submitted by the form for the Select element if the item is selected. If the Selected keyword is included, the item will be the default item in the list. The text between the two tags is what is displayed in the list. This may be the same as the Value attribute but does not have to be. Here's an example of an Option tag:

```
<option value = "Washington">George</option>
```

This item will display in the list as `George`, but if it is selected, the value submitted will be `Washington`.

For the sort option, there are only two choices: by catalog number and by price. Therefore, a Radio element will be fine or, to be more precise, two Radio elements. The syntax is

```
<input type="radio" name="name" value="value">
```

`Value` is the data submitted to the server if the Radio button is selected. By creating two or more Radio buttons with the same `Name` attribute, the buttons will automatically be linked so that only one can be selected at a time.

Loading the `Select` list with items presents a challenge. You cannot know ahead of time which countries and categories will be available in the stamps database, so the `<option>` elements cannot be hard-coded into the HTML page. Rather, it will be necessary to open the database and generate a list of `<option>` elements, one for each country/category in the database.

Now you come to the code for the user input page, which I called Sales.asp. Here's what the page must do:

1. Display the page heading.
2. Open the sales.mdb database.
3. Create a `Recordset` that contains the Country field for all records.
4. Go through the table, creating a list of the country entries.
5. Keep a count of how many records there are for each country and another count of the total number of countries.
6. Create a Form element that will use the `POST` method to submit the data. The target file will be Stampdata2.asp, a page that you will create next.
7. Create a `Select` element that contains the list of countries, as well as an additional `All Countries` entry (which will be the default).
8. Create the two Radio elements for the sort order.

Listing 20.2 presents the code for Sales.asp. The various procedures used, such as opening a `Connection` object and populating a `RecordSet`, are covered in the previous two chapters. You can refer back to them if you need to brush up on the details.

20

LISTING 20.2   THE CODE IN SALES.ASP

```
<html>
<head>
<title>Stamp Web Database</title>
</head>
<body>
<h2>Stamps for Sale</h2>
<h4>by Peter G. Aitken</h4>
<hr>
<%
dim rs ' the RecordSet object
dim temp ' temporary buffer
dim count ' for counting entries for a country
dim num ' for counting countries
dim cl() ' for countries and counts
' The sales.mdb database has been opened in
' global.asa. The reference is stored in
' session("sdb")
' Get the Country field, all records,
' sorted by country.
set rs = session("sdb").execute _
    ("select country from stamps order by country") %>
<% ' Move to the first record.
rs.movefirst
' Put the first country in the array.
num = 1
count = 1
redim cl(1,num)
cl(0,num) = rs.fields("Country").Value
cl(1,num) = count
temp = rs.fields("Country").Value
' Now loop through recordset.
rs.movenext
do while not rs.eof %>
<% if temp = rs.fields("Country").Value then
    ' Same as previous country - increment count.
    count = count + 1
else
    ' New country.
    cl(1,num) = count
    num = num + 1
    redim preserve cl(1,num)
    cl(0,num) = rs.fields("Country").Value
    cl(1,num) = 1
    temp = rs.fields("Country").Value
    count = 1
end if
rs.movenext
loop
```

```
' Now num has the number of countries and
' cl() has the country names and counts.
' Load them into a Select element.
%>
<form method="POST" action="stampdata2.asp">
Which country/category do you want to view?
 <select name="country" size="1">
    <option selected value="All countries">All countries</option>
    <% for i = 1 to num %>
    <option value="<%= cl(0,i) %> "><%= cl(0,i) %>
    (<%= cl(1,i) %> items)</option>
    <% next  %>
 </select></p>
 <p>Sort list by:
 <input type="radio" value="catno" checked name="sort">Catalog number
    <input type="radio" name="sort" value="price">Price </p>
 <p><input type="submit" value="Send Request" name="B1"></p>
<hr>

</form>
</body>
</html>
```

The Custom Data Page

The next task is to create Stampdata2.asp, which is the ASP page that the user input page
sends its data to. This is the custom data page that will search the database and display
only those records that the user requested. Take a look at some of the things the script in
the page must do.

First, the script must retrieve the data posted from the Sales.asp page, which informs the
page of the records to display and how to sort them. This is done with the Request
object's Form collection:

```
c = Request.Form("Country")
s = Request.Form("sort")
```

After this code executes, the variable c will contain a string indicating which country to
view, and the variable s will contain information on the sort order.

Next is the matter of which fields to display in the results table. The database contains a
Date field, which is the date the item was added to the database. Clearly, the user does
not need to see this data. Also, what about the Country field? If the user selected to view
only a single country, there is no need to display the Country information with each
record. I created two strings of field names, as shown here:

```
fl1 = "LotNo, Country, CatNo, Description, CatValue, Price, Image"
fl2 = "LotNo, CatNo, Description, CatValue, Price, Image"
```

20

Then, depending on the listing requested by the user, one or the other of these will be used in the SQL request. The SQL request must also specify the sort order. If the user requested to view all countries, the records should be sorted first by country and then by either price or catalog number, as requested by the user. The desired sort order, along with the fields to retrieve, is incorporated into an SQL request as follows:

```
if c = "All countries" then
    cmd = "select " & fl1 & " from stamps order by country," & s
else
    cmd = "select " & fl2 & " from stamps where country = '" & c
    cmd = cmd & "' order by val(" & s & ")"
end if %>
```

SORTING NUMBERS

In this database, I have used a Text field to store data that is often numeric in nature: the catalog numbers. This can cause a problem when sorting on this field. Text fields are sorted based on the characters in the data, not their numeric value. For example, 101 will be placed before 9 because the character 1 precedes the character 9. That the number 101 is greater than the number 9 is ignored. To sort things in numeric order, which is what you want, it's necessary to have the data treated as a number. This is done with the Val() function, which converts text to the corresponding number. For example, val("25") evaluates to 25, val("17b") evaluates to 17, and val("hello") evaluates to 0. By including val() in the SQL statement,

```
    ... ORDER BY Val(s)
```

you instruct the RecordSet to sort the records based on the numerical value of the field and not its text value.

You can see how this works. Suppose the user requests to see listings for Canada, sorted by price. The resulting SQL request would be

```
select LotNo, CatNo, Description, CatValue, Price, Image
from stamps where country = 'Canada' order by price
```

After the SQL request has been built, creating the RecordSet requires only the following single statement:

```
set rs = session("sdb").execute(cmd)
```

The remainder of the code is mostly straightforward and performs the tasks of moving through all the records in the RecordSet and for each record, displaying the value of each field. As before, I used standard HTML table formatting syntax to display the results in a table.

There are some special formatting needs. It is nice to have the `CatValue` and `Price` data displayed in the proper format, as currency. This can be done with the VBScript function `FormatCurrency`. An `If` statement can check for these two fields and apply the formatting as needed.

The Image field also needs special consideration. The way the data is stored in this field is simply the filename with no path or extension (because all images are JPG files). Also, only some records have an entry in the Image field. Therefore, the script must check for a nonempty Image field and then add the `.jpg` extension. Finally, the `Server.MapPath` method must be called to map the image path properly. Because all images are kept in the images folder, this relative path must be added as well.

The code for applying the currency formatting and mapping the image file paths is shown here:

```
<% if rs(i).name = "CatValue" or rs(i).name = "Price" then
    ' format for currency.
    if isNumeric(rs.fields(i).value) then %>
        <%= formatcurrency(rs.fields(i).value) %>
    <% end if %>
<% elseif rs(i).name = "Image" then
    ' Add link to image.
    img = rs.fields(i).value
    if img <> "" then
        img = "images\" & img & ".jpg"
        img = server.mappath(img) %>
        <a href="<%= img %>">Image</a>
    <% end if %>
<% else %>
    <%= rs.fields(i).value %>
<% end if %>
```

LINKING TO IMAGES

You can display an image in two general ways. One is to display it directly on the page by placing an <img> tag at the desired location in the HTML document:

```
<img src="filename">
```

For the database, however, displaying images in the table would cause problems with the overall formatting because the images are not all the same size. Also, image download time can be a problem, so why force users to wait for images they might not want to see? Better to link to the image, using the standard tag:

```
<a href="filename">
```

Although you might think that hyperlinks should be to HTML or ASP pages only, you can also link directly to a JPG or GIF file.

20

The final page, shown in Figure 20.3, displays a list of records. Listing 20.3 presents the page's HTML and script.

FIGURE 20.3

Displaying a selected set of records.

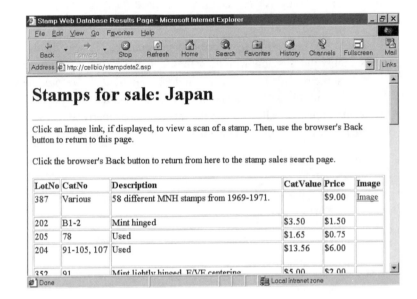

LISTING 20.3 STAMPDATA2.ASP

```
<html>
<head>
<title>Stamp Web Database Results Page</title>
</head>
<body>
<%

dim cmd ' the sql command string.
dim sdb ' the Connection object.
dim rs ' the RecordSet object.
dim img ' image name.
dim fl1, fl2 ' field lists.
' Open the sales.mdb database
' Get the request sent by sales.asp
c = Request.Form("Country")
s = Request.Form("sort")
' These are the fields to retrieve for an
' all countries listing.
fl1 = "LotNo, Country, CatNo, Description, CatValue, Price, Image"
' These are the fields to retrieve for a
' single country listing.
fl2 = "LotNo, CatNo, Description, CatValue, Price, Image"
if c = "All countries" then
```

```
     cmd = "select " & fl1 & " from stamps order by country," & s
else
     cmd = "select " & fl2 & " from stamps where country = '" & c
     cmd = cmd & "' order by val(" & s & ")"
end if %>
<h1> Stamps for sale: <%= c %></h1><hr>
Click an Image link, if displayed, to view a scan of a stamp.
Then, use the browser's Back button to return to this page.<p>
Click the browser's Back button to return from here to the
stamp sales search page.<p>
<% set rs = session("sdb").execute(cmd)
' Get the number of fields in the table.
numfields=rs.fields.count
' Create a table with one column per field. %>
<table border = 1>
<tr>
<% for i = 0 to numfields -1 %>
<td><b><%= rs(i).name %></b></td>
<% next %>
</tr>
<% ' Move to the first record.
rs.movefirst
' Loop for each record in the RecordSet.
do while not rs.eof %>
<tr>
<% ' Populate the row with field values.
for i = 0 to numfields - 1 %>
<td valign=top>
<% if rs(i).name = "CatValue" or rs(i).name = "Price" then
     ' format for currency.
     if isNumeric(rs.fields(i).value) then %>
          <%= formatcurrency(rs.fields(i).value) %>
     <% end if %>
<% elseif rs(i).name = "Image" then
     ' Add link to image.
     img = rs.fields(i).value
     if img <> "" then
          img = "images\" & img & ".jpg"
          img = server.mappath(img) %>
          <a href="<%= img %>">Image</a>
     <% end if %>
<% else %>
     <%= rs.fields(i).value %>
<% end if %>
 </td>
<% next %>
</tr>
<% ' Go to next record.
rs.movenext
```

20

continues

LISTING 20.3   CONTINUED

```
loop %>
</table>
</body>
</html>
```

I will be the first to admit that this is a simple Web database application. Sometimes that's all you need—no point in making something more complicated than necessary. Your Web database projects might be more involved, but you have learned all the basic techniques for Web database programming.

Perhaps you were surprised at how little programming it took to create this project? This is due in part to the power and simplicity of the ADO data model. For the database end of your Web database projects, you should learn as much about ASO as possible.

Summary

I hope you were as pleasantly surprised as I was. Creating a fully functional Web database application is not all that difficult. Between Active Server Pages and the ADO technology, almost all the details are hidden from you. You can concentrate on designing active database pages that meet the needs of your users without having to worry about the nitty-gritty details of database manipulation.

Q&A

Q Which parts of an SQL SELECT statement are required, and which are optional?

A You must specify which fields to retrieve and which table to use in a SELECT statement. The WHERE and ORDER BY clauses are optional.

Q How can you test your ASP application without actually uploading it to your Web server?

A By installing the Microsoft Personal Web Server on your local computer. The PWS lets you run and test your ASP scripts as if they were uploaded to your "real" server.

Q **You are writing an ASP database application in which two or more ASP pages access the same database. Where should the connection to the database be established, and why?**

A You should create the Connection object at the session level in the Session_OnStart event procedure. Then, store its reference as a Session-level variable. This permits all pages in the application to access the database connection and saves the overhead of having each page set up its own connection.

Workshop

Quiz

1. If the following values are contained in a Text field, what is the default order they will be sorted in?

    101b

    95

    10004g

    6x

2. Suppose your database contains a field name with a space in it. What must you do to include the field name in a SQL SELECT statement?

3. For fastest operation, which fields should your database table be indexed on?

4. How can you display a numerical value formatted as currency?

20

DAY 21

Common Gateway Interface Programming with Visual Basic

The Common Gateway Interface (CGI) was the first standard that defines how information can be passed back and forth between a Web user and an application program on the server. It is still widely used and has very broad support, so any Web developer should know how to use it. Today you will learn about

- The fundamentals of CGI
- A comparison of the two CGI types
- The differences between regular Visual Basic applications and CGI applications written in Visual Basic
- How to use the standard input and output streams in Visual Basic
- How to read environment variables
- A complete Visual Basic CGI demonstration

What Is the Common Gateway Interface?

The original, and perhaps still the most important, task of Web servers is to deliver static HTML files to their clients. As the Web developed, it was soon realized that a Web server could do much more if there was some way that the users could interact with programs running on the server. Many of the techniques you have learned in this book are related to this—Active Server Pages, for example. At this point, you should have no doubt about the power or value of interacting with the server to create dynamic content!

Before ASP, before DHTML, back when almost all Web servers were still running the UNIX operating system, programmers developed the first technology that permitted clients to interact with programs on the server. It is called the *common gateway interface* (CGI).

Even though CGI was the first technology for providing an interface between servers and clients, it is still widely used. If you have spent any time at all on the Web, I am sure you have used a CGI program, although you were probably not aware of it. The fundamental idea is the same as with Active Server Pages: The client sends information to the server, which then runs a program that generates the response sent to the user.

The server program that generates the script can be written in nearly any programming language, although the most widely used is Perl, because of its excellent text-processing capabilities. Yes, you can also write a CGI program in Visual Basic. There are two somewhat different CGI standards.

Standard CGI

The original CGI implementation is now called *standard CGI*. It was developed to run on computers running UNIX. The CGI technology defined standards for several necessary steps:

- How information is transferred between the Web server and the CGI program
- What information the Web server supplies to the CGI program and in what format
- What information can be returned by a CGI program and in what format

Standard CGI makes use of two operating-system features to transfer data between the server and CGI program. One is the standard input and output streams, and the other is environment variables. Figure 21.1 illustrates the arrangement.

This works very well, but in the past it left some programmers out in the cold. Specifically, graphical programming languages such as Visual Basic and Delphi did not provide a way to access the standard input and output streams (although current versions do). To fill this gap, the Windows CGI specification was developed.

FIGURE 21.1

Standard CGI uses the standard input/output streams (stdin and std-out) and environment variables to transfer information.

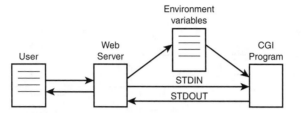

THE CGI-BIN DIRECTORY

Traditionally, many Web sites keep their CGI programs in a folder named CGI-BIN.

Windows CGI

The Windows CGI specification follows the standard CGI specification very closely, differing mainly in the way information is passed back and forth between the server and CGI program. Rather than use the memory-based standard input and output streams, Windows CGI uses temporary files. Take a look at the fundamentals of this process.

1. A client submits some information from an HTTP form. The information includes the path and name of the CGI program that the information is to be processed by. This is called a *Windows CGI request*.

2. The server locates the specified CGI program and then places the data to be passed in a file called the *CGI profile file*. Generally, such files are given the .INI extension.

3. The server executes the CGI program and passes the name of the CGI profile file as its command-line argument.

4. The CGI program opens the CGI profile file and reads the data. Code in the CGI program performs the necessary processing—accessing a database, or whatever.

5. The CGI program writes its response to the CGI output file. The name of this file is specified in the CGI profile file, so the server knows where to locate the output file.

6. The server reads the CGI output file and sends the data back to the client. All temporary files are then deleted.

Figure 21.2 details the entire process.

21

FIGURE 21.2

The sequence of events in processing a Windows CGI request.

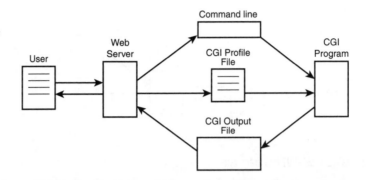

> **CGI AND DATABASE ACCESS**
>
> Can you use the CGI technology to provide database access on the Web? Absolutely! Remember, CGI is only the technology that connects the user, via the server, to your CGI program. What goes on inside your CGI program is independent and depends on the capabilities of the programming language you are using, the server software, and the operating system. If you are running on a Microsoft server, you can use Visual Basic and ActiveX Data Objects to connect a CGI application to a database, just as you did with Active Server Pages in Chapter 20, "Implementing a Web Database Application."

Which CGI Should You Use?

Both CGI standards work perfectly well, and technically there is no reason to choose one over the other (at least, that I am aware of). However, some practical matters should be considered.

Perhaps most important is that the Microsoft Personal Web Server (PWS) does not support Windows CGI. This means that you cannot test Win CGI applications on your own computer unless you happen to be running the Internet Information Server on Windows NT. PWS fully supports standard CGI, so testing is possible for anyone running Windows 95/98.

Another factor is that many Web services do not support Win CGI. Your Win CGI application must be published on a site that does offer such support, of course, so you need to check with the Web site administrator. To the best of my knowledge, standard CGI is universally supported.

One factor in favor of Win CGI is that it's easier to debug. A Win CGI server can be set to debug mode, in which the temporary files used to transfer information are not deleted. By examining these files, you can often figure out the sources of various program bugs.

MAPPING YOUR CGI DIRECTORY

Executable CGI programs are usually kept in their own directory on the Web server, traditionally cgi-bin. This directory must have the proper permissions set to execute CGI programs. In the Personal Web Server, you must open the Advanced page and select the /cgi-bin virtual directory. This virtual directory must be mapped to the physical directory where you keep your CGI executables (usually c:\inetpub\wwwroot\cgi-bin), and the Execute access permission must be turned on. This is done by clicking the Edit Properties button on the PWS Advanced page and making the required entries.

On any Web server, a CGI directory can be mapped to run either Win CGI applications or standard CGI applications, but not both.

What's the bottom line? I suggest that you use standard CGI unless you have a specific reason to use Windows CGI. The broader acceptance of this technique is a compelling argument. I will cover both in this chapter so that you'll have the ability to use either in your Visual Basic CGI programs.

CGI Applications in Visual Basic

Although you can create CGI applications in Visual Basic, you should know that they are unlike almost any Visual Basic application you have created before. There are some factors you must take into account, and some other issues that might not be essential but should be considered even so.

One essential thing to remember is that a CGI application has no visual interface. It runs on the server, where (trust me) no one is sitting there watching it. It is launched by the server, reads data from the CGI profile file, and then sends its output to another file. You will not use Visual Basic forms or controls—just code.

FORMLESS VISUAL BASIC APPLICATIONS

To create a code-only, no-forms Visual Basic application, start a Standard EXE project and add a code module to it. Then select the project's one form and use the Project|Remove command to delete it from the project. Add a procedure named Main to the module; this is where execution will start when the program runs.

21

Furthermore, there is no one to respond to a CGI application. The only input it will receive is from the CGI profile file. You cannot display a message box and expect someone to click the OK button! In other words, a CGI program cannot be interactive in any way; it needs to simply run on its own.

The preceding considerations are essential for any CGI program. Some other considerations are important, although not essential. Perhaps most critical is to remember that Web responses are usually slow enough without your CGI program introducing additional delays. Web users do not like delays, and a good way to drive visitors away from your site is to leave them sitting there staring at the hourglass cursor while your program does something. Your CGI program should do its job as quickly as possible and should avoid performing tasks, such as using OLE automation objects, that are known to be slow.

Do	**Don't**
DO make sure that your Visual Basic CGI application requires no user input at all—no dialog boxes, no message boxes, and no error messages.	**DON'T** neglect to enable global error trapping in your Visual Basic GCI applications.

Error trapping is another area of concern. Be sure that error trapping is turned on throughout the program so that the default error message box will never be displayed. Remember, there is no one to respond to them! Error messages, if any, must be written to the output file so that the user will see them in his or her browser. You might also want to write error messages to an error log file on the server so that you will be aware of error conditions that need fixing.

Using Windows CGI

The server sends information to a Windows CGI program, using the command line and the profile file. You need to understand both of these to use Win CGI.

Getting Command-Line Arguments

Command-line arguments are something that Visual Basic programs rarely need to be concerned with. A *command-line argument* is an argument typed after the program name on the command line, which is how programs used to be started in DOS. Suppose, for example, that you wrote a program named SORTFILE that would open a file, sort its contents, and write the sorted data to a new file. You could write the program to obtain its information (the two filenames) from the command line. Then the user would type the following at the command prompt:

```
SORTFILE infile.dat outfile.dat
```

The `infile.dat` and `outfile.dat` are two command-line arguments. Code in the program could retrieve this information, enabling the program to run without need for further input from the user.

When a Web server starts a CGI program, it uses the command line to pass the name of the profile file to the program. In a Visual Basic program, command-line arguments are available from the `Command$` function, separated by spaces if there is more than one argument. Because the CGI profile filename is the first and only command-line argument, it is easy to retrieve from the return value of the `Command$` function.

OLDER WIN CGI SERVERS

Some older Windows-based HTTP servers start CGI applications with a more complex command line that includes not only the CGI profile filename, but also the names of the input and output files and some other parameters. You might need to plan for the possibility that these other items will be passed on the command line unless you are sure that your CGI program will be executed only on the newer servers.

Therefore, one of the first things that a CGI program must do when it starts is to read its command-line arguments and retrieve the name of the CGI profile file. The function `GetCGIFileName()`, presented in Listing 21.2, does just this. Because this filename will be needed by other parts of the program (namely, the function `GetProfileKey` presented later in Listing 21.2), it is stored in a global variable named `gCGIFileName`.

This function returns `True` on success and `False` if there was no command-line argument to retrieve.

LISTING 21.1 THE FUNCTION `GETCGIFileName` RETRIEVES THE FIRST COMMAND-LINE ARGUMENT

```
Private Function GetCGIFileName() As Boolean

' Gets the first command-line argument which
' should be the CGI profile filename. Places argument
' in the global variable gCGIFileName. Returns True
' on success, False if no argument was passed.

Dim s As String, p As Integer

s = Trim(Command$)
If s = "" Then
    GetCGIFileName = False
```

continues

21

LISTING 21.1   CONTINUED

```
      Exit Function
End If

' If there is more than one argument,
' get only the first one.

p = InStr(s, " ")
If p = 0 Then
    gCGIFileName = s
Else
    gCGIFileName = Left(s, p - 1)
End If

GetCGIFileName = True

End Function
```

The CGI Profile File

As described earlier in this chapter, information being passed from the server to the CGI program is placed in the CGI profile file. This is a plain text file that has a format similar to the INI files used in earlier versions of the Windows operating system. The file is divided into a number of sections, some of which are required and some of which are optional.

The basic format of the file is as follows:

```
[section1]
name1=value1
name2=value2
[section2]
name3=value3
...
```

Sections are identified by the section name in brackets. Within each section are *name=value* pairs that supply the actual data. There are eight possible sections in the CGI Profile file, some of which are optional and some of which are always present. Table 21.1 briefly describes these.

TABLE 21.1 CGI PROFILE FILE SECTIONS

Section	Data
[CGI]	Information about the CGI version, query string, request method, path to CGI application, and similar information.
[ACCEPT]	Information on which MIME data types the client can accept.
[SYSTEM]	The name of the output file, the name of the content file, time information.
[FORM LITERAL]	Optional. Decoded data from an HTMP form POST method.
[FORM EXTERNAL]	Optional. If any form data is too long or contains control characters or double quotes, it cannot be returned in the [FORM LITERAL] section but rather is placed in a file. This section contains information on the file where such data is located.
[FORM HUGE]	Optional. Use for binary data that is too long for the [FORM EXTERNAL] section. Specifies the offset of the data in the content file and its length.
[FORM FILE]	Optional. Specifies a list of files where uploaded data has been placed.
[EXTRA HEADERS]	Additional headers sent by the client.

WHAT IS MIME?

MIME stands for *Multipurpose Internet Mail Extensions*. This is a specification developed for exchanging different types of documents with Internet mail. Assigning standardized descriptions to different types of content makes it easier to determine what programs support which types. The MIME types you see most often are

- text/plain: A plain text document
- text/html: A text document with HTML tags
- image/gif: A GIF image
- image/jpeg: A JPEG image
- audio/basic: Basic audio data (.au files)
- audio/wav: WAV-format sound data
- audio/x-midi: MIDI-formatted sound data
- video/quicktime: A QuickTime format video file
- video/mpeg: A MPEG format video file
- application/octet-stream: Arbitrary 8-bit data
- application/x-java-class: A Java applet
- application/msword: A Microsoft Word document

21

Reading Data from the CGI Profile File

Because the CGI profile file is formatted like a Windows INI file, you can use a function in the Windows API to read data from it. This function, GetPrivateProfileString, was originally designed for reading regular Windows INI files. Its declaration is as follows:

```
Public Declare Function GetPrivateProfileString Lib "kernel32" _
    Alias "GetPrivateProfileStringA" (ByVal lpApplicationName _
    As String, ByVal lpKeyName As Any, ByVal lpDefault As _
    String, ByVal lpReturnedString As String, ByVal nSize As _
    Long, ByVal lpFileName As String) As Long
```

lpApplicationName is the name of the section of the INI file, without the brackets.

lpKeyName is the name of the key whose value you want returned. If a null is passed for this argument, the function returns a list of all the keys in the specified section.

lpDefault is the default value to return if the specified key is not found in the specified section of the file.

lpReturnedString is a buffer where the returned value is placed.

nSize is the size, in bytes, of the buffer lpReturnedString.

lpFileName is the name, including path, to the INI file.

The return value of this function is a type Long giving the number of characters copied to the return buffer. The way this API function works might seem strange to you. This is because, like all API functions, it is written in C. It's easy to use in a Visual Basic program, though. You must include the preceding declaration at the module level in your code. Then, declare a fixed-length string to serve as the return buffer.

```
Const BUFLEN = 64
Dim buf as String * BUFLEN, retlen as Long
retlen = GetPrivateProfileString(section, key, default, buf, _
    BUFLEN, INIFileName)
```

Next, extract the return value as follows:

```
keyvalue = left(buf, retlen)
```

STRINGS IN C

The C language handles strings differently from Basic. Whereas a Basic string contains information about its own length, C strings do not. Rather, the end of a string is marked by the null character (chr$(0)). When GetPrivateProfileString is used with no key value, to return a list of all the keys in a section, the individual keys are returned in the buffer separated by single null characters, with a pair of nulls at the end.

Because the CGI program you will develop will need to read CGI profile files, you can use GetPrivateProfileString to create a Basic function that will read the value associated with a specific section and key in a CGI profile file. The function is called GetProfileKey, and it is shown in Listing 21.1. It takes as its two arguments the key and section names and returns the associated value or, if there is no such section/key combination, a blank string. If the blank value for key is passed, the function returns a listing of all the keys in the specified section of the CGI profile file.

LISTING 21.2   GetProfileKey READS A VALUE FROM THE CGI PROFILE FILE

```
Private Function GetProfileKey(key As String, _
    section As String) As String

' Returns the value for key in section in the
' CGI profile file whose name is in the global
' variable gCGIFileName.

Const BUFLEN = 1024
Dim buf As String * BUFLEN
Dim keylen As Long

If key = "" Then ' Get all keys
    keylen = GetPrivateProfileString(section, 0&, "", _
        buf, BUFLEN, gCGIFileName)
Else
    keylen = GetPrivateProfileString(section, key, "", _
        buf, BUFLEN, gCGIFileName)
End If

If keylen > 0 Then
    GetProfileKey = Left(buf, keylen)
Else
    GetProfileKey = ""
End If

End Function
```

Using Standard CGI

As I have already mentioned, standard CGI uses the operating-system environment variables and the stdin stream to pass information to the CGI program. Then the CGI program uses the stdout stream to pass the output back to the server, which then sends it to the user.

21

Environment Variables

An *environment variable* can be thought of as a global variable that is part of a CGI process and lasts as long as the process is in existence. Each environment variable has a name and a value. For example, during a CGI session the server creates an environment variable named SCRIPT_NAME and assigns it the value of the local portion of the URL.

In Visual Basic, you read environment variables by using the Environ function. The syntax is

```
val = Environ(name)
```

Name is the name of the variable whose value you want to retrieve. If there is no variable with the specified *name*, an empty string is returned.

Table 21.2 describes the environment variables used by standard CGI. Know that as the technology advances, new variables will be added to this list.

TABLE 21.2 STANDARD CGI ENVIRONMENT VARIABLES

Variable	Description
Server-Related Variables	
GATEWAY_INTERFACE	The version number of the server's CGI implementation (for example, CGI/1.1).
SERVER_NAME	The fully qualified domain name of the server.
SERVER_SOFTWARE	The name and version of the Web server software.
Request-Related Variables	
AUTH_TYPE	The type of authentication used.
CONTENT_LENGTH	The length in bytes of the supplemental data sent as part of a POST request.
CONTENT_TYPE	The MIME type of the supplemental data sent as part of a POST request.
HTTP_ACCEPT	A comma-delimited list of the MIME data types that the client can accept.
HTTP_KEEP_ALIVE	If present, this indicates that the client wants to reuse the connection later.
HTTP_REFERRER	The URL of the document that referred the user to the CGI program.
HTTP_USER_AGENT	Information on the requesting Web client, including product code name, version, and operating system.

Variable	Description
REMOTE_ADDR	The IP address of the client computer from where the request is coming. If a proxy server is being used, its IP address is returned.
REMOTE_HOST	The fully qualified domain name of the client computer from where the request is coming. Not always available because many client computers do not have a domain name.
REMOTE_USER	If AUTH_TYPE is set, this variable holds the validated user-name.
REQUEST_METHOD	The method used by the client to make the request (for example, POST or GET).
SERVER_PORT	The TCP port through which the request came (usually 80).
SERVER_PROTOCOL	The name and version of the Web protocol used to make the request (for example, HTTP/1.1)

Path-Related Variables
These environment variables are related to the query portion of a request URL.

SCRIPT_NAME	The location part of a URL in a request.
PATH_INFO	The extra part of the URL path.
PATH_TRANSLATED	The physical path corresponding to the extra path information, based on the server's document mapping.
QUERY_STRING	The query string part of the URL.

Suppose that a POST request were made to the following:

```
/cgi-bin/search.exe/catalog?part=frammis
```

Then these variables would have the following values:

```
SCRIPT_NAME: /cgi-bin/search.exe
PATH_INFO: /catalog
PATH_TRANSLATED: c:\inetpub\wwwroot\sales (e.g., depends on server)
QUERY_STRING: part=frammis
```

The Standard Input Stream

Although Visual Basic does not have its own tools for reading the standard input stream (stdin), you can turn to the Windows API for all the required tools. Think of stdin as a special type of file; in fact, data is read from stdin by using an API function that also can

21

read files. First, however, you must get a handle to stdin with the function `GetStdHandle`. Its declaration is as follows:

```
Public Declare Function GetStdHandle Lib "kernel32" _
    (ByVal nStdHandle As Long) As Long
```

The argument `nStdHandle` specifies which handle you want. Table 21.3 lists the three possible values. You will use the standard output handle later for writing to stdout. The standard error handle is for displaying error information; you will not be using it.

TABLE 21.3 VALUES FOR THE `nStdHandle` ARGUMENT TO `GetStdHandle`

Constant	Value	Handle Returned
STD_OUTPUT_HANDLE	-11&	Standard output
STD_INPUT_HANDLE	-10&	Standard input
STD_ERROR_HANDLE	-12&	Standard error

After you have obtained the handle for stdin, you use the API function `ReadFile` to get the data. The declaration of this function is

```
Private Declare Function ReadFile Lib "kernel32" _
    (ByVal hFile As Long, ByVal lpBuffer As Any, _
    ByVal nNumberOfBytesToRead As Long, _
    lpNumberOfBytesRead As Long, _
    ByVal lpOverlapped As Any) As Long
```

`hFile` is the stdin handle obtained from `GetStdHandle`.

`lpbuffer` is a string variable where the data read from stdin will be placed.

`nNumberOfBytesToRead` is the number of bytes to read. Its value should be one less that the size of `lpbuffer`.

`lpNumberOfBytesRead` is a type `Long` where the function returns the actual number of bytes read from stdin.

`lpOverlapped` is used for reading files only. For your purposes, you will simply pass a value of zero.

The following code fragment shows how you would use these two functions to read from stdin. Note that the string variable used to receive the data is padded with spaces before being passed to the API function.

```
Dim buf as string, BytesRead As Long, hStdIn As Long
buf = Space(5000)
hStdIn = GetStdHandle(STD_INPUT_HANDLE)
ReadFile hStdIn, buf, Len(buf) - 1, BytesRead, 0&
```

The standard input stream is used to supply the supplemental data sent as part of a POST request. The stdin stream is not always used. With a GET request, for example, stdin is empty, and the user data is obtained in the QUERY_STRING environment variable. When POST is used, the CONTENT_TYPE and CONTENT_LENGTH environment variables contain information about the size and format of the data available through stdin.

Data in stdin is formatted as follows:

- Spaces are replaced by plus signs.
- Names and values are separated by equal signs.
- Entries are separated by ampersands.

Here's an example:

```
return=20&term=dogs+cats&list=all
```

In the sample program, you'll see how code can separate the individual values from the stream.

The Standard Output Stream

After a CGI program has read the input information from the environment variables and (if required) stdin, it must generate the output that is to be sent back to the client. The output is sent to the standard output stream (stdout) from where the server reads it and sends it to the client. Data is written to stdout by using the WriteFile API function:

```
Private Declare Function WriteFile Lib "kernel32" _
    (ByVal hFile As Long, ByVal lpBuffer As Any, _
    ByVal nNumberOfBytesToWrite As Long, _
    lpNumberOfBytesWritten As Long, _
    ByVal lpOverlapped As Any) As Long
```

hFile is the handle of stdout and is obtained with GetStdHandle, as explained earlier in the chapter.

lpBuffer is a string variable containing the data to be written.

nNumberOfBytesToWrite is the number of bytes to write, the length of lpBuffer.

lpNumberOfBytesWritten is where the function returns the actual number of bytes written.

lpOverlapped is not used when writing to stdout; pass a value of 0.

Here is a code fragment showing how it is done (where temp holds the text to be written to stdout):

21

```
Dim hStdout As Long, BytesWritten As Long
hStdout = GetStdHandle(STD_OUTPUT_HANDLE)
Call WriteFile(hStdout, (temp), Len(temp), BytesWritten, 0&)
```

What exactly are you writing to stdout from a CGI program? In essence, you are writing the entire HTML page that the user will see: everything from the opening <HTML> tag to the closing </HTML> tag. That's not all, however. The response sent to stdout must include some HTTP response headers required by the server. The first part is required and follows this syntax:

```
Protocol/Version Status Reason
```

Protocol and *version* will be HTTP/1.0. The *Status* portion is a three-digit numerical code describing the results of the request, and *Reason* is a brief text description of the result. Here is a typical HTTP response:

```
HTTP/1.0 200 OK
```

The status code numbers are divided into categories, based on the first digit. These are

- 1xx: Informational
- 2xx: Successful
- 3xx: Redirection
- 4xx: Client error
- 5xx: Server error

Table 21.4 describes the most frequently needed response codes.

TABLE 21.4 HTTP RESPONSE CODES

Code	Reason	Details
200	Okay	Request fulfilled successfully.
204	No content	The request was fulfilled, but there is no content to return to the client.
301	Moved permanently	The requested resource has been assigned a new permanent URL as specified in the header field (see Table 21.5). Use that URL for future requests.
302	Moved temporarily	The requested resource has been assigned a temporary URL. Use the current URL for future requests.
304	Not modified	The requested document has not been modified since the date specified in the If Modified Since field of the GET request.

Code	Reason	Details
400	Bad request	The request was impossible to carry out (for example, bad syntax).
401	Unauthorized	The request requires user authentication.
404	Not found	The requested resource cannot be found.
500	Server error	Unexpected server error.
502	Bad gateway	The requested server or gateway program is not responding.
503	Service unavailable	The server is temporarily overloaded and cannot handle the request.

Following the first line of the HTTP response, the response can optionally contain one or more headers that provide additional information to the client. Table 21.5 describes the most commonly needed headers.

TABLE 21.5 HTTP RESPONSE HEADERS

Header	Information
Location: *absoluteURL*	The absolute URL or the requested resource.
Server: *product*	The software used by the server.
Last-modified: *HTTP-date*	The date and time the resource was last modified.
Expires: *HTTP-date*	The date and time the response originated.
Content-encoding: *encoding*	The encoding used for the message body.
Content-length: *length*	The length of the data, in bytes.
Content-type: *type*	The MIME type of the data.

Here is an example of a complete HTTP response that uses several of the optional headers to provide additional information. Note that a blank line always exists between the last header and the beginning of the HTML.

```
HTTP/1.0 200 OK
Server: Microsoft-IIS/4.0
Date: Friday, 9-OCT-1998 10:15:00 GMT
Last-modified: Thursday, 8-OCT-1998 21:35:30 GMT
Content-type: text/html

<HTML>
<HEAD>
<TITLE>Example of HTTP Response</TITLE>
</HEAD>
<BODY>
```

21

```
Hello
</BODY></HTML>
```

The technique just described creates what is called a *direct response*. The Web server interprets the data as a complete HTTP response that can be sent to the client without further processing. Any response sent to stdout that starts with HTTP/ is considered to be a direct response.

You can also send an *indirect response* by starting the data with any one of the following headers:

```
Content-type:
Location:
URI:
Status:
```

When the server recognizes an indirect response, it processes it to create a completely formed HTTP response before sending it to the client.

A Demonstration

Now that you understand the way CGI programs work, it's time for a demonstration. This program runs perfectly under the Personal Web Server and should also run under any other type of Web server. It consists of an HTML page that permits the user to enter some information, as shown in Figure 21.3. When the user clicks the Submit button, the data is sent to the server by using the POST method. Note that as written, the form assumes that the CGI program SCGIDEMO.EXE is located in the /cgi-bin directory. If your Web server is set up differently, you will have to change this. Listing 21.3 shows the complete HTML code for this page.

LISTING 21.3   CONTENTS OF SCGITEST.HTM

```html
<html>

<head>
<meta http-equiv="Content-Type" content="text/html; charset=iso-8859-1">
<title>Testing standard CGI</title>
</head>

<body>

<p>This form tests the standard CGI application SCGIDEMO.EXE.</p>

<form method="POST" action="/cgi-bin/scgidemo.exe">
  <p>Your name: <input type="text" name="Name" size="29" value></p>
  <p>Your city: <input type="text" name="City" size="30" value></p>
  <p>What's your favorite hobby?
```

```
    <input type="text" name="Hobby" size="23" value></p>
    <p>Please enter your email address:
    <input type="text" name="email" size="20" value></p>
    <p><input type="submit" value="Submit" name="B1">
    <input type="reset" value="Reset"
    name="B2"></p>
</form>
</body>
</html>
```

FIGURE 21.3

The HTML data entry page SCGITEST.HTM.

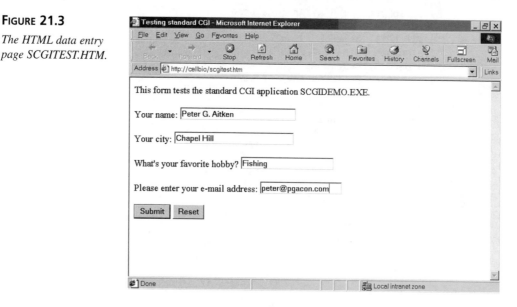

The CGI program, SCGITEST, accepts the data posted by the user and displays it in the user's browser. The program also retrieves the values of several environment variables and displays them as well. Listing 21.4 presents the code for the CGI program. You can easily modify this code to display other environment variables if you are curious. Figure 21.4 shows the response.

WATCH YOUR DECLARATIONS

Be sure to use the declarations of WriteFile and ReadFile that are presented here in the listings and not the ones from the Visual Basic API Text Viewer. Those have errors, and if you use them, your program will not function properly.

21

LISTING 21.4   THE CODE IN SCGIDEMO

```vb
Option Explicit

Public Declare Function GetStdHandle Lib "kernel32" _
    (ByVal nStdHandle As Long) As Long
Private Declare Function WriteFile Lib "kernel32" _
    (ByVal hFile As Long, ByVal lpBuffer As Any, _
    ByVal nNumberOfBytesToWrite As Long, _
    lpNumberOfBytesWritten As Long, _
    ByVal lpOverlapped As Any) As Long
Private Declare Function ReadFile Lib "kernel32" _
    (ByVal hFile As Long, ByVal lpBuffer As Any, _
    ByVal nNumberOfBytesToRead As Long, _
    lpNumberOfBytesRead As Long, _
    ByVal lpOverlapped As Any) As Long

' Constants for retrieving system
' stdin and stdout handles
Public Const STD_OUTPUT_HANDLE = -11&
Public Const STD_INPUT_HANDLE = -10&

' Flag that is True if the HTML headers have
' already been written to the output.
Public HeadersWritten As Boolean

' Collection to keep parameter values.
Dim params As New Collection

Sub Main()

Dim i As Integer

HeadersWritten = False

' Load the parameters.
GetParams

' Start the output file.
CGI_Out ("<H1>Testing the standard CGI program SCGIDEMO.EXE</H1>")
CGI_Out ("<p>The data submitted to the standard CGI program: </p>")

' Display the parameter values.
For i = 1 To params.Count - 1
    CGI_Out ("<p>" & params(i) & "</p>")
Next i

CGI_Out ("Some environment variables are:<p>")
CGI_Out ("SERVER_SOFTWARE: " & Environ("SERVER_SOFTWARE") & "<br>")
CGI_Out ("SERVER_NAME: " & Environ("SERVER_NAME") & "<br>")
```

```vb
CGI_Out ("HTTP_ACCEPT: " & Environ("HTTP_ACCEPT") & "<br>")
CGI_Out ("HTTP_REFERRER: " & Environ("HTTP_REFERRER") & "<br>")
CGI_Out ("HTTP_USER_AGENT: " & Environ("HTTP_USER_AGENT") & "<br>")
CGI_Out ("SCRIPT_NAME: " & Environ("SCRIPT_NAME") & "<br>")
CGI_Out ("PATH_INFO: " & Environ("PATH_INFO") & "<br>")
CGI_Out ("PATH_TRANSLATED: " & Environ("PATH_TRANSLATED") & "<br>")
CGI_Out ("QUERY_STRING: " & Environ("QUERY_STRING") & "<br>")

' Finish it off.
Call CGI_Out("<hr></body></html>")

End Sub

Public Sub CGI_Out(s As String)

    Dim BytesWritten As Long, temp As String
    Static hStdout As Long
    Dim x As Long, dummy As Long

    dummy = 0

    ' If this is the first call to CGI_Out,
    ' write the HTTP response header.
    If Not HeadersWritten Then
        temp = "Content-type: text/html" & vbCrLf & vbCrLf
        HeadersWritten = True
    Else
        temp = ""
    End If

    temp = temp & s

    ' If we do not already have a handle to stdout, get it.
    If hStdout = 0 Then
        hStdout = GetStdHandle(STD_OUTPUT_HANDLE)
    End If

    Call WriteFile(hStdout, (temp), Len(temp), BytesWritten, dummy)

End Sub

Public Function CGI_In() As String

Static buf As String
Dim BytesRead As Long
Static hStdIn As Long

Select Case Environ("REQUEST_METHOD")
    ' If it was not a POST method, the query string
    ' is in an environment variable.
```

continues

21

LISTING 21.4 CONTINUED

```
            Case "GET", "PUT", "HEAD":
                CGI_In = Environ("QUERY_STRING")
            Case "POST":
            ' Only with POST do we need to read stdin.
                If (buf <> "") Then
                    CGI_In = buf
                    Exit Function
                End If
                buf = Space(5000)
                If (hStdIn = 0) Then
                    hStdIn = GetStdHandle(STD_INPUT_HANDLE)
                End If
                ReadFile hStdIn, buf, Len(buf) - 1, BytesRead, 0&
                ' Trim off spaces and training chr$(0).
                buf = Trim$(buf)
                buf = Left$(buf, Len(buf) - 1)
                CGI_In = buf
    End Select

End Function

Public Sub GetParams()

' Reads the parameters and puts them in the
' params collection.

Dim p As String, pos As Integer
Dim Name As String, Val As String

p = CGI_In()

Do While (Len(p) > 0)
    If ((Right$(p, 1) = Chr$(13)) Or (Right$(p, 1) = _
        Chr$(10))) Then
            p = Mid$(p, 1, Len(p) - 1)
    Else
        Exit Do
    End If
Loop

Do
    ' Look for =.
    pos = InStr(p, "=")
    If (IsNull(pos) Or pos = 0) Then
        Exit Do
    End If

    Name = Left$(p, pos - 1)
    Val = Mid$(p, pos + 1)
```

```
    pos = InStr(Val, "&")
    If (IsNull(pos) Or pos = 0) Then
        p = ""
    Else
        Val = Left$(Val, pos - 1)
        p = Mid$(p, Len(Val) + Len(Name) + 3)
    End If

    ' Clean up data.
    Name = Clean(Name)
    Val = Clean(Val)
    ' Handle duplicate keys.
    On Error GoTo DupKeyError
    ' Add data to collection.
    params.Add Item:=Name & "=" & Val, Key:=Name
    On Error GoTo 0

    Loop
    Exit Sub

DupKeyError:
    If Err.Number = 457 Then ' Duplicate - skip.
        Resume Next
    Else
        Exit Sub
    End If

End Sub

Private Function Clean(dirty As String) As String

Dim pos As Integer, i As Integer
Dim temp As String, buf As String

' Make a local copy.
buf = dirty

' Replace + signs with spaces.
Do
    pos = InStr(buf, "+")
    If (pos = 0 Or IsNull(pos)) Then Exit Do
    buf = Left$(buf, pos - 1) & " " & Mid$(buf, pos + 1)
Loop

' Convert %XX hex codes to ASCII.
Do
    pos = InStr(buf, "%")
    If (pos = 0 Or IsNull(pos)) Then Exit Do
    temp = "&H" + Mid$(buf, pos + 1, 2)
    buf = Left$(buf, pos - 1) & Chr$(CInt(temp)) & _
        Mid$(buf, pos + 3)
```

21

continues

LISTING 21.4   CONTINUED

```
Loop

Clean = buf

End Function
```

FIGURE 21.4

The response of the CGI program.

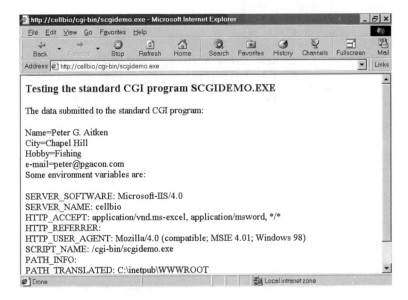

> **DRAWING A BLANK?**
>
> There's no guarantee that all these environment variables will always contain information. Some submissions do not include parameters relevant to some environment variables, so trying to read them will just return a blank.

Summary

The most attractive thing about the CGI standard is that it is almost universally supported. Almost any Web server in use will let you run CGI programs. Some of the other dynamic-content techniques presented in this book, such as Active Server Pages and DHTML, are easier to use and more powerful than CGI, but they are limited to certain Web servers. As a Web developer, you need to understand CGI so that you will not be limited.

The standard CGI implementation uses environment variables and the standard input/output streams for communication between the server and the CGI program. The Windows CGI implementation uses the command line and temporary files. Because modern versions of Visual Basic provide access to the standard input/output streams, you should never have any need to use the Windows CGI approach.

Q&A

Q What is the primary advantage of using CGI to provide dynamic Web content over other technologies such as Active Server Pages and DHTML?

A CGI is a widely supported standard and can be used on just about any Web server in existence. The other more modern technologies are supported only by Microsoft Web servers.

Q Can a CGI program use ActiveX Data Objects (ADO) to provide Web database connectivity?

A It depends. Although CGI is supported on essentially all Web servers, ADO is a Microsoft technology that is not as widely supported.

Q In standard CGI, is some user information always sent to the CGI application by the standard input stream?

A No, only when data is sent with the POST method is the standard input stream used. With GET, all user data is sent by means of environment variables.

Q What are the two types of HTTP responses that a CGI application can pass to the server?

A A direct response is complete and is not processed by the server before being sent to the client. Any response that starts with HTTP/ is treated as a direct response by the server. An indirect response is processed by the server to add the required headers before being sent to the client.

Workshop

Quiz

1. How can a Visual Basic program read from the standard input stream?
2. How can a Visual Basic program read the value of an environment variable?
3. When using the Windows CGI technology, how does the CGI program obtain the name of the CGI profile file?

21

4. In standard CGI, how would the CGI program know whether the client used POST or GET to send the data?

5. In a direct-response HTTP response, the first line must start with HTTP/1.0. What follows next?

Exercise

Use Visual Basic to write a CGI "guestbook" application. This is a Web page that lets users register, entering information such as their name and email address. Save each user's information in a database.

WEEK 3

In Review

I'd like to pat you on the back and shake your hand. You deserve hearty congratulations for finishing all 21 lessons in this book. It was a lot of material to cover, but that is simply a reflection of all the powerful tools that Visual Basic brings to Web and Internet development. During this third week, you learned about some of the most powerful aspects of Visual Basic Web technology, including Active Server Pages and database connectivity. With this information under your belt, along with the information from the first two weeks, you are now ready to start creating your own Web applications, using Visual Basic and its related technologies.

Where You Have Been

The first part of this week showed you how to use the WebBrowser control to add full Web-browsing capabilities to your Visual Basic application. Using this control, you created a custom Web browser that limits users to a list of selected Web sites. Next, you saw how Active Server Pages and VBScript can be combined to create powerful, interactive Web applications. You also saw how these methods can be used to connect a Web page to a database, one of the most popular types of Web application. Finally, you learned how Visual Basic can be used to write common gateway interface applications (CGI). Because CGI is one of the most widely supported Web standards, this means you have the ability to create Visual Basic applications that will run on just about any Web server out there.

Now that you have completed all these lessons, it's time for you to start working on your own. Perhaps there's a Web application you need to write as part of your job, or maybe you just want to add some pizzazz to your personal Web site. Whatever the Web programming task, Visual Basic can handle it—and so can you!

Appendix A

Answers

Day 1, "Saying Hello to the World"

1. What is the function of a domain name server?

   A domain name server looks up the IP address associated with a particular domain name.

2. How can you identify an HTML tag in a hypertext document?

   All HTML tags are enclosed in angle brackets `<like this>`.

3. What is a hyperlink?

   A hyperlink is a tag in an HTML document that links to another document or to a different location in the same document.

4. Describe three important functions of the tags in an HTML document.

   To control formatting, to display images, and to define hyperlinks.

5. What is the function of a browser program?

   To display an HTML document with all the formatting, images, and hyperlinks that are defined by the document's HTML tags.

6. What is TCP/IP?

TCP/IP stands for Transmission Control Protocol/Internet Protocol. It is the basic protocol by which information is transmitted over the Internet.

7. What does the last part of a domain name mean?

In the United States, the last part of the domain name usually identifies the type of organization: commercial, educational, and so on. In other countries, it identifies the country.

Day 2, "Making Sense of ActiveX"

1. What is the simplest way to reuse code in a Visual Basic program?

The simplest way to reuse code is to put the code in a procedure or function.

2. What are the five types of ActiveX projects available in Visual Basic?

These types of ActiveX projects can be created in Visual Basic:

ActiveX EXE

ActiveX DLL

ActiveX Document Exe

ActiveX Document Dll

ActiveX Control

3. What is the name of Microsoft's security system for ActiveX components?

The security system is Authenticode.

4. How does the end user control whether active components are downloaded?

The end user controls active component download by setting the browser's security options. Component download is then controlled based on the security options and the nature of the component's digital signature.

5. What is the advantage of including a timestamp when you apply a digital signature to a component?

If a component's signature includes a timestamp, even if the publisher's certificate has expired, the user can verify that the component was signed when the certificate was still valid.

Day 3, "Creating and Using an ActiveX Control"

A

1. Name two containers in which ActiveX controls can run.

   An ActiveX control can be contained in a Visual Basic form and the Internet Explorer browser.

2. Can you access a control's Extender properties in its initialize event procedure?

   No. The Extender object is not available when the initialize event procedure is fired.

3. What are the required Extender properties?

   The required Extender properties are five properties that all container objects are required to provide in their Extender object: Name, Visible, Parent, Cancel, and Default.

4. What happens when your ActiveX control has a property with the same name as an Extender property? How do you access the two properties?

   It is called a *collision* when your ActiveX control has a property with the same name as an Extender property. Use the Object keyword to access the control's property: MyControl.Tag accesses the Extender property, and MyControl.Object.Tag accesses the control property.

5. If you deploy your ActiveX control to your Web page, how can you prevent other developers from downloading it and using it in their own projects?

   You can prevent unauthorized people from using your controls in their own projects by generating a license file when you compile the project. Without this file, other developers will not be able to use your control in their projects, although they will be able to view those Web pages that use the control.

6. How do you include an ActiveX control on a Web page?

   To include an ActiveX control on a Web page, you must insert an <OBJECT> tag in the page's HTML. The tag must include information identifying the object and the location where installation files can be downloaded from.

Day 4, "Advanced ActiveX Control Techniques"

1. How would you create a read-only property in an ActiveX control?

   Write a `Property Get` procedure for the property, but don't create a corresponding `Property Let` procedure.

2. What is the first event to fire when an instance of an ActiveX control is created?

   The `Initialize` event.

3. When does the `ReadProperties` event fire?

   Every time an instance of the control is created, *except* the first time.

4. Does the `UserControl` object ever receive mouse events?

   Yes, if the user clicks on an area of the UserControl that isn't covered by a constituent control, or if the constituent control itself at that location doesn't detect mouse events.

5. How does a browser identify VBScript code and tell it apart from other elements of the page?

   VBScript code is identified by the `<script></script>` tags that enclose it.

6. What are ambient properties, and for what are they used?

   Ambient properties are provided by the container object to provide "hints" about how a control in the container should display itself. A control can read these properties to determine things such as the container's `BackColor` property and then set its own properties accordingly.

Day 5, "Real-World ActiveX"

1. Can you use the Property Page Wizard to add properties to an ActiveX control?

   No. You must write the code to define the properties first. Then the Property Page Wizard will create a property page for those properties.

2. In property page code, how can you determine whether the developer has selected more than one control?

   You can determine whether the developer selected more than one control by reading the `SelectedControls.Count` property, which returns the number of currently selected controls.

3. Where should you place code that writes to and reads from a property bag?

Code that writes to and reads from a property bag must go in the UserControl's `ReadProperties` and `WriteProperties` event procedures, respectively.

4. How would you display a bitmap image as the background of a UserControl?

Set the UserControl's `Picture` property to the desired image.

Day 6, "Understanding ActiveX Documents"

1. Which type of ActiveX document project runs faster, a DLL or an EXE?

An ActiveX document DLL executes faster because it runs in-process with the container.

2. Which Visual Basic control *cannot* be placed on a UserDocument in an ActiveX document project?

The OLE Container control.

3. How many individual ActiveX documents can an ActiveX document project have?

There is no limit to the number of ActiveX documents in a project.

4. Where would you declare a global variable that needs to be visible to all ActiveX documents in a project?

Declare global variables in the project's code module.

5. When does a UserDocument's `Activate` event occur?

Trick question! Whereas forms have `Activate` events, UserDocuments do not.

6. How can an ActiveX document determine what type of container it's executing in?

By calling `TypeName(UserDocument.Parent)` and examining the return value. Possible return values are `IwebBrowserApp` (Internet Explorer), `Section` (Microsoft Binder), and `Window` (Tool Window).

Day 7, "ActiveX Documents—Beyond the Basics"

1. Suppose that your ActiveX document has a menu and you want to temporarily disable its display in the container object without actually deleting the menu from the project. How could this be done?

By setting the menu item's `NegotiatePosition` property to `0 - None`.

2. To have your ActiveX document automatically resize itself to fit the container's viewport, what property values do you need to obtain?

The `ViewPortWidth` and `ViewPortHeight` properties, which give the current size of the container's viewport.

3. Are all of an ActiveX document's properties automatically saved in the property bag?

No. You must execute the `WriteProperty` method for each property value you want to save.

4. How does the container object know that one or more property values have changed and might need saving?

You tell it by executing the `PropertyChanged` method.

5. Do all the distribution files for an ActiveX document project require digital signing?

No. Only the CAB file must be signed. The VBD files do not require signing.

6. When an `AsyncRead` request has been completed, where is the retrieved data located?

In a file on the local hard disk.

Day 8, "Migrating Regular Visual Basic Applications to ActiveX"

1. Is the `End` statement permitted in an ActiveX document?

No. `End` is one of the few Basic statements that are illegal in an ActiveX document.

2. When you convert a standard application to an ActiveX document application, do you always get one UserDocument for each form?

No. Although at least one form must be converted to UserDocument, other forms can remain as forms, depending on the needs of the application.

3. What is the UserDocument object's `Show` method used for?

Trick question! The UserDocument does not have a `Show` method. It does have a `Show` event, which is fired each time the user navigates to the document.

4. After running the ActiveX Document Migration Wizard, can you immediately compile and deploy the new ActiveX document application?

No, the new application must be thoroughly tested first.

Day 9, "Understanding Dynamic HTML"

1. Can you use regular Visual Basic controls on a DHTML page?

   It depends. You can use ActiveX controls on a DHTML page, but you cannot use non-ActiveX controls.

2. When adding text to a DHTML page, how do you start a new paragraph?

   By pressing Enter.

3. How many individual pages can a DHTML application contain?

   There is no limit to the number of pages in a DHTML application.

4. How do you define a group of Option elements so that only one at a time can be on?

   By assigning the same Name property to all the elements.

5. When placing text on a DHTML page, what point sizes are available?

   Trick question! On an HTML page, text size is not specified in points, but rather in relative size values of 1–7.

Day 10, "Putting the *Dynamic* into DHTML"

1. How are DHTML event names different from standard Visual Basic event names?

   Almost all DHTML event names begin with on, followed by the name of the event. Instead of Click, therefore, you have OnClick.

2. Which of the Event object's properties are *not* read-only.

   CancelBubble, KeyCode, and ReturnValue

3. When does a DHTML element's LostFocus event fire?

   Trick question! DHTML elements do not have the LostFocus event, but rather OnBlur. It fires when the element loses the focus.

4. How do you stop an event from bubbling farther up in the object hierarchy?

   By setting the Event object's CancelBubble property to True.

5. What is the HTML stream?

   The HTML stream refers to the order in which elements occur within the HTML text and may be different from the apparent order of the elements as displayed on the page.

6. What is necessary if you want to be able to access and manipulate an element in code?

   The element must have a unique ID assigned to it.

7. How do you access element properties that affect its appearance?

By means of its `Style` collection.

8. What are the two ways to provide navigation capabilities in a DHTML page?

By using the Hyperlink element or by using the `BaseWindow` object's `Navigate` method.

9. Which element in a DHTML application does *not* use a Style collection?

The `Document` object does not have a `Style` collection.

Day 11, "The Internet Transfer Control"

1. What transfer protocols can the ITC use?

File Transfer Protocol (FTP) and Hypertext Transfer Protocol (HTTP).

2. What event is fired when the ITC completes a download?

The `StateChanged` event.

3. How can your program know that an error has occurred in the ITC?

The `StateChanged` event will be fired and passed the `icError` argument.

4. What method is used to obtain data from the ITC's buffer during an asynchronous data transfer?

The `GetChunk` method.

5. Does the ITC's `Execute` method always use the URL in the control's `URL` property?

No. It uses the `URL` property only if a URL is not passed to the method as an argument.

Day 12, "Using the ITC for FTP"

1. Can anyone log on to an FTP site?

Generally, yes. Most FTP sites permit anonymous logon, which allows anyone to download selected files but not to perform any other FTP commands.

2. What standard password should be sent when you log on to an FTP site as an anonymous user?

Your email address.

3. Can the Internet Transfer control be used to create an FTP server?

No. It can be used as an FTP client only. You need specialized FTP server software to create an FTP site.

4. Do all FTP sites have URLs that start with `ftp`?

No. Most do, but there is no requirement for an FTP site's URL to start with `ftp`.

Day 13, "Crawling the Web: Creating a Web Search Engine"

1. What is a termination rule? Why is it important?

A termination rule provides a set of one or more conditions under which a Web robot will terminate operation. Without an appropriate termination condition, a robot could continue indefinitely under certain conditions.

2. Are the instructions in a robot exclusion file mandatory?

No. It is up to the programmer to create a robot that reads and follows the instructions in a robot exclusion file.

3. How can you identify the start of a hyperlink tag in an HTML document?

A hyperlink tag always starts with `<a href=`.

Day 14, "Email in Visual Basic"

1. What `MAPIMessages` control event is fired when a mail message is received?

Trick question! The `MAPIMessages` control has no events.

2. What is the first thing that a Visual Basic program must do before accessing email with the MAPI controls?

Use the `MAPISession` control's `SignOn` method to establish a MAPI session.

3. How do you determine whether the `MAPIMessages` control downloads all messages or only unread messages?

By setting the `FetchUnreadOnly` property to `True` or `False`.

4. After executing the `Fetch` method, how can you determine how many messages were downloaded?

By reading the `MAPIMessages` control's `MsgCount` property.

5. When examining a specific message that has been received, how can you tell whether it has any attachments with it?

By reading the `MAPIMessages` control's `AttachmentCount` property.

Day 15, "Understanding the WebBrowser Control"

1. Which of the WebBrowser control's events can you use to enable and disable the application's Forward and Back buttons?

   The `CommandStateChange` event.

2. How do you know that the WebBrowser control has loaded all its data?

   When the `ReadyState` property returns the value `READYSTATE_COMPLETE`.

3. Can you use the `DownloadComplete` event to tell that the WebBrowser control has completed loading an HTML page?

   No. The `DownloadComplete` event also fires when a download is cancelled by the user or terminated because of an error.

4. How would you navigate to a new URL without adding the current URL to the history list?

   Call the `Navigate` method, passing the value `navNoHistory` as the `Flags` argument.

Day 16, "Creating a Customized Web Browser"

1. How do you display the WebBrowser control's toolbar?

   Trick question! The WebBrowser control does not have its own toolbar. If you want a toolbar, the Visual Basic application must provide it.

2. Ideally, when should a browser's Stop button be enabled?

   Only when the WebBrowser control's `Busy` property is `True`.

3. The user clicks on a hyperlink in the displayed page. Is it possible to prevent the browser from navigating to that URL?

   Yes, by using the `BeforeNavigate2` event procedure to check the URL and cancel the operation if desired.

Day 17, "Client-Side Scripting with VBScript"

1. How do you identify VBScript code in an HTML page?

   VBScript code must be enclosed in `<SCRIPT>...</SCRIPT>` tags. The first tag should identify the scripting language in use, as in `<SCRIPT LANGUAGE = "vbscript">`.

A

2. What graphics capabilities does VBScript have?

None.

3. Your VBScript program needs a variable to hold a number whose value will range between -2500 and +4500. Which data type should you use?

Trick question! VBScript has only a single data type, Variant, that is used for all numeric, string, and object data.

4. Is the following array declaration legal in VBScript?

```
Dim array(5 to 15)
```

No. All VBScript arrays start at index 0.

5. How can VBScript code access information about the loaded document?

By accessing the properties of the Document object.

6. How can VBScript code write text to the HTML page?

By calling the Document object's Write or WriteLn methods.

Day 18, "Creating Dynamic Content with Active Server Pages"

1. How can an ASP application determine whether a client's browser supports frames?

By creating a BrowserType component and examining the Frames property.

2. To create an object in an ASP script, do you use VBScript's CreateObject method?

No. You must use the Server object's CreateObject method.

3. How can an ASP script convert regular text into HTML encoded text for viewing in the client's browser?

With the Server object's HTMLEncode method.

4. From the client's point of view, what is the main difference between the GET and POST methods?

GET is limited to sending 255 bytes of data to the server, whereas POST has no length limitation.

5. What does the #include directive do?

It inserts the contents of one file into an ASP or HTML page at the specified location.

Day 19, "Connecting to a Database with ASP"

1. How would a database-aware Web application obtain input from the user?

   By displaying an HTML form for the user to enter data and then by sending the data to the server with GET or POST.

2. Do all database applications permit the user to enter, delete, and edit data?

   No. Decision support applications permit the user to view data, but not to change it.

3. In the ADO model, which object represents the link between your program and the database file?

   The Connection object.

4. After populating a RecordSet object, how do you know how many fields it contains?

   From the Fields collection's Count property.

5. Give two ways to tell whether a RecordSet is empty.

   If the RecordCount property is 0, and if both the BOF and EOF properties are True.

Day 20, "Implementing a Web Database Application"

1. If the following values are contained in a Text field, what is the default order they will be sorted in?

   101b

   95

   10004g

   6x

   They will be sorted in the following order:

   10004g

   101b

   6x

   95

A

2. Suppose your database contains a field name with a space in it. What must you do to include the field name in a SQL SELECT statement?

   Enclose it in brackets.

3. For fastest operation, which fields should your database table be indexed on?

   Any fields whose data will be used to sort the records.

4. How can you display a numerical value formatted as currency?

   Use the formatcurrency function.

Day 21, "Common Gateway Interface Programming with Visual Basic"

1. How can a Visual Basic program read from the standard input stream?

   By using API functions. Use GetStdHandle first to get the handle of stdin; then use ReadFile to read data from the stream.

2. How can a Visual Basic program read the value of an environment variable?

   By using the Environ() function.

3. When you are using the Windows CGI technology, how does the CGI program obtain the name of the CGI profile file?

   The name of the CGI profile file is passed on the application command line and is retrieved using Visual Basic's Command$ function.

4. In standard CGI, how would the CGI program know whether the client used POST or GET to send the data?

   By reading the REQUEST_METHOD environment variable.

5. In a direct-response HTTP response, the first line must start with HTTP/1.0. What follows next?

   A numerical result code indicating that the request was processed successfully or, if not, the nature of the error.

INDEX

Symbols

<!- - tag, 101, 393
#include directive (reusing ASP script), 431-432
<%= ... %> tag, 419
<%...%> tag, 419
<a href> tag, 13, 310, 473
- -> tag, 393

A

Abandon method, 425
About dialog box, 378
absolute mode (DHTML pages), 230
[ACCEPT] CGI profile file section, 487

access
  ASP server files, 436-439
    CreateTextFile and OpenTextFile methods, 437
    FileSystemObject object, 436
    FSO (FileSystemObject) model, 436
    reading and writing files example, 438-439
    TextStream object, 436-438
  public methods and properties, 161-162
AccessKeys property, 64
AccessType property, 269
accounts (email)
  configuring, 336-339
  multiple, 339
ACTION attribute (<FORM> tag), 432

Active Server Pages. *See* ASP
ActiveX
  advantages, 37
  components, 38, 49
  controls. *See* ActiveX controls
  Data Objects (ADO)
    Connection object, 452-455
    connection strings, 453-454
    Fields collection (RecordSet object), 457
    object model, 451-452
    OLE DB, 450
    RecordSet object, 455-457
  digital signing, 42
    Authenticode certificate, 43-44
    components, 46-47
    software, 44-45

FREE ISSUE!

The Ultimate Add-on Tool for Microsoft Visual Basic

As part of your purchase, you are eligible to receive a free issue of *Visual Basic Programmer's Journal*, the leading magazine for Visual Basic programmers.

There's a lot to know about Visual Basic and its improved development tools. And *VBPJ* is the only magazine devoted to giving you the timely information you need with articles on subjects like:

- When—and how—to use the latest data access technologies
- How DHTML and the Web affect the way you develop and deploy apps
- Which new Visual Basic features save time—and which to avoid
- Creating reusable code with Visual Basic classes

But don't let the development information stop with your free issue. When you subscribe to *VBPJ*, we'll also send you a **FREE** CD-ROM – with three issues of *VBPJ* in electronically readable format, plus all the source code & sample apps from each issue.

Filled with hands-on articles and indispensable tips, tricks and utilities, *Visual Basic Programmer's Journal* will save your hours of programming time. And, *VBPJ* is the only magazine devoted to making VB programmers more productive.

A single tip can more than pay for a year's subscription.

Send for your free issue today.

MY GUARANTEE

If at any time I do not agree that *Visual Basic Programmer's Journal* is the best, most useful source of information on Visual Basic, I can cancel my subscription and receive a full refund.

☐ **YES!** Please rush me the next issue of *Visual Basic Programmer's Journal* to examine without obligation. If I like it, I'll pay the low rate of $22.95,* for a full year—eleven additional issues plus the annual *Buyers Guide* and *Enterprise* issue, (for a total of fourteen). Also, with my paid subscription, I'll receive a **FREE** gift—three issues (with sample apps and code) of *VBPJ* on CD-ROM! If I choose not to subscribe, I'll simply write cancel on my bill and owe nothing. The free issue is mine to keep with your compliments.

Name: _____

Company: _____

Address: _____

_____

City: _____ State: _____ Zip: _____

* Basic annual subscription rate is $34.97. Your subscription is for 12 monthly issues plus two bonus issues. Canada/Mexico residents please add $18/year for surface delivery. All other countries please add $44/year for air mail delivery. Canadian GST included. Send in this card or fax your order to 415.853.0230. Microsoft and Visual Basic are registered trademarks and ActiveX is a trademark of Microsoft Corporation.

8039

FREE ISSUE!

Find out for yourself what *Visual Basic Programmer's Journal* can do for you.

Visual Basic is the most productive Windows development environment. Get the most out of it by learning from the experts that write for ***Visual Basic Programmer's Journal.***

Check out select articles online at http://www.devx.com